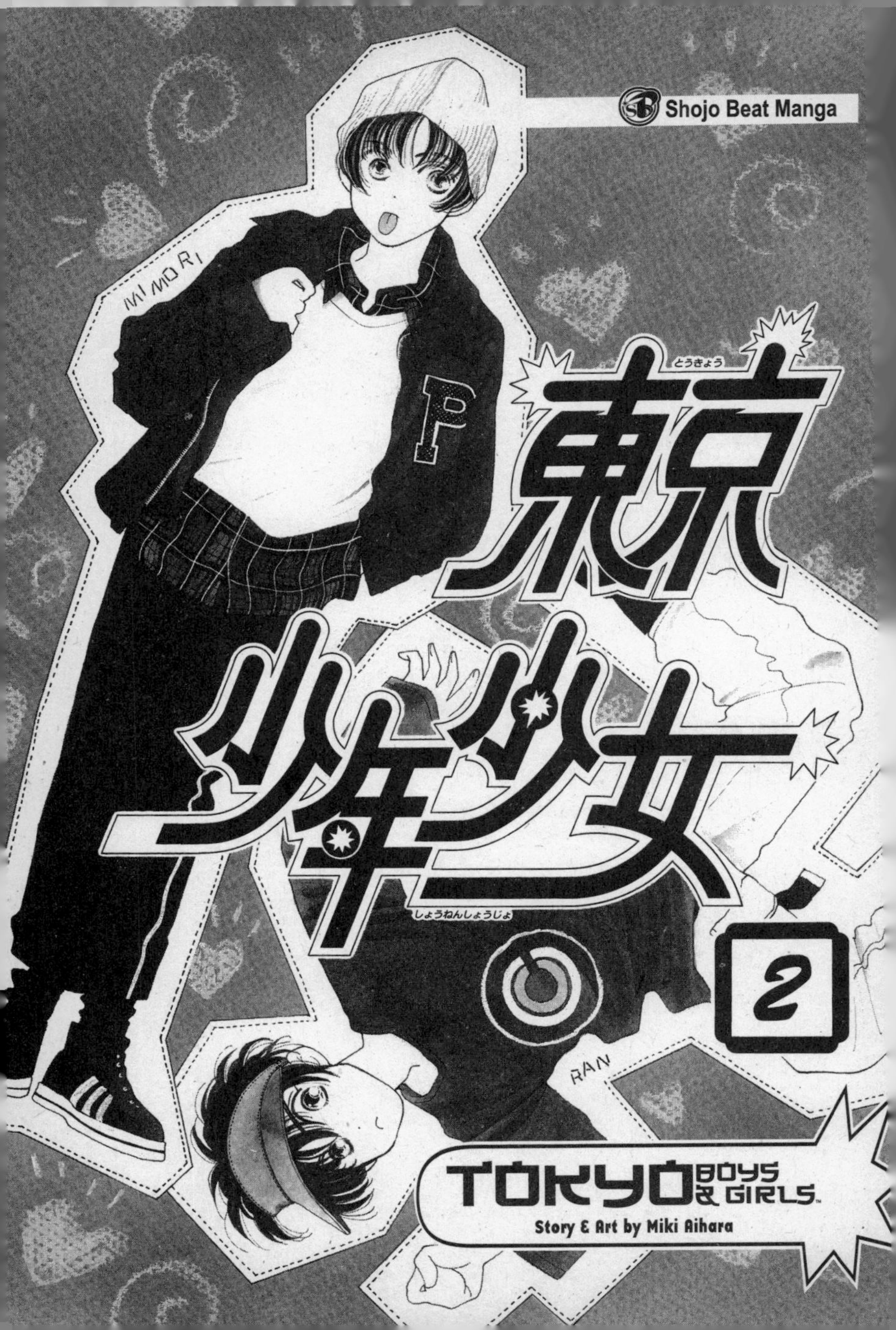

Shojo Beat Manga
MIMORI
とうきょう
東京
少年少女
しょうねんしょうじょ
2
RAN
TOKYO BOYS & GIRLS
Story & Art by Miki Aihara

TOKYO BOYS & GIRLS™

CONTENTS

The Story Thus Far

♥ On her first day of high school, Mimori makes friends with the beautiful Nana and looks forward to a great year. Soon, however, she has three different boys ganging up to destroy her. Haruta, a tough guy rumored to be part of a biker gang, wants revenge for something Mimori did to him in grade school. Best friends Kuniyasu and Shingyoji had designed a video game for a contest with a million-yen prize, but Mimori accidentally ruins their only disk.

When Mimori asks Haruta what happened in grade school, she discovers that he was "Haru," a boy who was viciously bullied. However, Mimori doesn't remember ever bullying him. Mimori finds herself thinking about Haruta more and more...when suddenly Kuniyasu announces that he wants to date her!

MAIN CHARACTERS

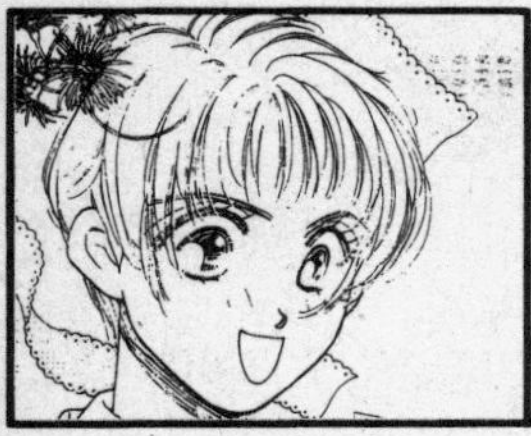

Mimori Kosaka

Class 1-A, Girls' Division, Meidai Attached High School. A sunny, enthusiastic girl. Maybe because of this, she seems to make a lot of mistakes.

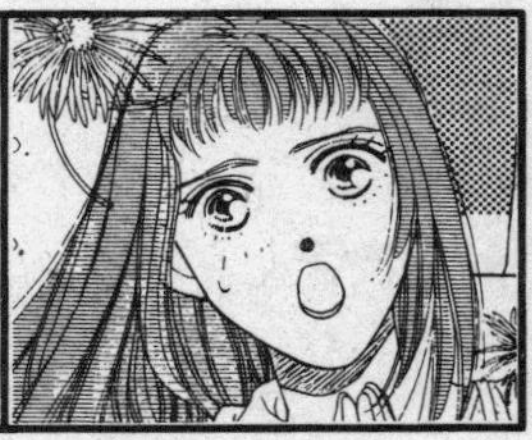

Nana Takaichi

Mimori's classmate. A very beautiful girl, she is the center of attention whenever boys are around. She's in love with Kuniyasu of Class 1-A, Boys' Division.

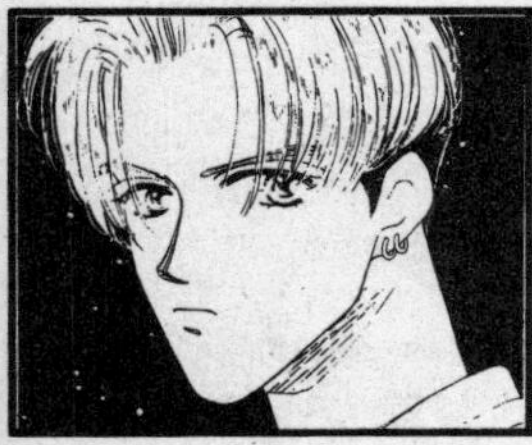

Atsushi Haruta

Class 1-A, Boys' Division. He went to elementary school with Mimori. He's intimidating now, but when he was little he was a target for bullies.

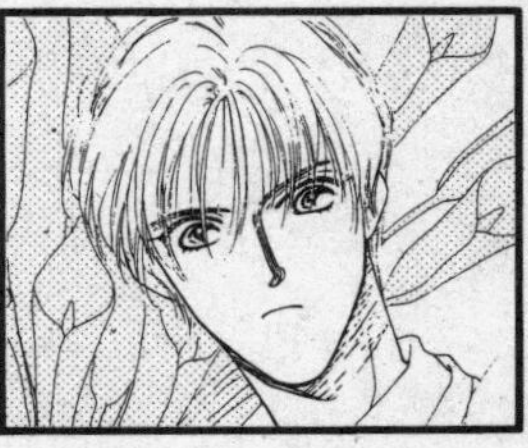

Kazukita Kuniyasu

Class 1-A, Boys' Division. Brainy, articulate, and, on top of that, handsome. He acts a bit cool toward girls.

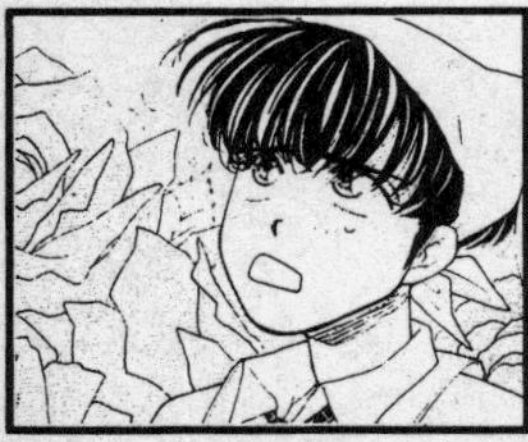

Ran Shingyoji

Class 1-A, Boys' Division. A hyperactive clown and Kazukita's best friend. He fell in love with Nana at first sight. Does he still hold a grudge against Mimori?

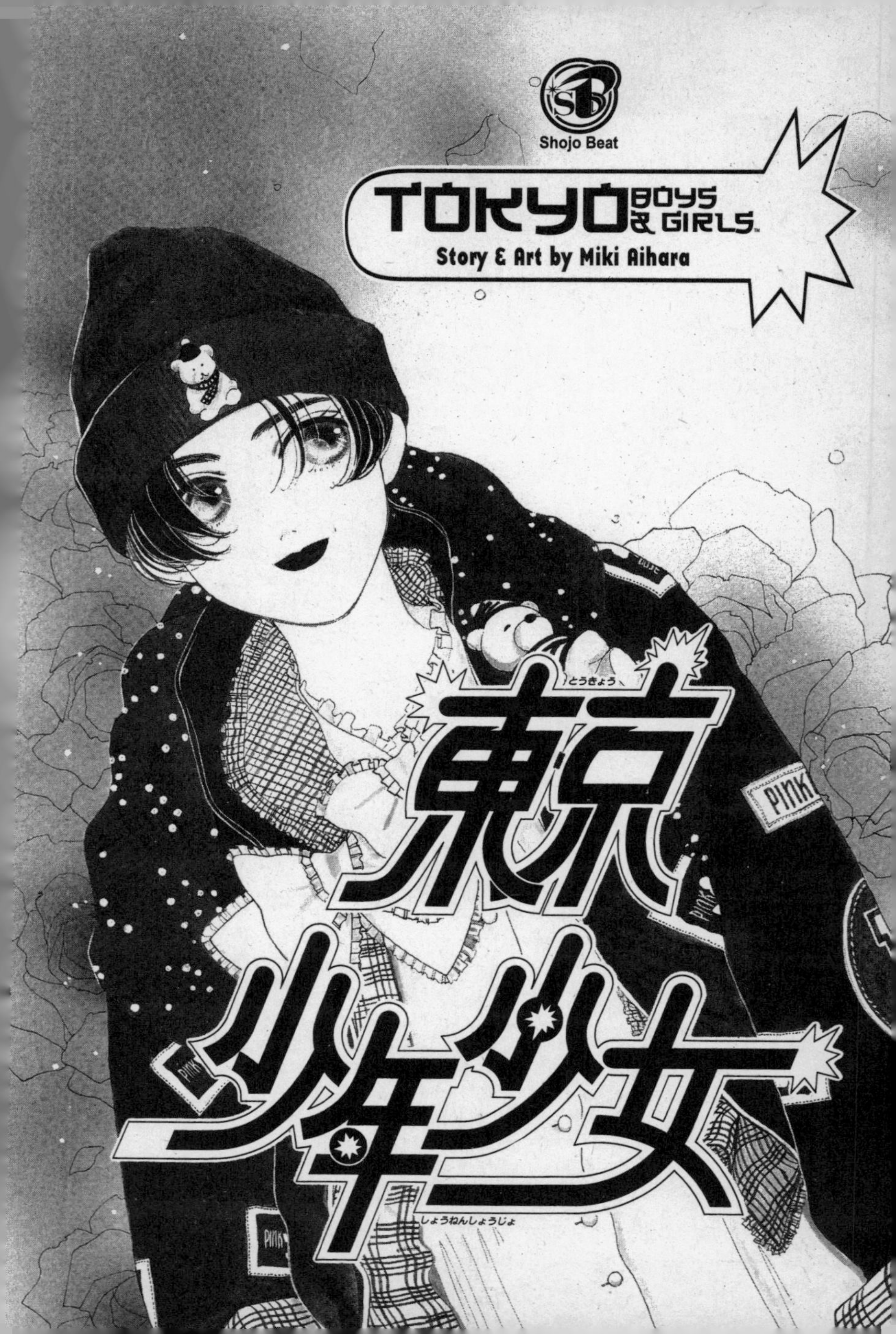
Shojo Beat
TOKYO BOYS & GIRLS
Story & Art by Miki Aihara
とうきょう
東京少年少女
しょうねんしょうじょ
PINK

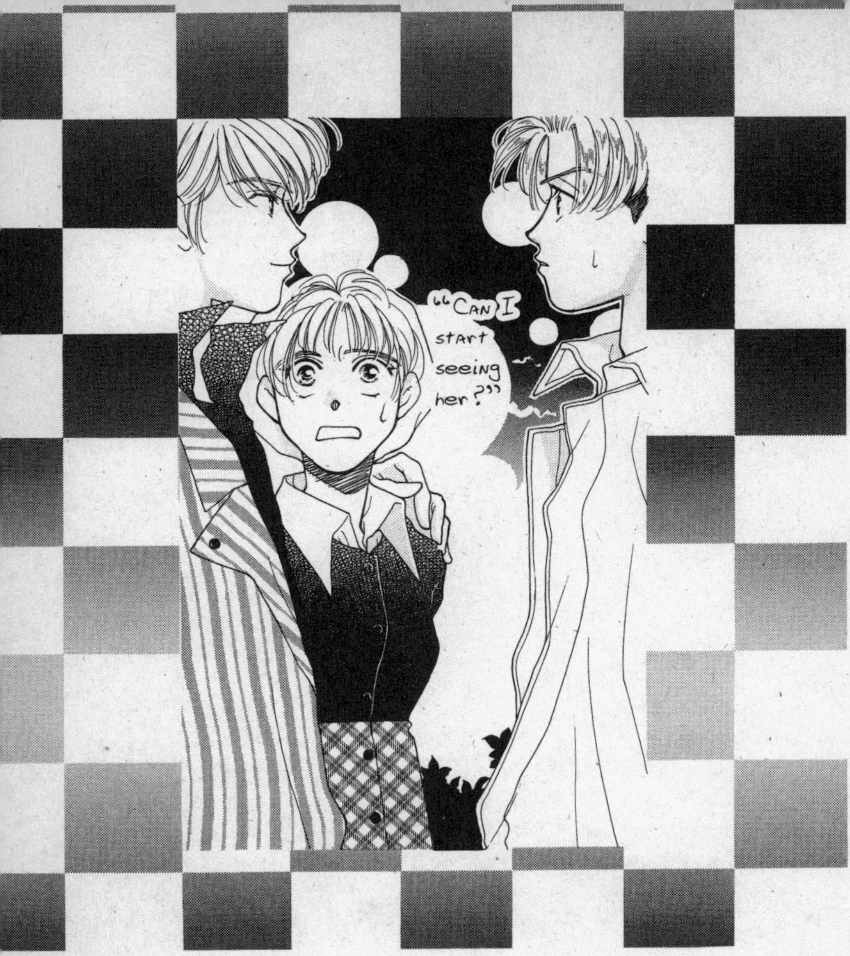
"Can I start seeing her?"

TOKYO GIRLS PROFILE NO. 2 NANA TAKAICHI

HEIGHT: 162 CM 44 KG (OR LESS)
BLOOD TYPE: B
FAMILY: FATHER, MOTHER, ELDER BROTHER (10 YEARS OLDER)
INTERESTS: SHOPPING, FALLING IN LOVE, BRAND-NAME EVERYTHING.
WHEN SHE WAS IN JUNIOR HIGH, SHE WAS THE IDOL OF ALL THE BOYS. SHE EVEN DATED A COLLEGE GUY. BUT HER REAL LOVE IS KUNIYASU.

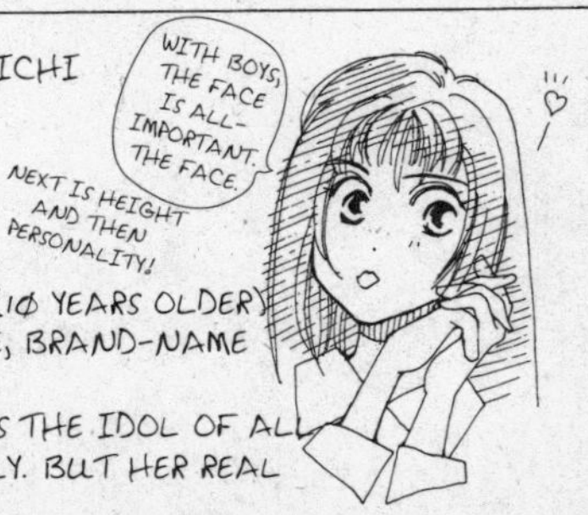
WITH BOYS, THE FACE IS ALL-IMPORTANT. THE FACE.
NEXT IS HEIGHT AND THEN PERSONALITY!

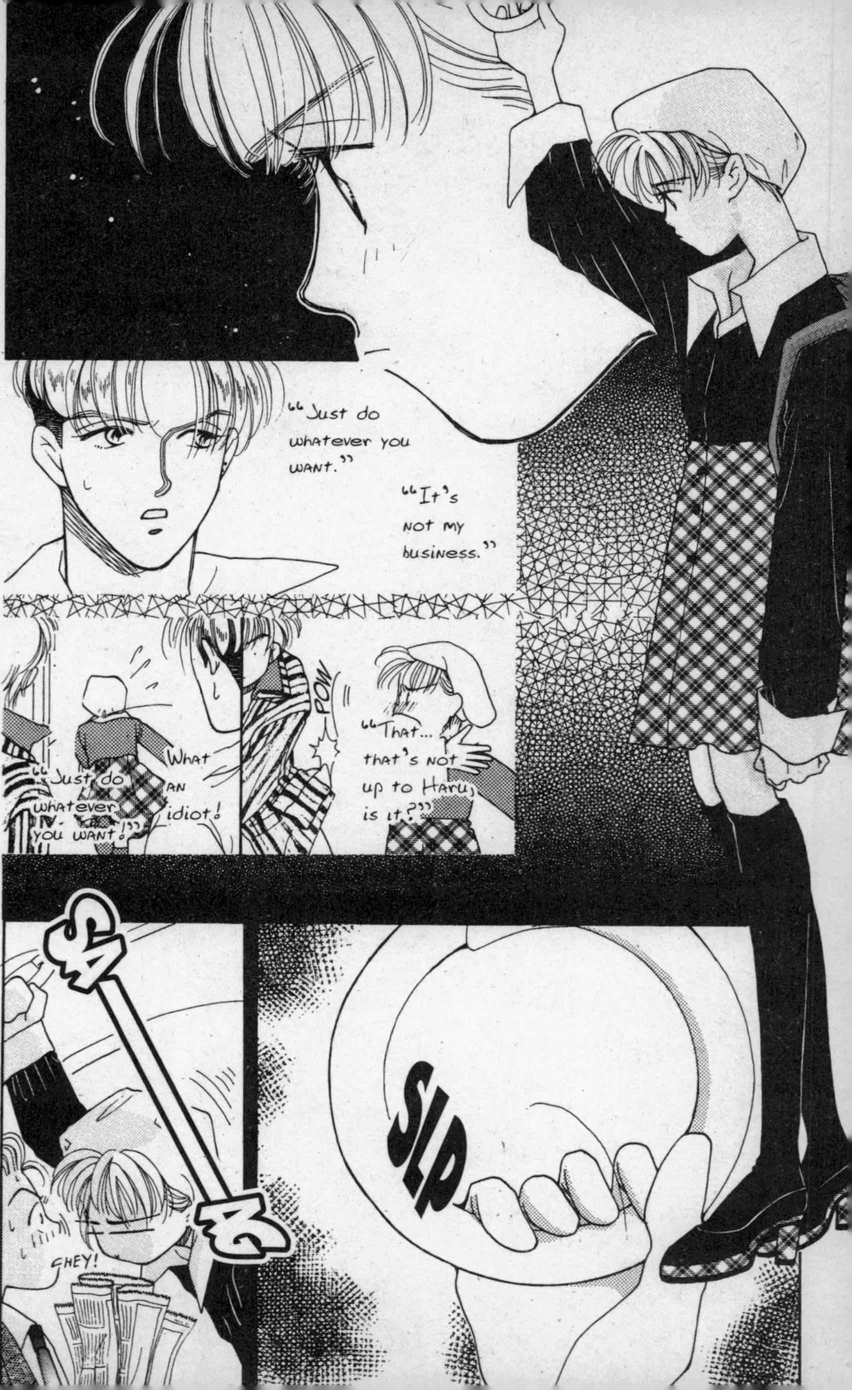
"Just do whatever you want."
"It's not my business."
POW
"That... that's not up to Haru, is it?"
What an idiot!
"Just do whatever you want!"
SLIP
SWAG
HEY!

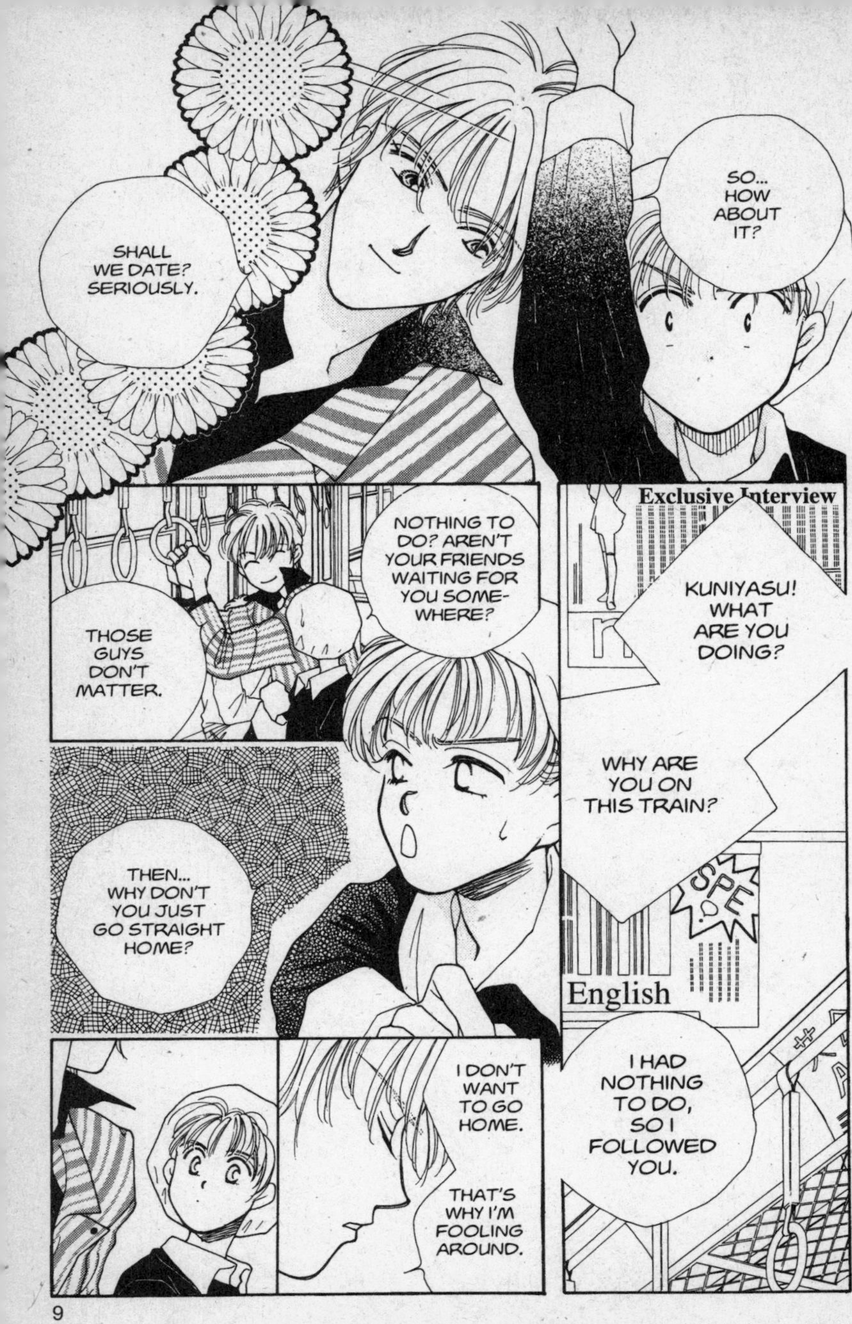
SO... HOW ABOUT IT?
SHALL WE DATE? SERIOUSLY.
Exclusive Interview
KUNIYASU! WHAT ARE YOU DOING?
WHY ARE YOU ON THIS TRAIN?
SPE
English
I HAD NOTHING TO DO, SO I FOLLOWED YOU.
NOTHING TO DO? AREN'T YOUR FRIENDS WAITING FOR YOU SOME-WHERE?
THOSE GUYS DON'T MATTER.
THEN... WHY DON'T YOU JUST GO STRAIGHT HOME?
I DON'T WANT TO GO HOME.
THAT'S WHY I'M FOOLING AROUND.

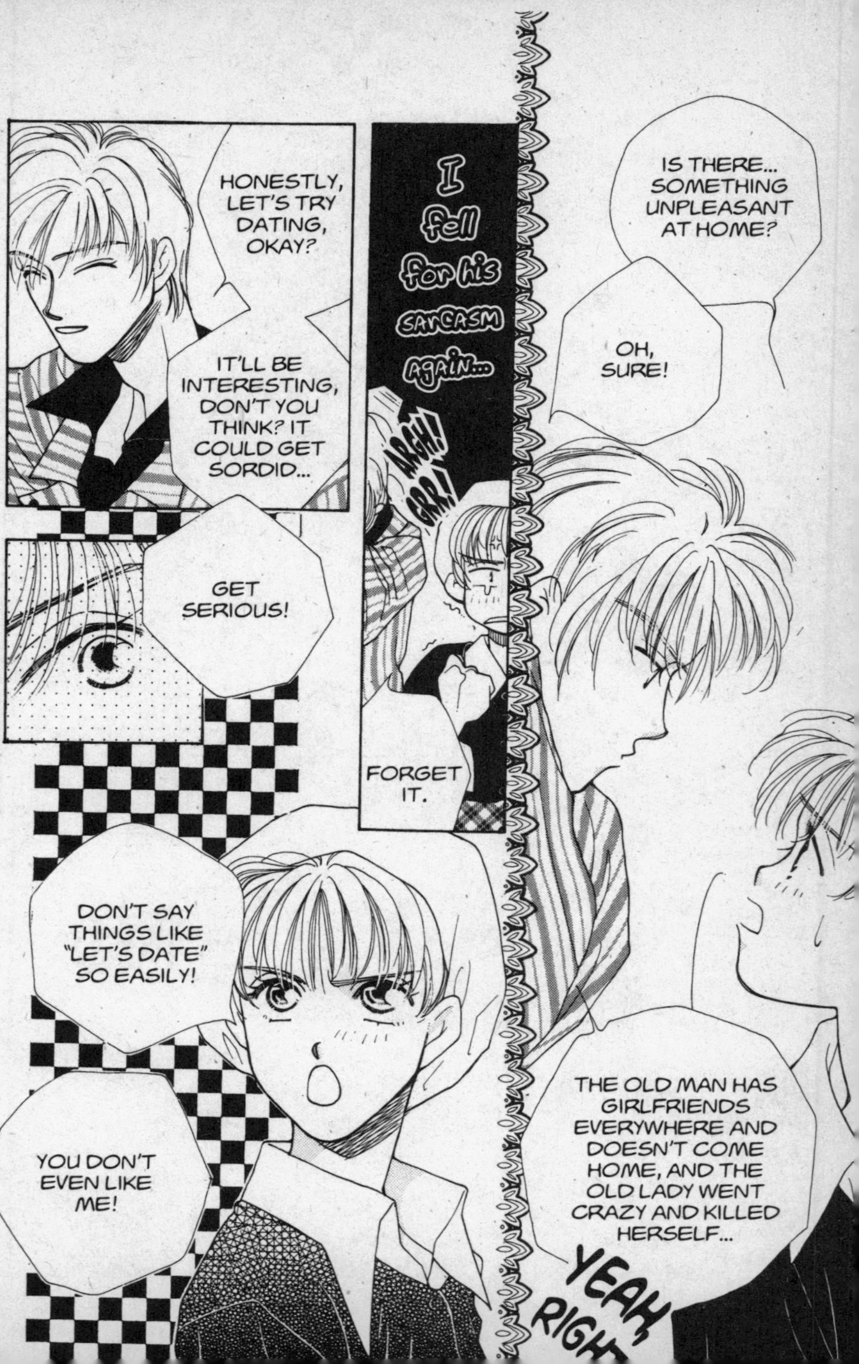
IS THERE... SOMETHING UNPLEASANT AT HOME?
OH, SURE!
THE OLD MAN HAS GIRLFRIENDS EVERYWHERE AND DOESN'T COME HOME, AND THE OLD LADY WENT CRAZY AND KILLED HERSELF...
YEAH, RIGHT
I fell for his sarcasm again...
ARGH! GRR!
FORGET IT.
HONESTLY, LET'S TRY DATING, OKAY?
IT'LL BE INTERESTING, DON'T YOU THINK? IT COULD GET SORDID...
GET SERIOUS!
DON'T SAY THINGS LIKE "LET'S DATE" SO EASILY!
YOU DON'T EVEN LIKE ME!

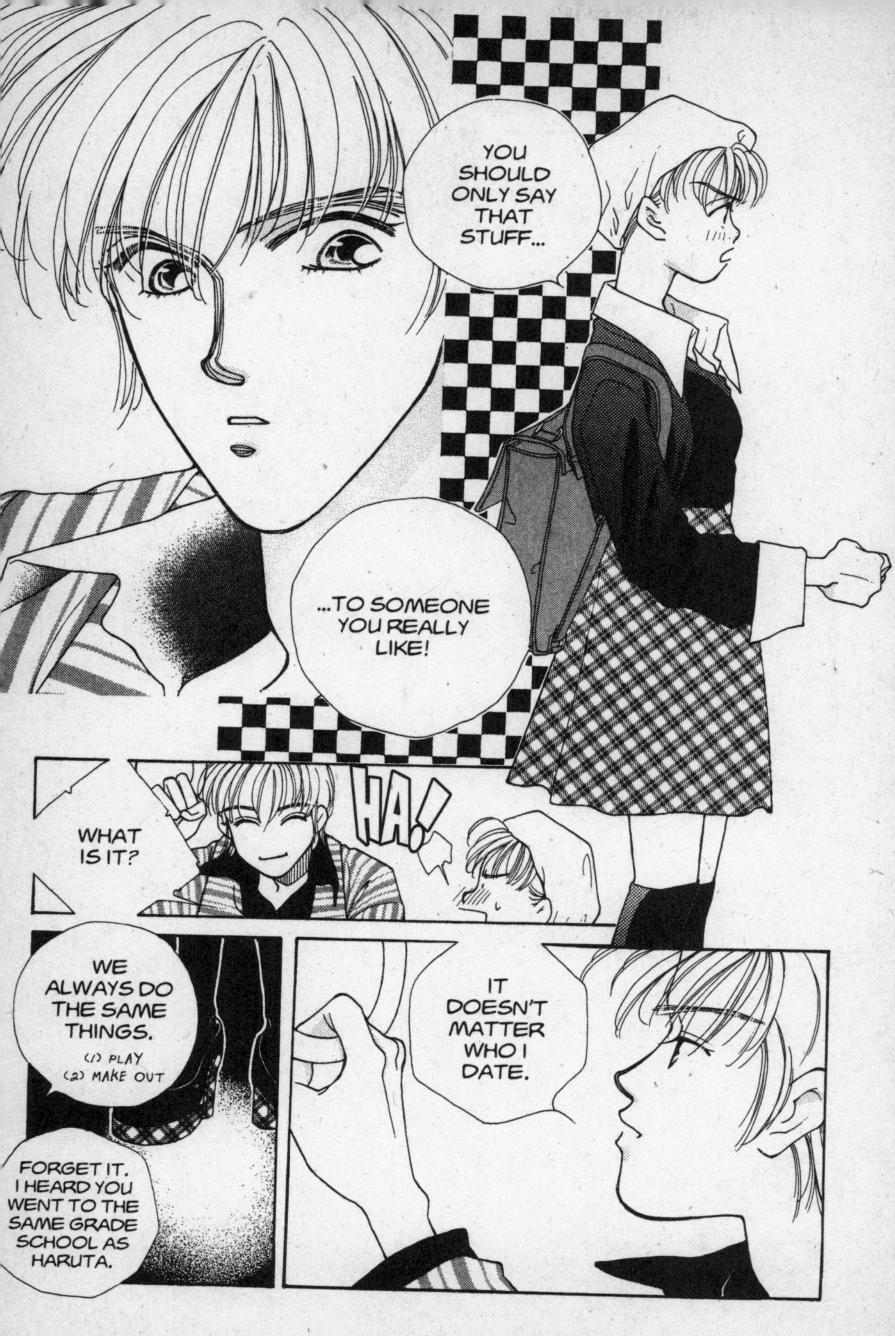
YOU SHOULD ONLY SAY THAT STUFF...
...TO SOMEONE YOU REALLY LIKE!
HA!
WHAT IS IT?
IT DOESN'T MATTER WHO I DATE.
WE ALWAYS DO THE SAME THINGS.
(1) PLAY
(2) MAKE OUT
FORGET IT. I HEARD YOU WENT TO THE SAME GRADE SCHOOL AS HARUTA.

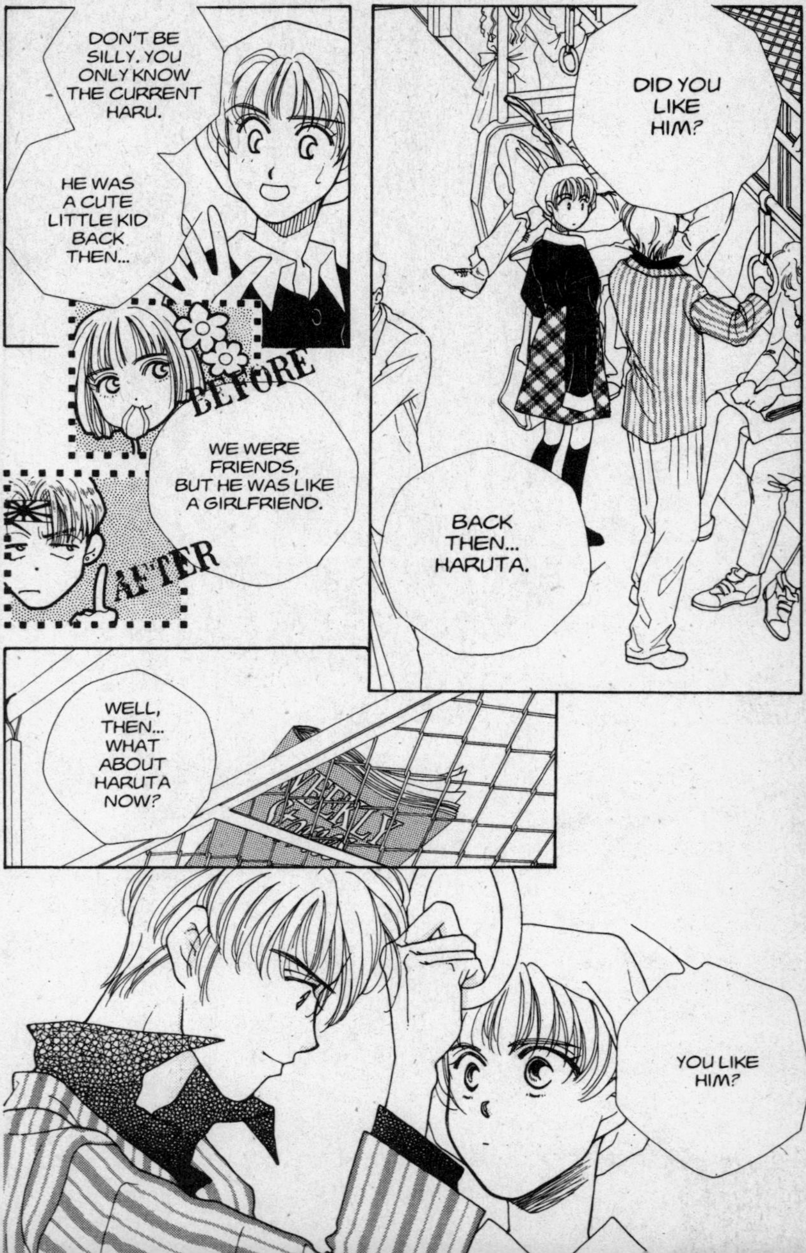
DID YOU LIKE HIM?
BACK THEN... HARUTA.
DON'T BE SILLY. YOU ONLY KNOW THE CURRENT HARU.
HE WAS A CUTE LITTLE KID BACK THEN...
BEFORE
WE WERE FRIENDS, BUT HE WAS LIKE A GIRLFRIEND.
AFTER
WELL, THEN... WHAT ABOUT HARUTA NOW?
YOU LIKE HIM?

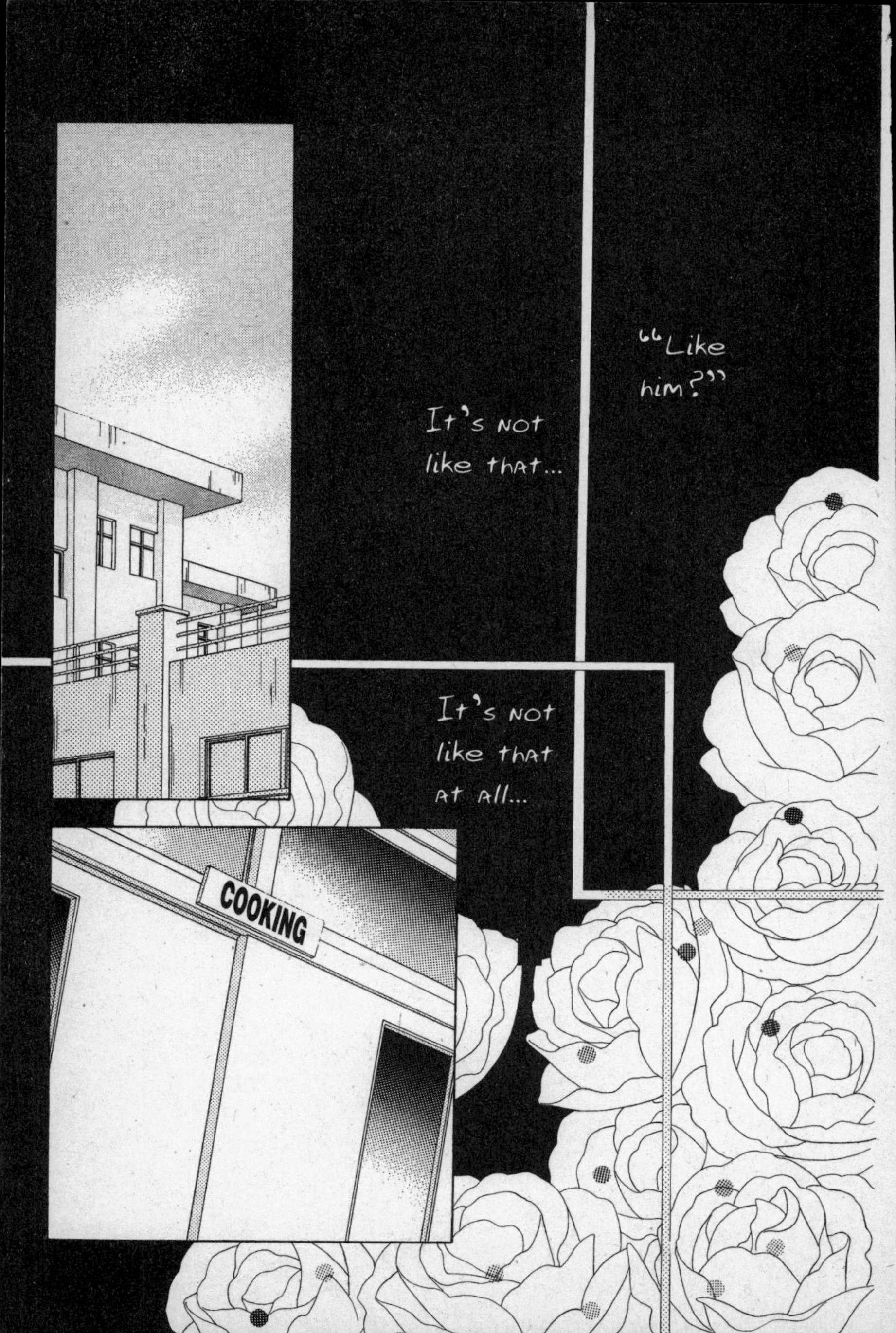
"Like him?"
It's not like that...
It's not like that at all...
COOKING

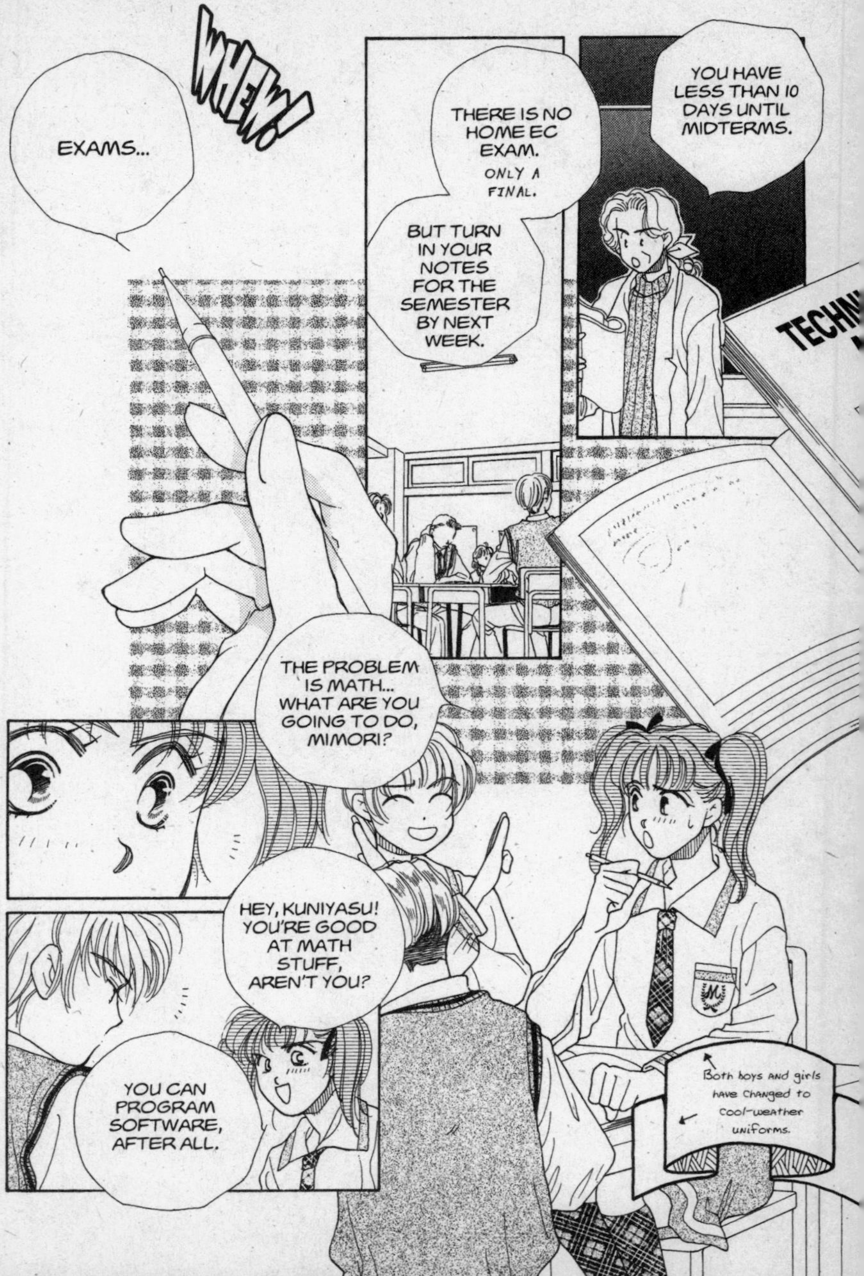
YOU HAVE LESS THAN 10 DAYS UNTIL MIDTERMS.
THERE IS NO HOME EC EXAM.
ONLY A FINAL.
BUT TURN IN YOUR NOTES FOR THE SEMESTER BY NEXT WEEK.
WHEW!
EXAMS...
THE PROBLEM IS MATH... WHAT ARE YOU GOING TO DO, MIMORI?
Both boys and girls have changed to cool-weather uniforms.
HEY, KUNIYASU! YOU'RE GOOD AT MATH STUFF, AREN'T YOU?
YOU CAN PROGRAM SOFTWARE, AFTER ALL.

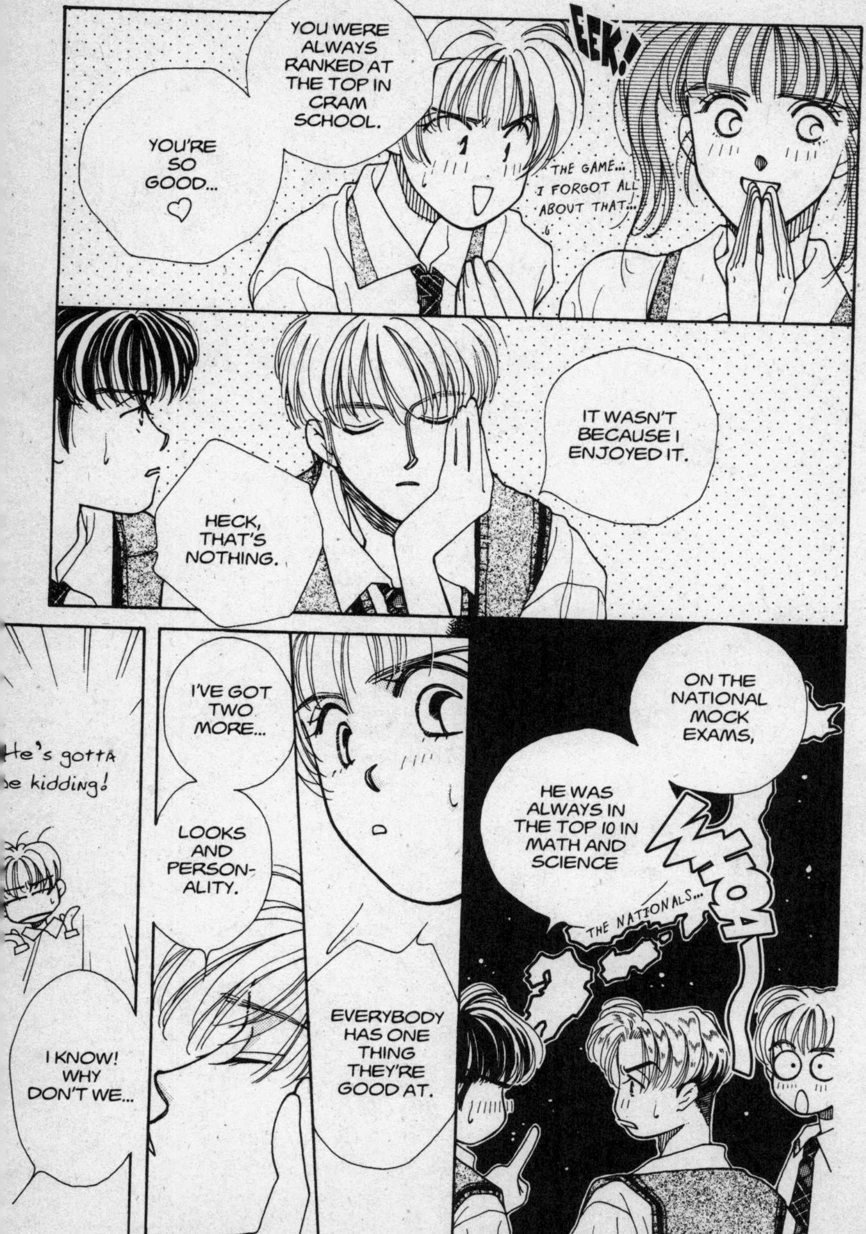
EEK!
THE GAME... I FORGOT ALL ABOUT THAT...
YOU WERE ALWAYS RANKED AT THE TOP IN CRAM SCHOOL.
YOU'RE SO GOOD... ♡
IT WASN'T BECAUSE I ENJOYED IT.
HECK, THAT'S NOTHING.
ON THE NATIONAL MOCK EXAMS,
HE WAS ALWAYS IN THE TOP 10 IN MATH AND SCIENCE
WHOA
THE NATIONALS...
I'VE GOT TWO MORE...
LOOKS AND PERSON-ALITY.
EVERYBODY HAS ONE THING THEY'RE GOOD AT.
He's gotta be kidding!
I KNOW! WHY DON'T WE...

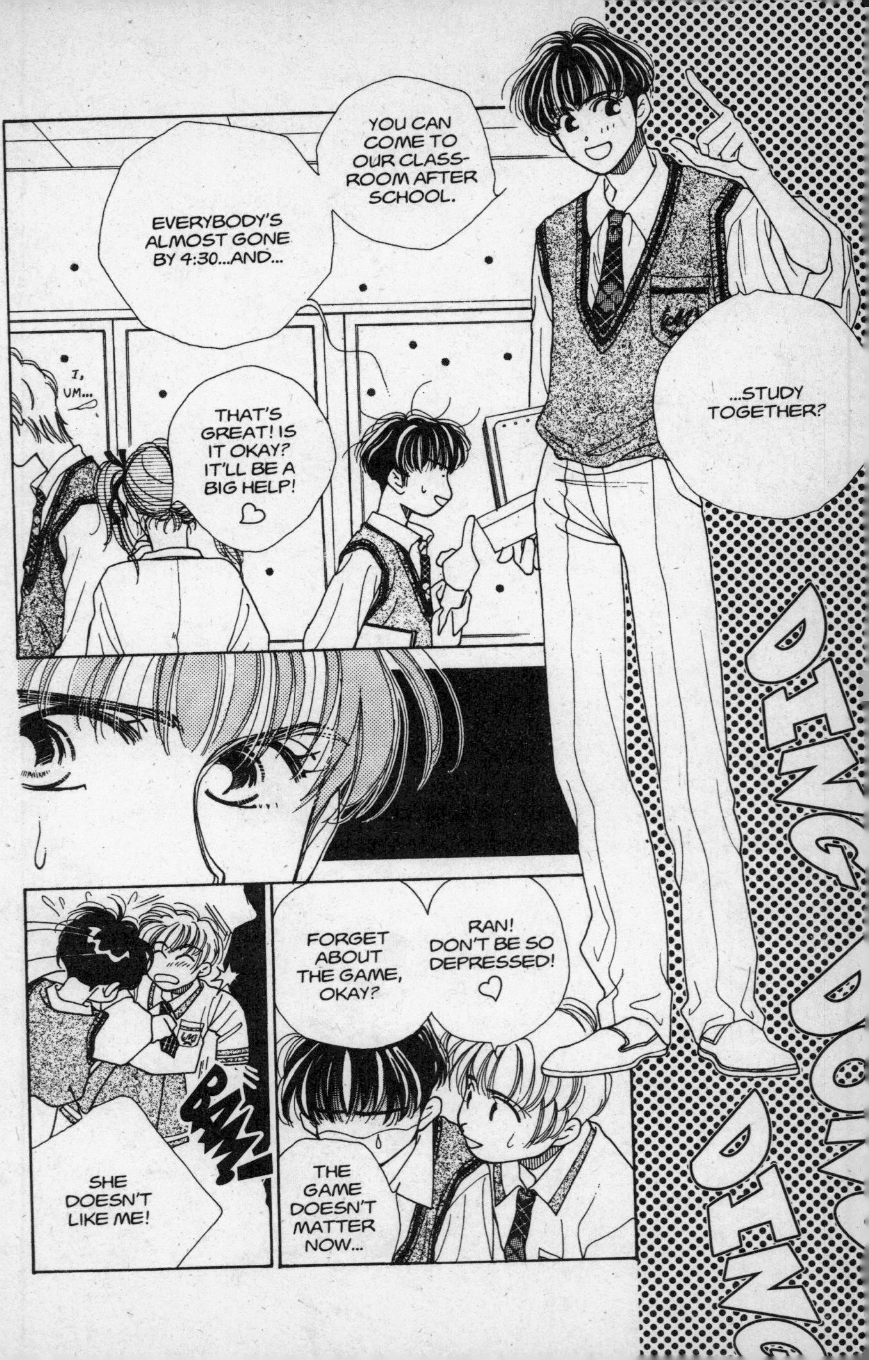
YOU CAN COME TO OUR CLASSROOM AFTER SCHOOL.
EVERYBODY'S ALMOST GONE BY 4:30...AND...
...STUDY TOGETHER?
DING DONG DING
THAT'S GREAT! IS IT OKAY? IT'LL BE A BIG HELP! ♡
I, UM...
RAN! DON'T BE SO DEPRESSED! ♡
FORGET ABOUT THE GAME, OKAY?
THE GAME DOESN'T MATTER NOW...
BAM!
SHE DOESN'T LIKE ME!

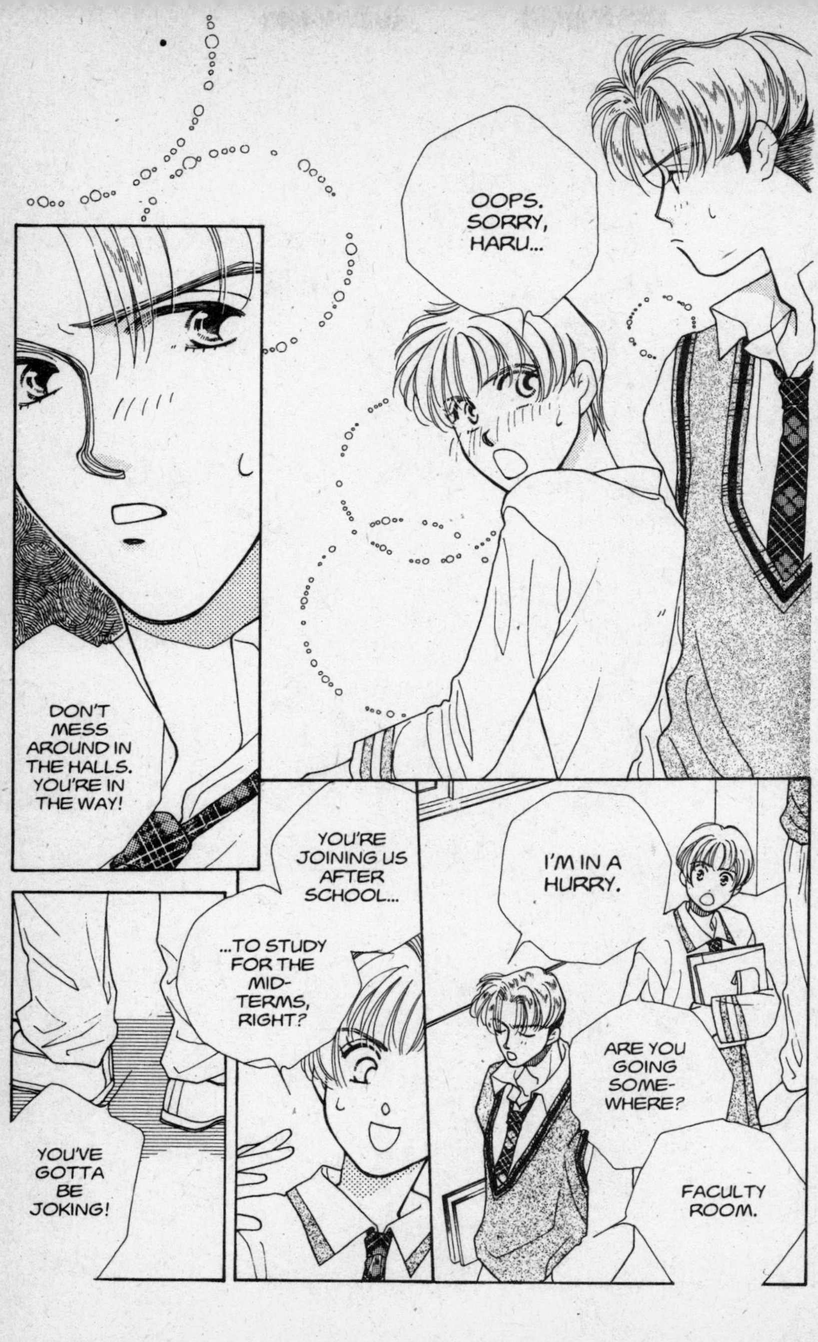
OOPS. SORRY, HARU...
DON'T MESS AROUND IN THE HALLS. YOU'RE IN THE WAY!
I'M IN A HURRY.
ARE YOU GOING SOME-WHERE?
FACULTY ROOM.
YOU'RE JOINING US AFTER SCHOOL...
...TO STUDY FOR THE MID-TERMS, RIGHT?
YOU'VE GOTTA BE JOKING!

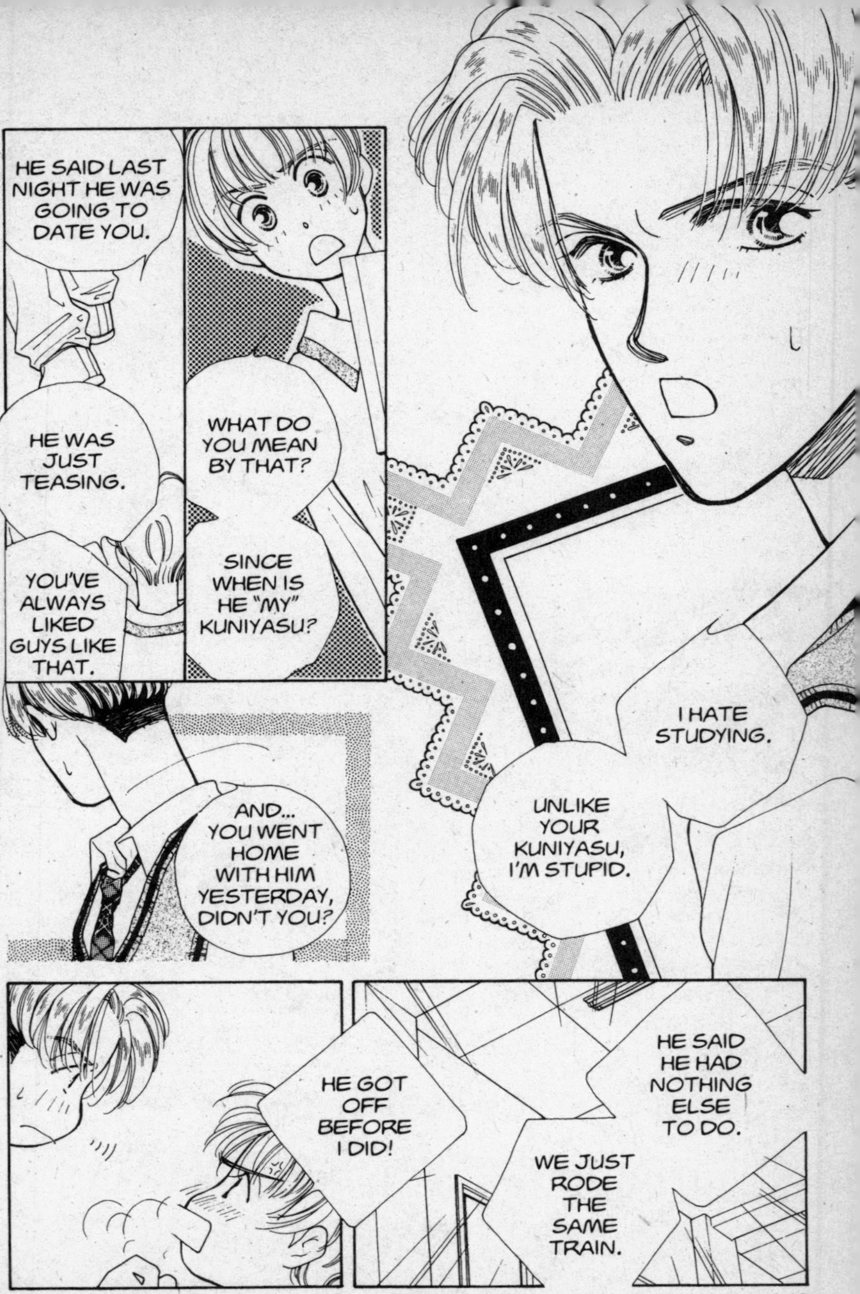
I HATE STUDYING.
UNLIKE YOUR KUNIYASU, I'M STUPID.
WHAT DO YOU MEAN BY THAT?
SINCE WHEN IS HE "MY" KUNIYASU?
HE SAID LAST NIGHT HE WAS GOING TO DATE YOU.
HE WAS JUST TEASING.
YOU'VE ALWAYS LIKED GUYS LIKE THAT.
AND... YOU WENT HOME WITH HIM YESTERDAY, DIDN'T YOU?
HE SAID HE HAD NOTHING ELSE TO DO.
WE JUST RODE THE SAME TRAIN.
HE GOT OFF BEFORE I DID!

TOKYO BOYS GIRLS

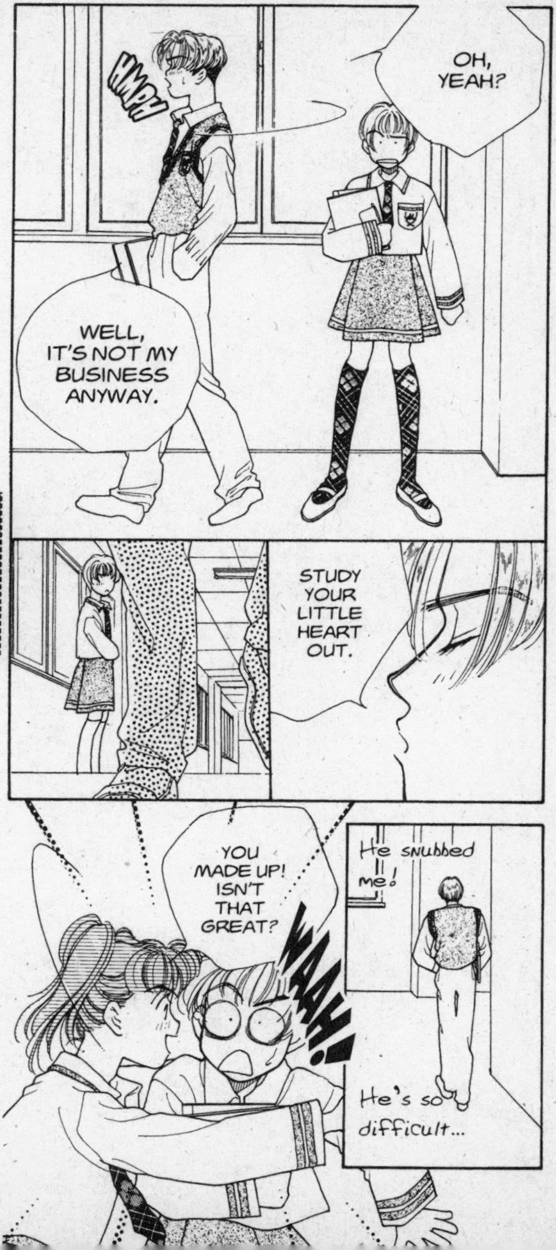
OH, YEAH?
HMMPH
WELL, IT'S NOT MY BUSINESS ANYWAY.
STUDY YOUR LITTLE HEART OUT.
He snubbed me!
He's so difficult...
YOU MADE UP! ISN'T THAT GREAT?
WAAH!!

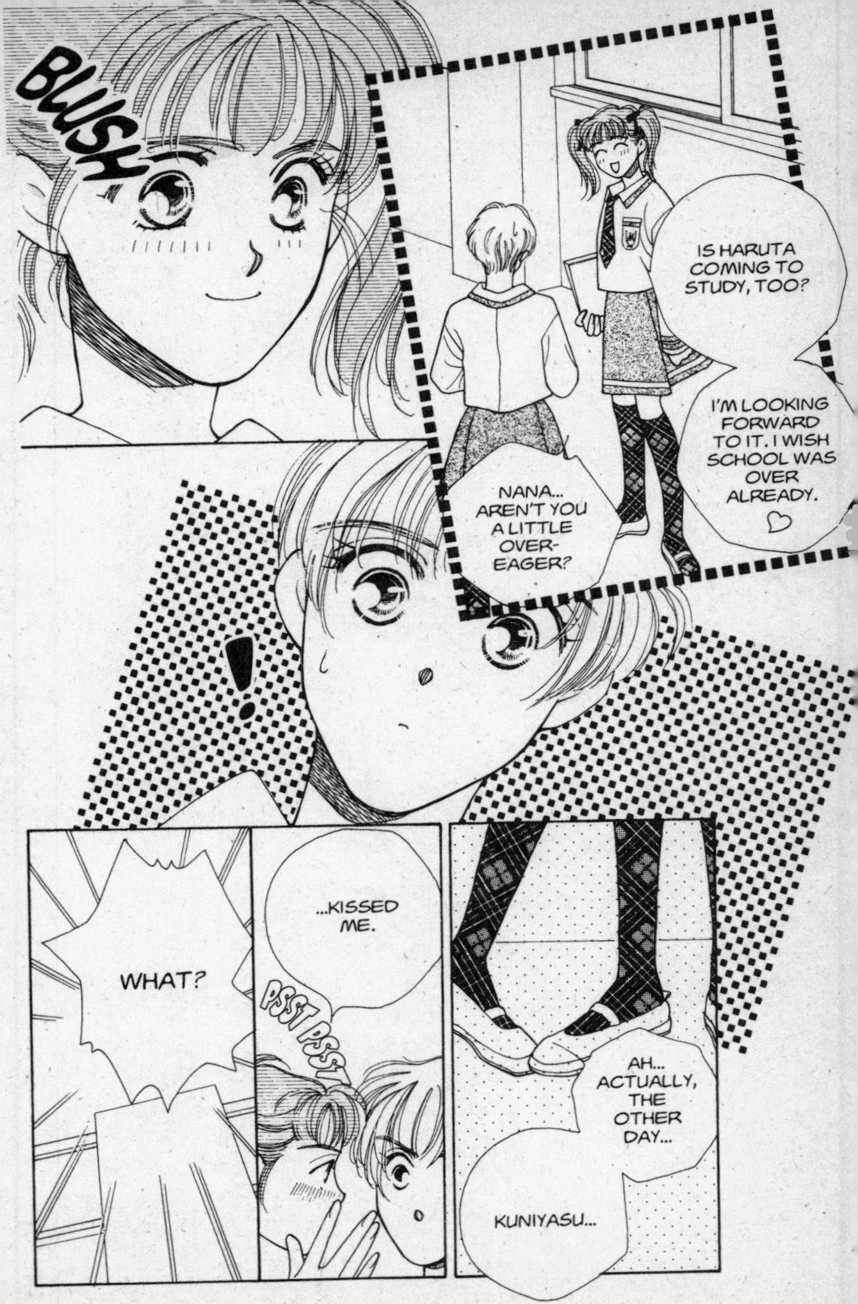
IS HARUTA COMING TO STUDY, TOO?
I'M LOOKING FORWARD TO IT. I WISH SCHOOL WAS OVER ALREADY. ♡
NANA... AREN'T YOU A LITTLE OVER-EAGER?
BLUSH
!
AH... ACTUALLY, THE OTHER DAY...
KUNIYASU...
...KISSED ME.
PSST PSST
WHAT?

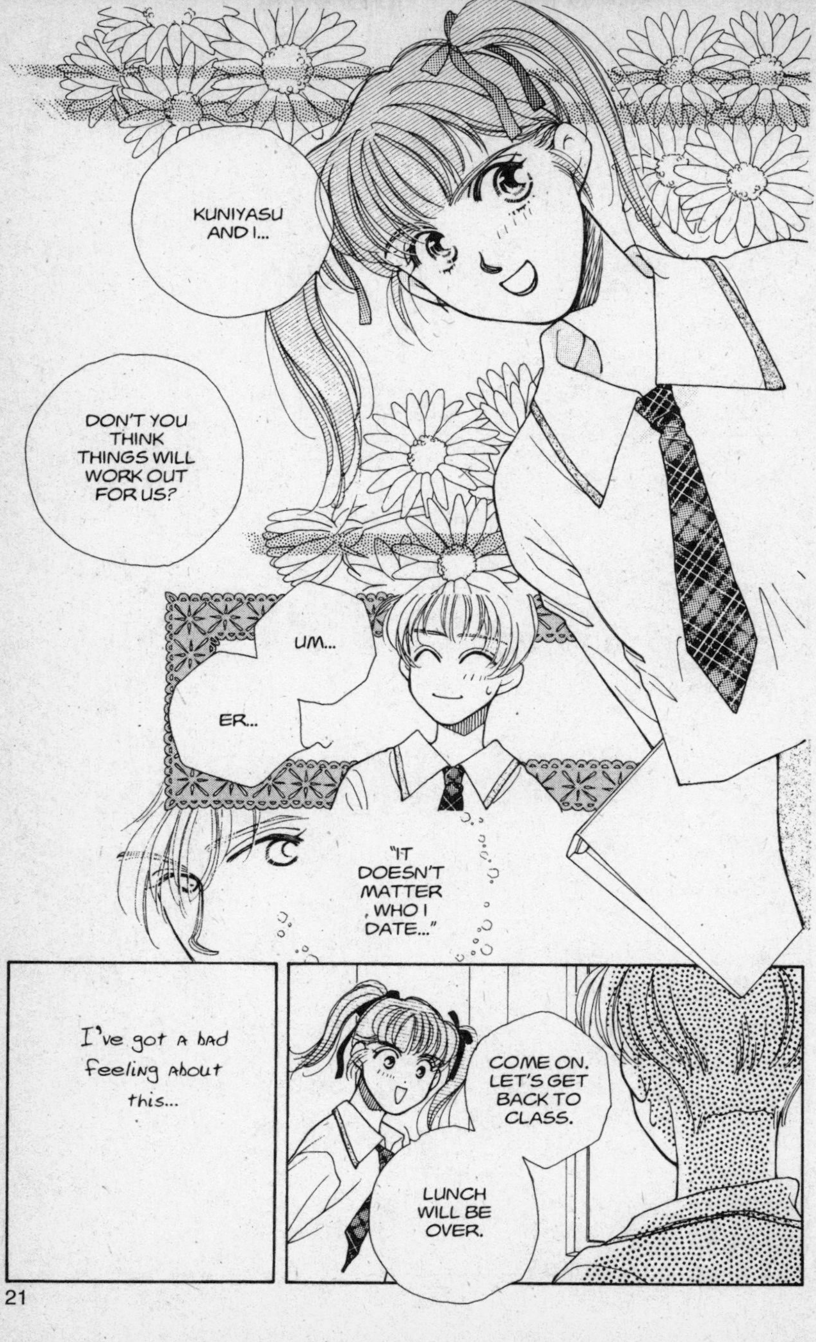
KUNIYASU AND I...
DON'T YOU THINK THINGS WILL WORK OUT FOR US?
UM...
ER...
"IT DOESN'T MATTER, WHO I DATE..."
COME ON. LET'S GET BACK TO CLASS.
LUNCH WILL BE OVER.
I've got a bad feeling about this...

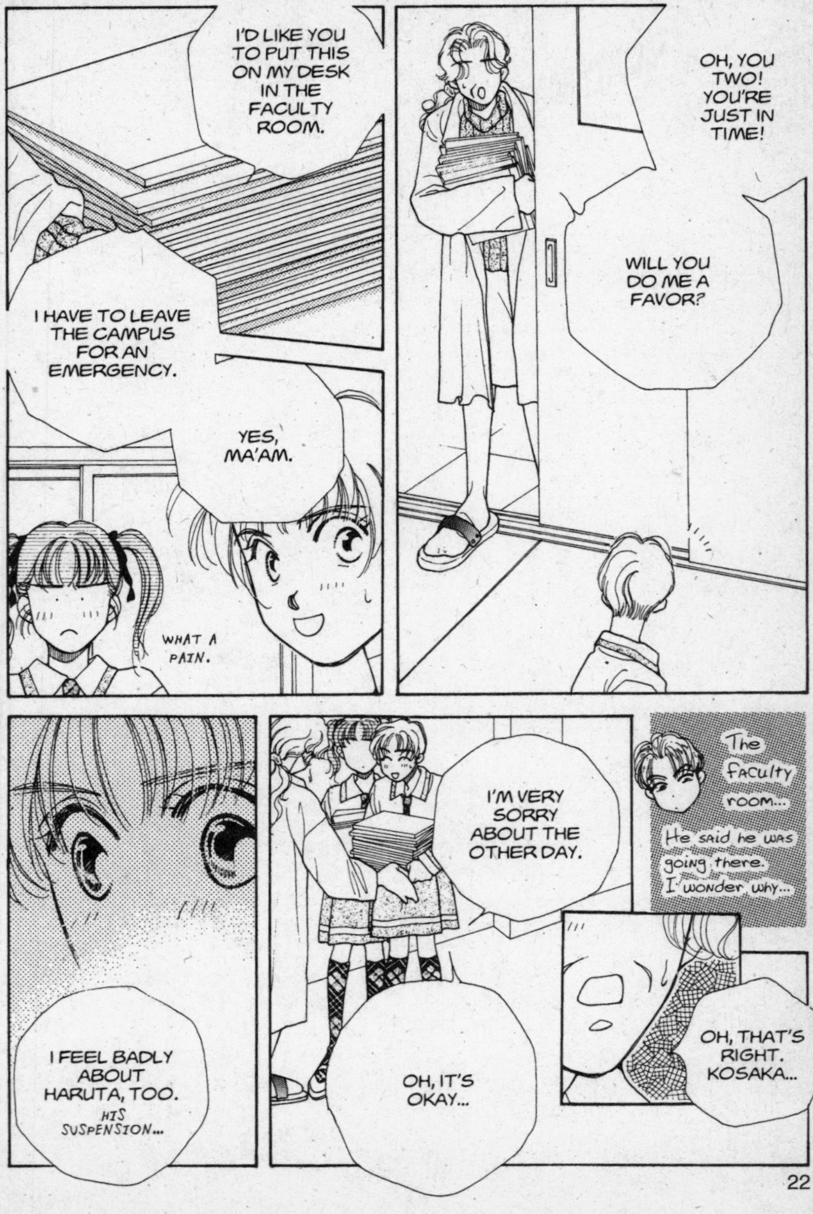
OH, YOU TWO! YOU'RE JUST IN TIME!
WILL YOU DO ME A FAVOR?
I'D LIKE YOU TO PUT THIS ON MY DESK IN THE FACULTY ROOM.
I HAVE TO LEAVE THE CAMPUS FOR AN EMERGENCY.
YES, MA'AM.
WHAT A PAIN.
The faculty room...
He said he was going there. I wonder why...
OH, THAT'S RIGHT. KOSAKA...
I'M VERY SORRY ABOUT THE OTHER DAY.
OH, IT'S OKAY...
I FEEL BADLY ABOUT HARUTA, TOO.
HIS SUSPENSION...

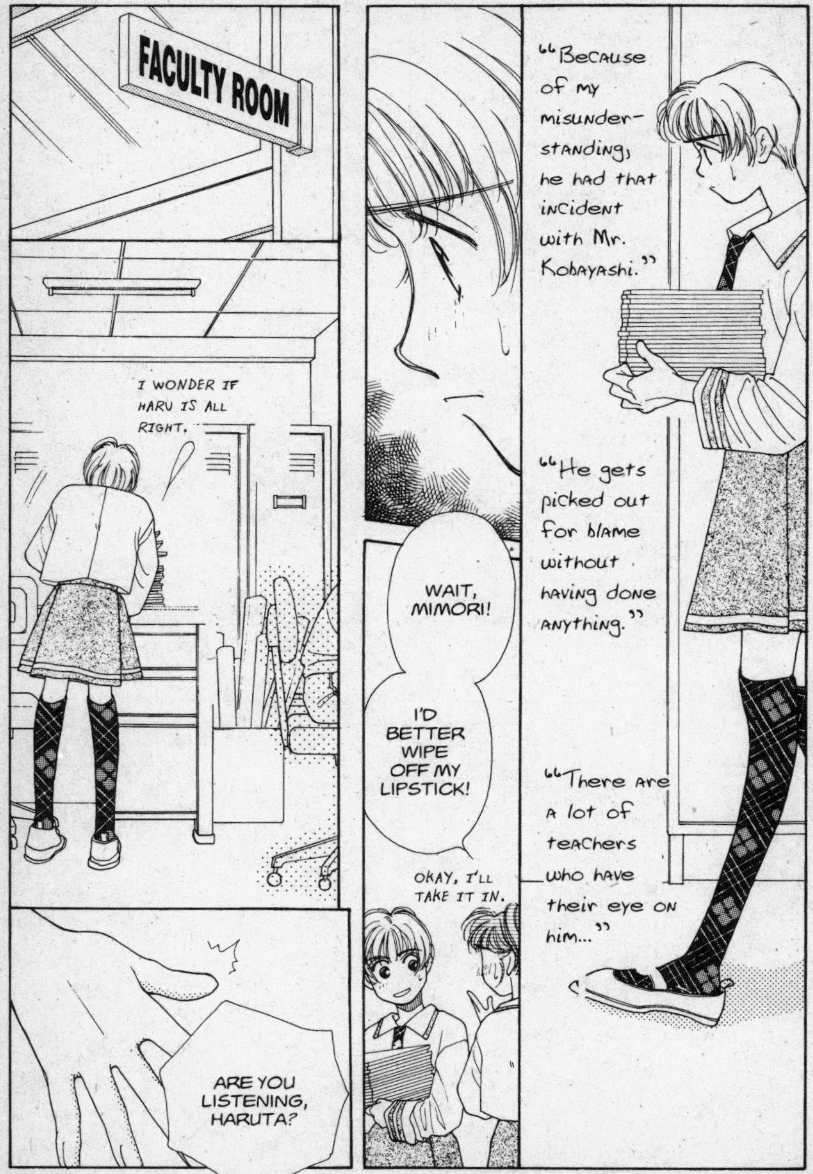

"Because of my misunderstanding, he had that incident with Mr. Kobayashi."
"He gets picked out for blame without having done anything."
"There are a lot of teachers who have their eye on him..."
WAIT, MIMORI!
I'D BETTER WIPE OFF MY LIPSTICK!
OKAY, I'LL TAKE IT IN.
FACULTY ROOM
I WONDER IF HARU IS ALL RIGHT.
ARE YOU LISTENING, HARUTA?

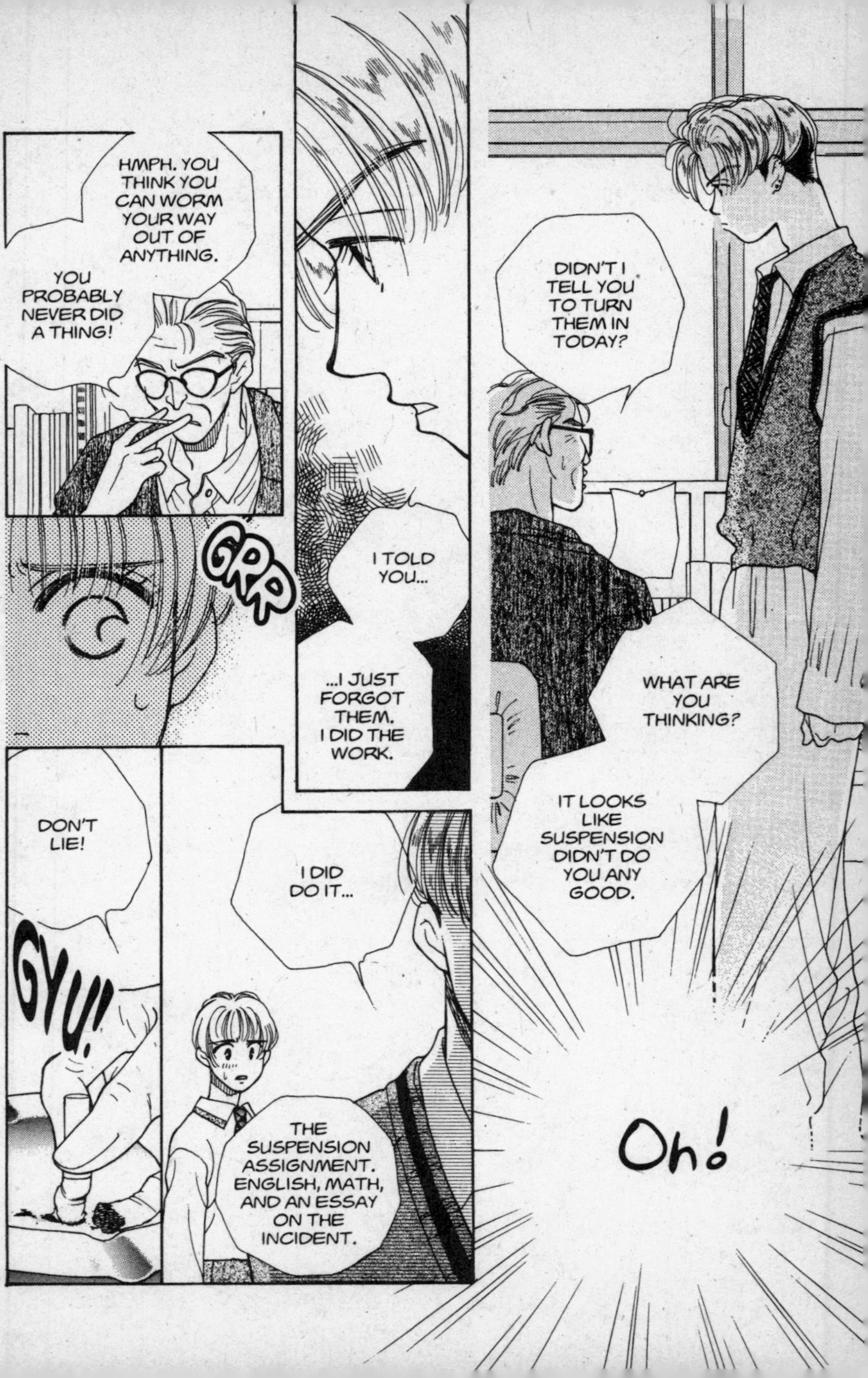
DIDN'T I TELL YOU TO TURN THEM IN TODAY?
WHAT ARE YOU THINKING?
IT LOOKS LIKE SUSPENSION DIDN'T DO YOU ANY GOOD.
I TOLD YOU...
...I JUST FORGOT THEM. I DID THE WORK.
HMPH. YOU THINK YOU CAN WORM YOUR WAY OUT OF ANYTHING.
YOU PROBABLY NEVER DID A THING!
GRR
I DID DO IT...
THE SUSPENSION ASSIGNMENT. ENGLISH, MATH, AND AN ESSAY ON THE INCIDENT.
DON'T LIE!
GYU!!
Oh!

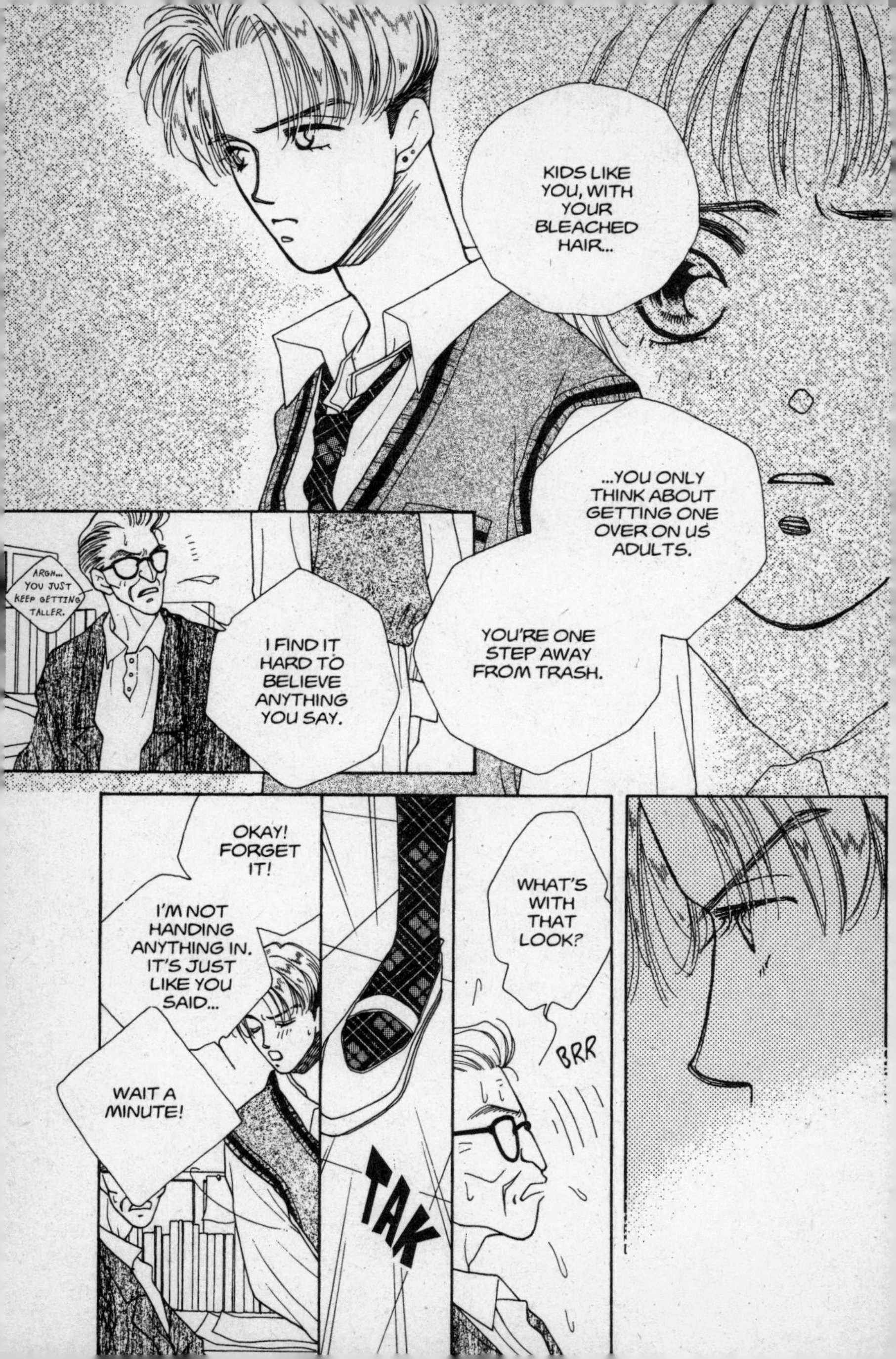
KIDS LIKE YOU, WITH YOUR BLEACHED HAIR...
...YOU ONLY THINK ABOUT GETTING ONE OVER ON US ADULTS.
YOU'RE ONE STEP AWAY FROM TRASH.
I FIND IT HARD TO BELIEVE ANYTHING YOU SAY.
ARGH... YOU JUST KEEP GETTING TALLER.
WHAT'S WITH THAT LOOK?
BRR
TAK
OKAY! FORGET IT!
I'M NOT HANDING ANYTHING IN. IT'S JUST LIKE YOU SAID...
WAIT A MINUTE!

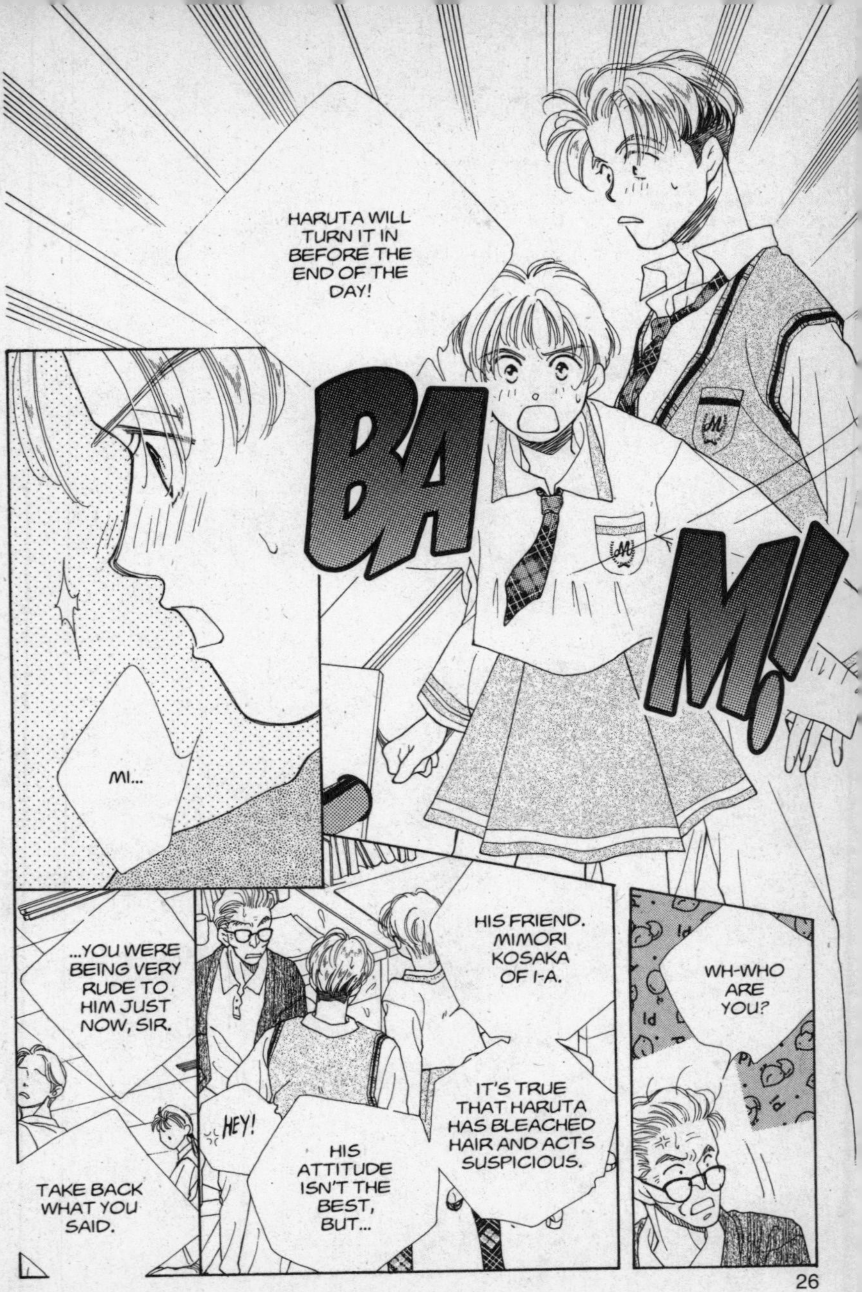
HARUTA WILL TURN IT IN BEFORE THE END OF THE DAY!
BAM!
MI...
WH-WHO ARE YOU?
HIS FRIEND. MIMORI KOSAKA OF I-A.
IT'S TRUE THAT HARUTA HAS BLEACHED HAIR AND ACTS SUSPICIOUS.
HIS ATTITUDE ISN'T THE BEST, BUT...
HEY!
...YOU WERE BEING VERY RUDE TO HIM JUST NOW, SIR.
TAKE BACK WHAT YOU SAID.

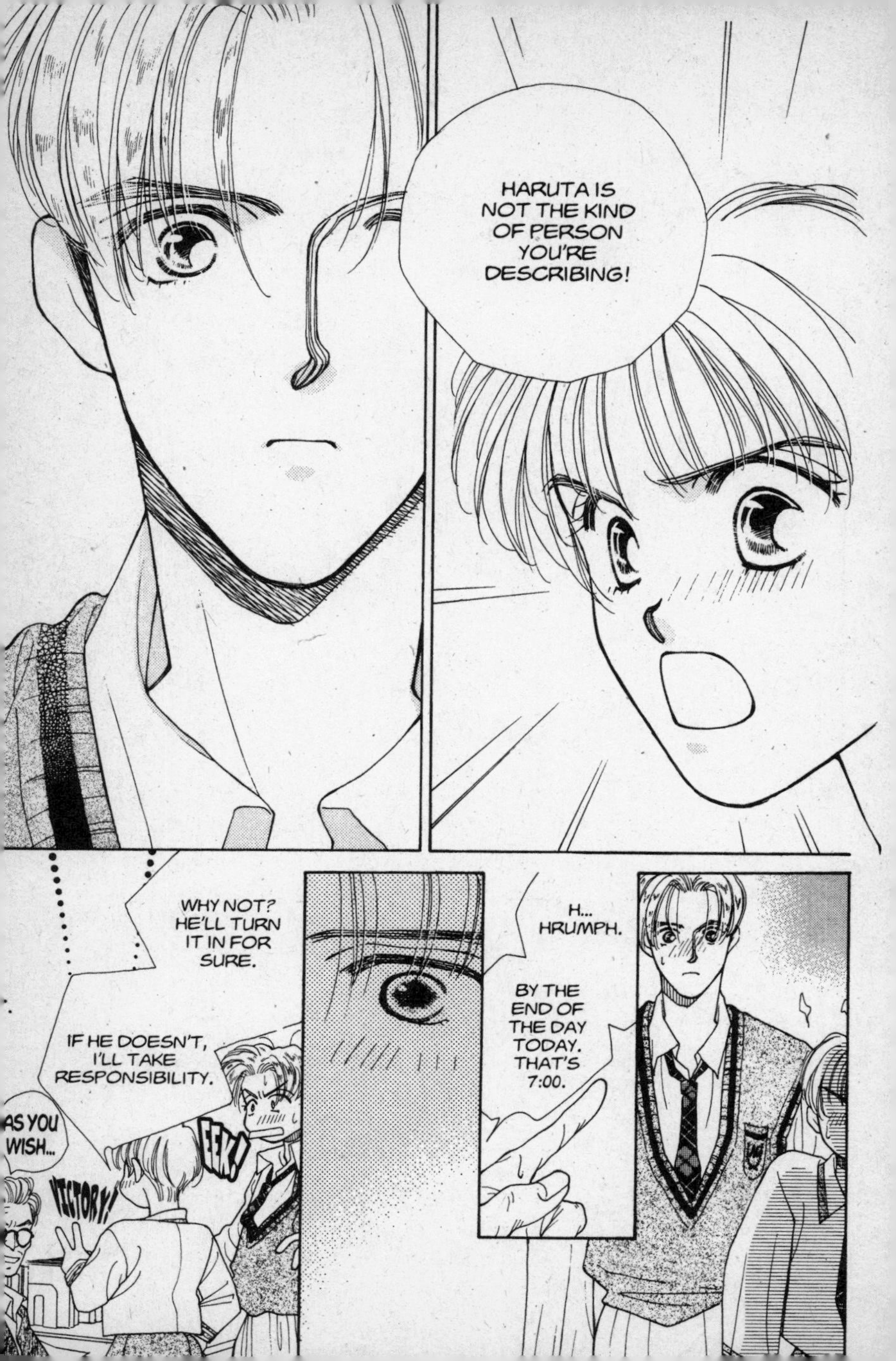
HARUTA IS NOT THE KIND OF PERSON YOU'RE DESCRIBING!
H... HRUMPH.
BY THE END OF THE DAY TODAY. THAT'S 7:00.
WHY NOT? HE'LL TURN IT IN FOR SURE.
IF HE DOESN'T, I'LL TAKE RESPONSIBILITY.
EEK!
AS YOU WISH...
VICTORY!

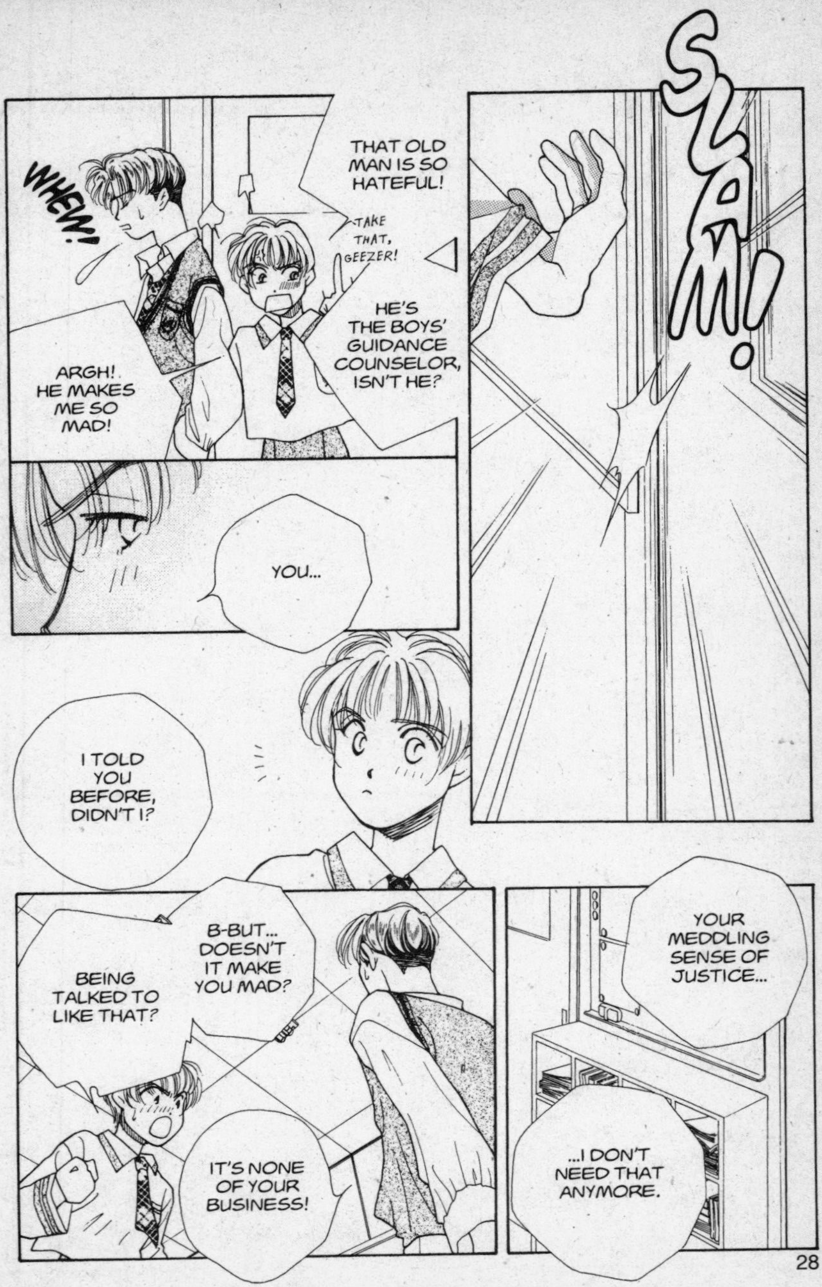
SLAM!
THAT OLD MAN IS SO HATEFUL!
TAKE THAT, GEEZER!
HE'S THE BOYS' GUIDANCE COUNSELOR, ISN'T HE?
WHEW!
ARGH! HE MAKES ME SO MAD!
YOU...
I TOLD YOU BEFORE, DIDN'T I?
YOUR MEDDLING SENSE OF JUSTICE...
...I DON'T NEED THAT ANYMORE.
B-BUT... DOESN'T IT MAKE YOU MAD?
BEING TALKED TO LIKE THAT?
IT'S NONE OF YOUR BUSINESS!

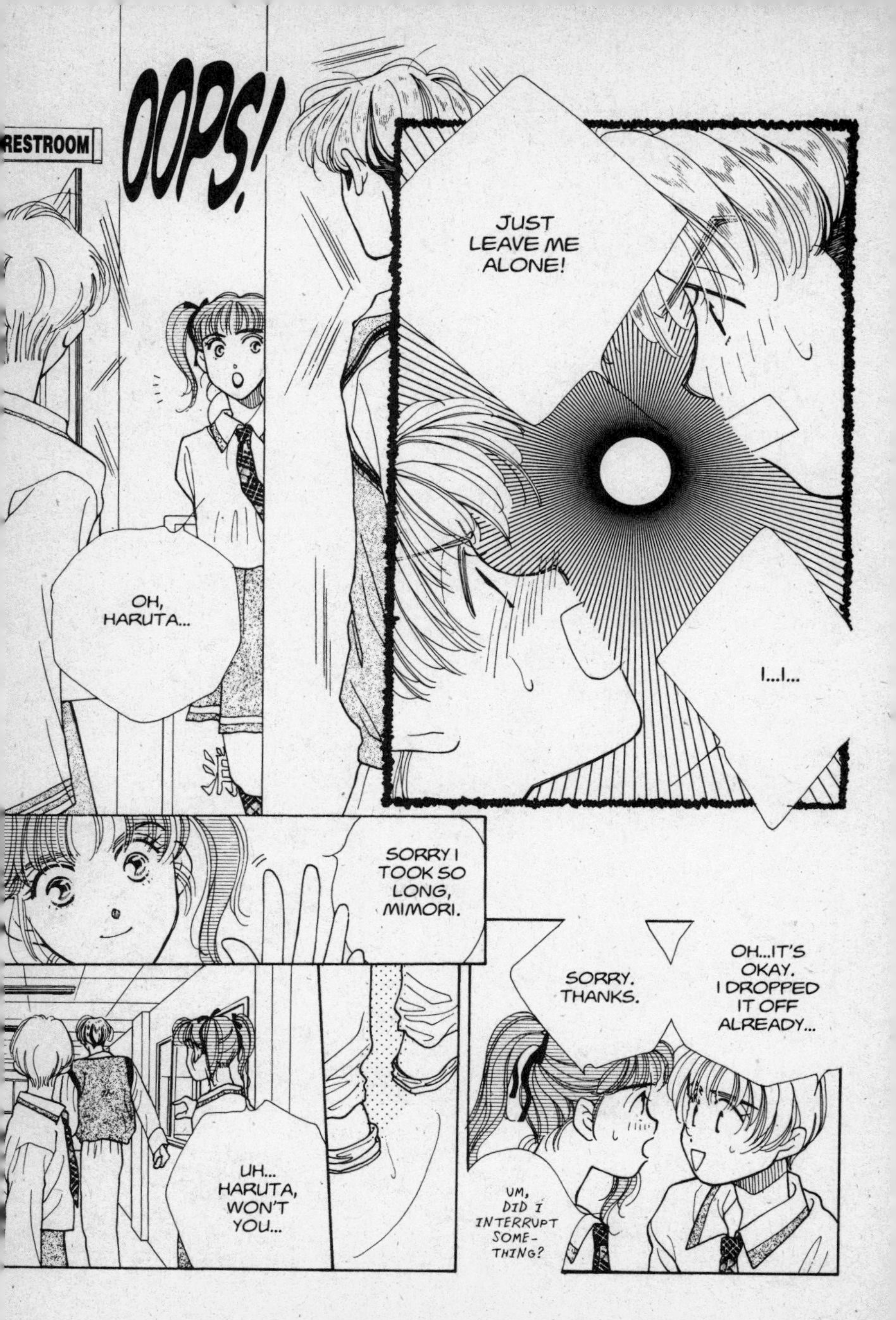
JUST LEAVE ME ALONE!
I...I...
OOPS!
RESTROOM
OH, HARUTA...
OH...IT'S OKAY. I DROPPED IT OFF ALREADY...
SORRY. THANKS.
UM, DID I INTERRUPT SOME-THING?
SORRY I TOOK SO LONG, MIMORI.
UH... HARUTA, WON'T YOU...

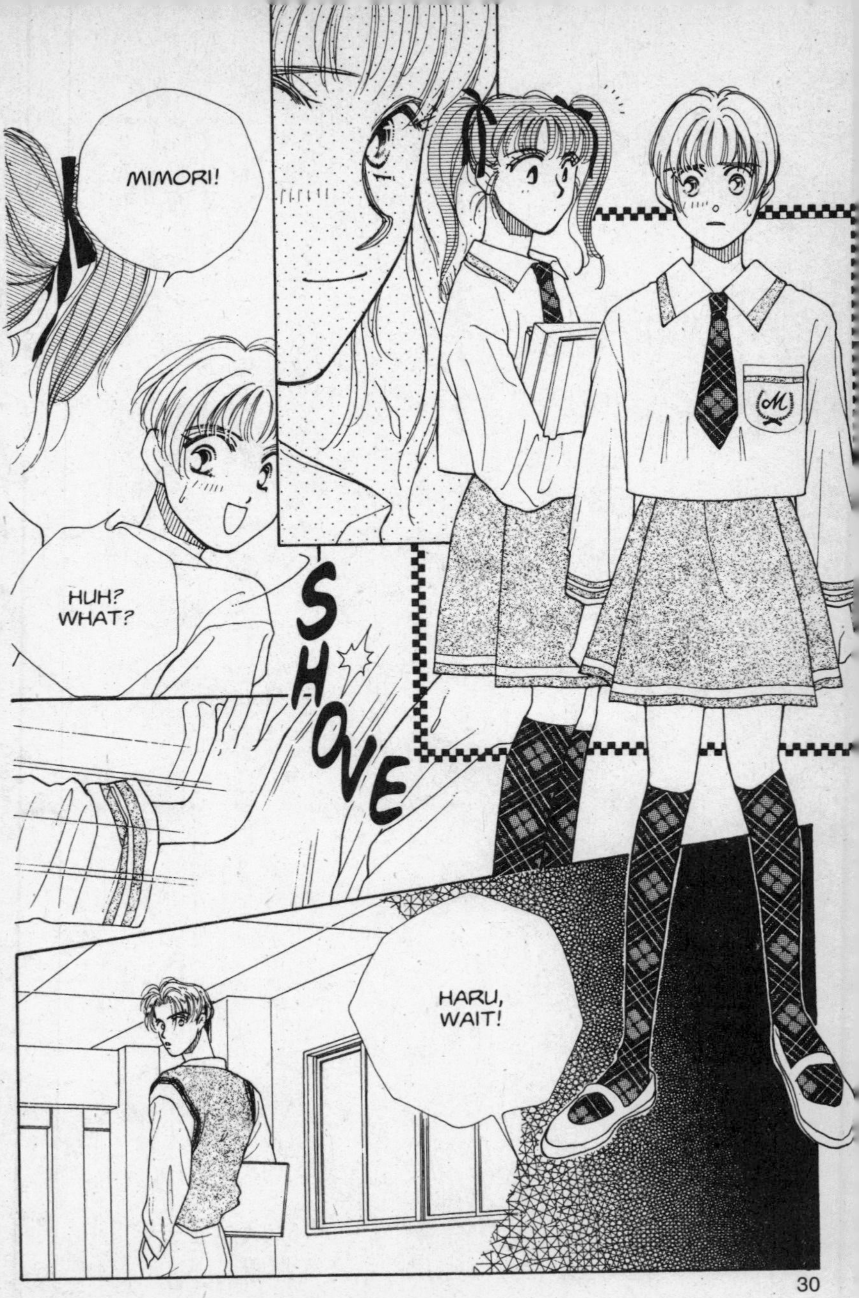
MIMORI!
HUH? WHAT?
SHOVE
HARU, WAIT!

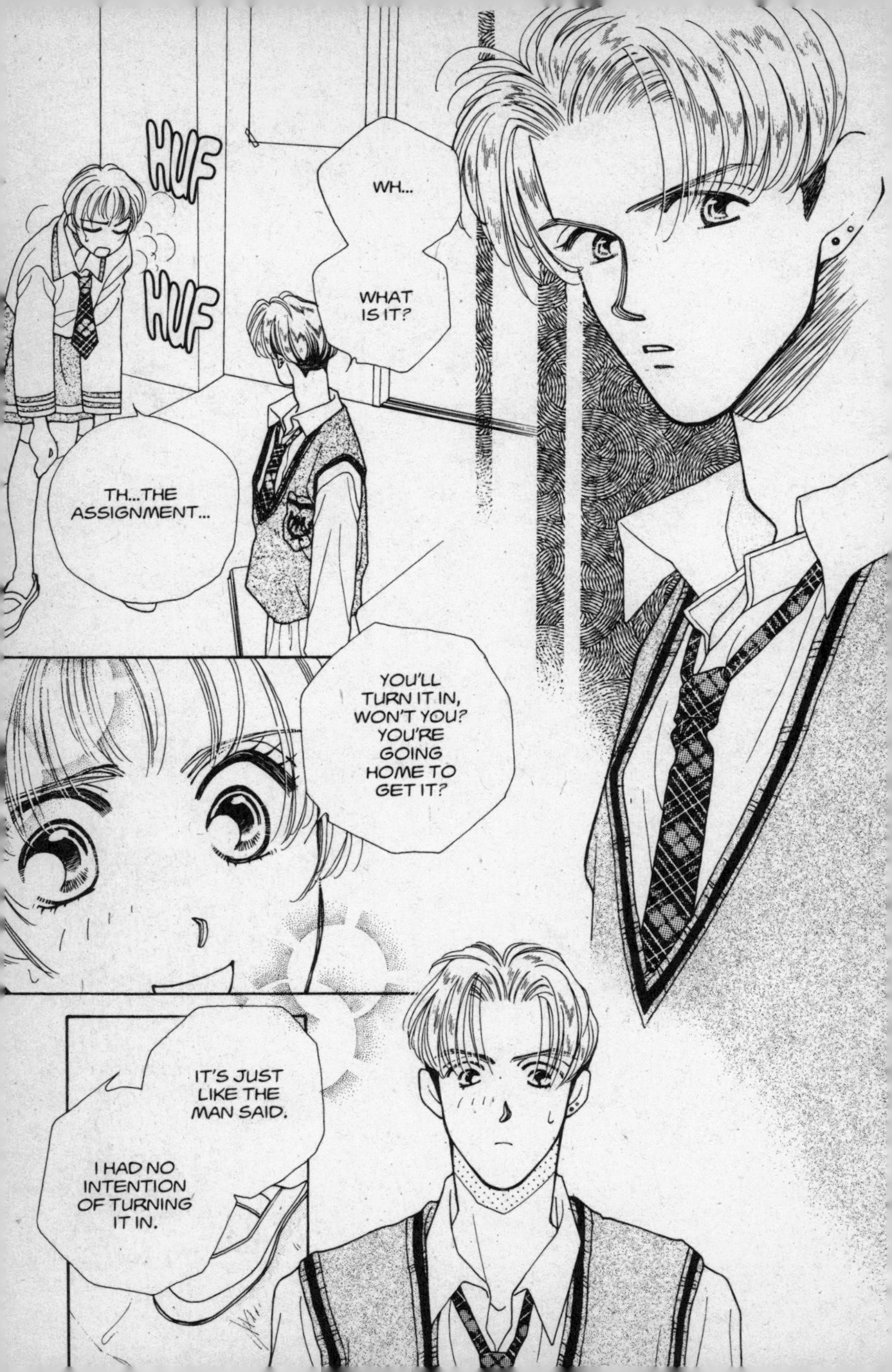
WH...
WHAT IS IT?
HUF
HUF
TH...THE ASSIGNMENT...
YOU'LL TURN IT IN, WON'T YOU? YOU'RE GOING HOME TO GET IT?
IT'S JUST LIKE THE MAN SAID.
I HAD NO INTENTION OF TURNING IT IN.

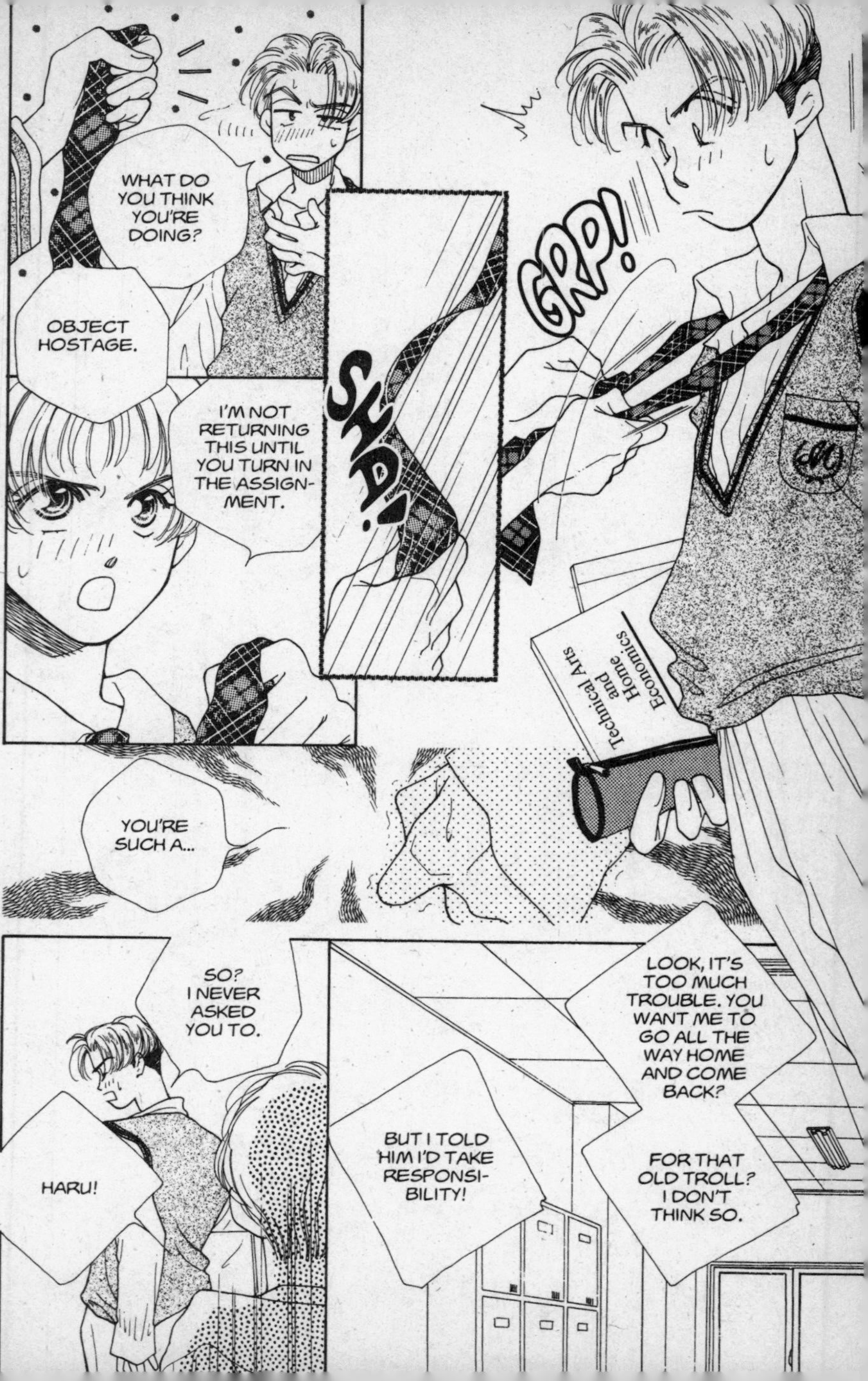
GRP!
Technical Arts and Home Economics
SHA!
WHAT DO YOU THINK YOU'RE DOING?
OBJECT HOSTAGE.
I'M NOT RETURNING THIS UNTIL YOU TURN IN THE ASSIGNMENT.
YOU'RE SUCH A...
LOOK, IT'S TOO MUCH TROUBLE. YOU WANT ME TO GO ALL THE WAY HOME AND COME BACK?
FOR THAT OLD TROLL? I DON'T THINK SO.
BUT I TOLD HIM I'D TAKE RESPONSIBILITY!
SO? I NEVER ASKED YOU TO.
HARU!

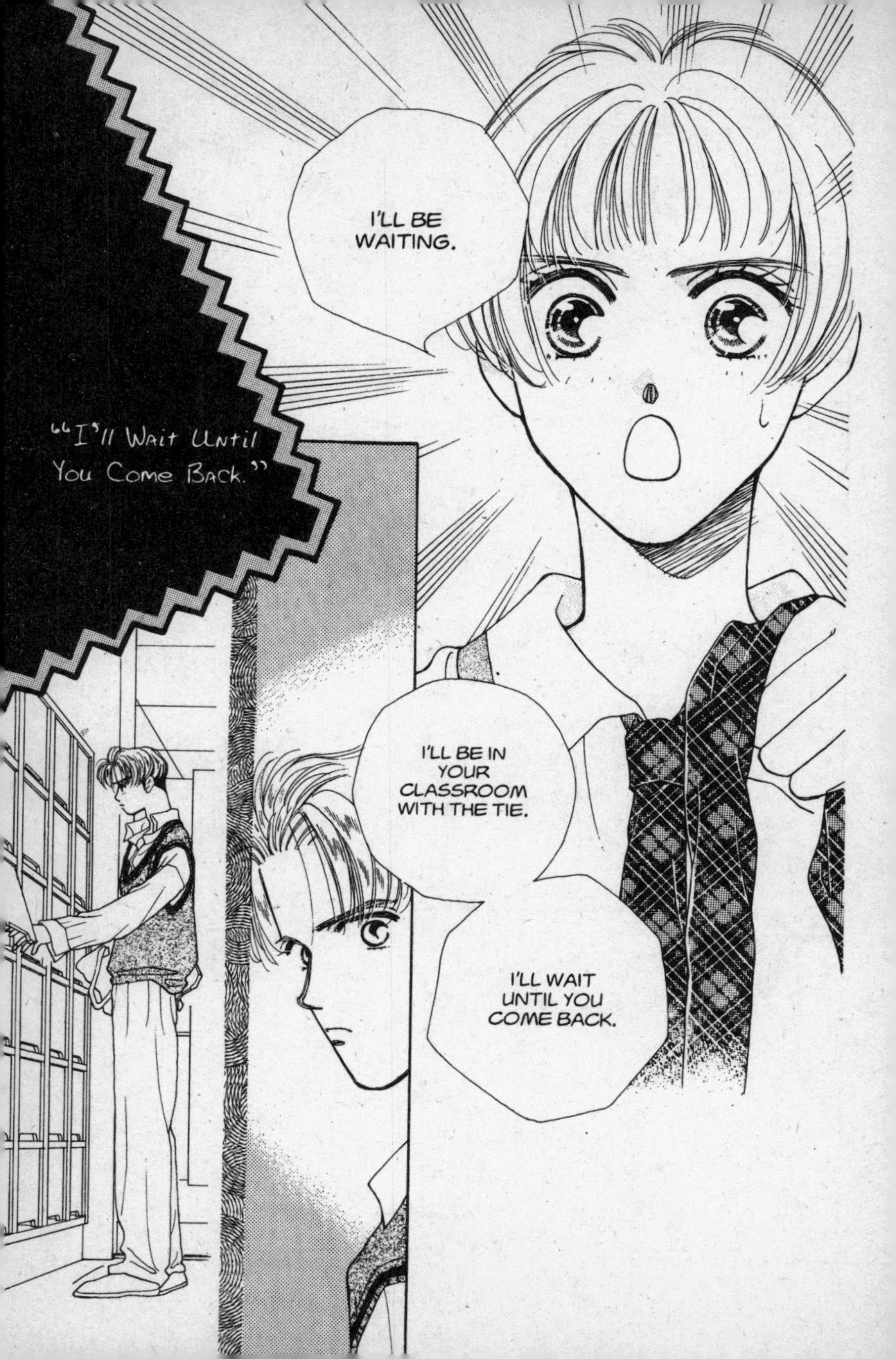
I'LL BE WAITING.
I'LL BE IN YOUR CLASSROOM WITH THE TIE.
I'LL WAIT UNTIL YOU COME BACK.
"I'll Wait Until You Come Back."

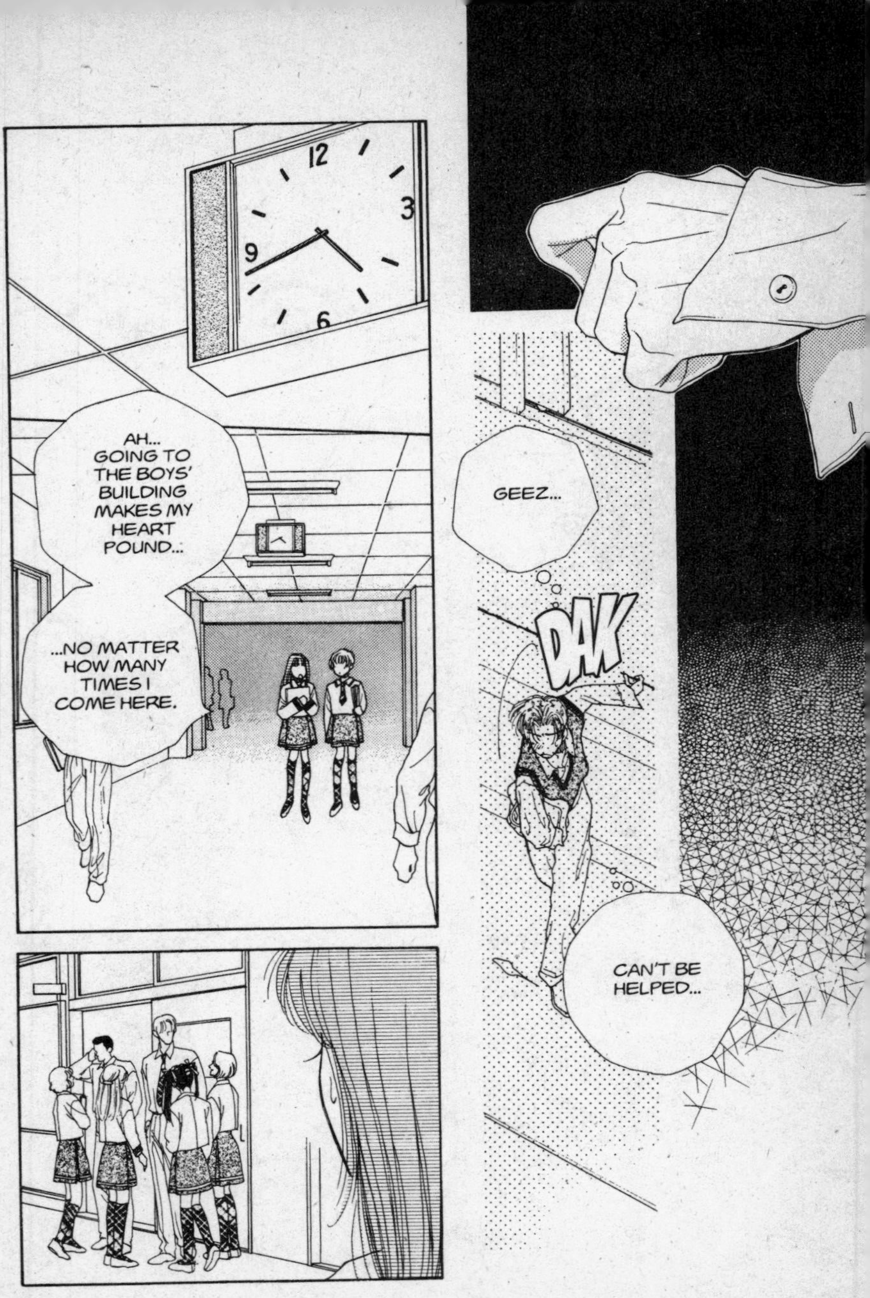
GEEZ...
DAK
CAN'T BE HELPED...
AH... GOING TO THE BOYS' BUILDING MAKES MY HEART POUND...
...NO MATTER HOW MANY TIMES I COME HERE.

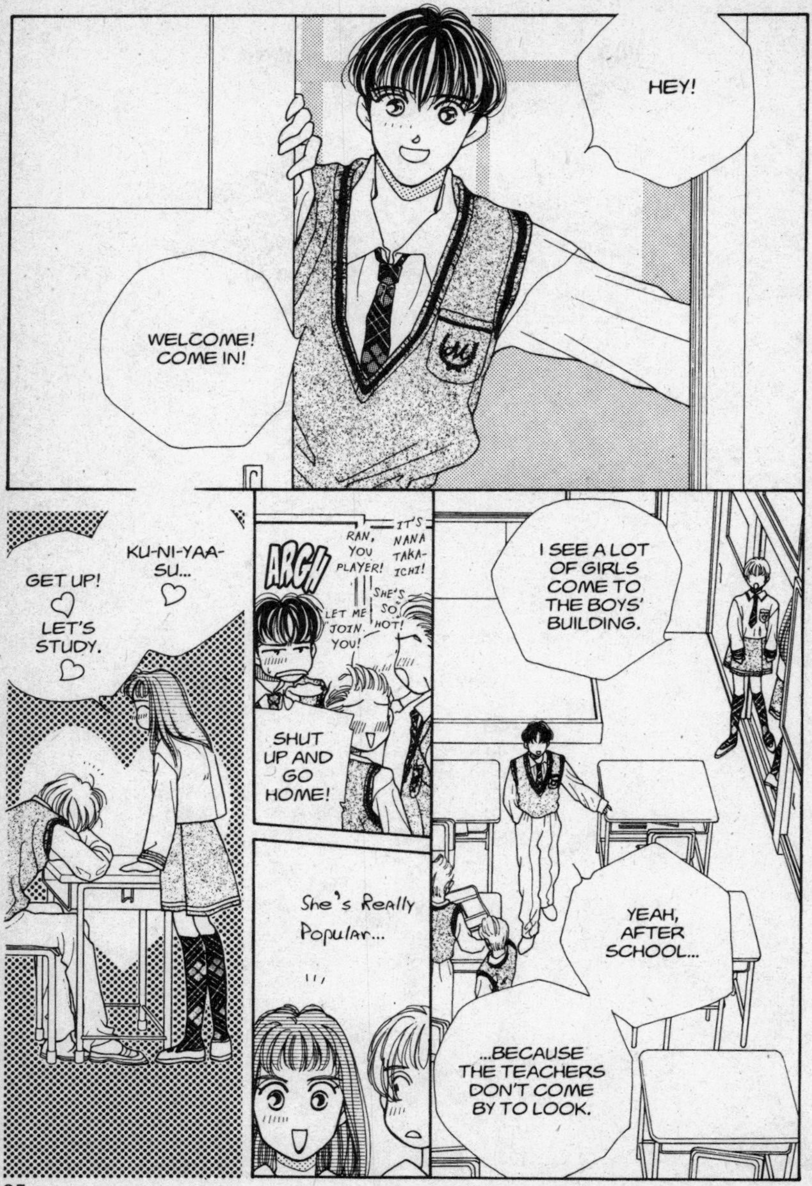
HEY!
WELCOME! COME IN!
I SEE A LOT OF GIRLS COME TO THE BOYS' BUILDING.
YEAH, AFTER SCHOOL...
...BECAUSE THE TEACHERS DON'T COME BY TO LOOK.
IT'S NANA TAKA-ICHI!
RAN, YOU PLAYER!
SHE'S SO HOT!
LET ME JOIN YOU!
ARGH
SHUT UP AND GO HOME!
She's Really Popular...
KU-NI-YAA-SU... ♡
GET UP! ♡ LET'S STUDY. ♡

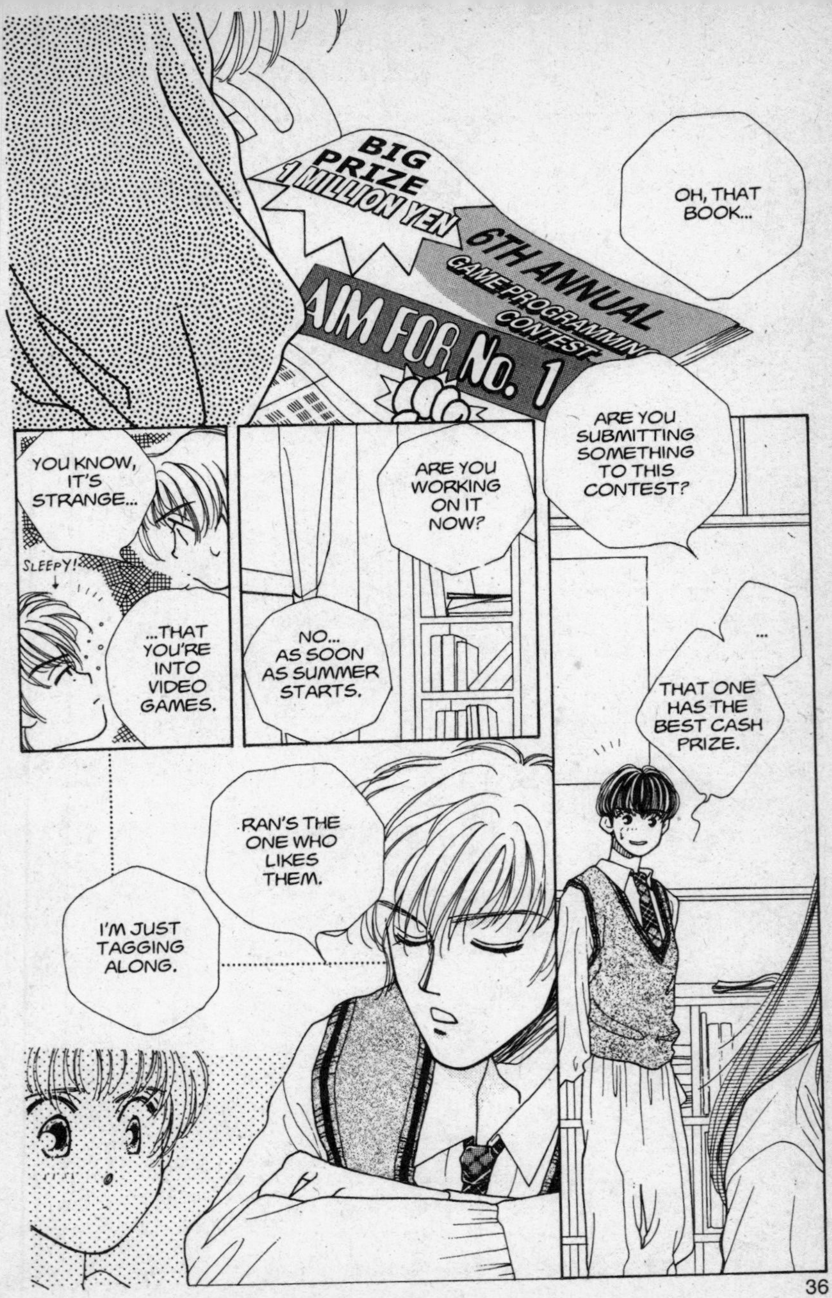
OH, THAT BOOK...
BIG PRIZE 1 MILLION YEN
6TH ANNUAL GAME PROGRAMMIN CONTEST
AIM FOR No. 1
ARE YOU SUBMITTING SOMETHING TO THIS CONTEST?
...
THAT ONE HAS THE BEST CASH PRIZE.
ARE YOU WORKING ON IT NOW?
NO... AS SOON AS SUMMER STARTS.
YOU KNOW, IT'S STRANGE...
SLEEPY!
...THAT YOU'RE INTO VIDEO GAMES.
RAN'S THE ONE WHO LIKES THEM.
I'M JUST TAGGING ALONG.

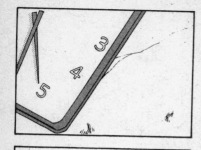

WHAT'S THAT?

YOU BROUGHT TWO NECKTIES?

WH-WHAT'S WRONG WITH THAT?

HEY, RAN, WHERE SHOULD WE SIT?

OH, ANYWHERE, ANYWHERE...

Haru...

OH, SO THAT'S IT! THE 3 GOES IN THERE...

RAN, ARE YOU USING THE FORMULA?

CREAK

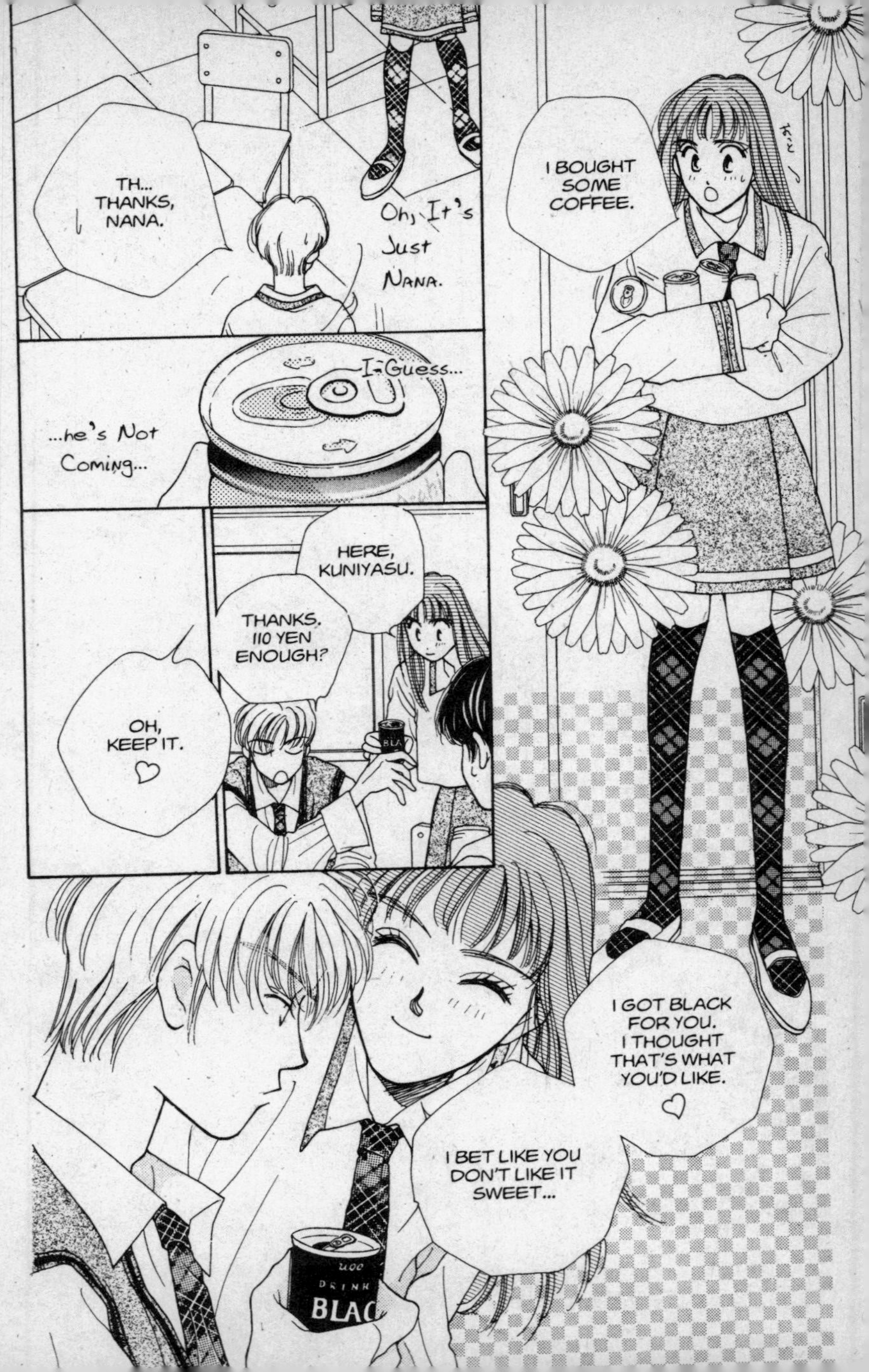
I BOUGHT SOME COFFEE.
TH... THANKS, NANA.
Oh, It's Just Nana.
I-Guess...
...he's Not Coming...
HERE, KUNIYASU.
THANKS. 110 YEN ENOUGH?
OH, KEEP IT. ♡
I GOT BLACK FOR YOU. I THOUGHT THAT'S WHAT YOU'D LIKE. ♡
I BET LIKE YOU DON'T LIKE IT SWEET...
DRINK BLAC

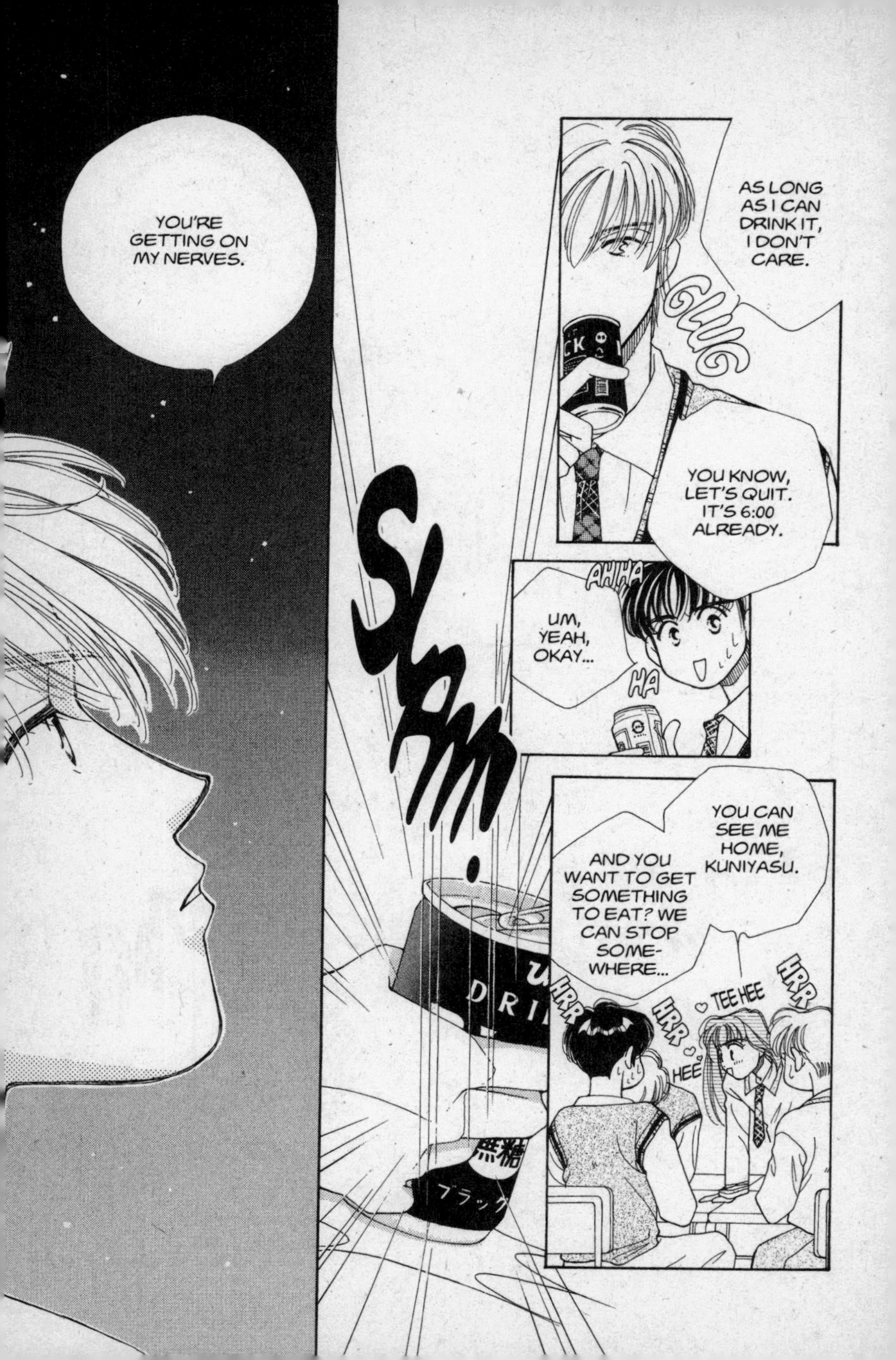
AS LONG AS I CAN DRINK IT, I DON'T CARE.
GLUG
YOU KNOW, LET'S QUIT. IT'S 6:00 ALREADY.
AHHA
UM, YEAH, OKAY...
HA
YOU CAN SEE ME HOME, KUNIYASU.
AND YOU WANT TO GET SOMETHING TO EAT? WE CAN STOP SOME-WHERE...
HRR
TEE HEE
HRR
HRR
HEE
SLAM!
無糖
ブラック
YOU'RE GETTING ON MY NERVES.

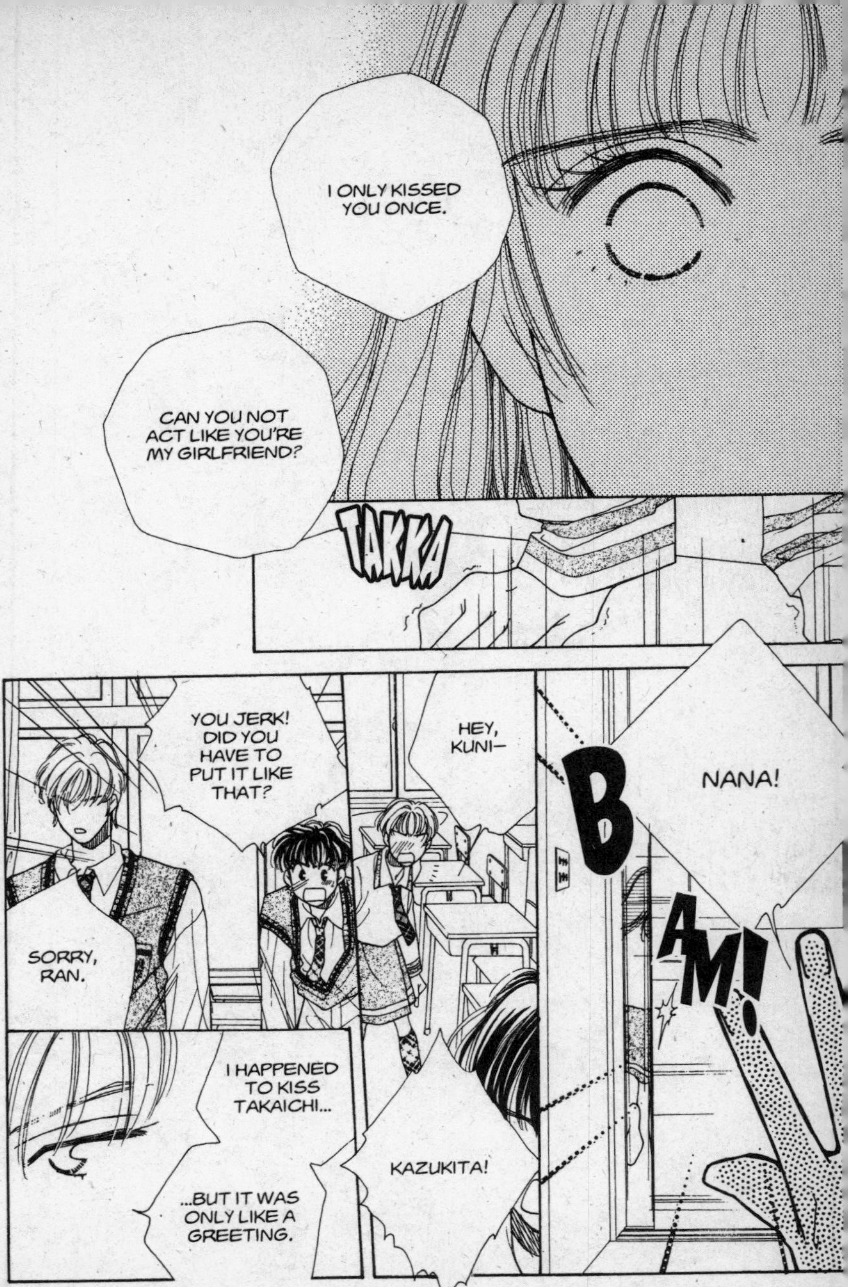

I ONLY KISSED YOU ONCE.
CAN YOU NOT ACT LIKE YOU'RE MY GIRLFRIEND?
TAKKA
BAM!
NANA!
KAZUKITA!
HEY, KUNI—
YOU JERK! DID YOU HAVE TO PUT IT LIKE THAT?
SORRY, RAN.
I HAPPENED TO KISS TAKAICHI...
...BUT IT WAS ONLY LIKE A GREETING.

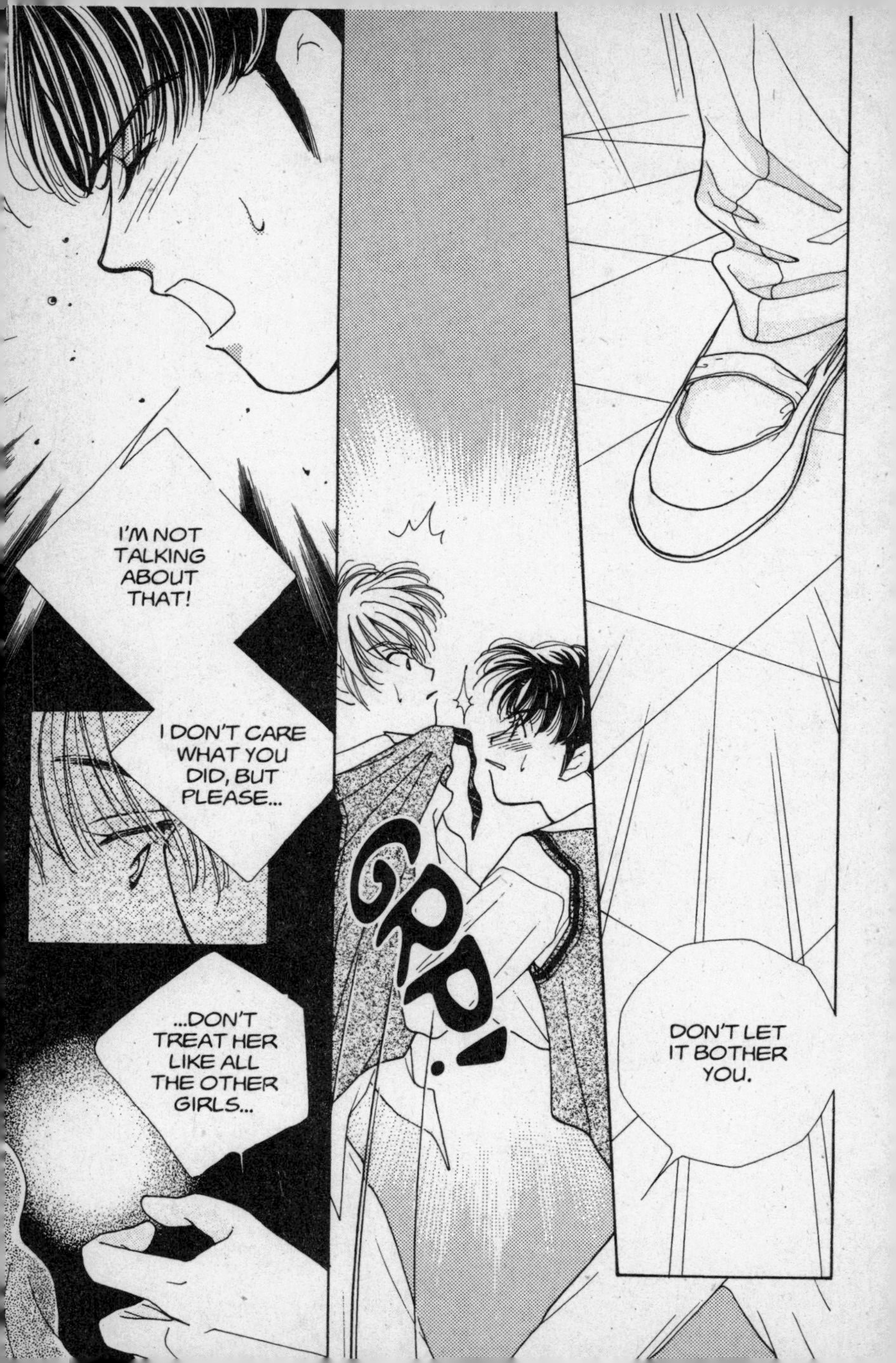
DON'T LET IT BOTHER YOU.
GRP!
I'M NOT TALKING ABOUT THAT!
I DON'T CARE WHAT YOU DID, BUT PLEASE...
...DON'T TREAT HER LIKE ALL THE OTHER GIRLS...

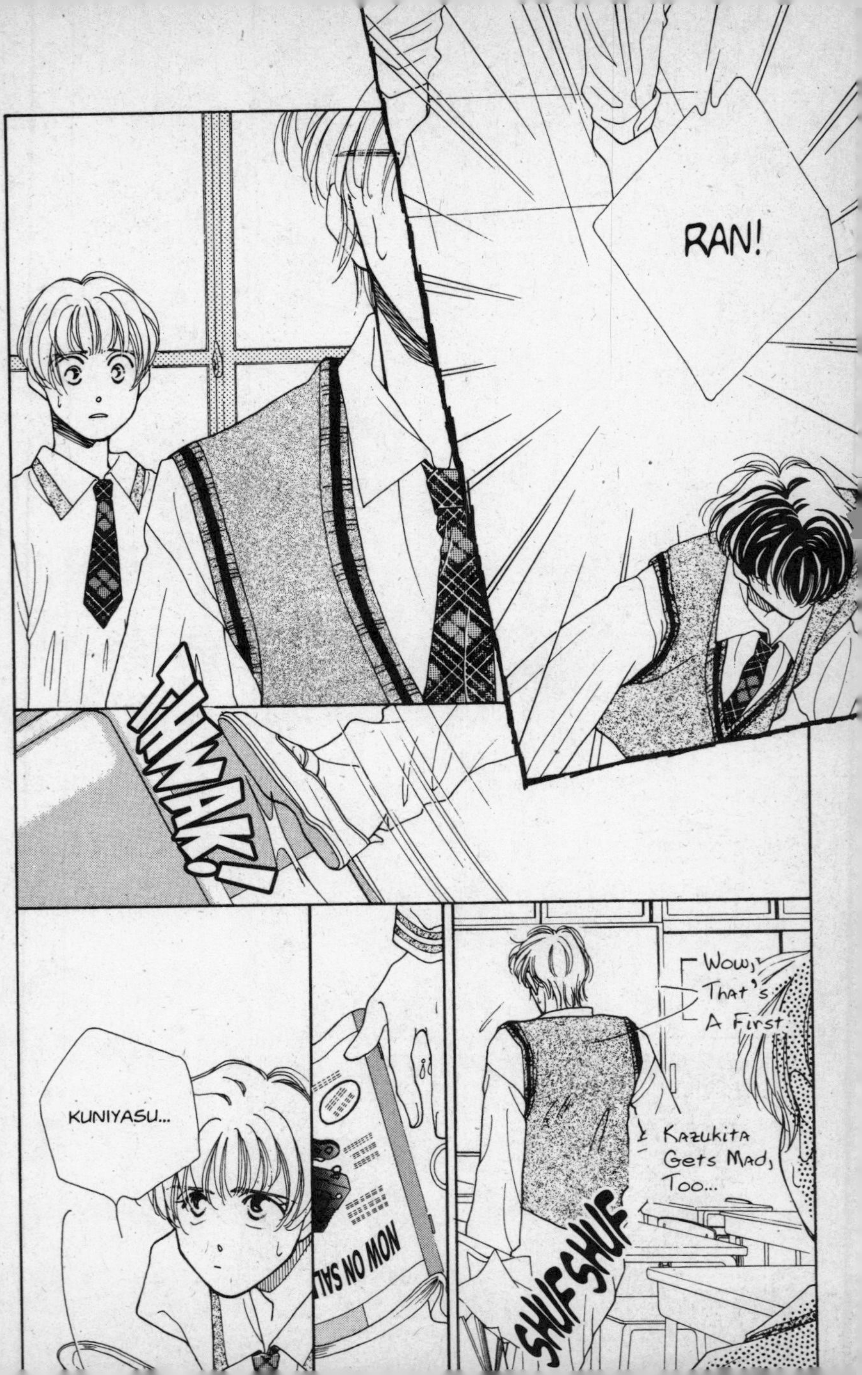
RAN!
THWAK!
Wow, That's A First.
Kazukita Gets Mad, Too...
SHUF SHUF
KUNIYASU...

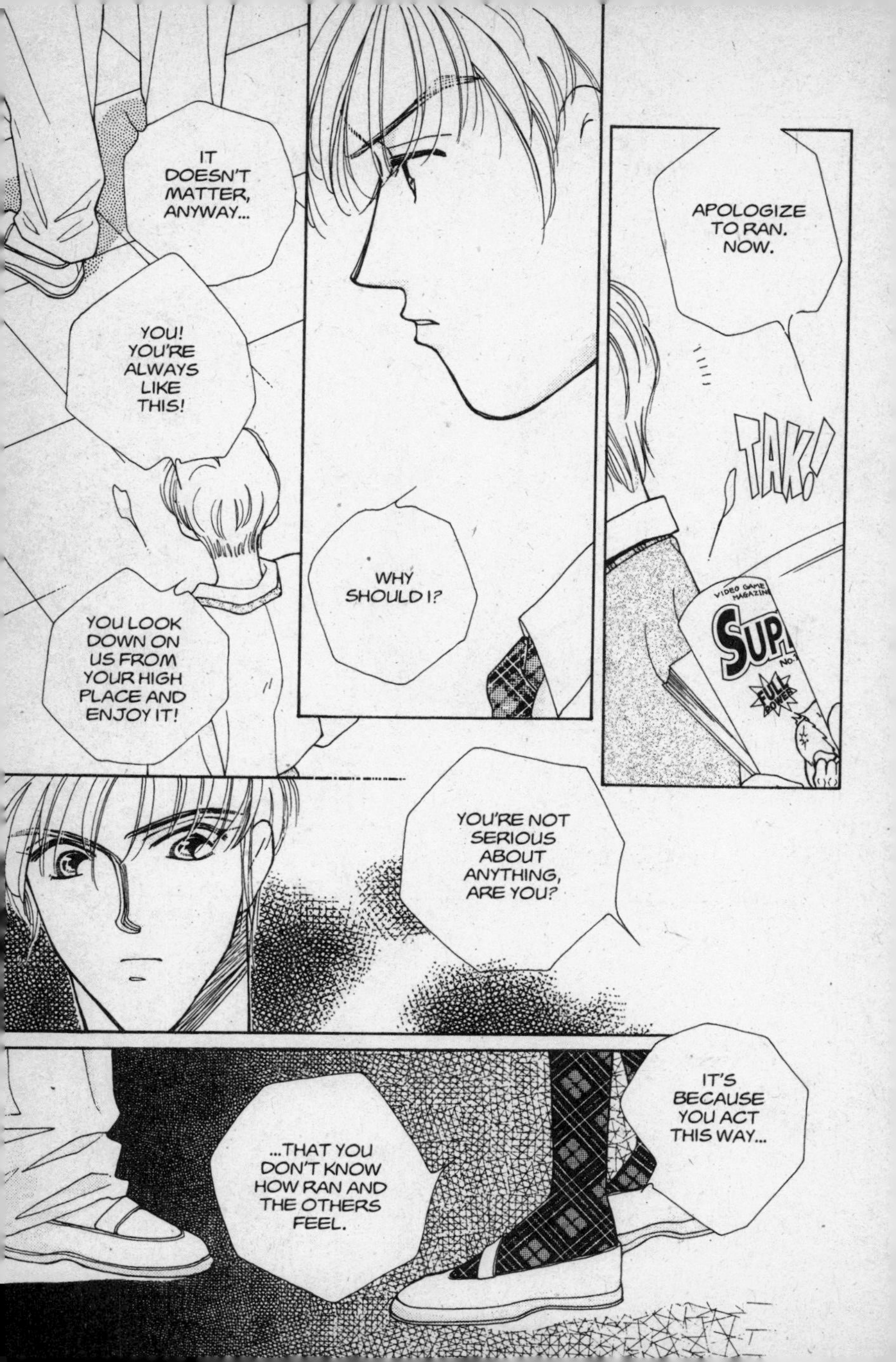
APOLOGIZE TO RAN. NOW.
TAK!
VIDEO GAME MAGAZINE
FULL POWER
WHY SHOULD I?
IT DOESN'T MATTER, ANYWAY...
YOU! YOU'RE ALWAYS LIKE THIS!
YOU LOOK DOWN ON US FROM YOUR HIGH PLACE AND ENJOY IT!
YOU'RE NOT SERIOUS ABOUT ANYTHING, ARE YOU?
IT'S BECAUSE YOU ACT THIS WAY...
...THAT YOU DON'T KNOW HOW RAN AND THE OTHERS FEEL.

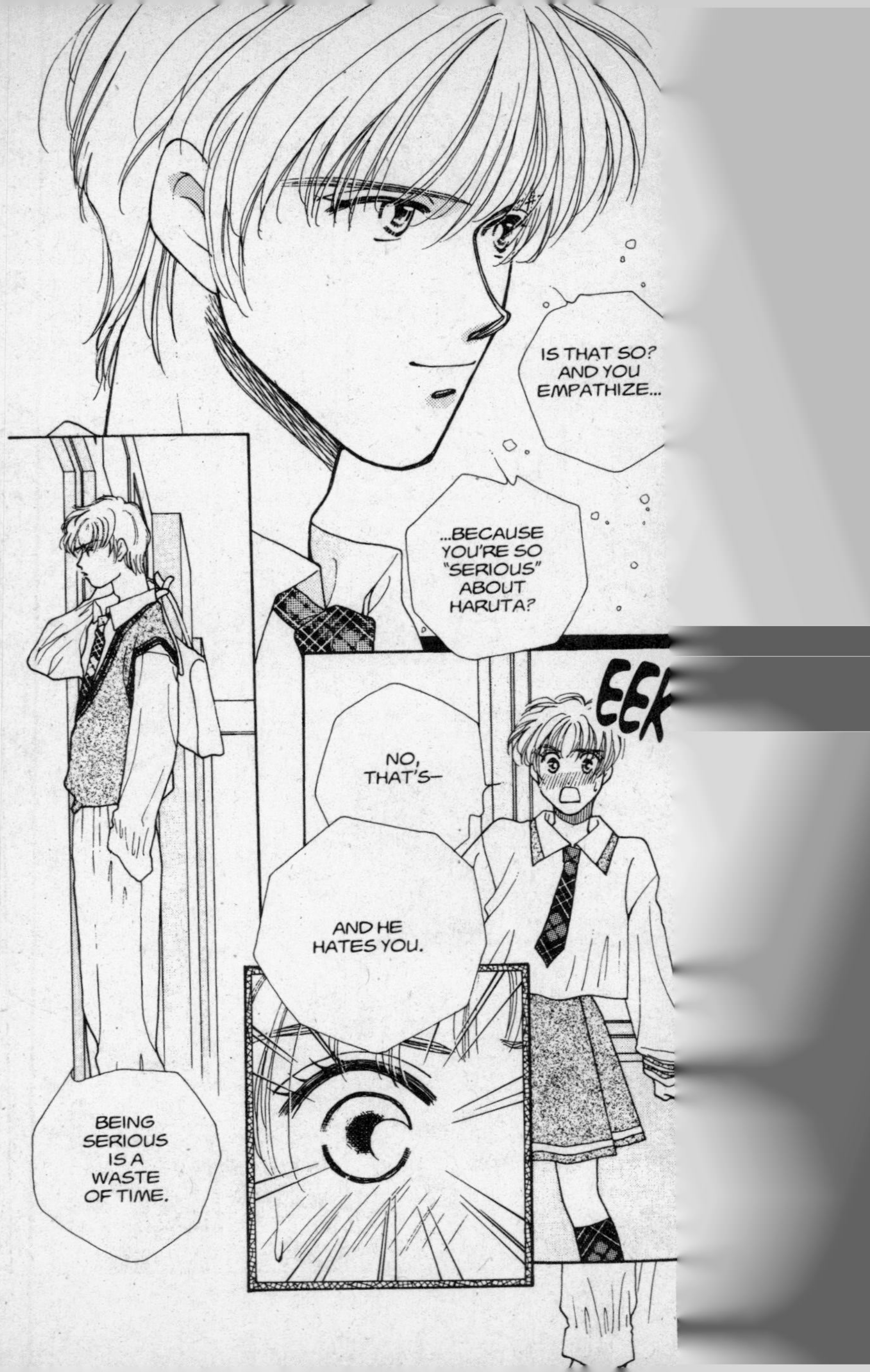
IS THAT SO? AND YOU EMPATHIZE...
...BECAUSE YOU'RE SO "SERIOUS" ABOUT HARUTA?
EEK
NO, THAT'S—
AND HE HATES YOU.
BEING SERIOUS IS A WASTE OF TIME.

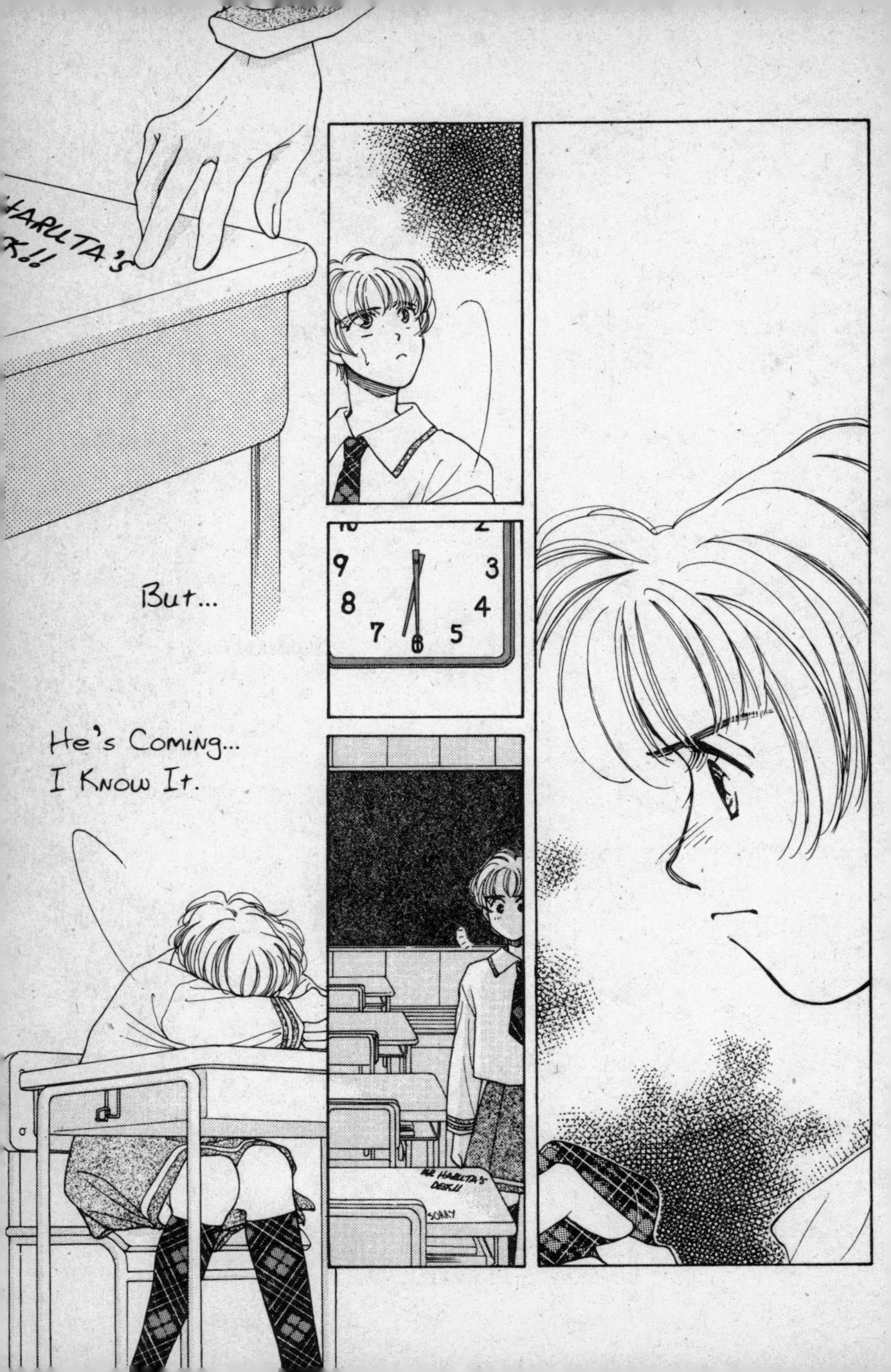

MR HARUTA'S DESK!!
SORRY
HARUTA'S
K!!
But...
He's Coming...
I Know It.

He'll
Come...

...for
Sure.

CREAK!

HUF HUF

HUF HUF

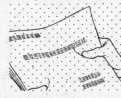

BOYS
1—A

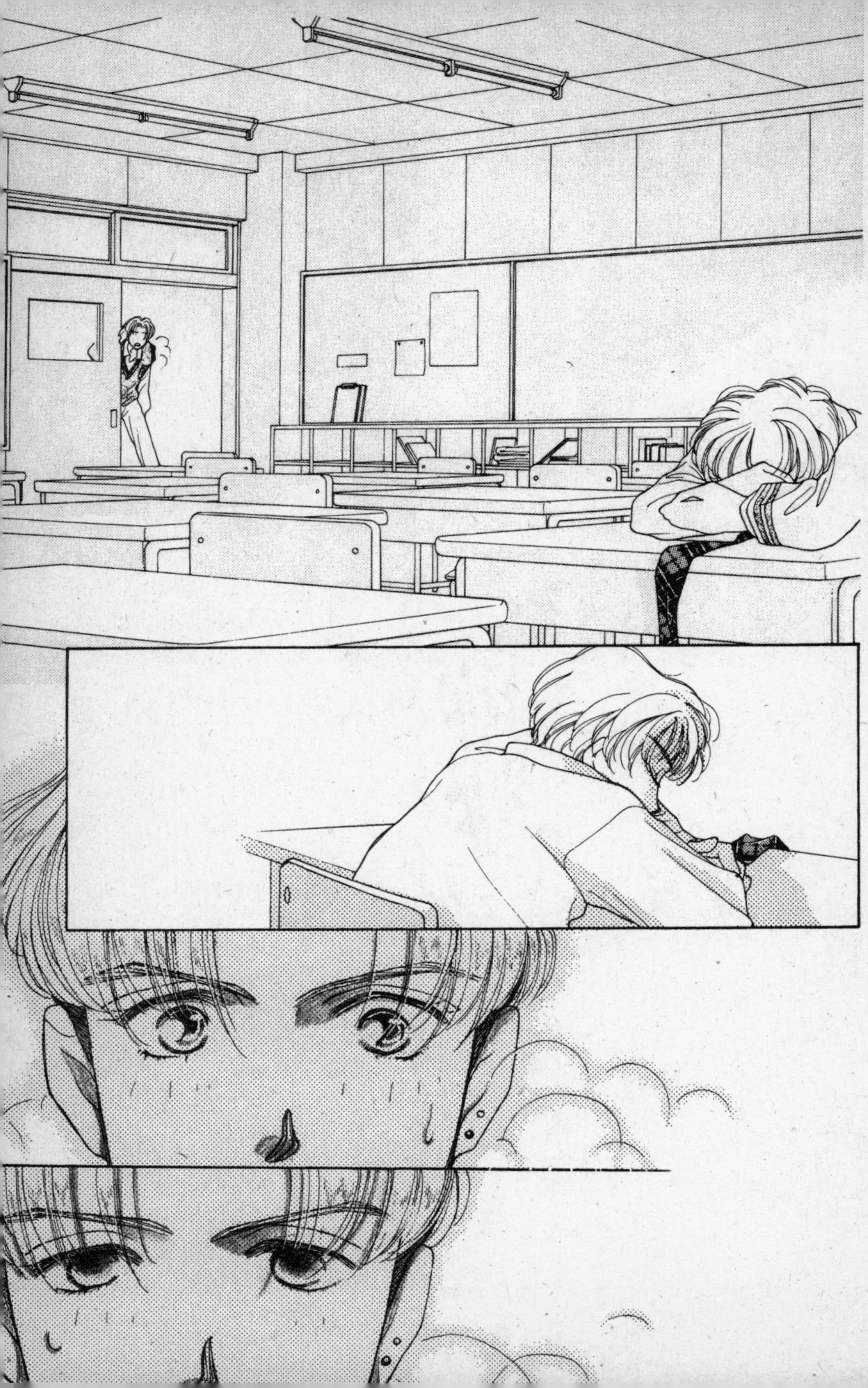

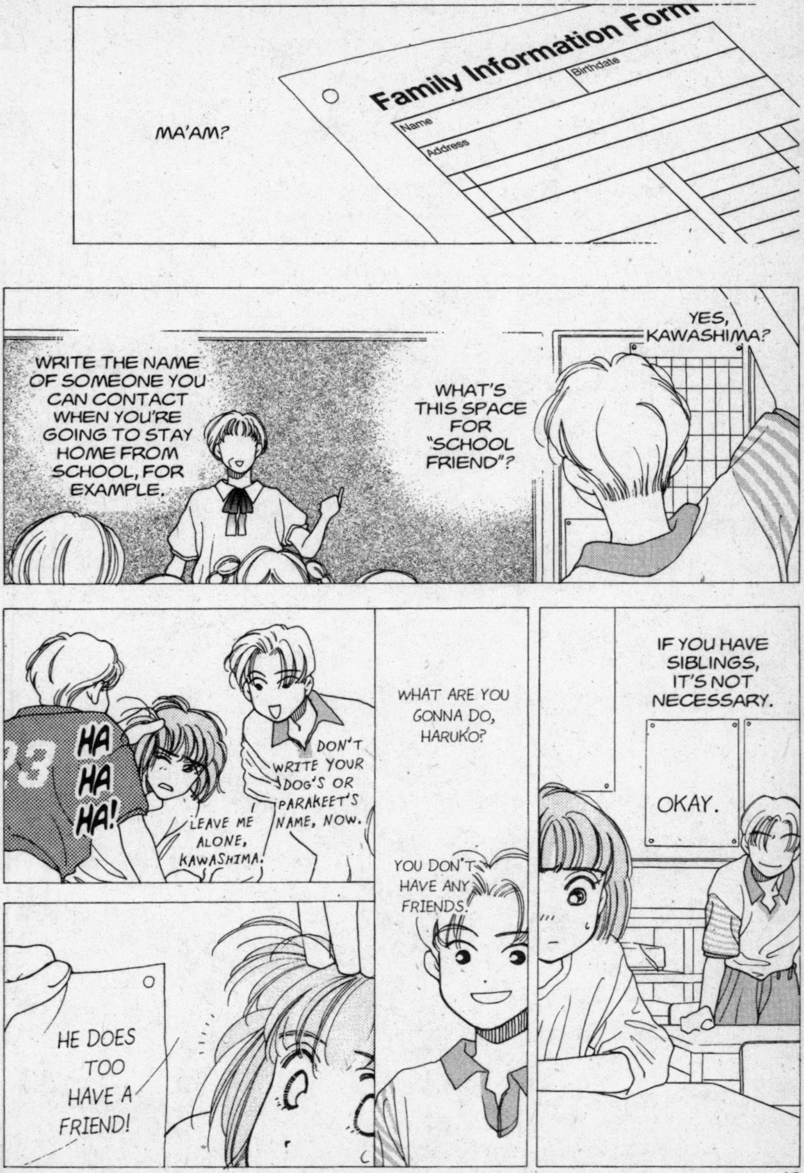
Family Information Form
Birthdate
Name
Address
MA'AM?
YES, KAWASHIMA?
WHAT'S THIS SPACE FOR "SCHOOL FRIEND"?
WRITE THE NAME OF SOMEONE YOU CAN CONTACT WHEN YOU'RE GOING TO STAY HOME FROM SCHOOL, FOR EXAMPLE.
IF YOU HAVE SIBLINGS, IT'S NOT NECESSARY.
OKAY.
WHAT ARE YOU GONNA DO, HARUKO?
YOU DON'T HAVE ANY FRIENDS.
DON'T WRITE YOUR DOG'S OR PARAKEET'S NAME, NOW.
HA HA HA!
LEAVE ME ALONE, KAWASHIMA!
HE DOES TOO HAVE A FRIEND!

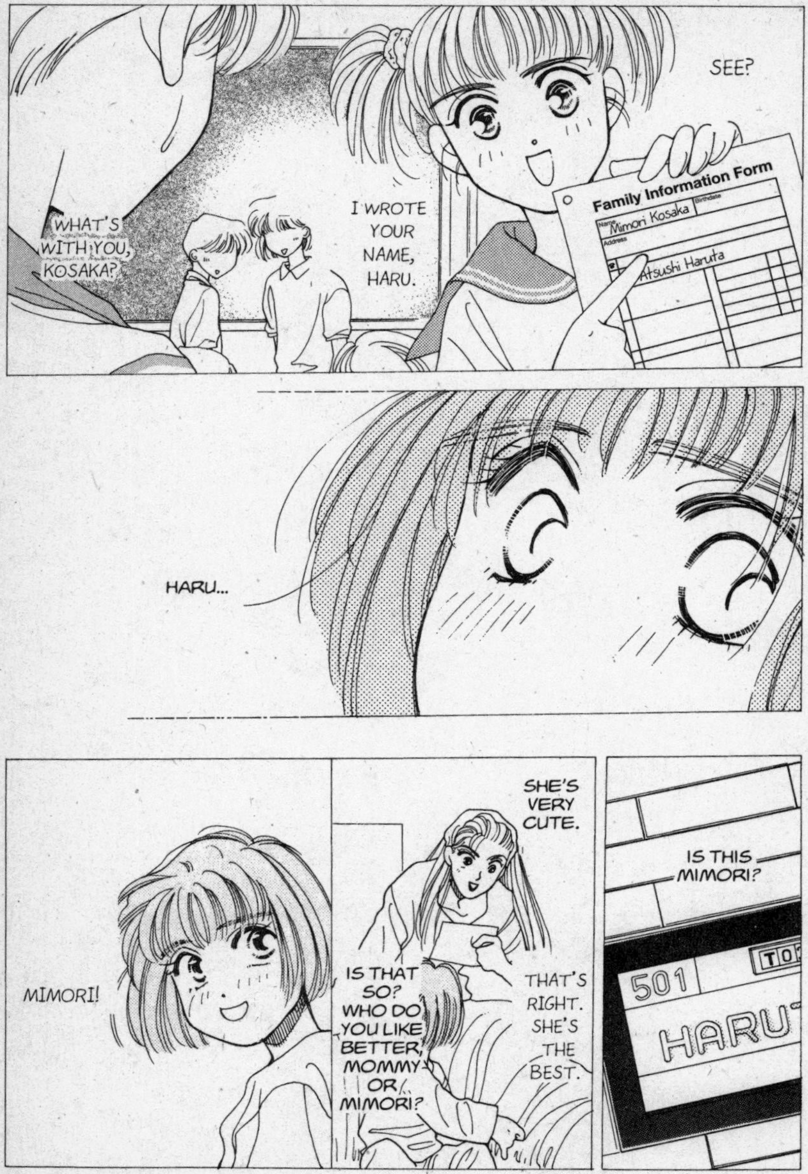
SEE?
Family Information Form
Name Mimori Kosaka
Birthdate
Address
Atsushi Haruta
I WROTE YOUR NAME, HARU.
WHAT'S WITH YOU, KOSAKA?
HARU...
IS THIS MIMORI?
501
HARU
SHE'S VERY CUTE.
THAT'S RIGHT. SHE'S THE BEST.
IS THAT SO? WHO DO YOU LIKE BETTER, MOMMY OR MIMORI?
MIMORI!

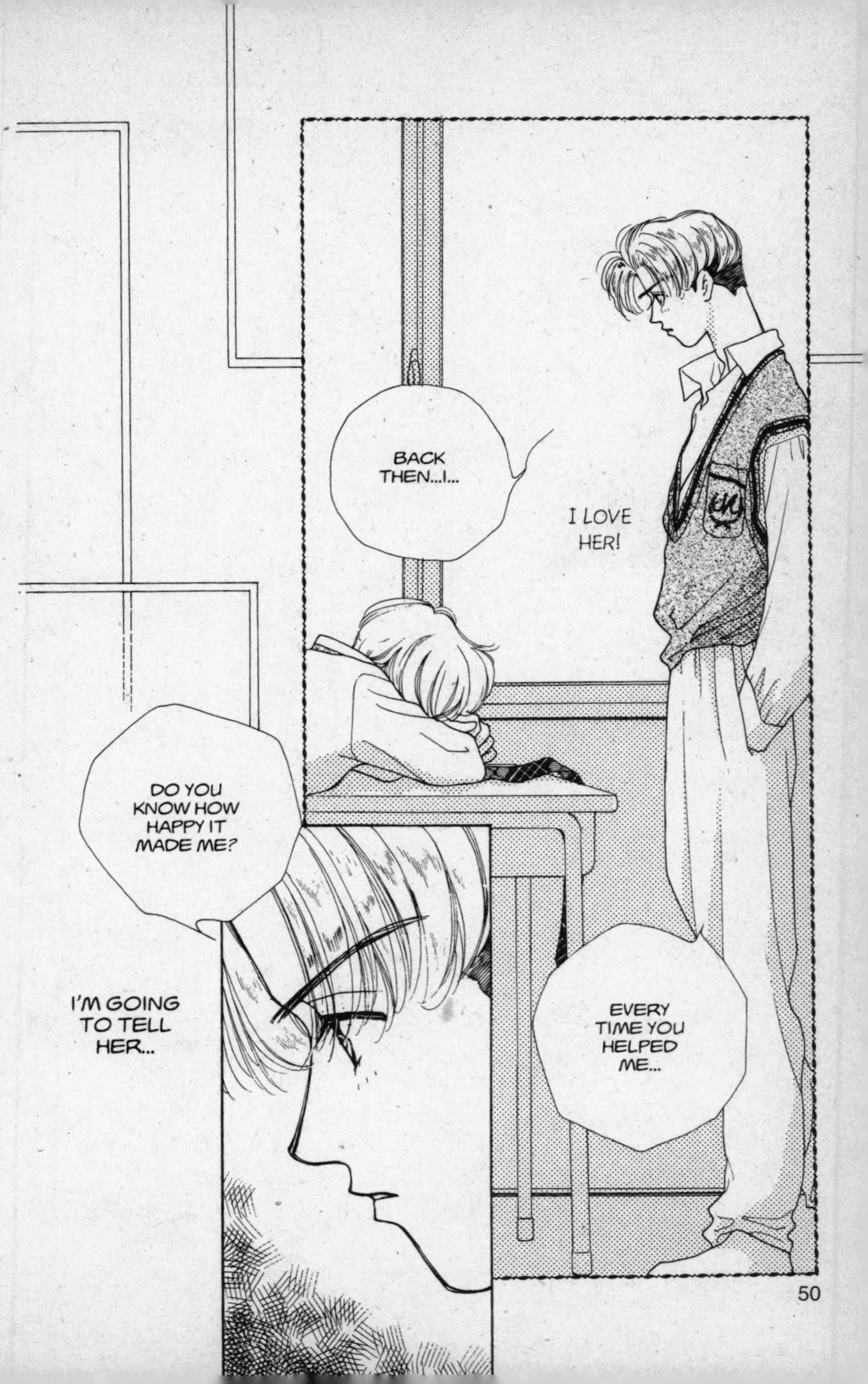
BACK THEN...I...
I LOVE HER!
EVERY TIME YOU HELPED ME...
DO YOU KNOW HOW HAPPY IT MADE ME?
I'M GOING TO TELL HER...

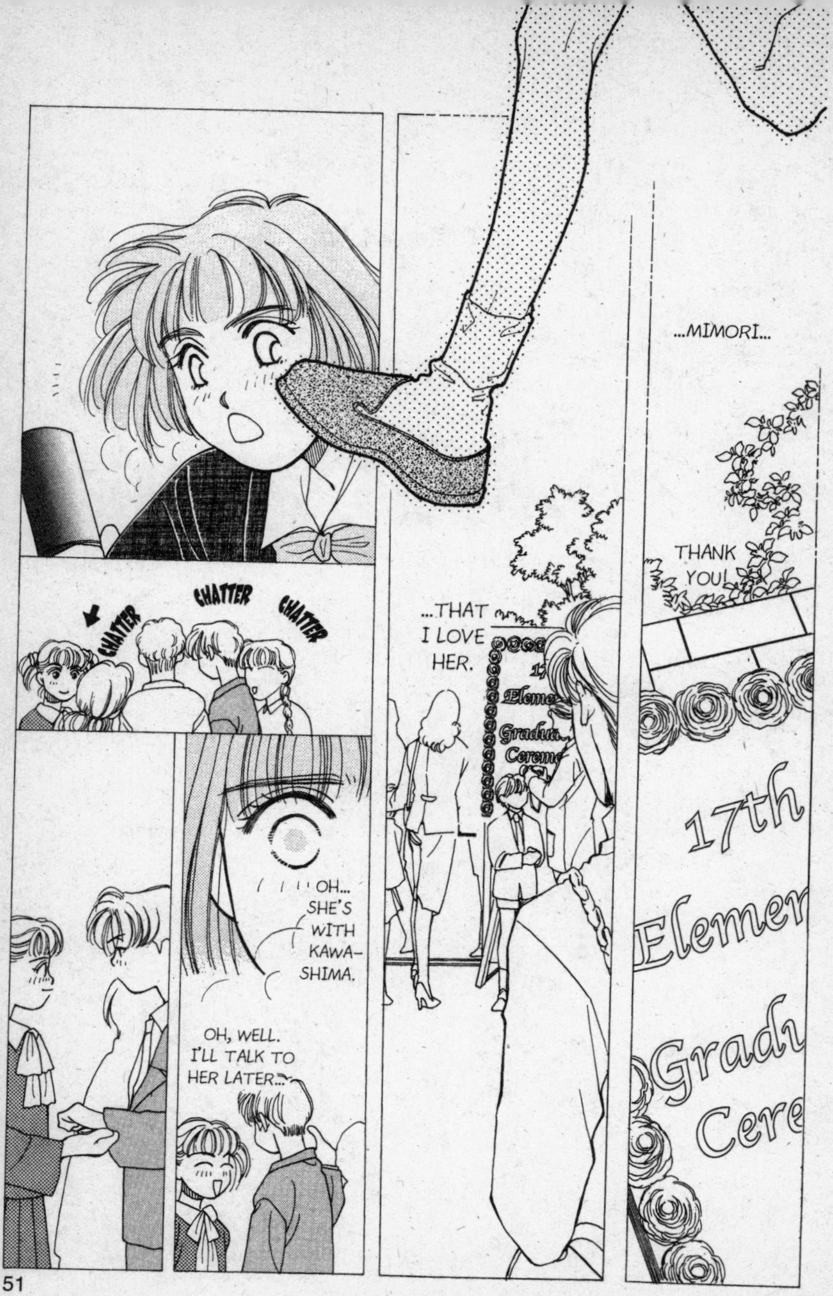
...MIMORI...
THANK YOU!
...THAT I LOVE HER.
CHATTER
CHATTER
CHATTER
OH... SHE'S WITH KAWA-SHIMA.
OH, WELL. I'LL TALK TO HER LATER...

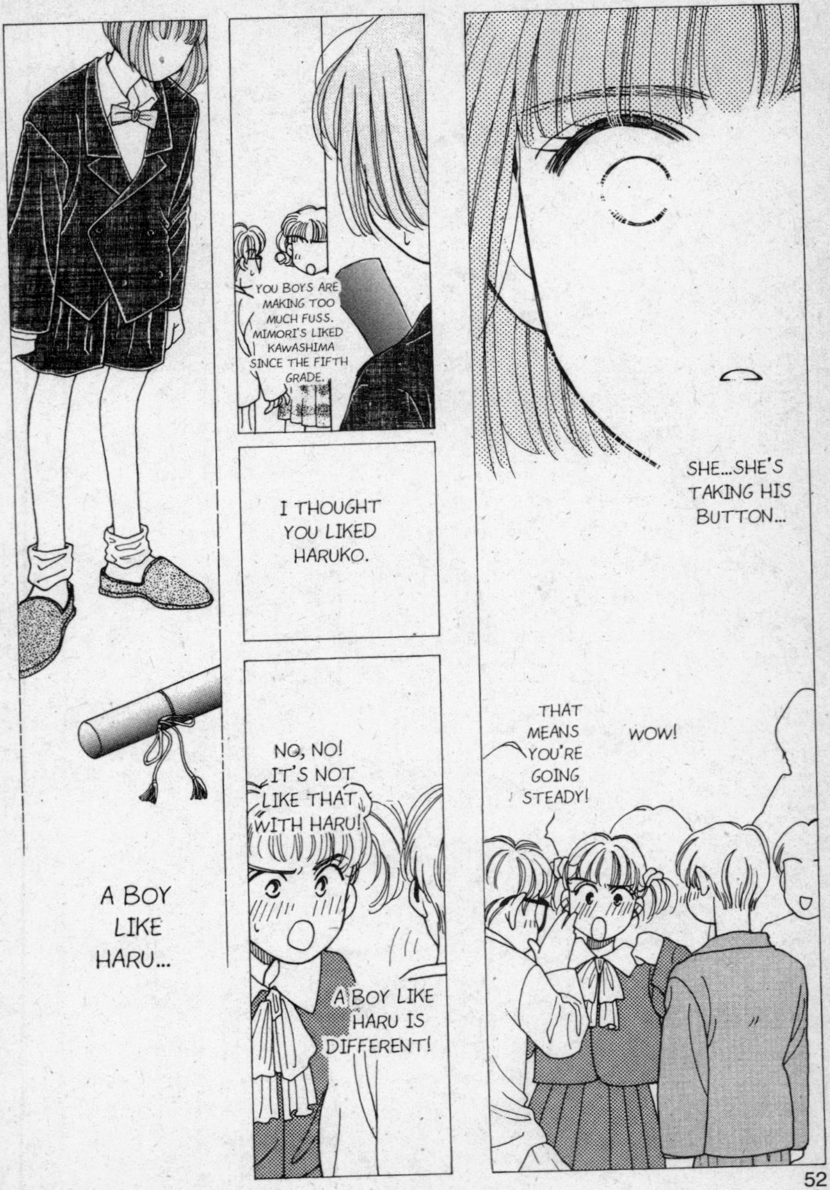
SHE...SHE'S TAKING HIS BUTTON...
WOW!
THAT MEANS YOU'RE GOING STEADY!
YOU BOYS ARE MAKING TOO MUCH FUSS. MIMORI'S LIKED KAWASHIMA SINCE THE FIFTH GRADE.
I THOUGHT YOU LIKED HARUKO.
NO, NO! IT'S NOT LIKE THAT WITH HARU!
A BOY LIKE HARU IS DIFFERENT!
A BOY LIKE HARU...

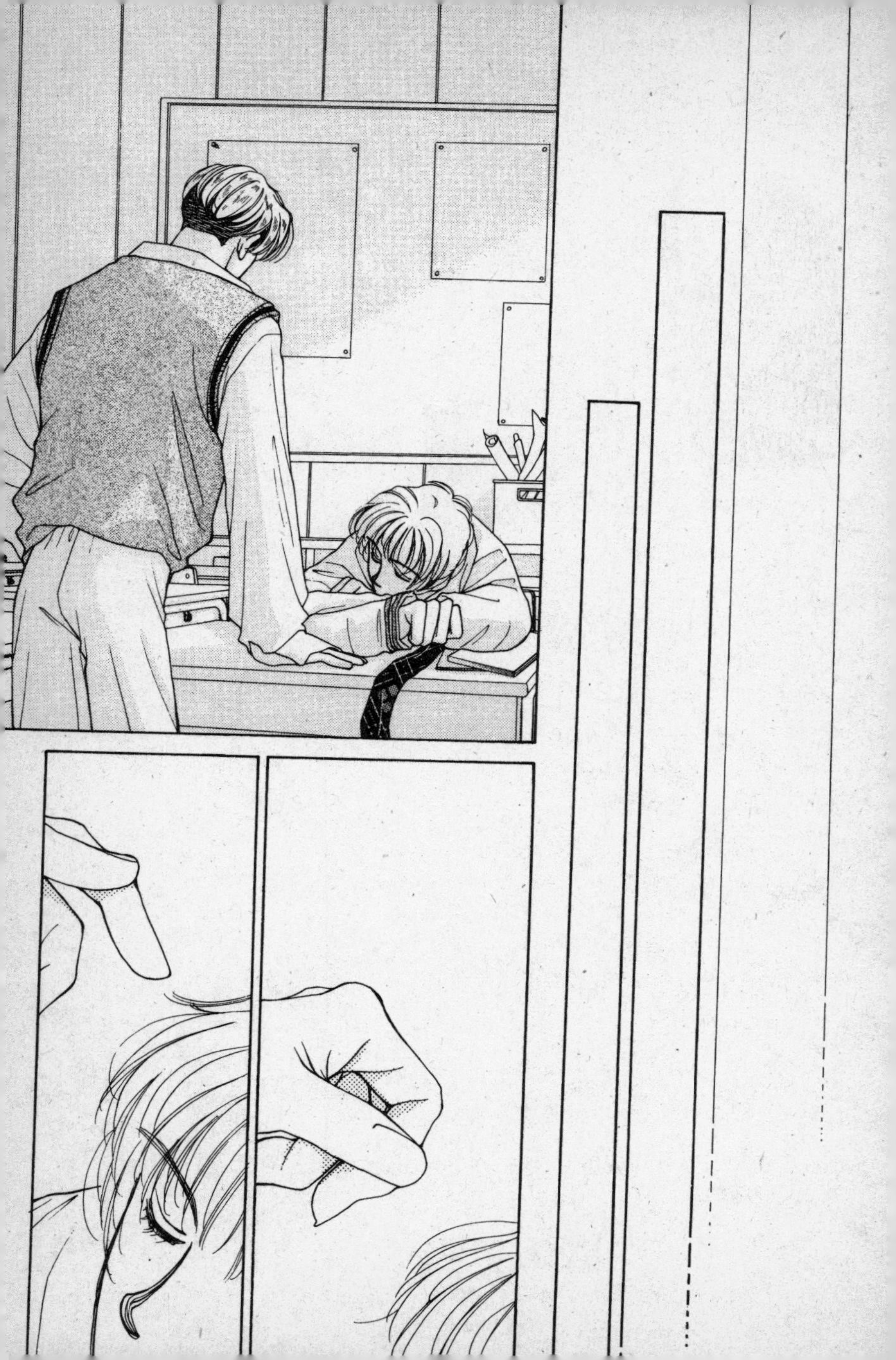

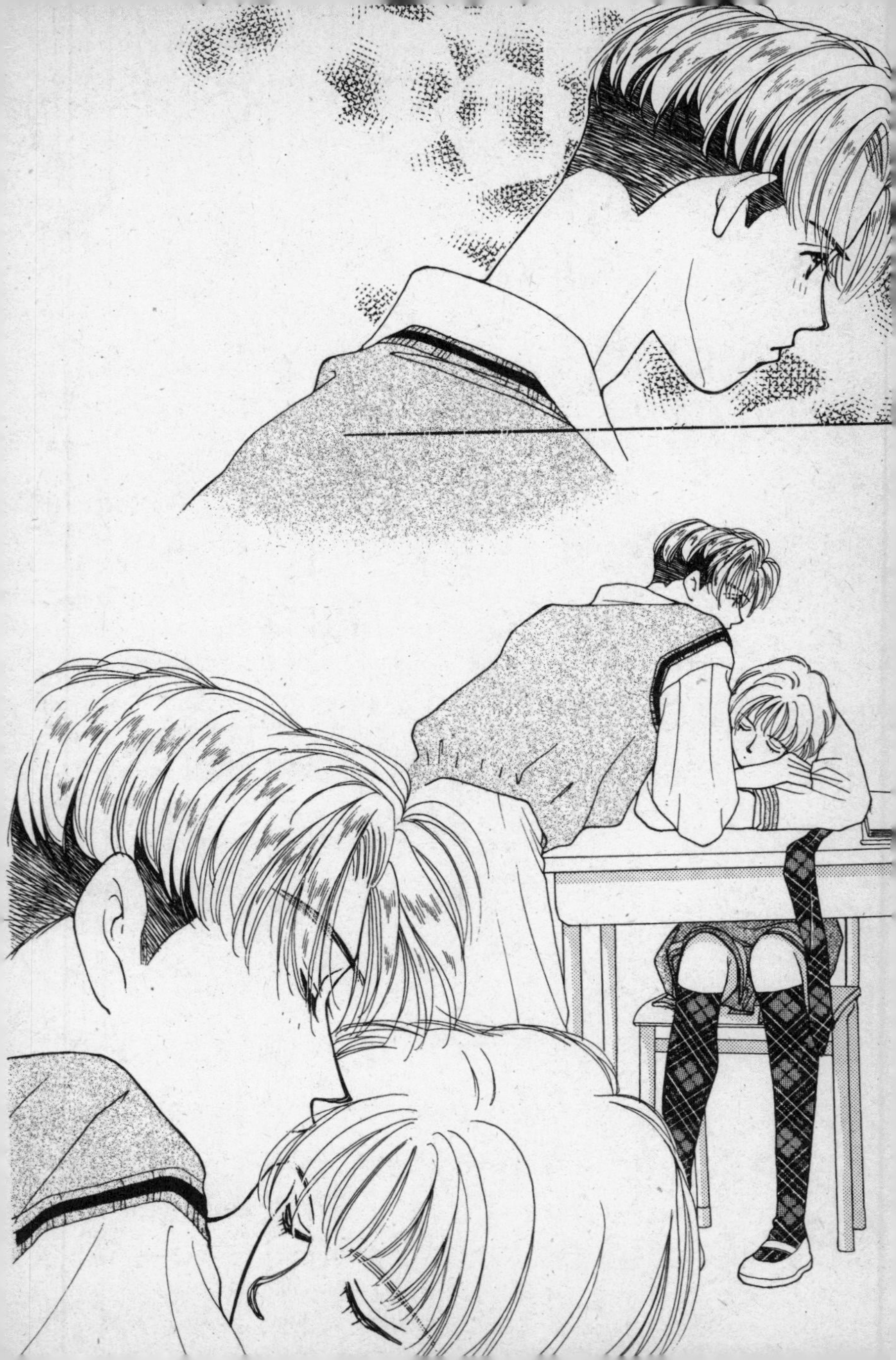

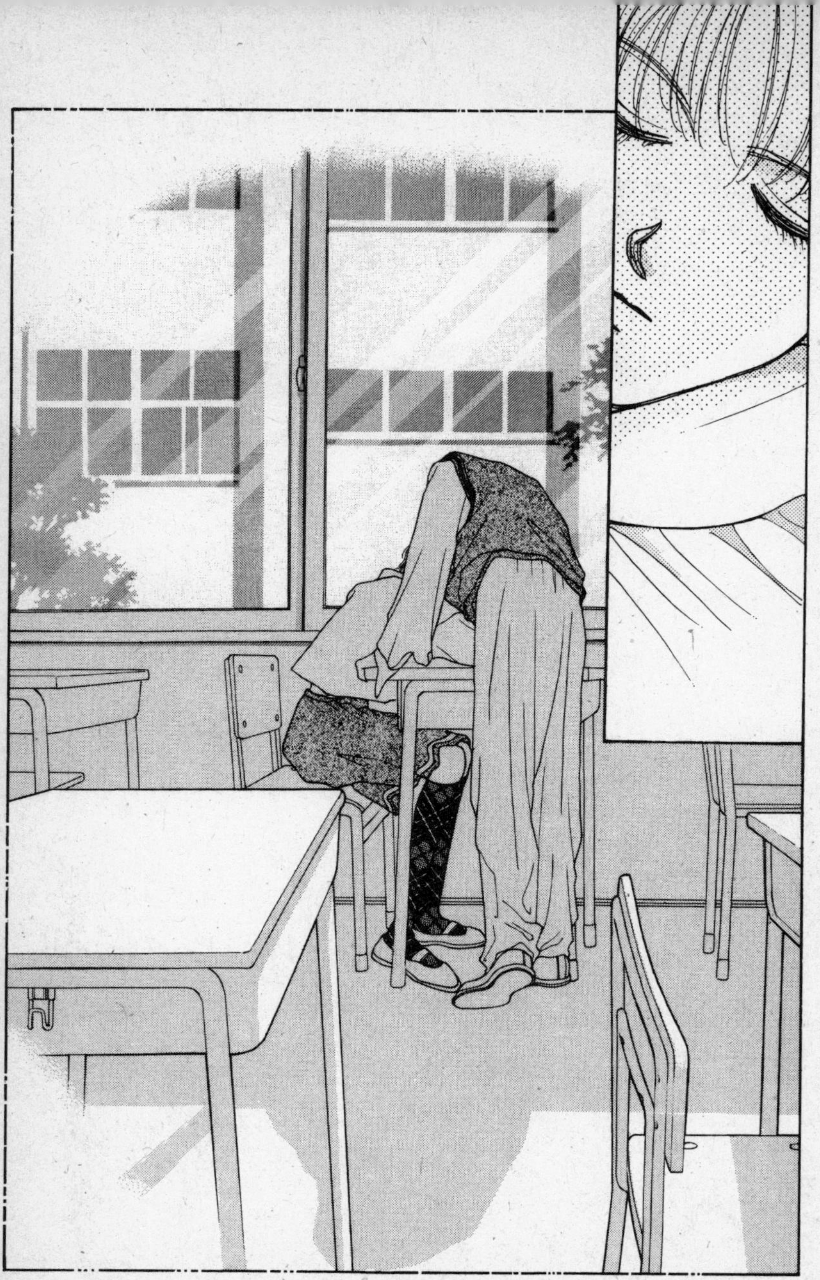

TAP!

I TURNED IN THE ASSIGNMENT.

I'M TAKING THIS.

BON
BON
BON

• TOKYO BOYS PROFILE NO. 2 • RAN SHINGYOJI

LIVES IN SETAGAYA-KU, TOKYO
HEIGHT: 164 CM (A CAUSE FOR CONCERN) WEIGHT: 50 KG
(AND RISING)
HEROES: DR. NAKAMATSU (AN INVENTOR), MUTSUGORO (A
FAMOUS ANIMAL LOVER)
BLOOD TYPE: A   FAMILY: FATHER, MOTHER, ELDER AND
YOUNGER SISTERS, GRANDMOTHER
INTERESTS: SPORTS AND GAMES. GOOD ENOUGH TO BE ON THE
CITY SOCCER TEAM IN JUNIOR HIGH, BUT AT THE END OF
8TH GRADE HE INJURED HIS KNEE AND HIS DOCTOR STOPPED
HIM FROM PLAYING. SO HE GAVE UP SOCCER. IT'S TRUE.

I COULD HAVE INCLUDED THIS STORY, BUT HE'S ONLY A
SUPPORTING CHARACTER... SO NO ROOM...

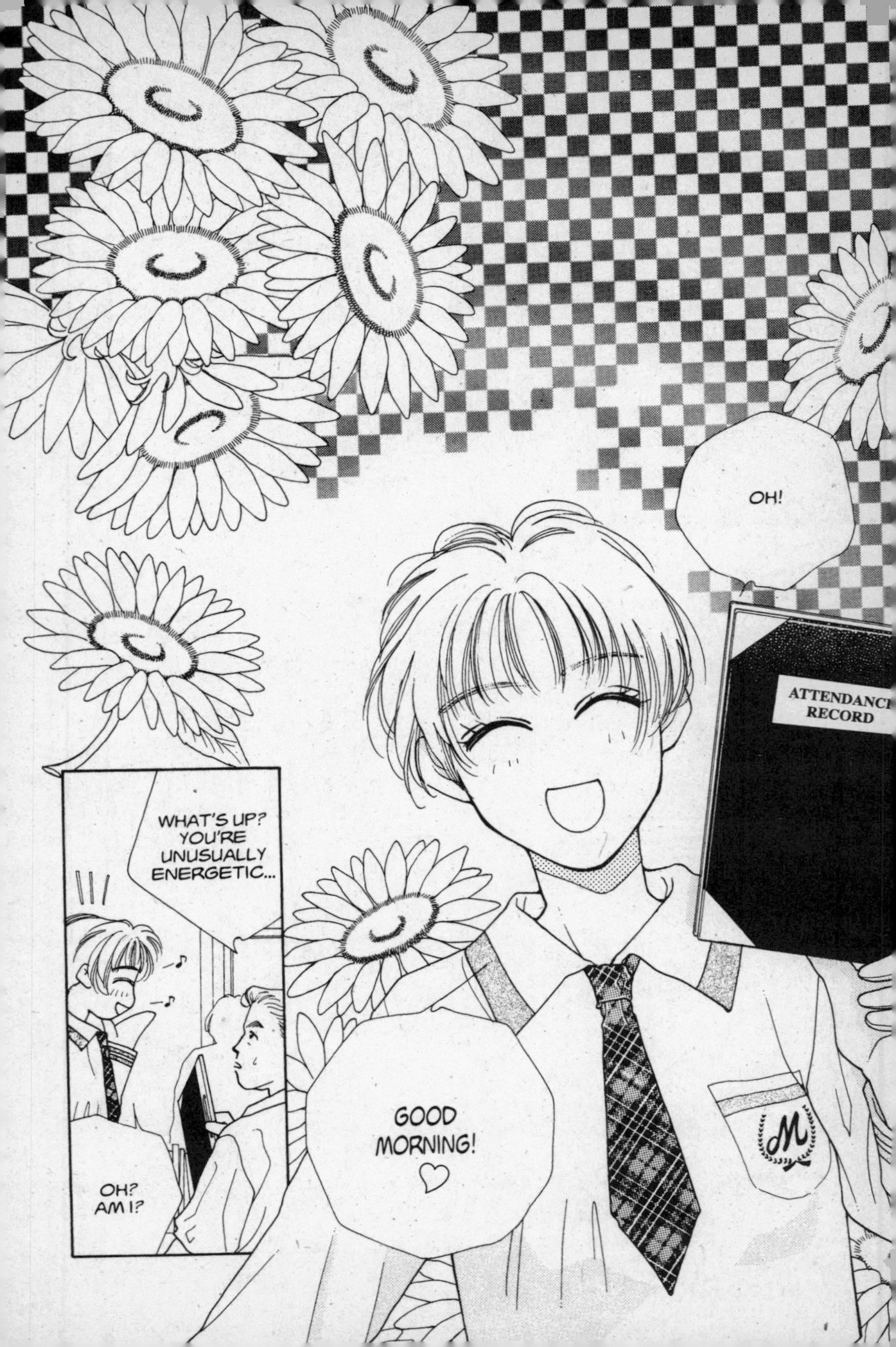
OH!
ATTENDANC
RECORD
GOOD MORNING! ♡
WHAT'S UP? YOU'RE UNUSUALLY ENERGETIC...
OH? AM I?

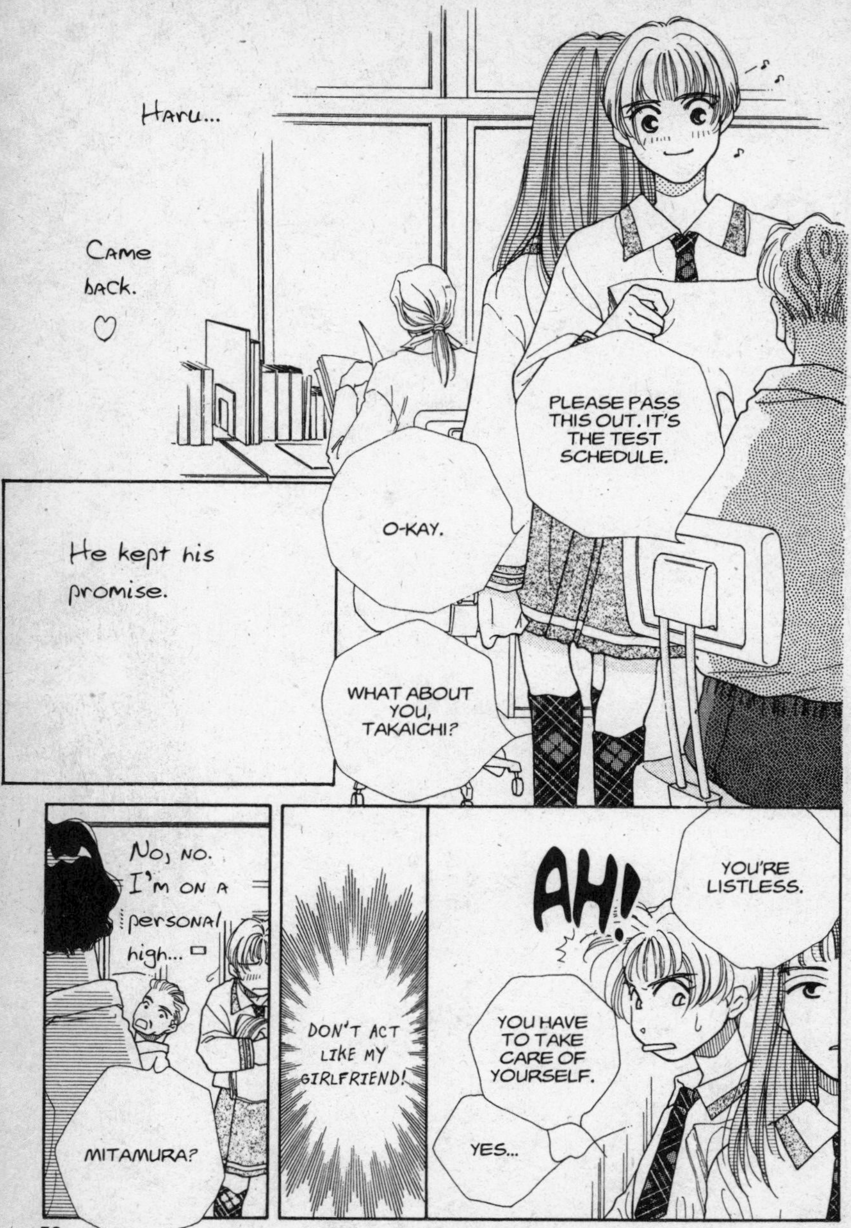

Haru...
Came back. ♥
PLEASE PASS THIS OUT. IT'S THE TEST SCHEDULE.
O-KAY.
WHAT ABOUT YOU, TAKAICHI?
He kept his promise.
AH!
YOU'RE LISTLESS.
YOU HAVE TO TAKE CARE OF YOURSELF.
YES...
DON'T ACT LIKE MY GIRLFRIEND!
No, no. I'm on a personal high...
MITAMURA?

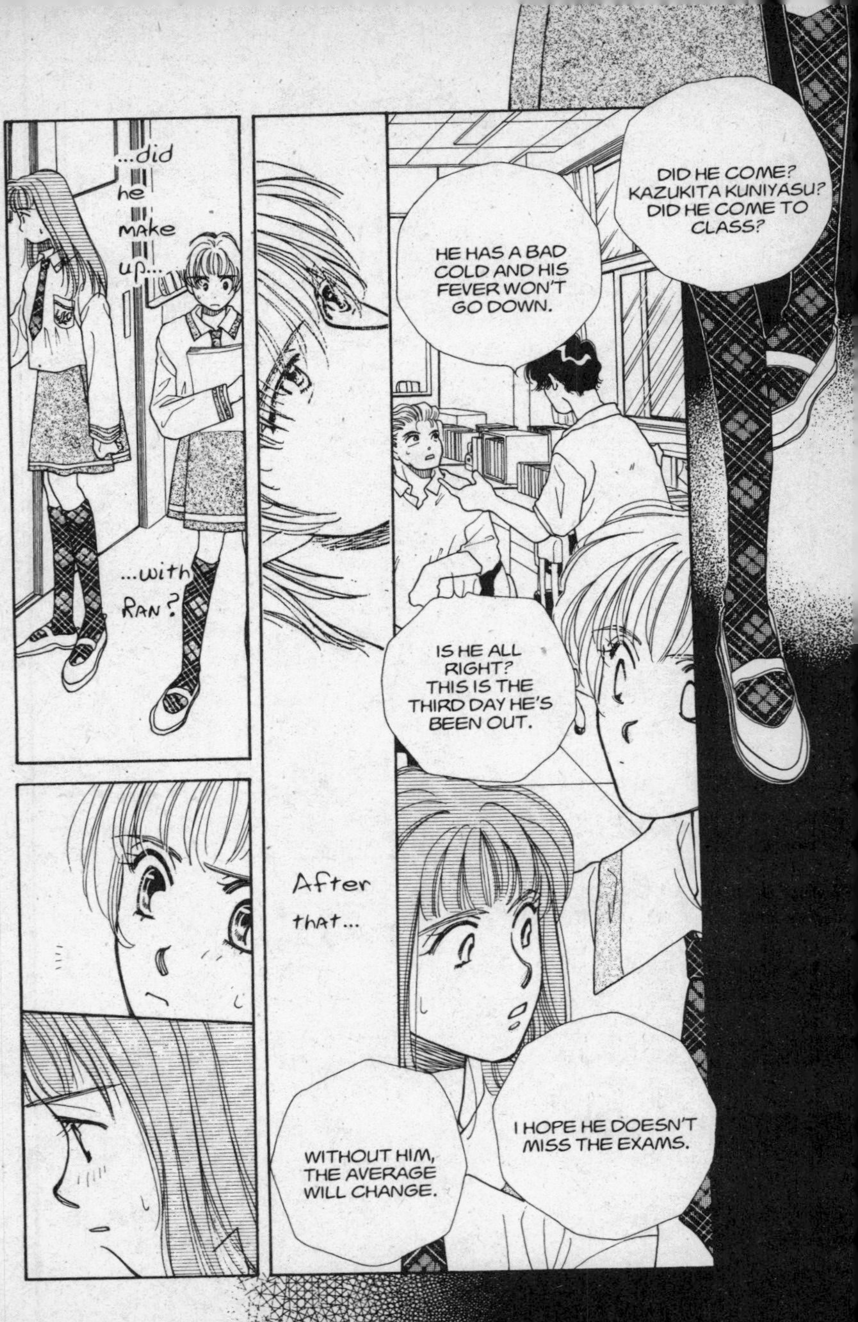
DID HE COME? KAZUKITA KUNIYASU? DID HE COME TO CLASS?
HE HAS A BAD COLD AND HIS FEVER WON'T GO DOWN.
IS HE ALL RIGHT? THIS IS THE THIRD DAY HE'S BEEN OUT.
I HOPE HE DOESN'T MISS THE EXAMS.
WITHOUT HIM, THE AVERAGE WILL CHANGE.
After that...
...did he make up...
...with Ran?

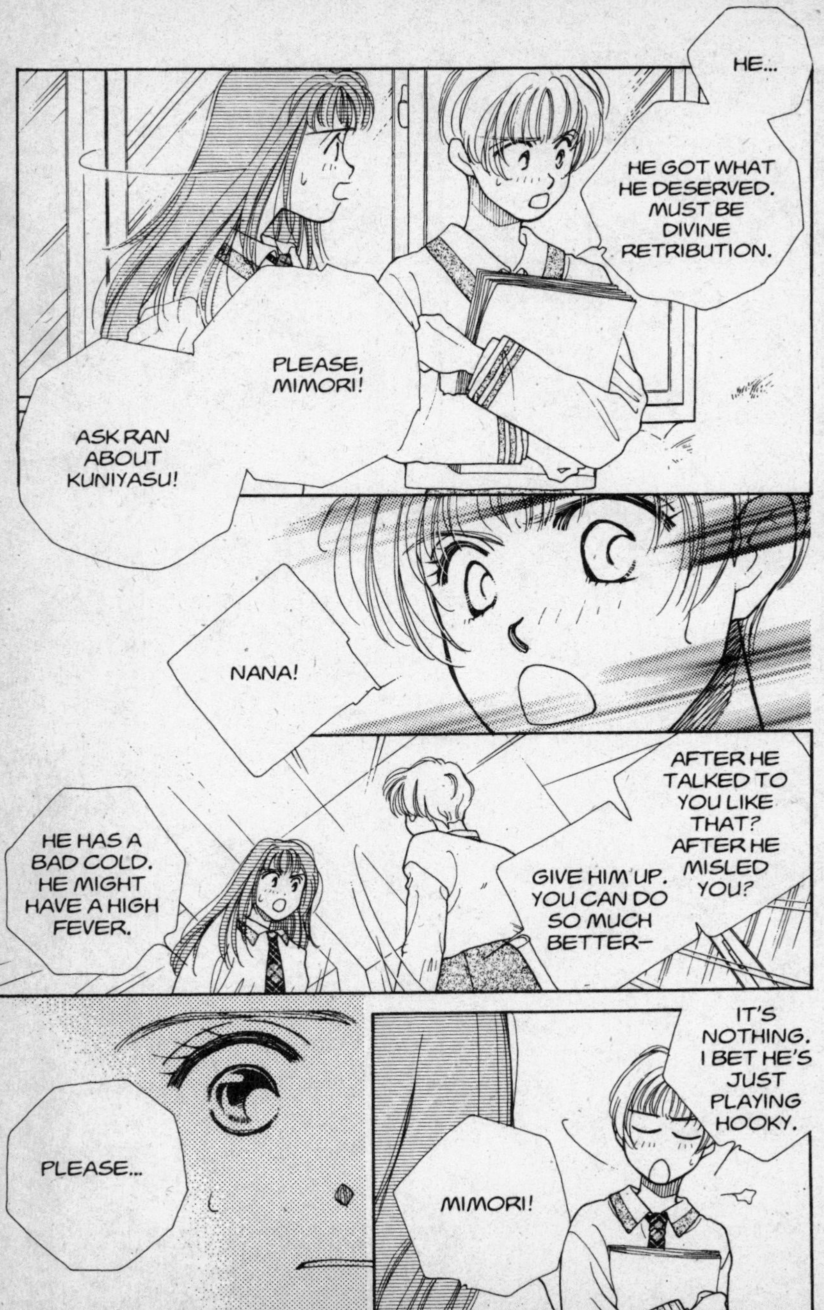
HE...
HE GOT WHAT HE DESERVED. MUST BE DIVINE RETRIBUTION.
PLEASE, MIMORI!
ASK RAN ABOUT KUNIYASU!
NANA!
AFTER HE TALKED TO YOU LIKE THAT? AFTER HE MISLED YOU?
GIVE HIM UP. YOU CAN DO SO MUCH BETTER–
HE HAS A BAD COLD. HE MIGHT HAVE A HIGH FEVER.
IT'S NOTHING. I BET HE'S JUST PLAYING HOOKY.
MIMORI!
PLEASE...

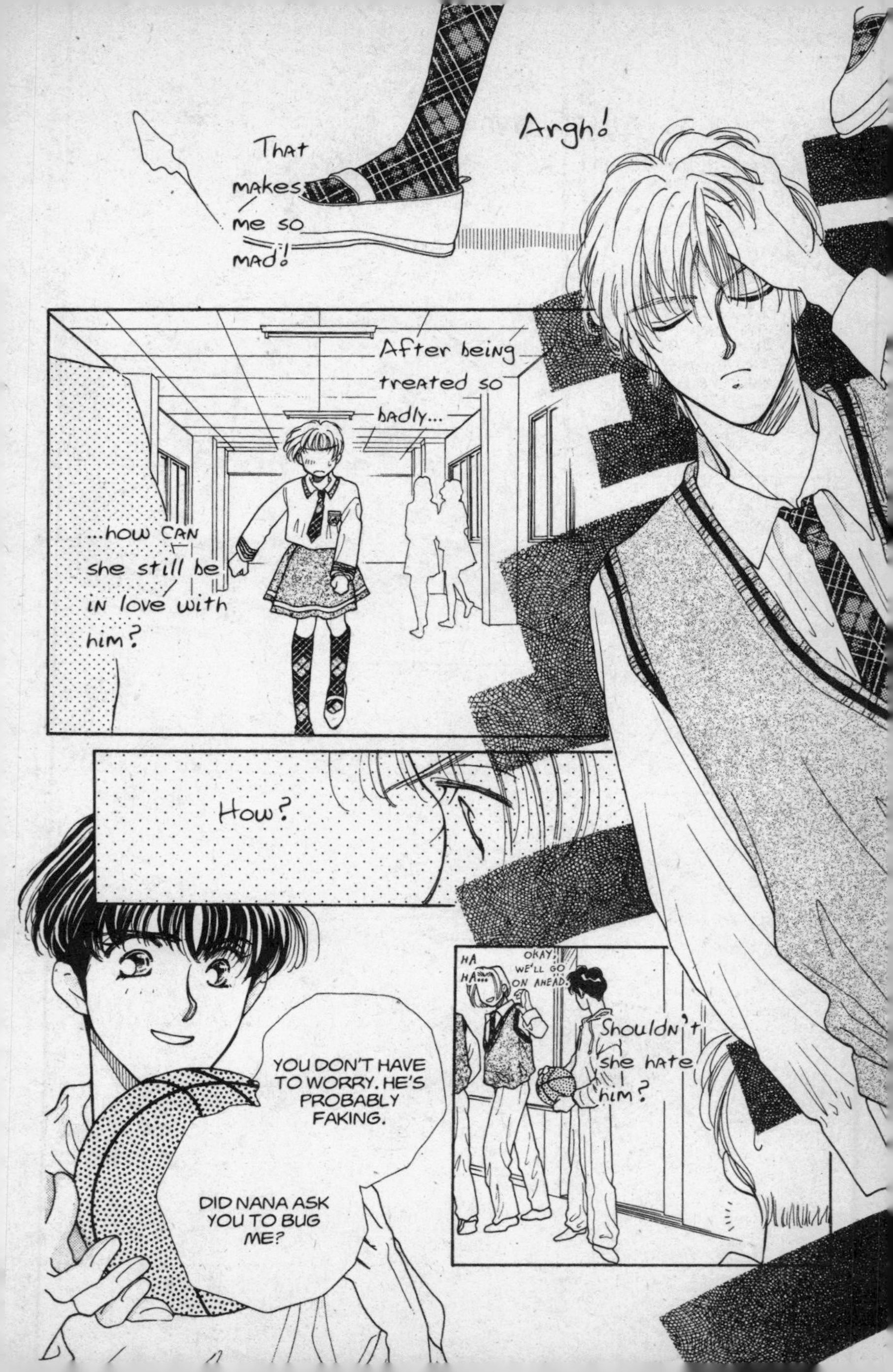
Argh!
That makes me so mad!
After being treated so badly...
...how CAN she still be in love with him?
How?
HA HA...
OKAY, WE'LL GO ON AHEAD.
Shouldn't she hate him?
YOU DON'T HAVE TO WORRY. HE'S PROBABLY FAKING.
DID NANA ASK YOU TO BUG ME?

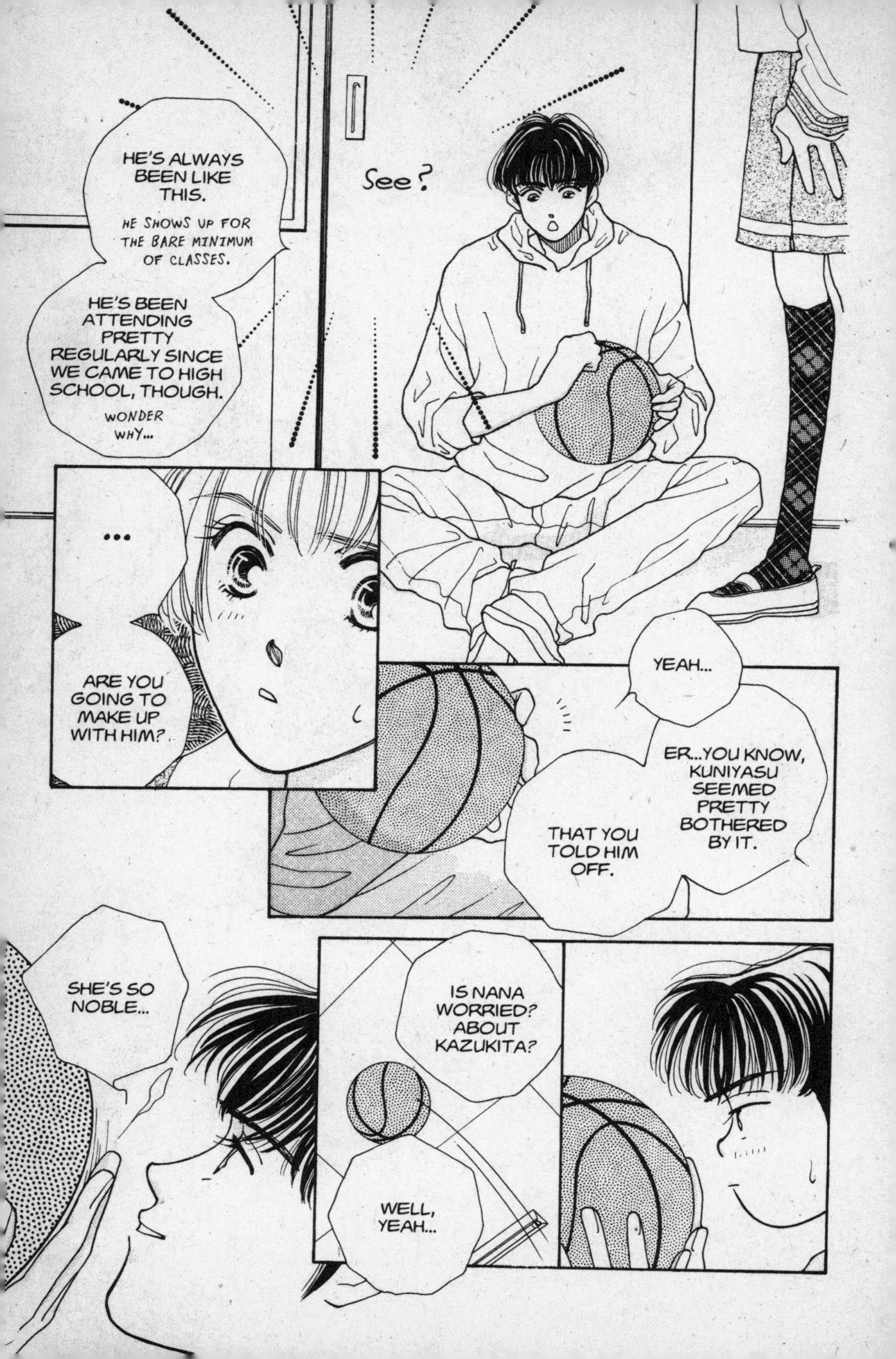

See?
HE'S ALWAYS BEEN LIKE THIS.
HE SHOWS UP FOR THE BARE MINIMUM OF CLASSES.
HE'S BEEN ATTENDING PRETTY REGULARLY SINCE WE CAME TO HIGH SCHOOL, THOUGH.
WONDER WHY...
...
ARE YOU GOING TO MAKE UP WITH HIM?
YEAH...
ER...YOU KNOW, KUNIYASU SEEMED PRETTY BOTHERED BY IT.
THAT YOU TOLD HIM OFF.
IS NANA WORRIED? ABOUT KAZUKITA?
WELL, YEAH...
SHE'S SO NOBLE...

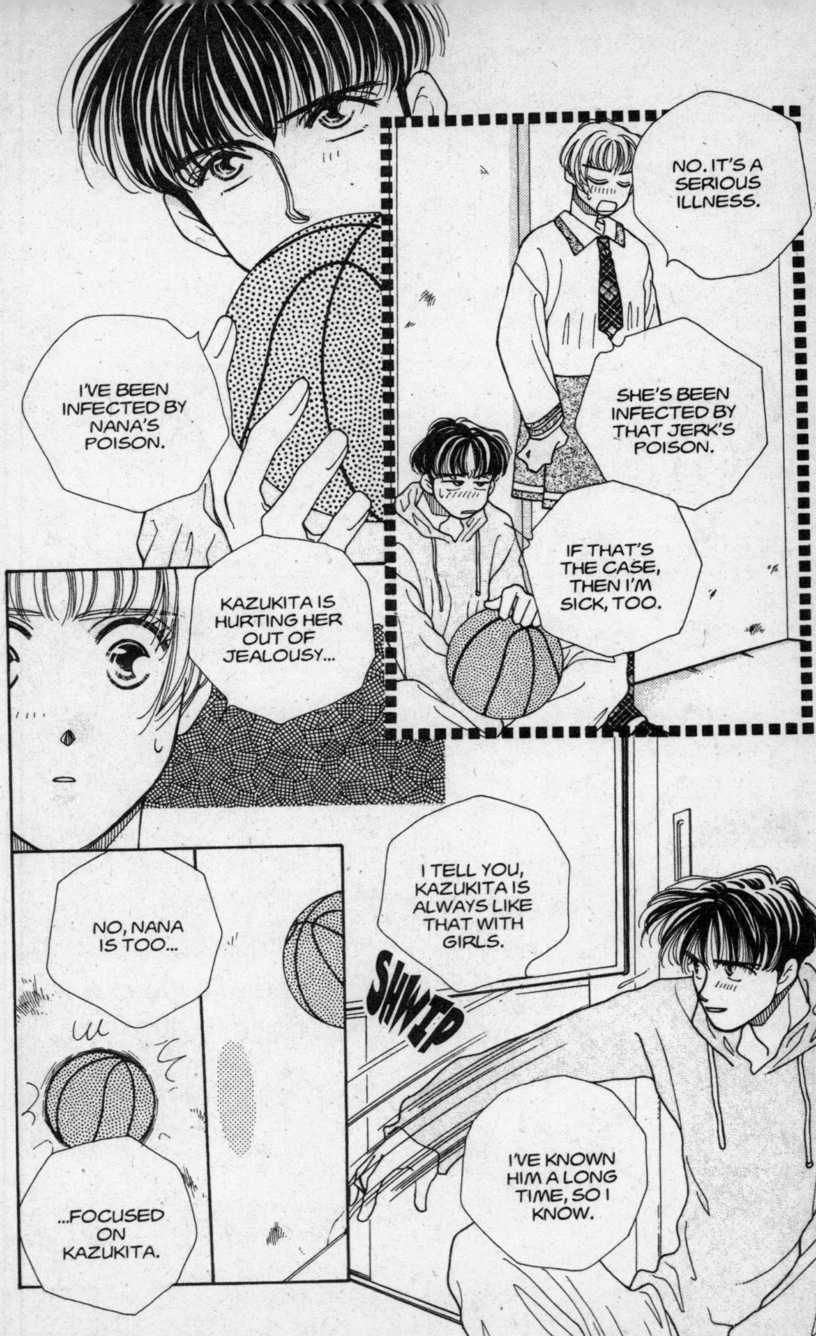
NO. IT'S A SERIOUS ILLNESS.
SHE'S BEEN INFECTED BY THAT JERK'S POISON.
IF THAT'S THE CASE, THEN I'M SICK, TOO.
I'VE BEEN INFECTED BY NANA'S POISON.
KAZUKITA IS HURTING HER OUT OF JEALOUSY...
I TELL YOU, KAZUKITA IS ALWAYS LIKE THAT WITH GIRLS.
SHWIP
I'VE KNOWN HIM A LONG TIME, SO I KNOW.
NO, NANA IS TOO...
...FOCUSED ON KAZUKITA.

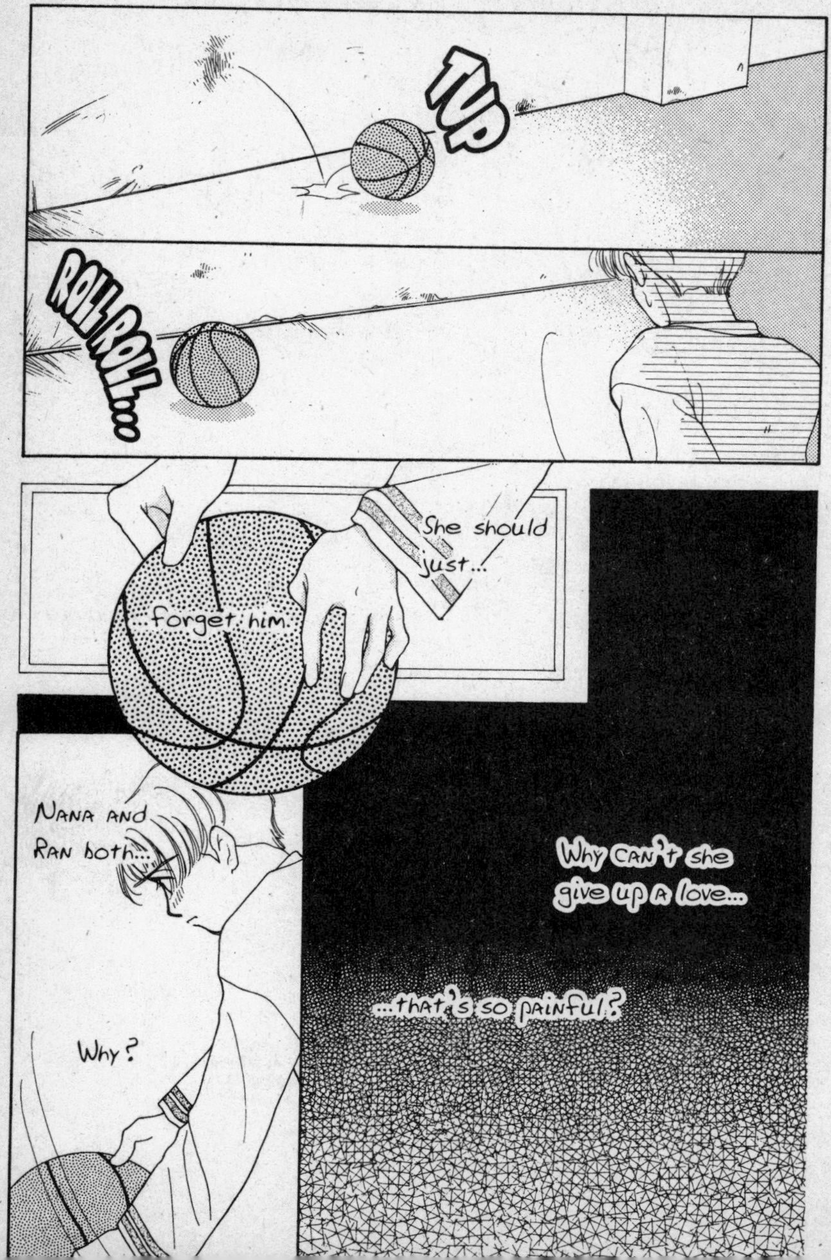
TUP
ROLLROLL...
She should just...
...forget him.
Why can't she give up a love...
...that's so painful?
Nana and Ran both...
Why?

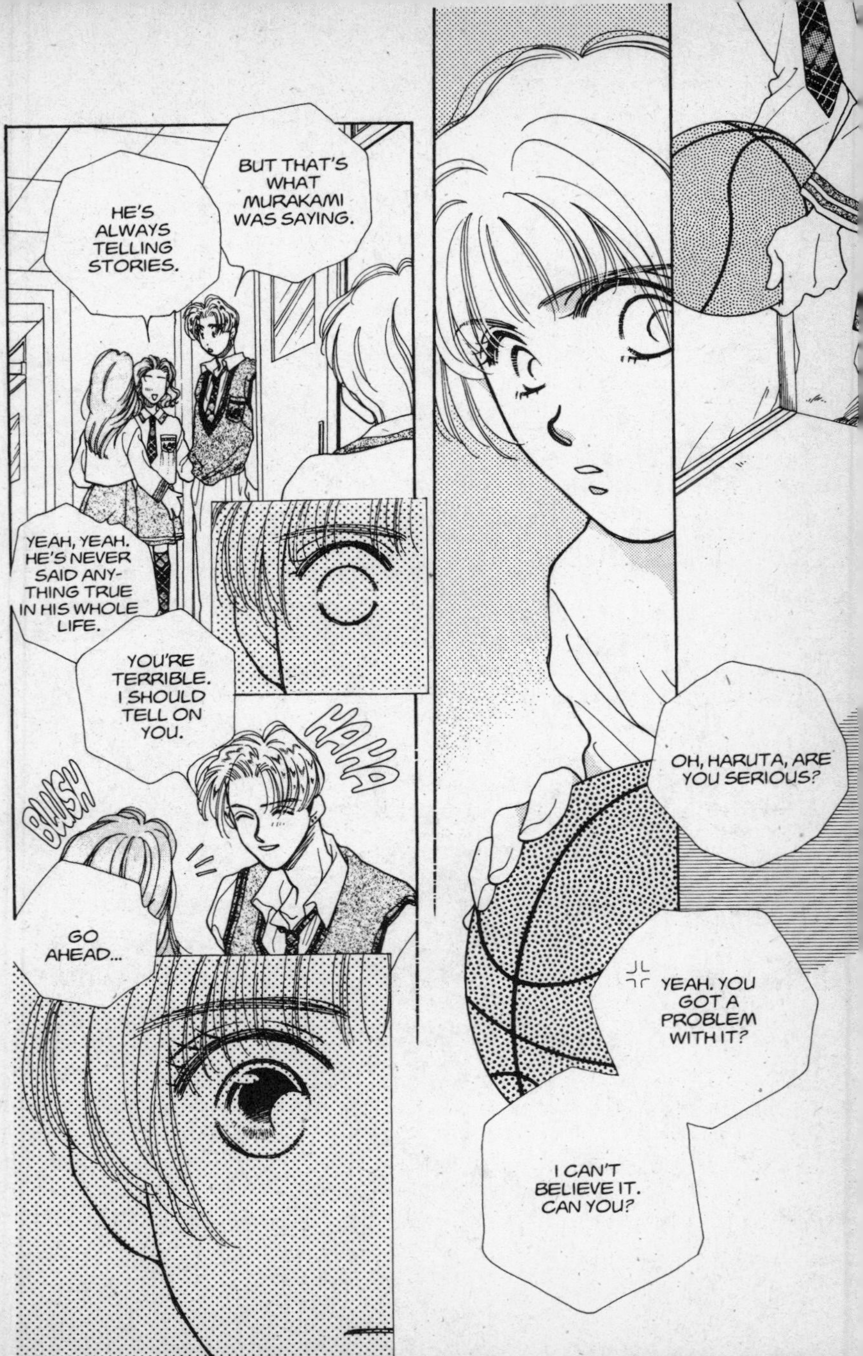
OH, HARUTA, ARE YOU SERIOUS?
YEAH. YOU GOT A PROBLEM WITH IT?
I CAN'T BELIEVE IT. CAN YOU?
BUT THAT'S WHAT MURAKAMI WAS SAYING.
HE'S ALWAYS TELLING STORIES.
YEAH, YEAH. HE'S NEVER SAID ANY-THING TRUE IN HIS WHOLE LIFE.
YOU'RE TERRIBLE. I SHOULD TELL ON YOU.
HAHA
BLUSH
GO AHEAD...

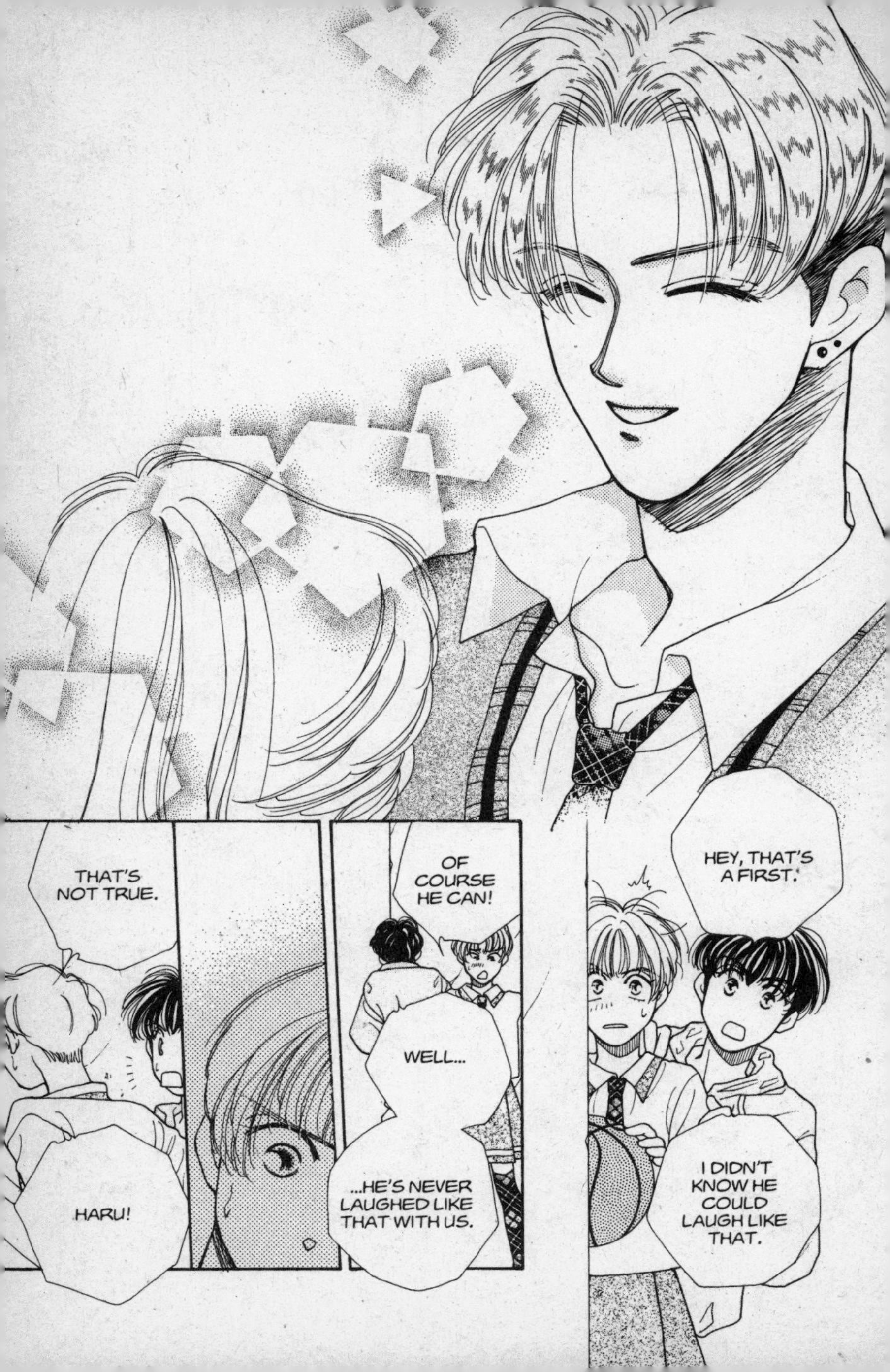
HEY, THAT'S A FIRST.
I DIDN'T KNOW HE COULD LAUGH LIKE THAT.
OF COURSE HE CAN!
WELL...
...HE'S NEVER LAUGHED LIKE THAT WITH US.
THAT'S NOT TRUE.
HARU!

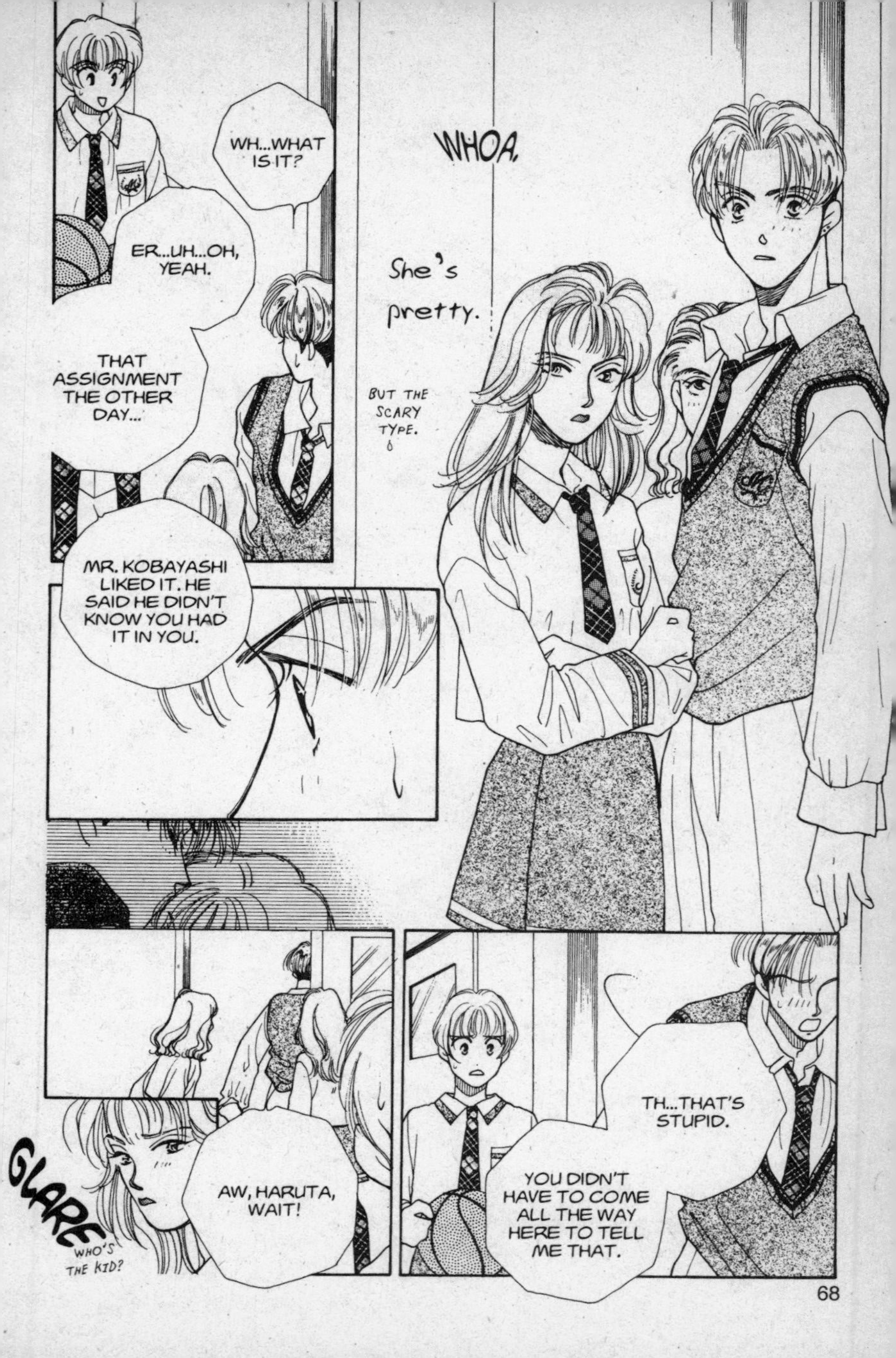
WHOA.
She's pretty.
BUT THE SCARY TYPE.
WH...WHAT IS IT?
ER...UH...OH, YEAH.
THAT ASSIGNMENT THE OTHER DAY...
MR. KOBAYASHI LIKED IT. HE SAID HE DIDN'T KNOW YOU HAD IT IN YOU.
TH...THAT'S STUPID.
YOU DIDN'T HAVE TO COME ALL THE WAY HERE TO TELL ME THAT.
AW, HARUTA, WAIT!
GLARE
WHO'S THE KID?

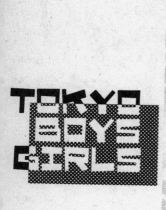

TOKYO BOYS & GIRLS

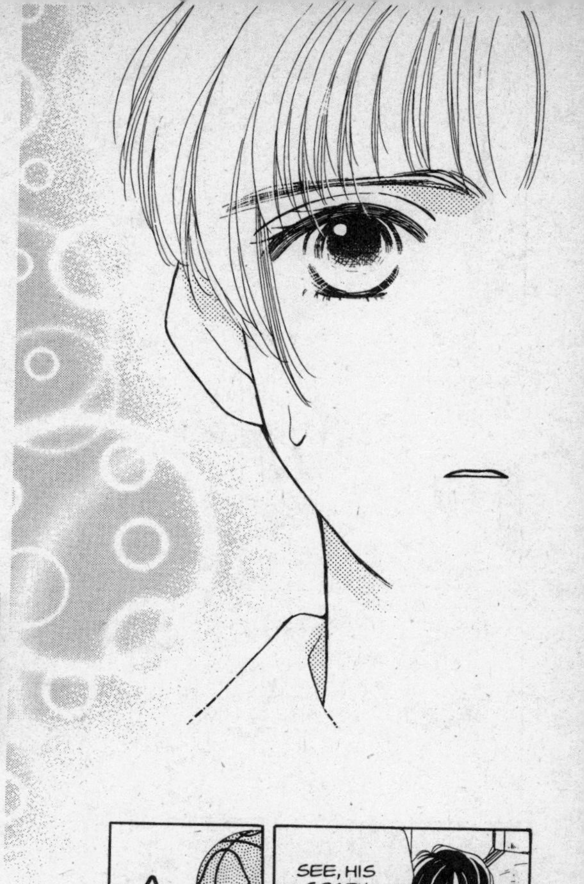

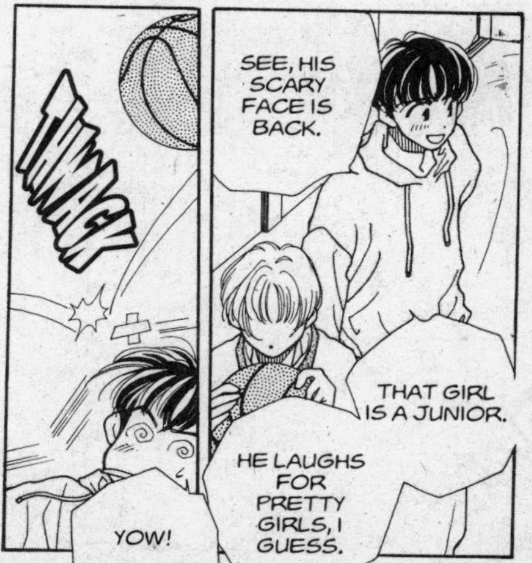
SEE, HIS SCARY FACE IS BACK.
THAT GIRL IS A JUNIOR.
HE LAUGHS FOR PRETTY GIRLS, I GUESS.
THWACK
YOW!

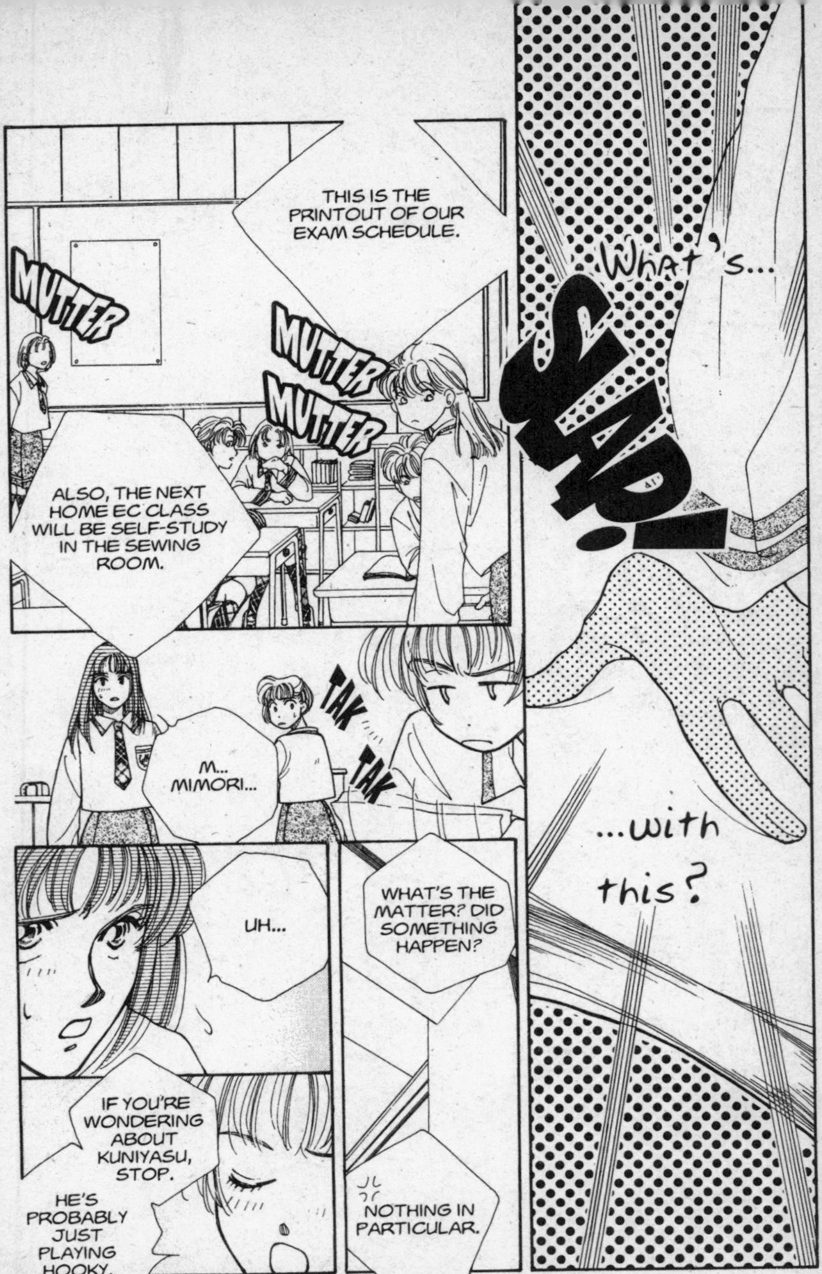
What's...
SNAP!
...with this?
THIS IS THE PRINTOUT OF OUR EXAM SCHEDULE.
MUTTER MUTTER
MUTTER
MUTTER
ALSO, THE NEXT HOME EC CLASS WILL BE SELF-STUDY IN THE SEWING ROOM.
TAK TAK
M... MIMORI...
WHAT'S THE MATTER? DID SOMETHING HAPPEN?
NOTHING IN PARTICULAR.
UH...
IF YOU'RE WONDERING ABOUT KUNIYASU, STOP.
HE'S PROBABLY JUST PLAYING HOOKY.

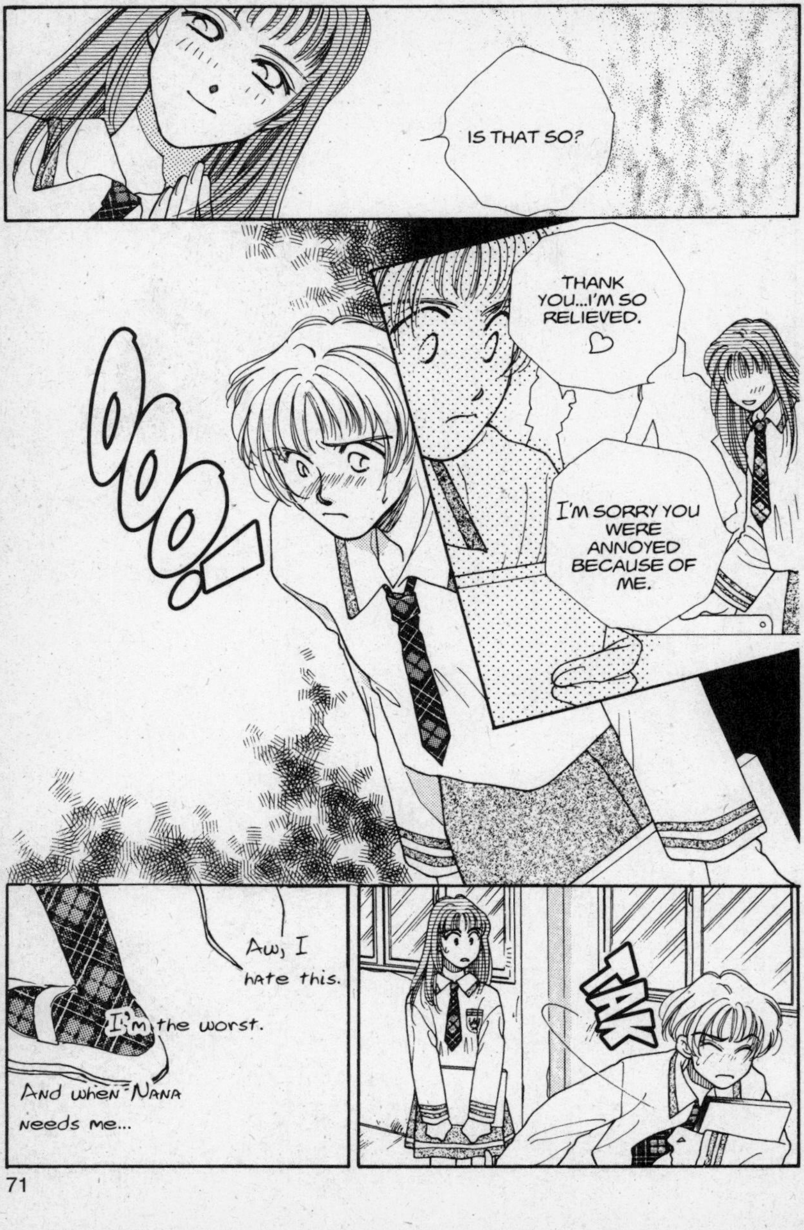
IS THAT SO?
THANK YOU...I'M SO RELIEVED. ♡
I'M SORRY YOU WERE ANNOYED BECAUSE OF ME.
OOO!
TAK
Aw, I hate this.
I'm the worst.
And when Nana needs me...

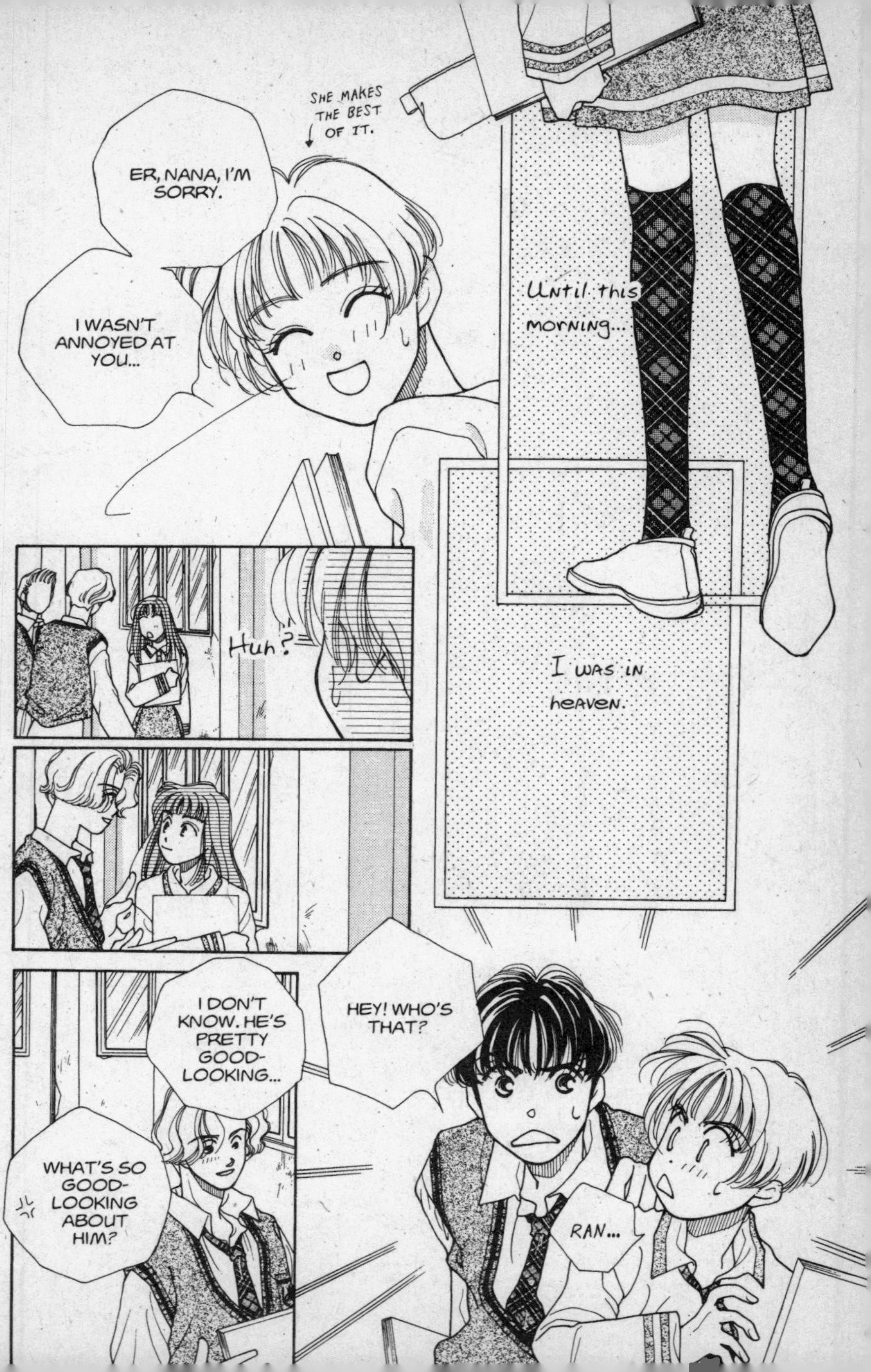

Until this morning...
I was in heaven.
SHE MAKES THE BEST OF IT.
ER, NANA, I'M SORRY.
I WASN'T ANNOYED AT YOU...
Huh?
HEY! WHO'S THAT?
RAN...
I DON'T KNOW. HE'S PRETTY GOOD-LOOKING...
WHAT'S SO GOOD-LOOKING ABOUT HIM?

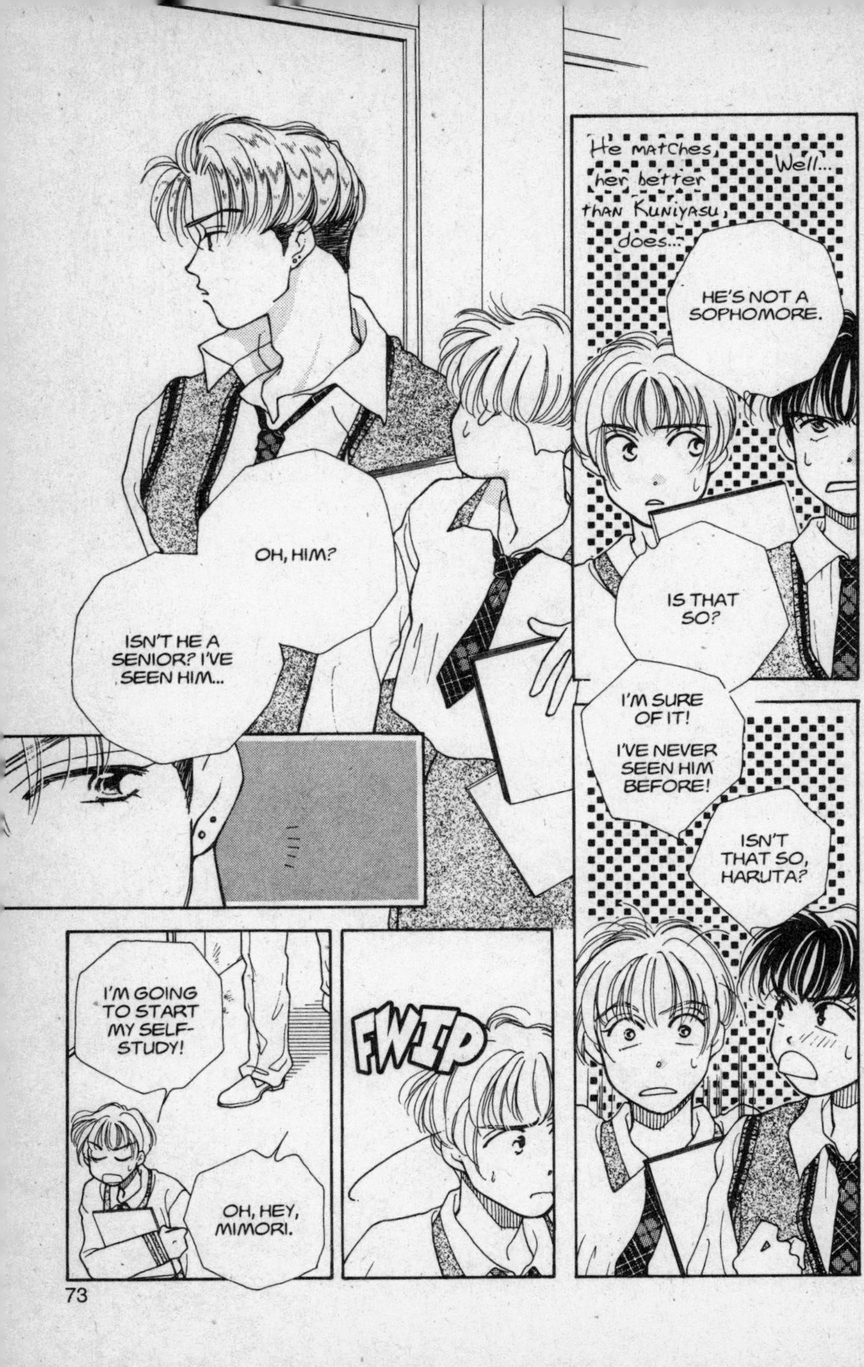
Well...
He matches, her better than Kuniyasu, does...
HE'S NOT A SOPHOMORE.
IS THAT SO?
I'M SURE OF IT!
I'VE NEVER SEEN HIM BEFORE!
ISN'T THAT SO, HARUTA?
OH, HIM?
ISN'T HE A SENIOR? I'VE SEEN HIM...
FWIP
I'M GOING TO START MY SELF-STUDY!
OH, HEY, MIMORI.

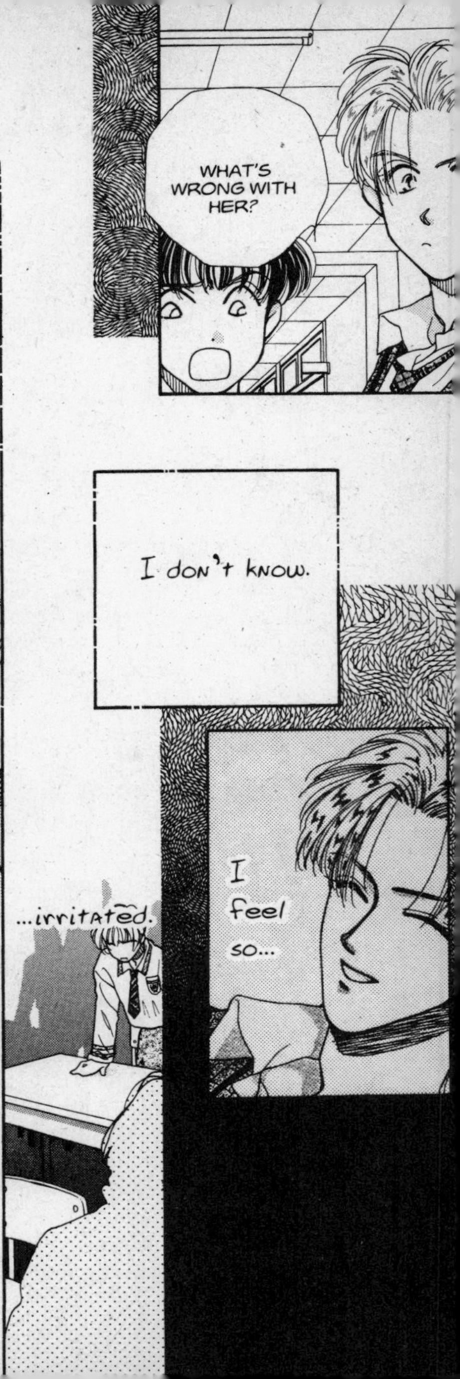
WHAT'S WRONG WITH HER?
I don't know.
I feel so...
...irritated.
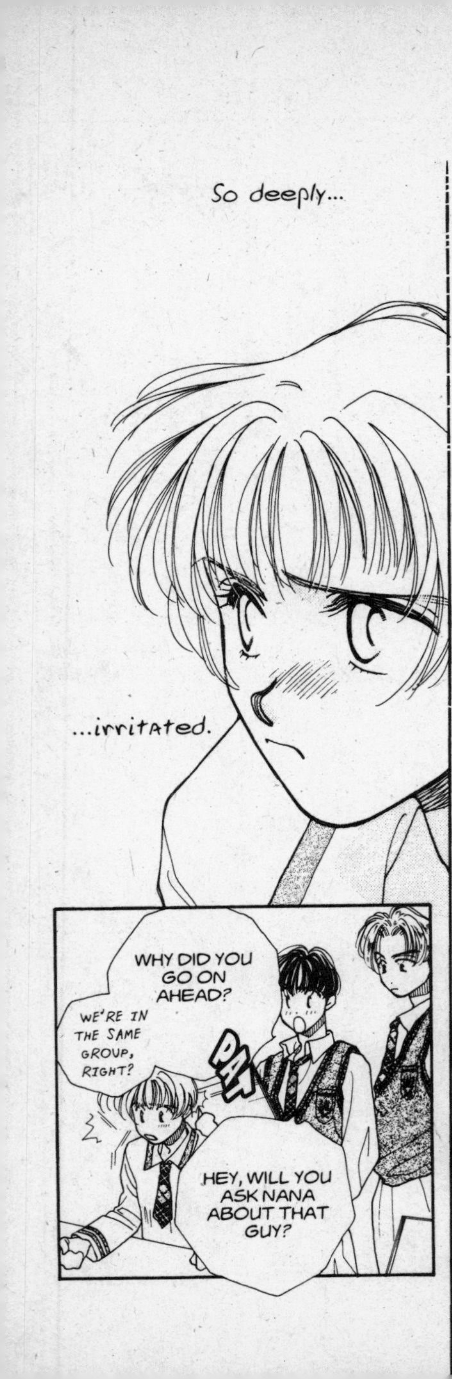
So deeply...
...irritated.
WHY DID YOU GO ON AHEAD?
WE'RE IN THE SAME GROUP, RIGHT?
PAT
HEY, WILL YOU ASK NANA ABOUT THAT GUY?

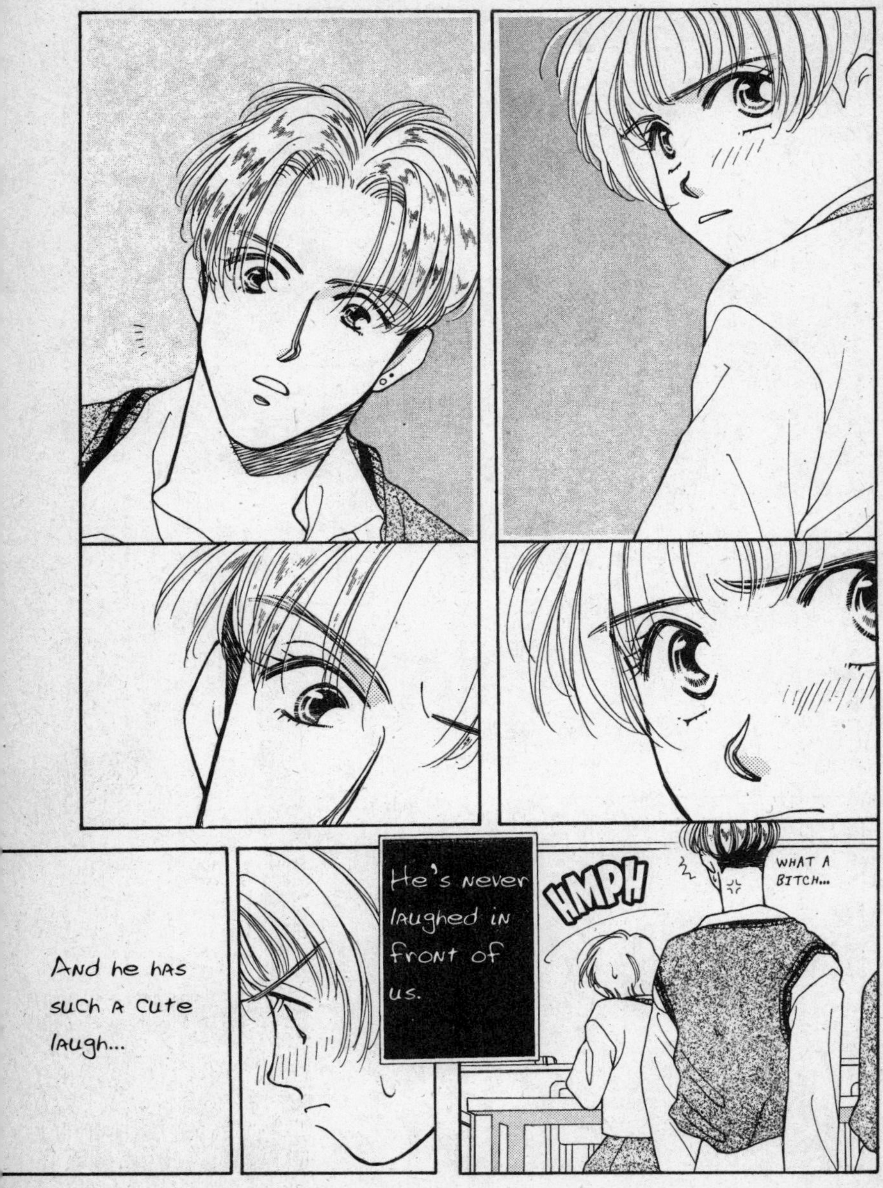
WHAT A BITCH...
HMPH
He's never laughed in front of us.
And he has such a cute laugh...

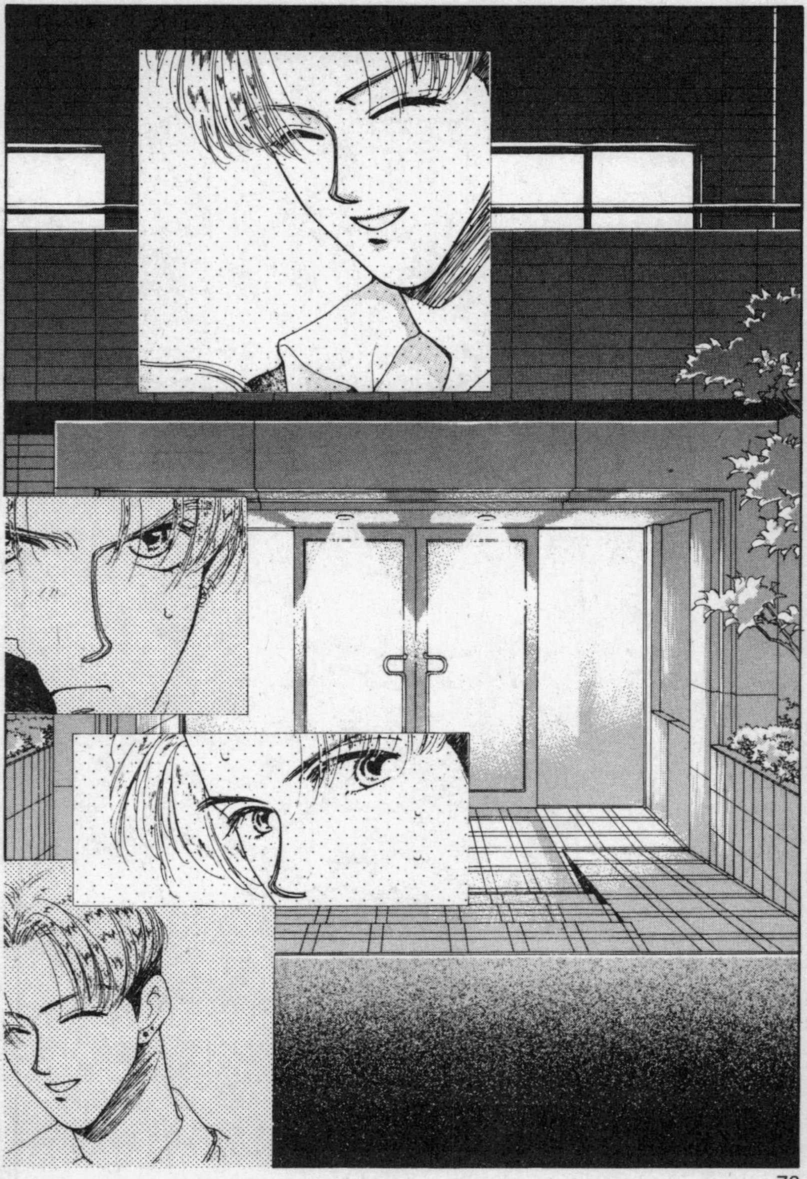

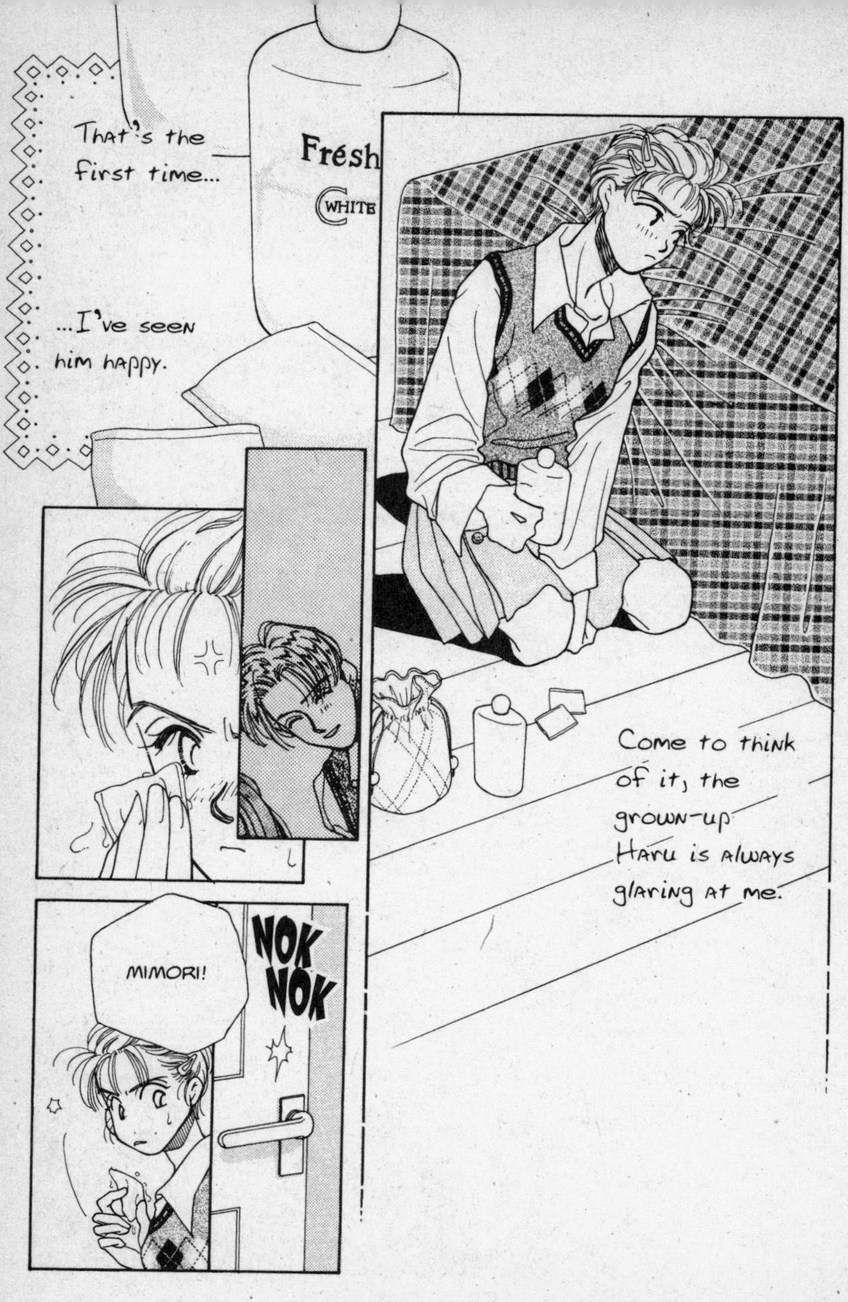

That's the first time...
...I've seen him happy.
Come to think of it, the grown-up Haru is always glaring at me.
NOK NOK
MIMORI!

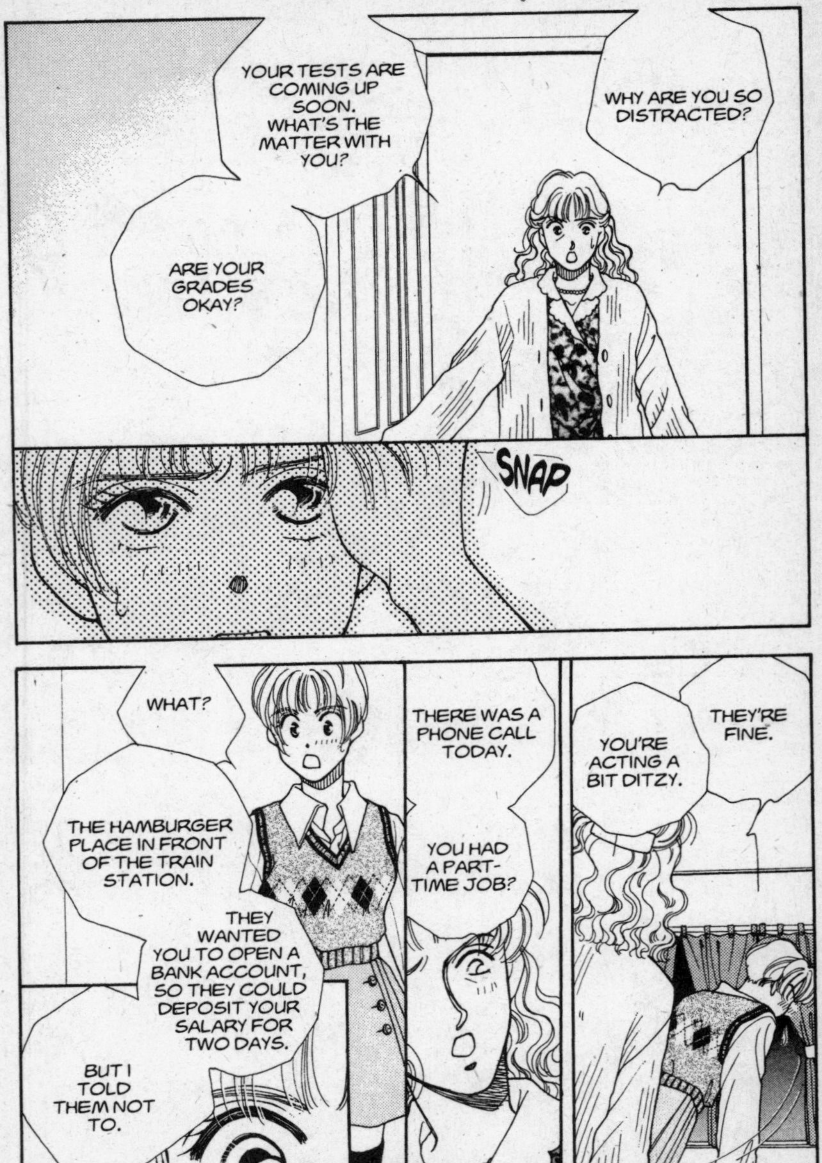
WHY ARE YOU SO DISTRACTED?
YOUR TESTS ARE COMING UP SOON. WHAT'S THE MATTER WITH YOU?
ARE YOUR GRADES OKAY?
SNAP
THEY'RE FINE.
YOU'RE ACTING A BIT DITZY.
THERE WAS A PHONE CALL TODAY.
YOU HAD A PART-TIME JOB?
WHAT?
THE HAMBURGER PLACE IN FRONT OF THE TRAIN STATION.
THEY WANTED YOU TO OPEN A BANK ACCOUNT, SO THEY COULD DEPOSIT YOUR SALARY FOR TWO DAYS.
BUT I TOLD THEM NOT TO.

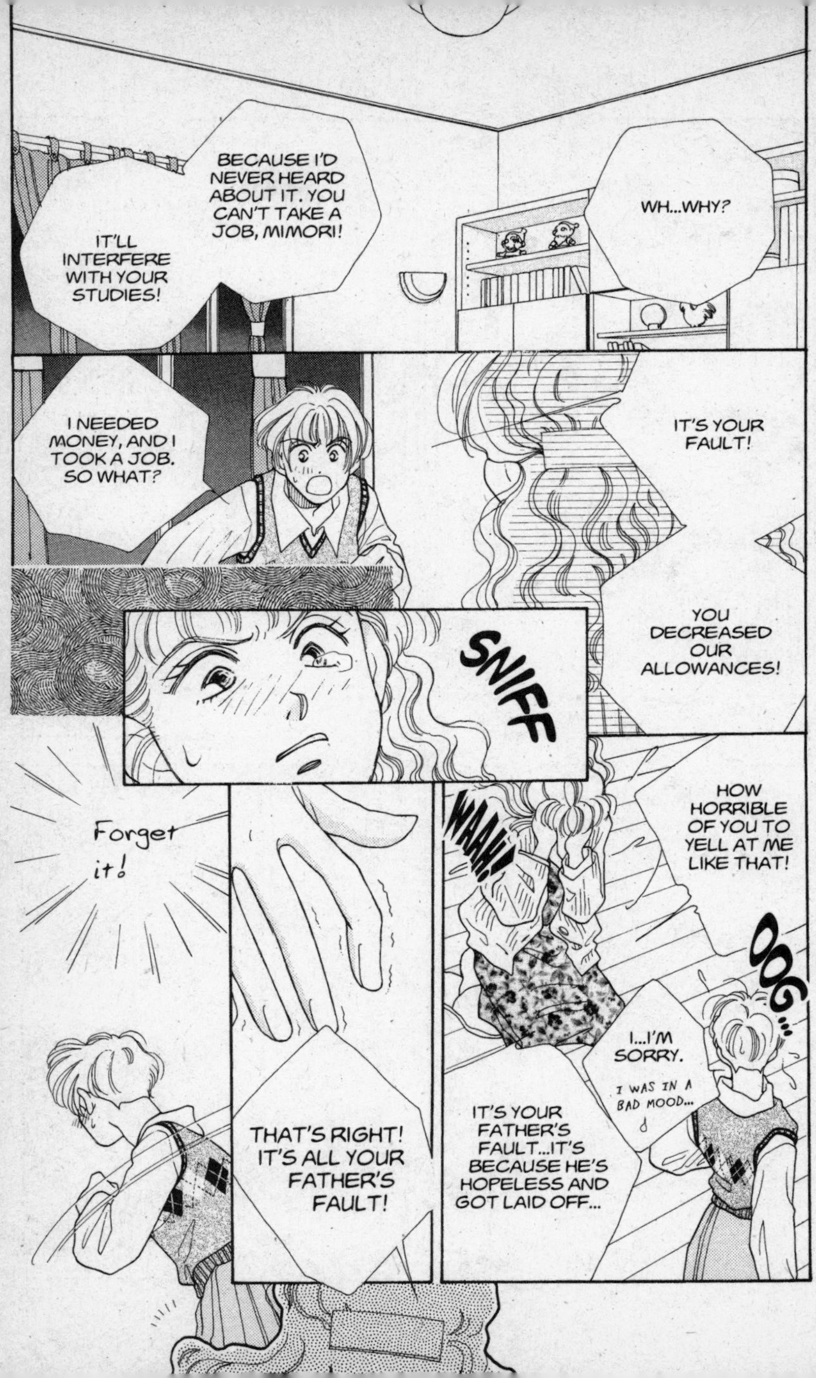
WH...WHY?
BECAUSE I'D NEVER HEARD ABOUT IT. YOU CAN'T TAKE A JOB, MIMORI!
IT'LL INTERFERE WITH YOUR STUDIES!
IT'S YOUR FAULT!
YOU DECREASED OUR ALLOWANCES!
I NEEDED MONEY, AND I TOOK A JOB. SO WHAT?
SNIFF
HOW HORRIBLE OF YOU TO YELL AT ME LIKE THAT!
WAAH!
OOG...
I...I'M SORRY.
I WAS IN A BAD MOOD...
IT'S YOUR FATHER'S FAULT...IT'S BECAUSE HE'S HOPELESS AND GOT LAID OFF...
THAT'S RIGHT! IT'S ALL YOUR FATHER'S FAULT!
Forget it!

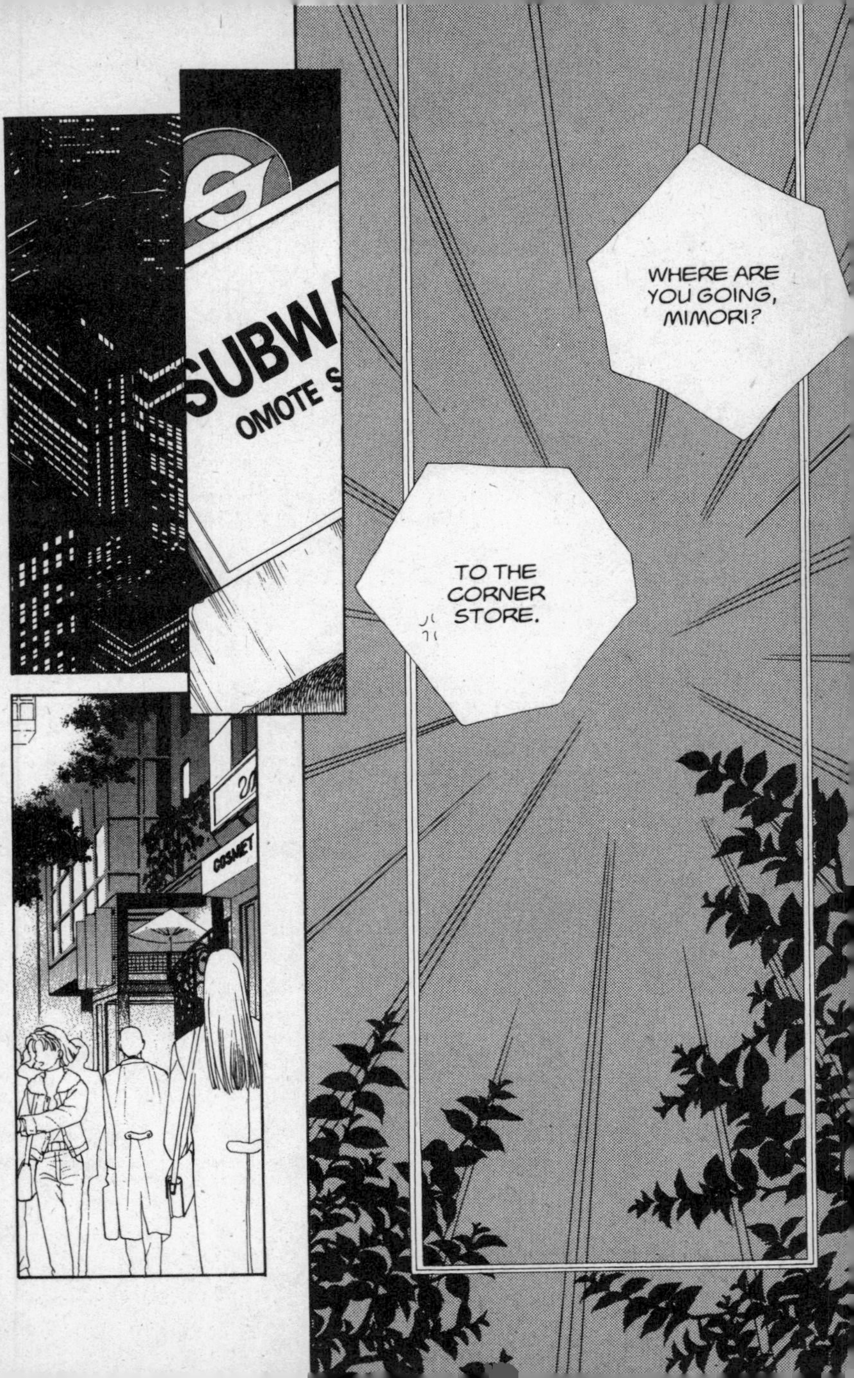
WHERE ARE YOU GOING, MIMORI?
TO THE CORNER STORE.
SUBW
OMOTE S
COSMET

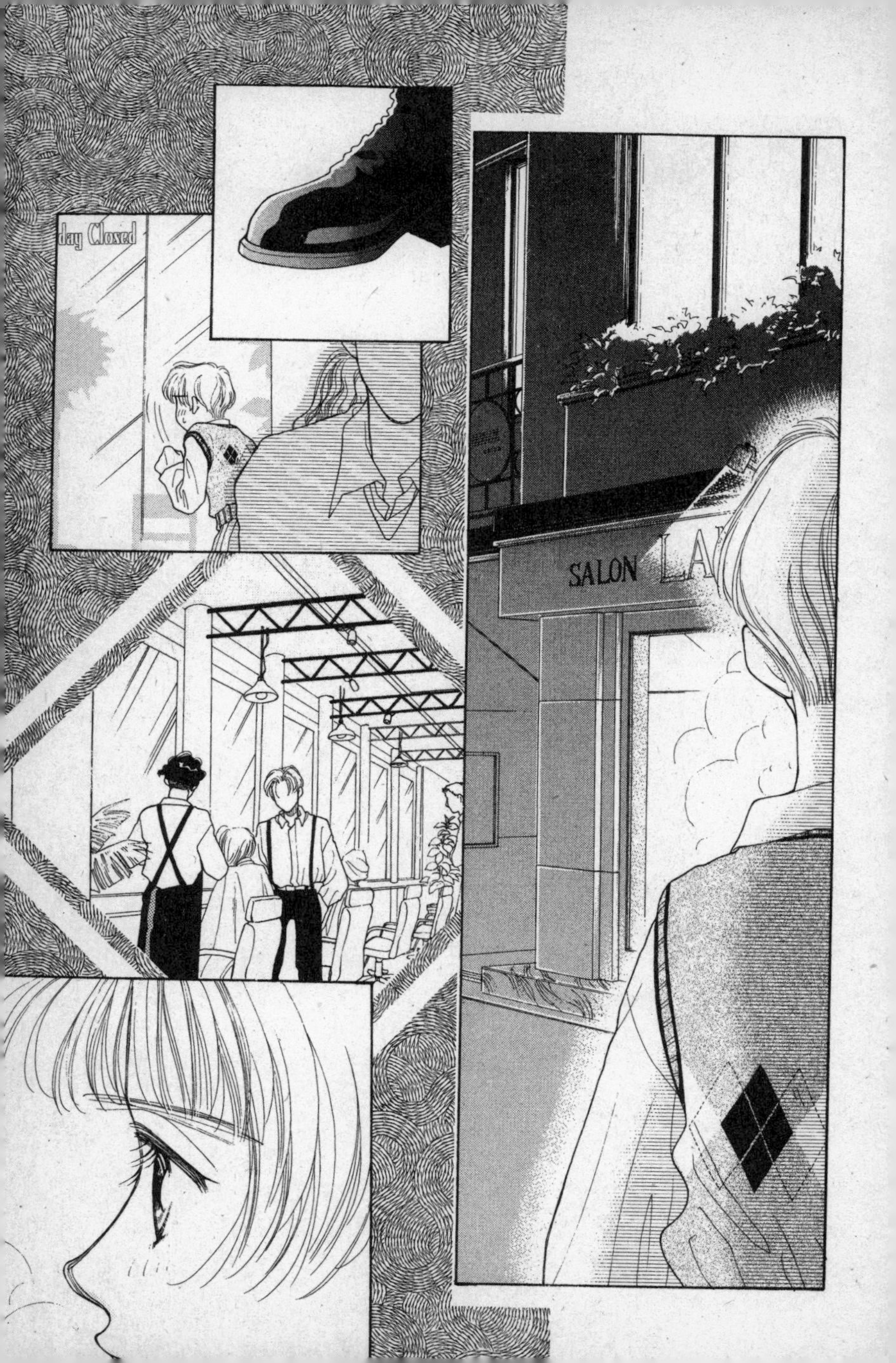
SALON LA
day Closed

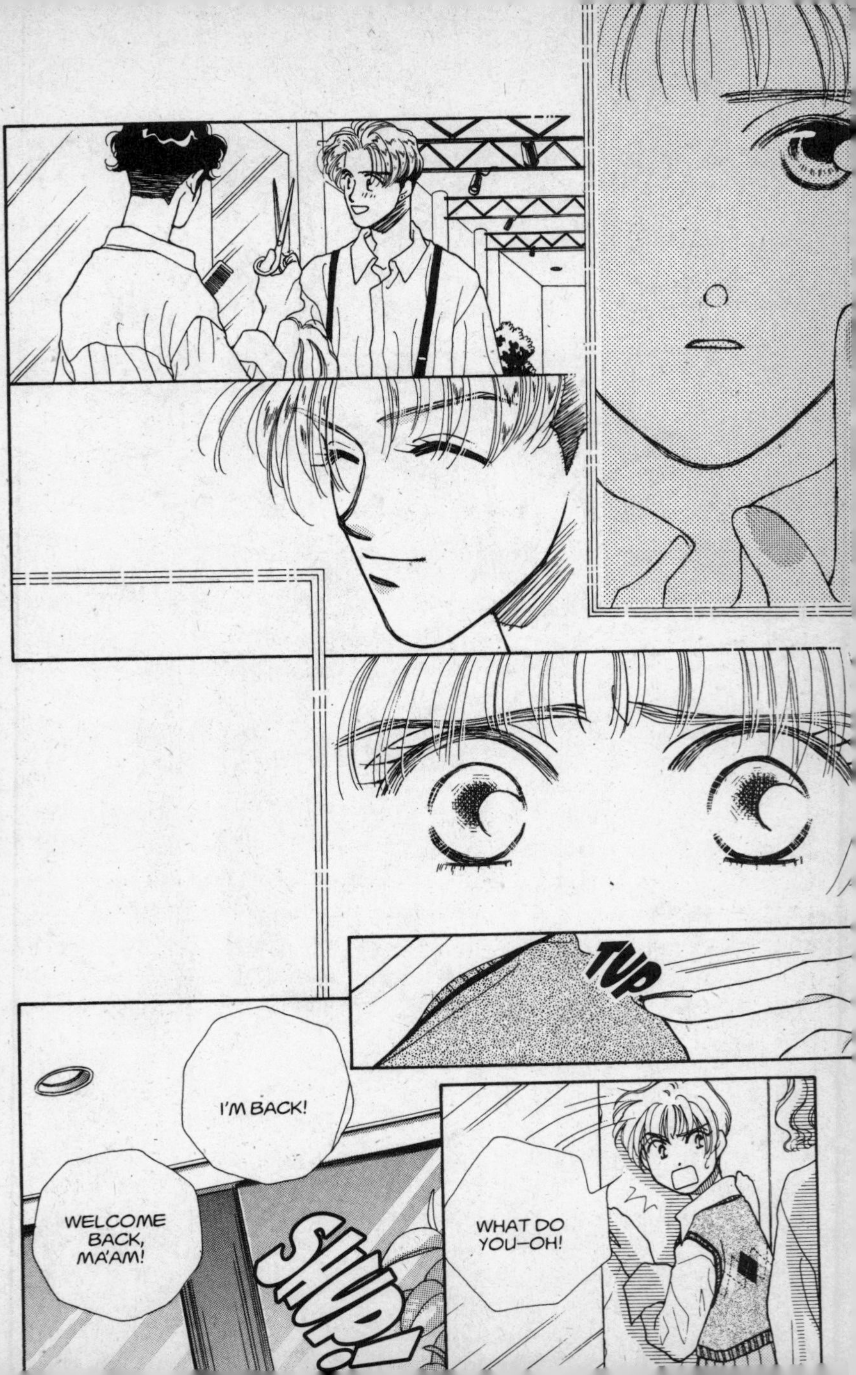
TUP
WHAT DO YOU—OH!
I'M BACK!
SHUP!
WELCOME BACK, MA'AM!

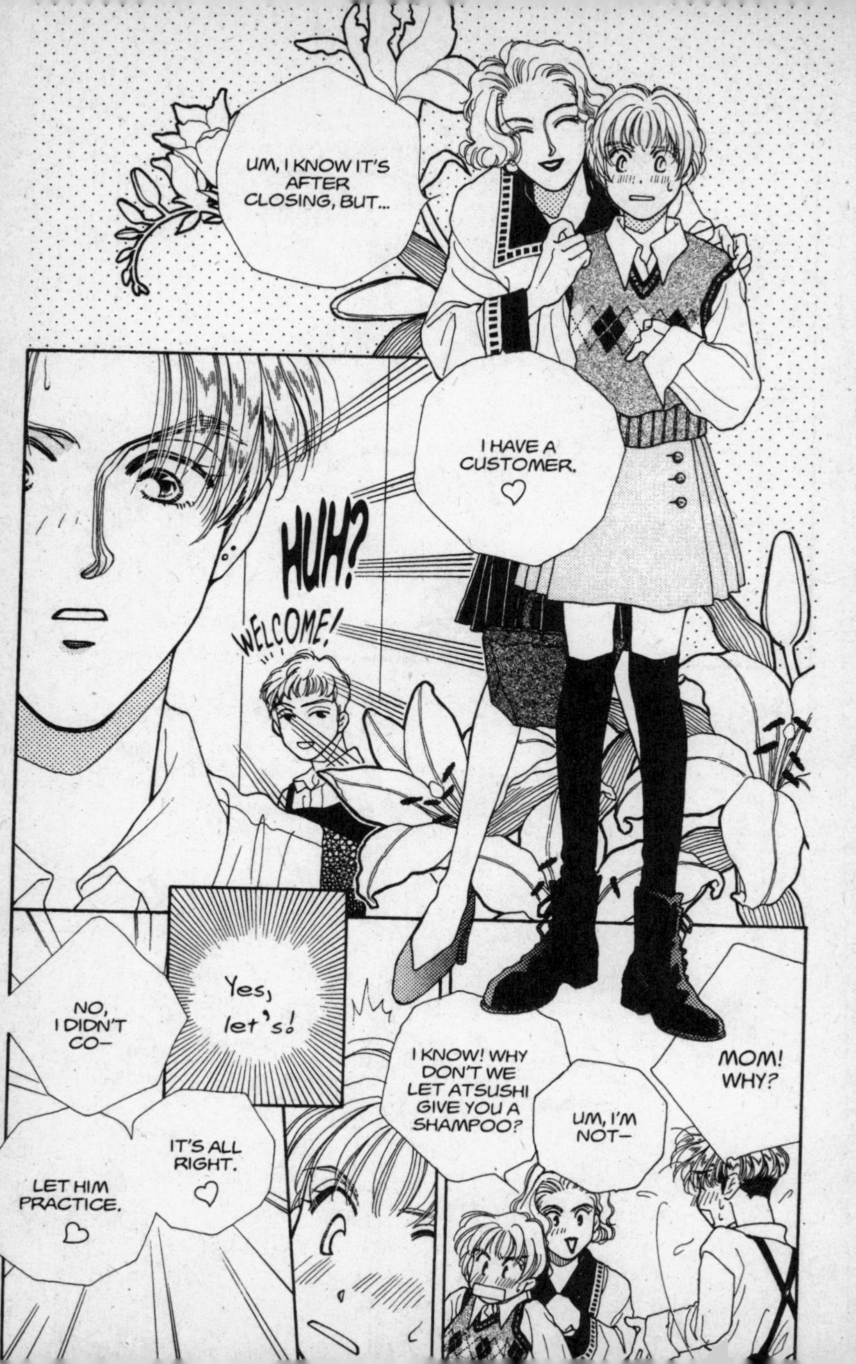
UM, I KNOW IT'S AFTER CLOSING, BUT...
I HAVE A CUSTOMER. ♡
HUH?
WELCOME!
MOM! WHY?
I KNOW! WHY DON'T WE LET ATSUSHI GIVE YOU A SHAMPOO?
UM, I'M NOT-
Yes, let's!
NO, I DIDN'T CO-
IT'S ALL RIGHT. ♡
LET HIM PRACTICE. ♡

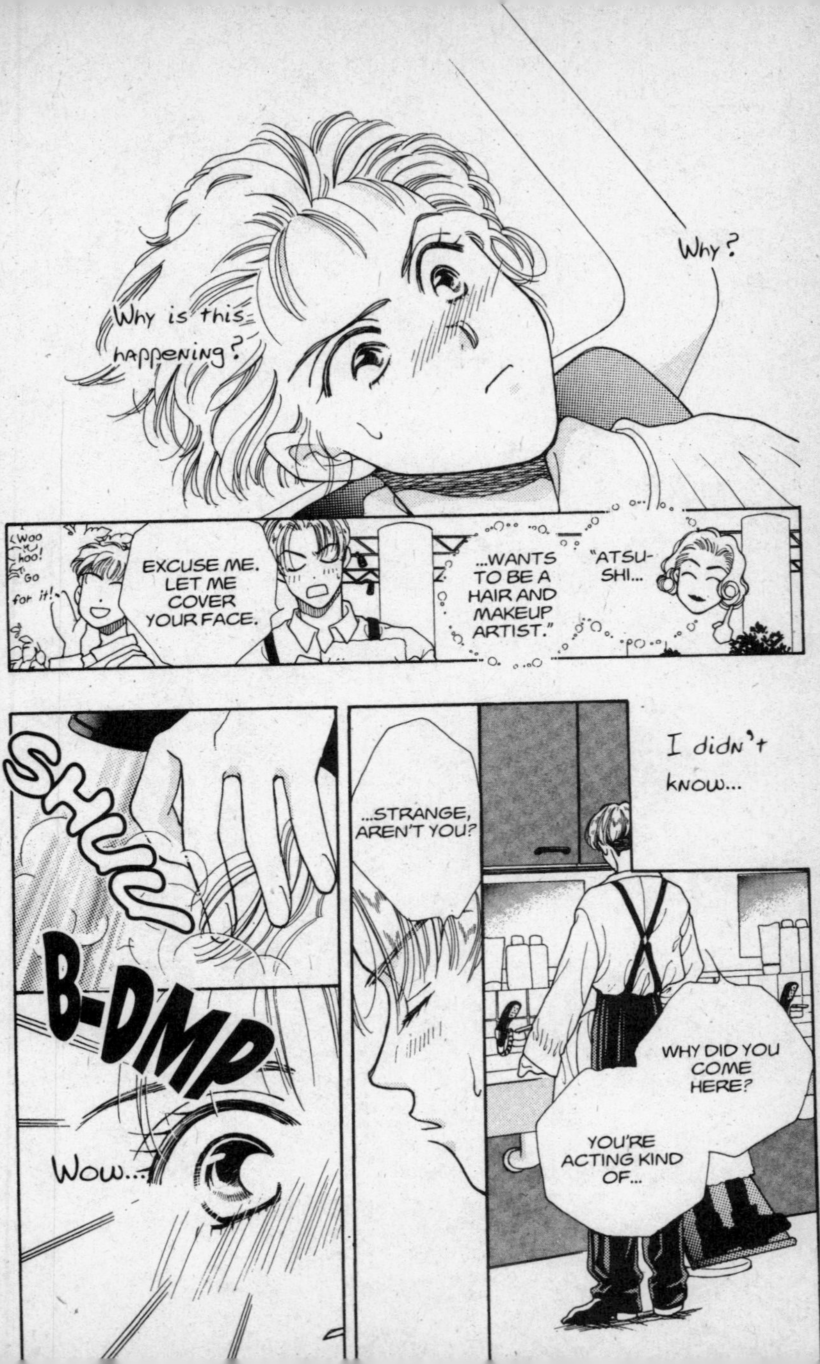
Why?
Why is this happening?
"ATSU-SHI...
...WANTS TO BE A HAIR AND MAKEUP ARTIST."
EXCUSE ME. LET ME COVER YOUR FACE.
Woo hoo! Go for it!
I didn't know...
WHY DID YOU COME HERE?
YOU'RE ACTING KIND OF...
...STRANGE, AREN'T YOU?
SHU
B-DMP
Wow...

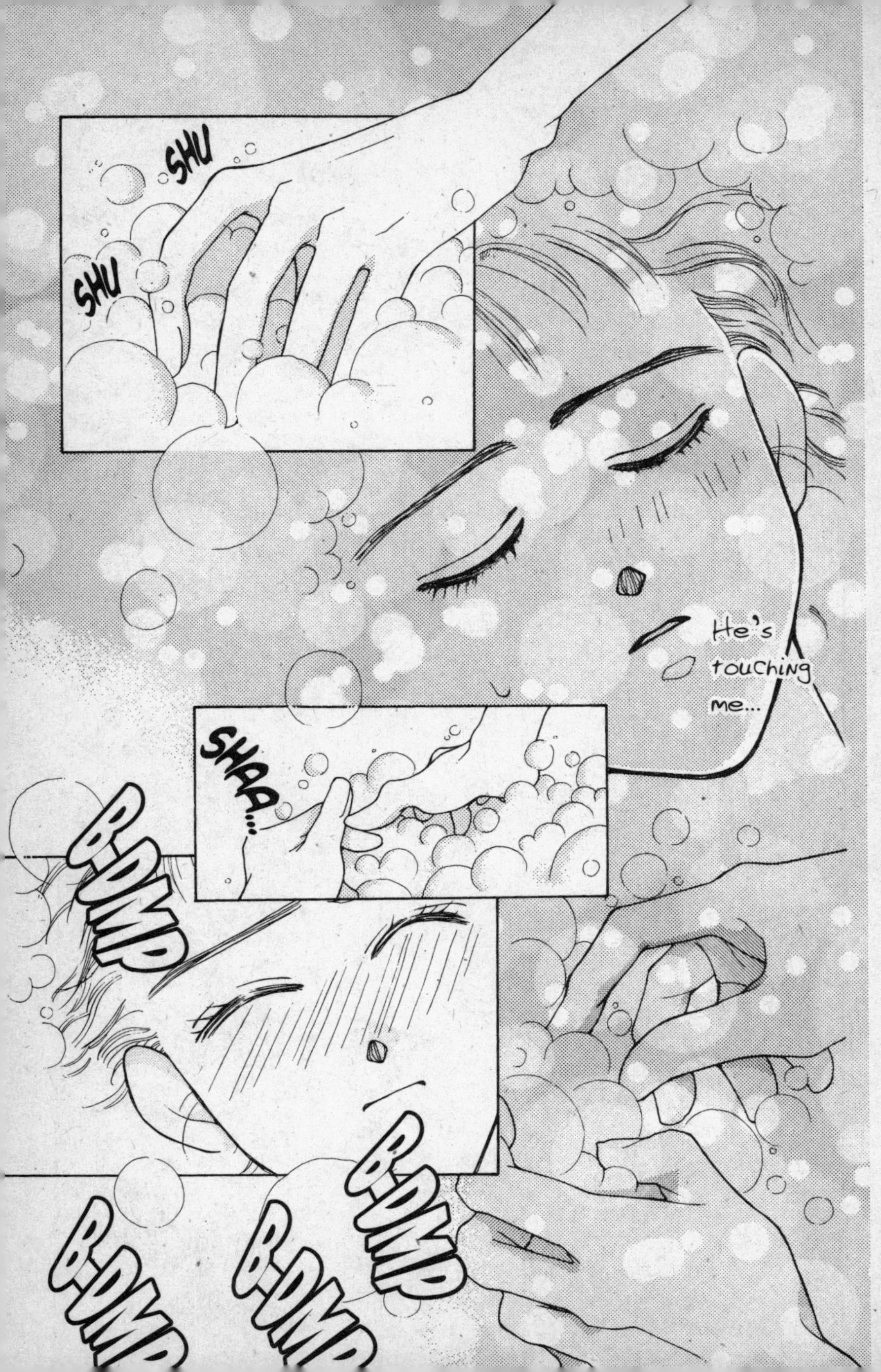
SHU SHU
He's touching me...
SHAA...
B-DMP
B-DMP B-DMP
B-DMP

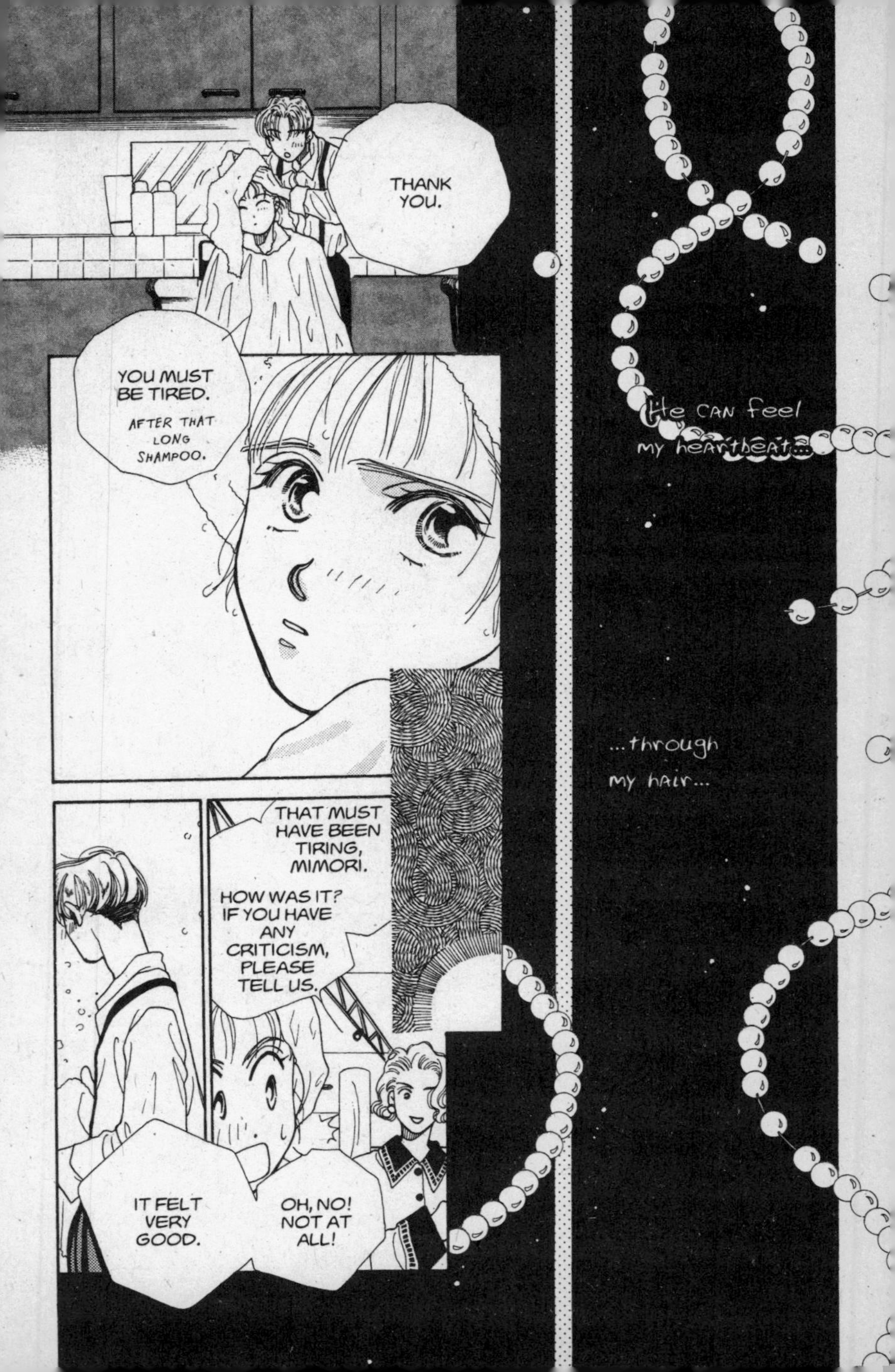
He can feel my heartbeat...
...through my hair...
THANK YOU.
YOU MUST BE TIRED.
AFTER THAT LONG SHAMPOO.
THAT MUST HAVE BEEN TIRING, MIMORI.
HOW WAS IT? IF YOU HAVE ANY CRITICISM, PLEASE TELL US.
OH, NO! NOT AT ALL!
IT FELT VERY GOOD.

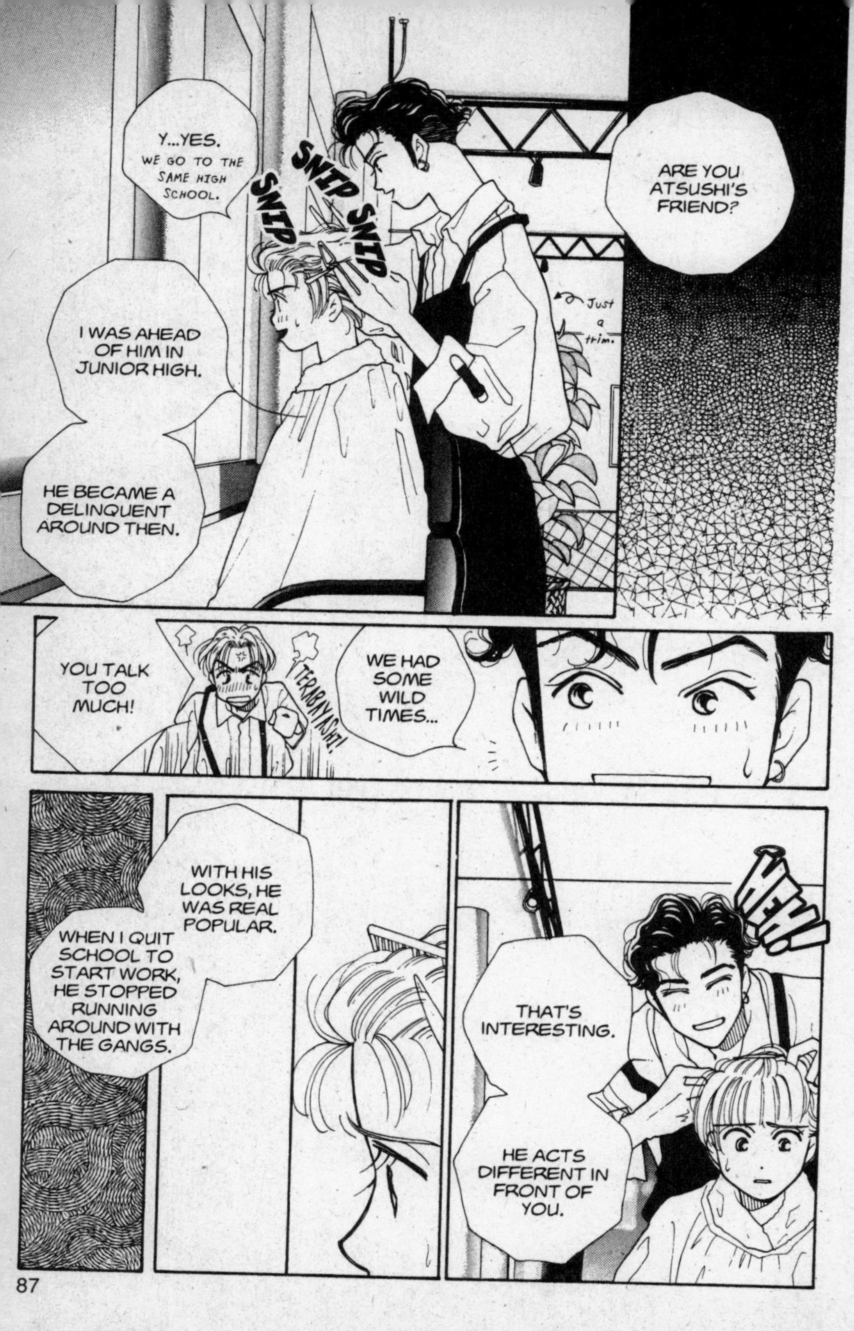
ARE YOU ATSUSHI'S FRIEND?
Y...YES. WE GO TO THE SAME HIGH SCHOOL.
SNIP SNIP
SNIP SNIP
Just a trim.
I WAS AHEAD OF HIM IN JUNIOR HIGH.
HE BECAME A DELINQUENT AROUND THEN.
WE HAD SOME WILD TIMES...
YOU TALK TOO MUCH!
TERABAYASHI!
HEH!
THAT'S INTERESTING.
HE ACTS DIFFERENT IN FRONT OF YOU.
WITH HIS LOOKS, HE WAS REAL POPULAR.
WHEN I QUIT SCHOOL TO START WORK, HE STOPPED RUNNING AROUND WITH THE GANGS.

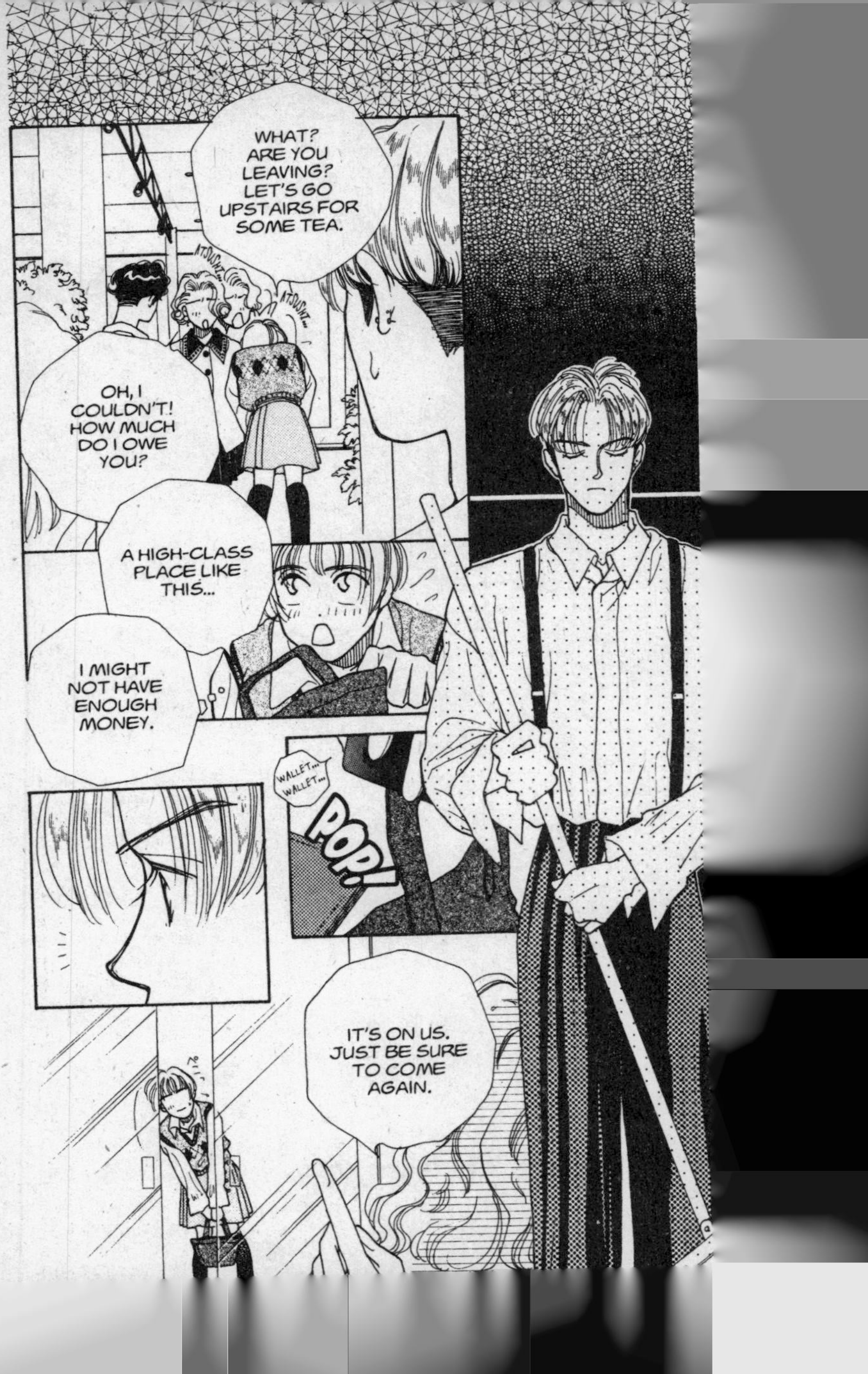
WHAT? ARE YOU LEAVING? LET'S GO UPSTAIRS FOR SOME TEA.
OH, I COULDN'T! HOW MUCH DO I OWE YOU?
A HIGH-CLASS PLACE LIKE THIS...
I MIGHT NOT HAVE ENOUGH MONEY.
WALLET... WALLET...
POP!
IT'S ON US. JUST BE SURE TO COME AGAIN.

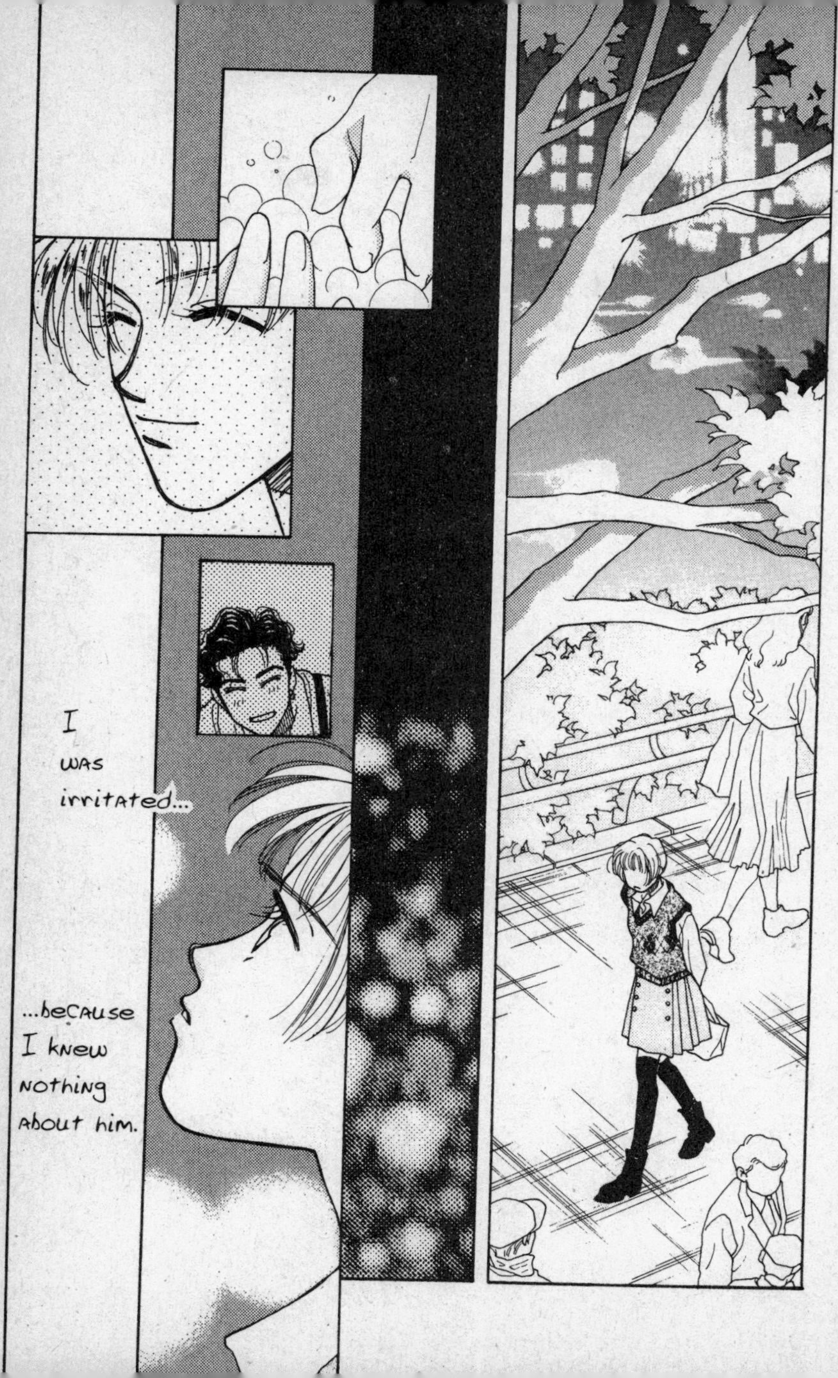
I was irritated...
...because I knew nothing about him.

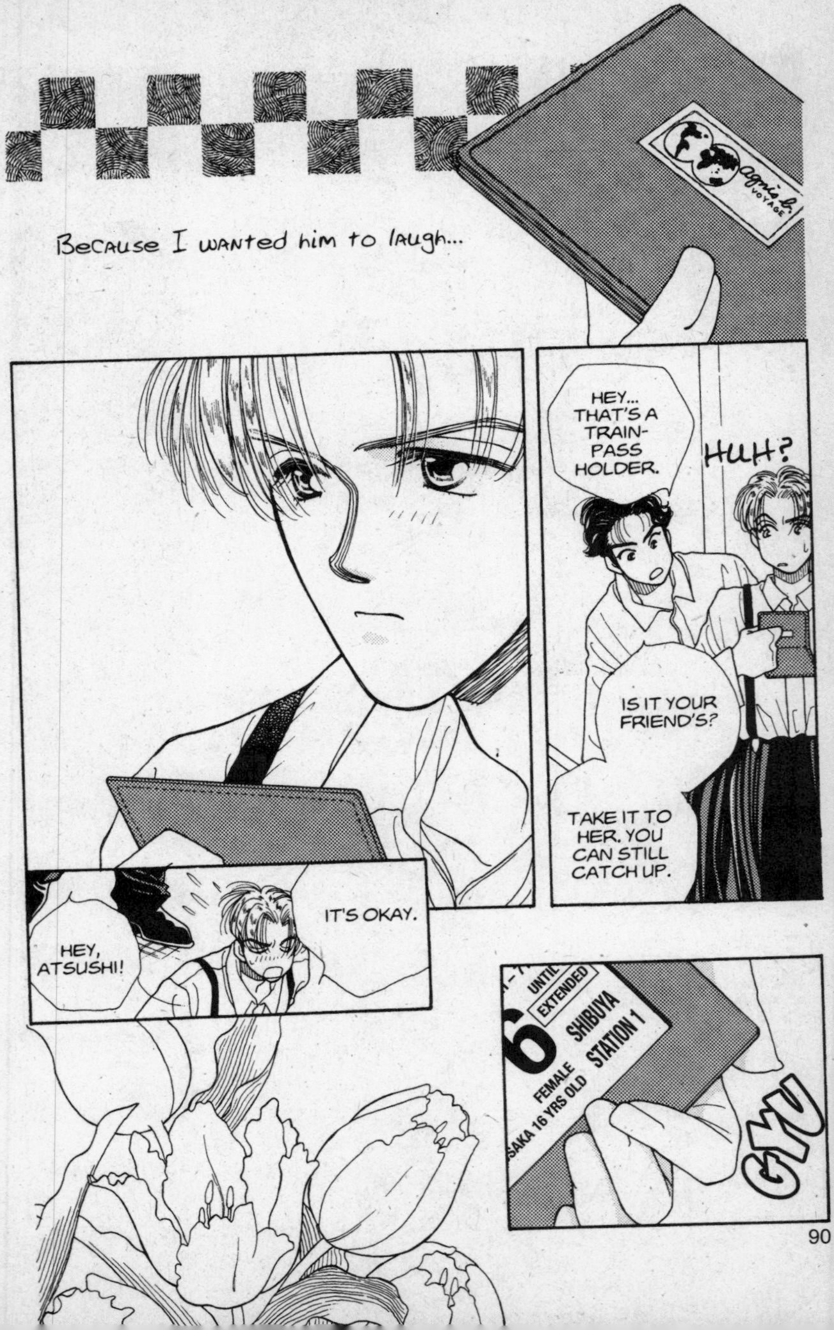
Because I wanted him to laugh...
agnès b.
VOYAGE
HEY... THAT'S A TRAIN-PASS HOLDER.
HUH?
IS IT YOUR FRIEND'S?
TAKE IT TO HER. YOU CAN STILL CATCH UP.
IT'S OKAY.
HEY, ATSUSHI!
UNTIL
EXTENDED
6
SHIBUYA
STATION 1
FEMALE
SAKA 16 YRS OLD
GYU

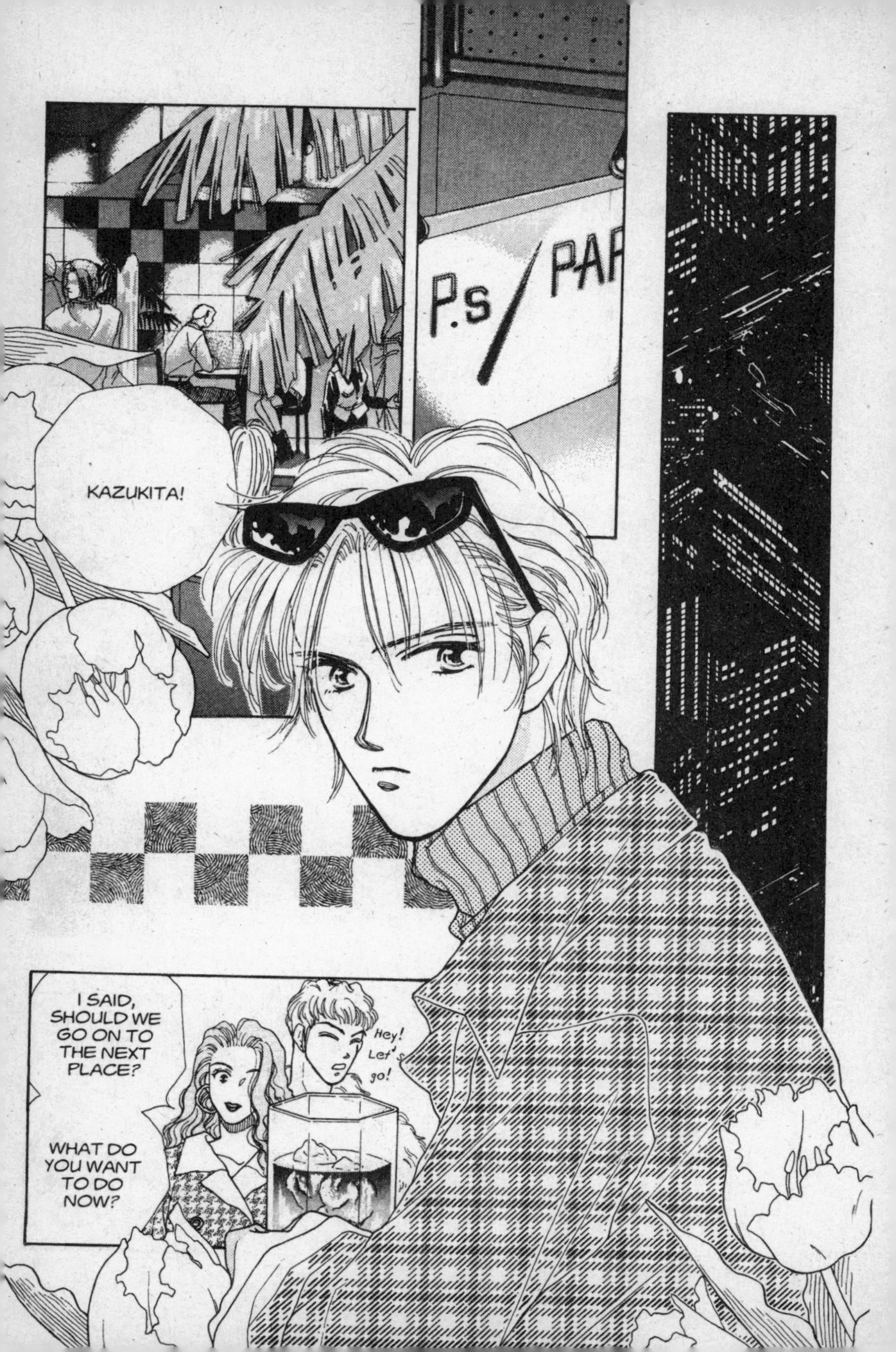
P.s / PAR
KAZUKITA!
I SAID, SHOULD WE GO ON TO THE NEXT PLACE?
Hey! Let's go!
WHAT DO YOU WANT TO DO NOW?

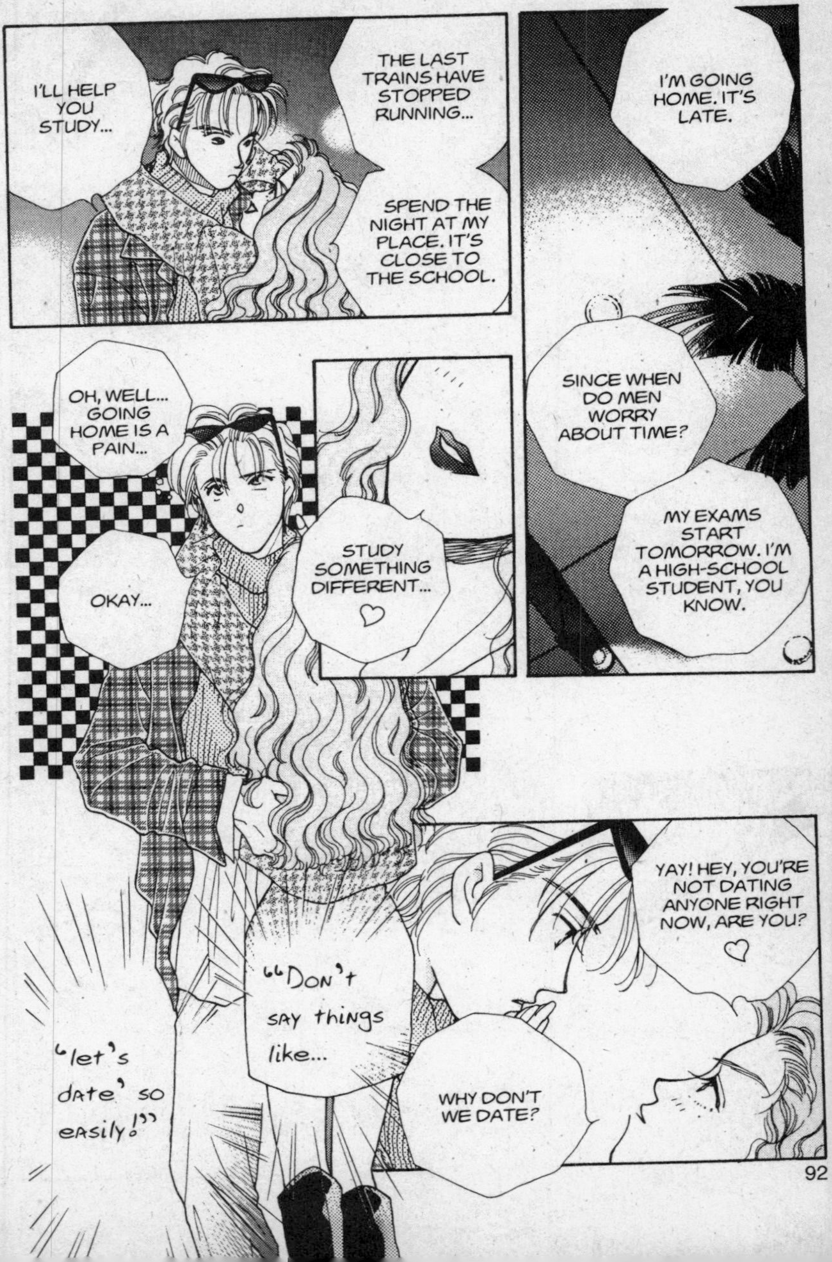
I'M GOING HOME. IT'S LATE.
SINCE WHEN DO MEN WORRY ABOUT TIME?
MY EXAMS START TOMORROW. I'M A HIGH-SCHOOL STUDENT, YOU KNOW.
THE LAST TRAINS HAVE STOPPED RUNNING...
SPEND THE NIGHT AT MY PLACE. IT'S CLOSE TO THE SCHOOL.
I'LL HELP YOU STUDY...
STUDY SOMETHING DIFFERENT... ♡
OH, WELL... GOING HOME IS A PAIN...
OKAY...
YAY! HEY, YOU'RE NOT DATING ANYONE RIGHT NOW, ARE YOU? ♡
WHY DON'T WE DATE?
"Don't say things like...
'let's date' so easily!"

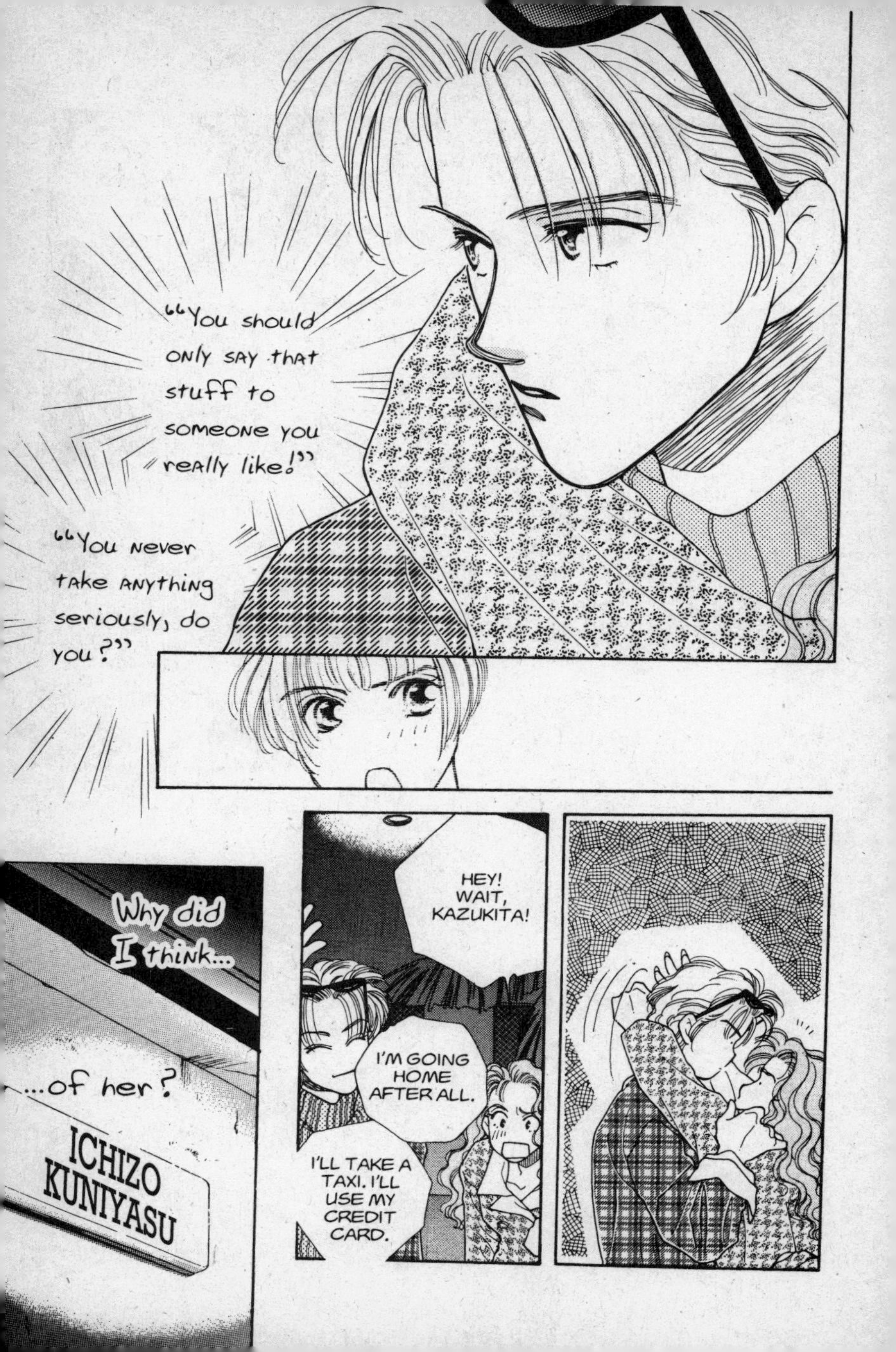
"You should only say that stuff to someone you really like!"
"You never take anything seriously, do you?"
HEY! WAIT, KAZUKITA!
I'M GOING HOME AFTER ALL.
I'LL TAKE A TAXI. I'LL USE MY CREDIT CARD.
Why did I think...
...of her?
ICHIZO KUNIYASU

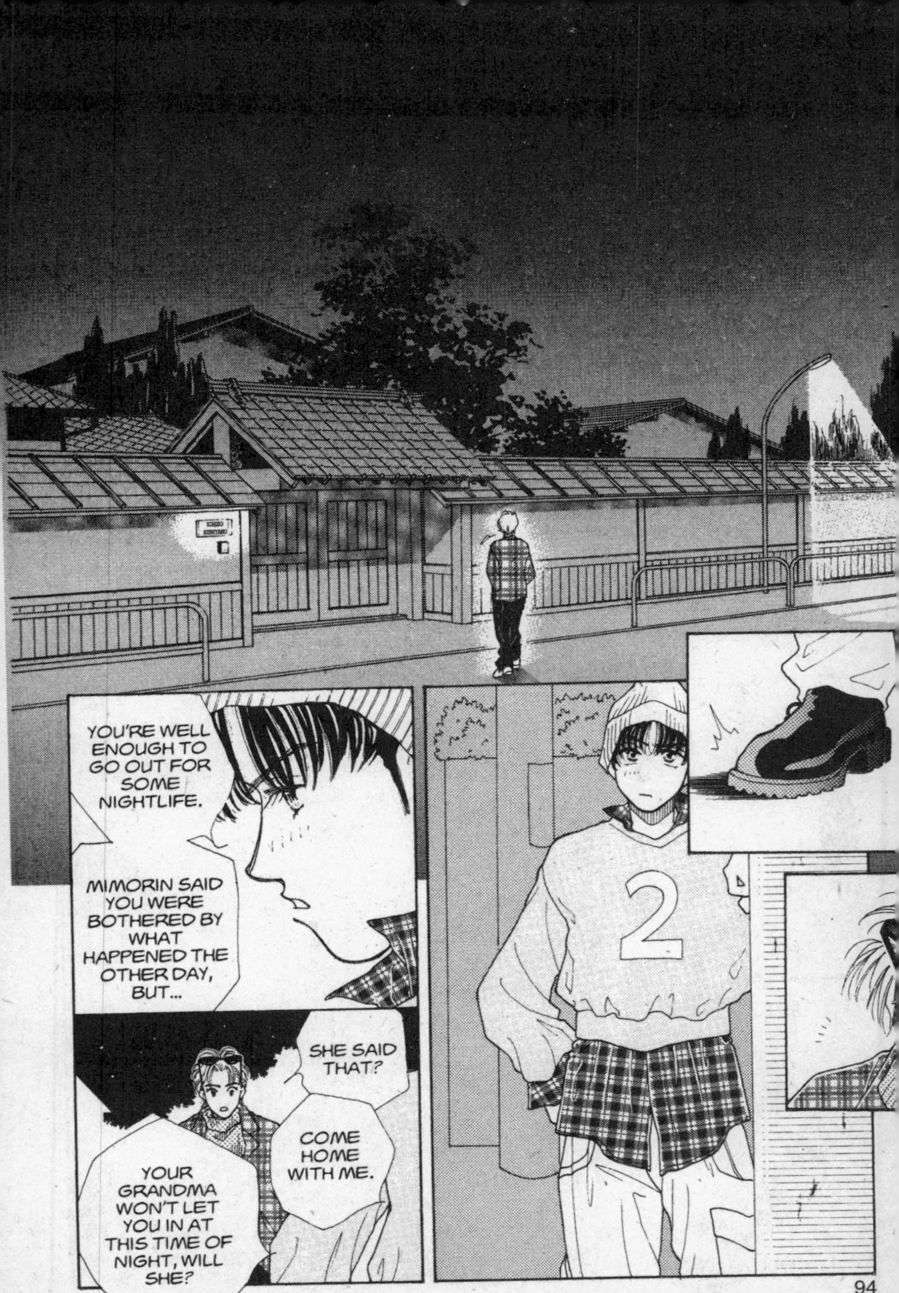
YOU'RE WELL ENOUGH TO GO OUT FOR SOME NIGHTLIFE.
MIMORIN SAID YOU WERE BOTHERED BY WHAT HAPPENED THE OTHER DAY, BUT...
SHE SAID THAT?
COME HOME WITH ME.
YOUR GRANDMA WON'T LET YOU IN AT THIS TIME OF NIGHT, WILL SHE?

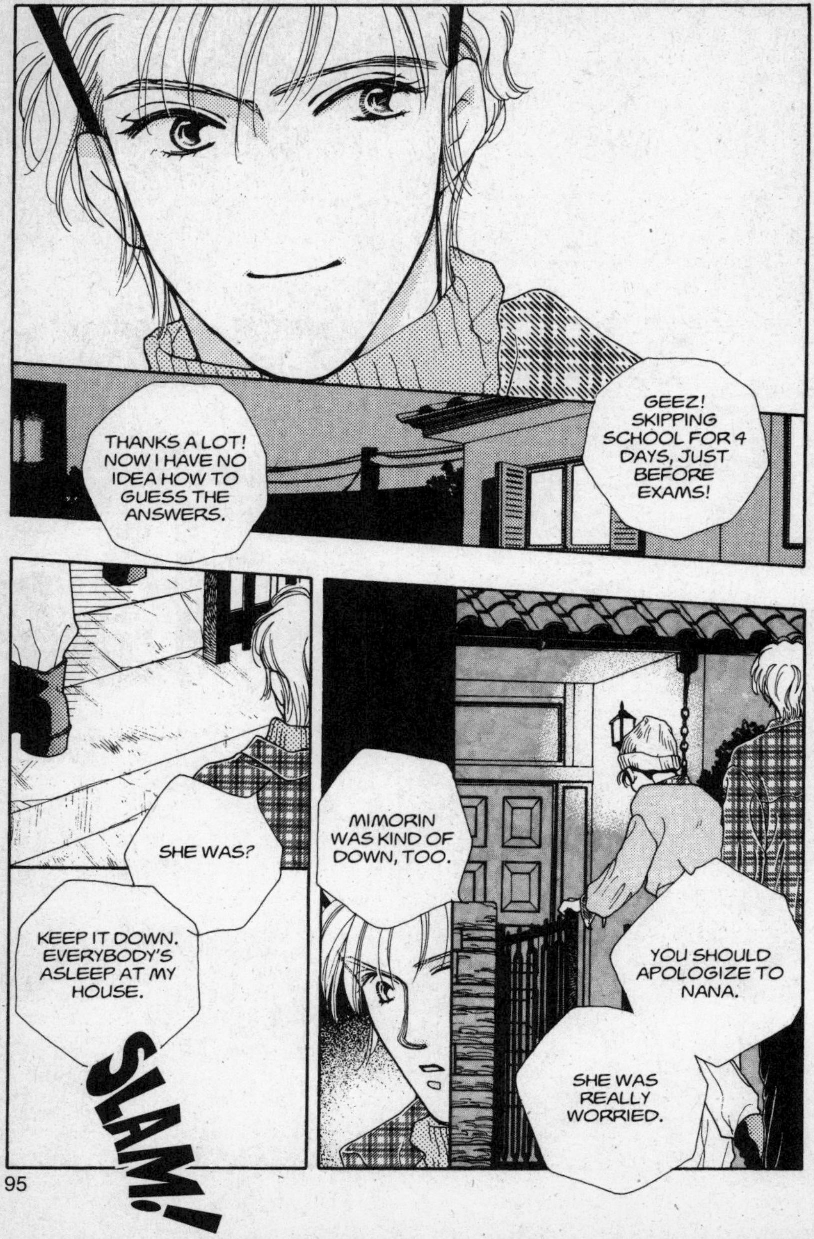
GEEZ! SKIPPING SCHOOL FOR 4 DAYS, JUST BEFORE EXAMS!
THANKS A LOT! NOW I HAVE NO IDEA HOW TO GUESS THE ANSWERS.
YOU SHOULD APOLOGIZE TO NANA.
SHE WAS REALLY WORRIED.
MIMORIN WAS KIND OF DOWN, TOO.
SHE WAS?
KEEP IT DOWN. EVERYBODY'S ASLEEP AT MY HOUSE.
SLAM!

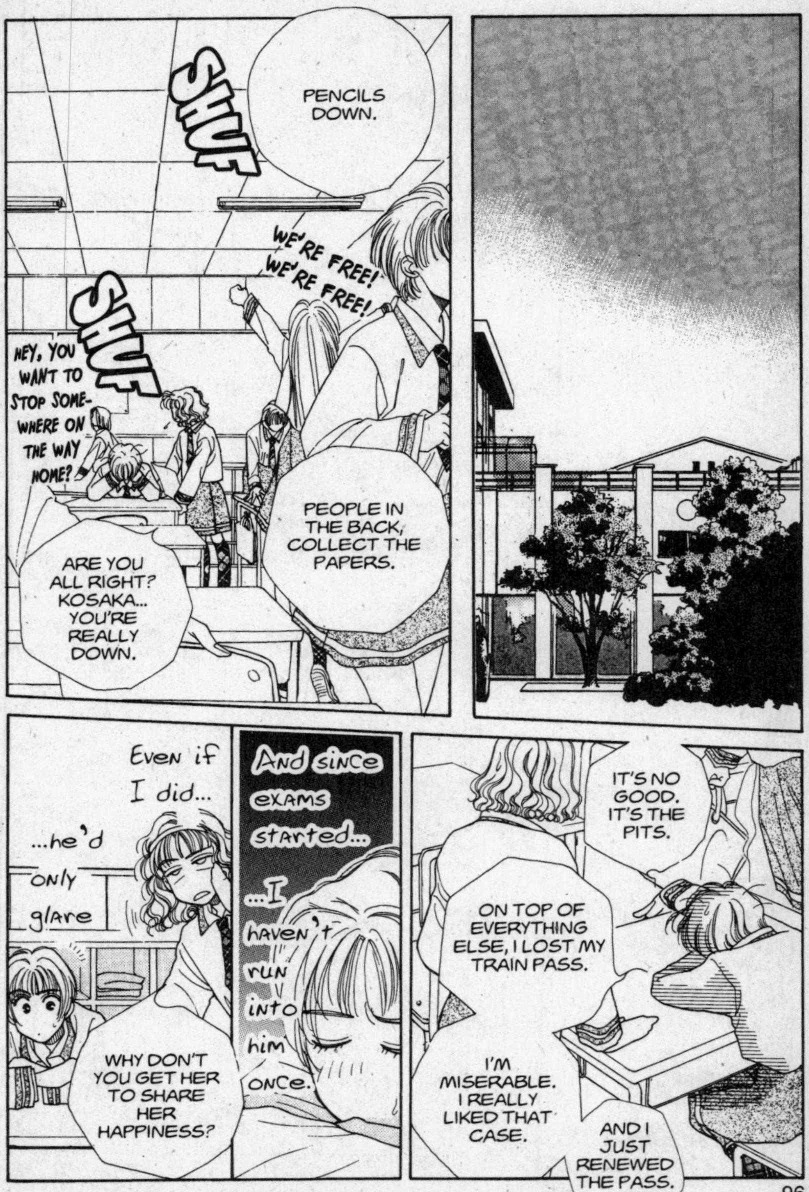
PENCILS DOWN.
SHUF
SHUF
WE'RE FREE! WE'RE FREE!
PEOPLE IN THE BACK, COLLECT THE PAPERS.
HEY, YOU WANT TO STOP SOME-WHERE ON THE WAY HOME?
ARE YOU ALL RIGHT? KOSAKA... YOU'RE REALLY DOWN.
IT'S NO GOOD. IT'S THE PITS.
ON TOP OF EVERYTHING ELSE, I LOST MY TRAIN PASS.
I'M MISERABLE. I REALLY LIKED THAT CASE.
AND I JUST RENEWED THE PASS.
And since exams started...
...I haven't run into him once.
Even if I did...
...he'd only glare
WHY DON'T YOU GET HER TO SHARE HER HAPPINESS?

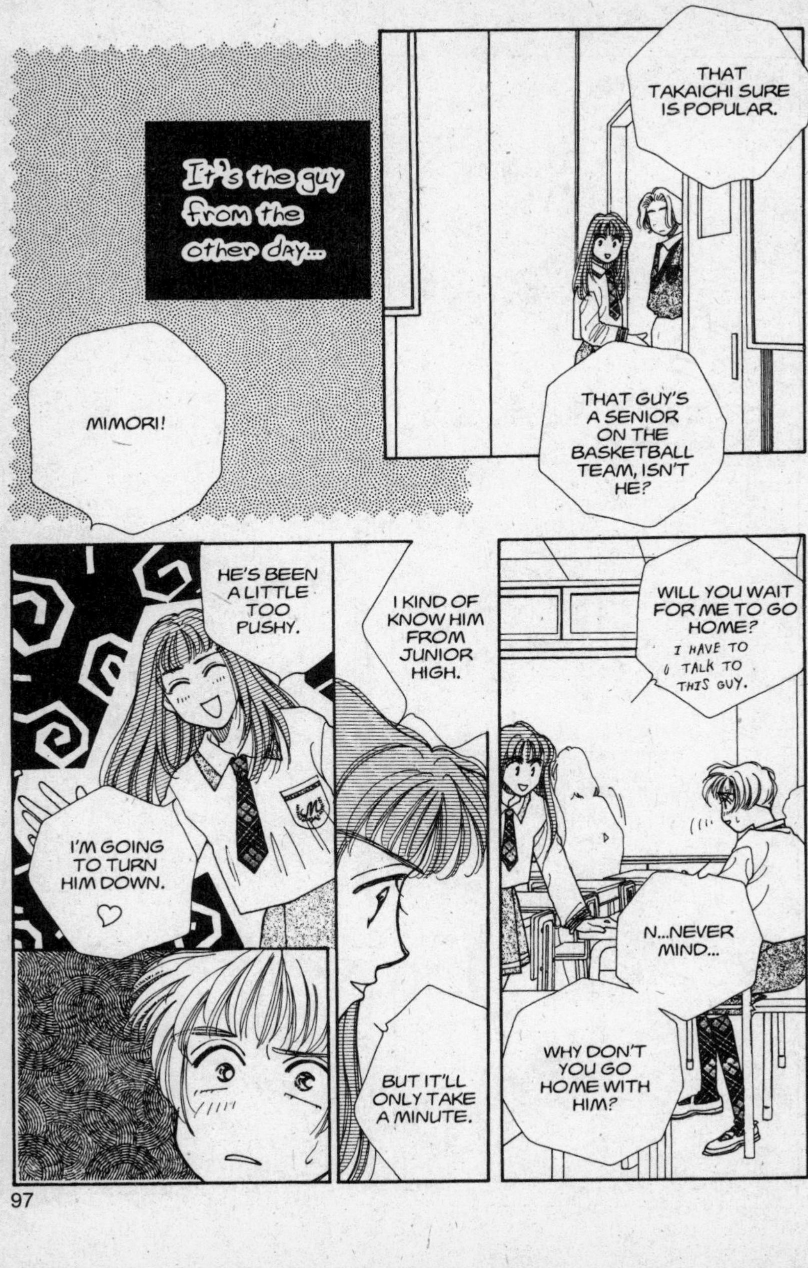
THAT TAKAICHI SURE IS POPULAR.
THAT GUY'S A SENIOR ON THE BASKETBALL TEAM, ISN'T HE?
It's the guy from the other day...
MIMORI!
WILL YOU WAIT FOR ME TO GO HOME?
I HAVE TO TALK TO THIS GUY.
N...NEVER MIND...
WHY DON'T YOU GO HOME WITH HIM?
I KIND OF KNOW HIM FROM JUNIOR HIGH.
BUT IT'LL ONLY TAKE A MINUTE.
HE'S BEEN A LITTLE TOO PUSHY.
I'M GOING TO TURN HIM DOWN. ♡

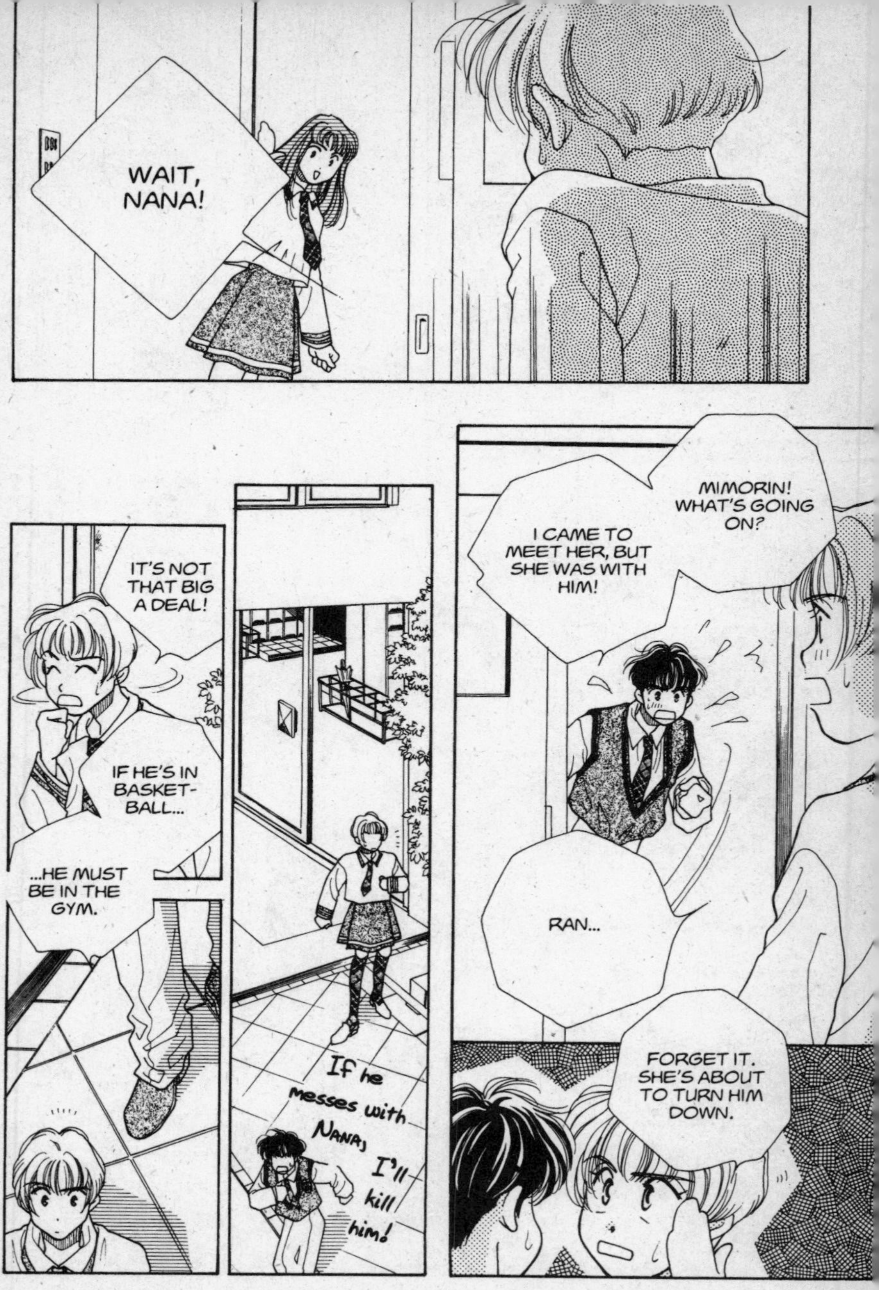
WAIT, NANA!
MIMORIN! WHAT'S GOING ON?
I CAME TO MEET HER, BUT SHE WAS WITH HIM!
RAN...
FORGET IT. SHE'S ABOUT TO TURN HIM DOWN.
If he messes with Nana, I'll kill him!
IT'S NOT THAT BIG A DEAL!
IF HE'S IN BASKET-BALL...
...HE MUST BE IN THE GYM.

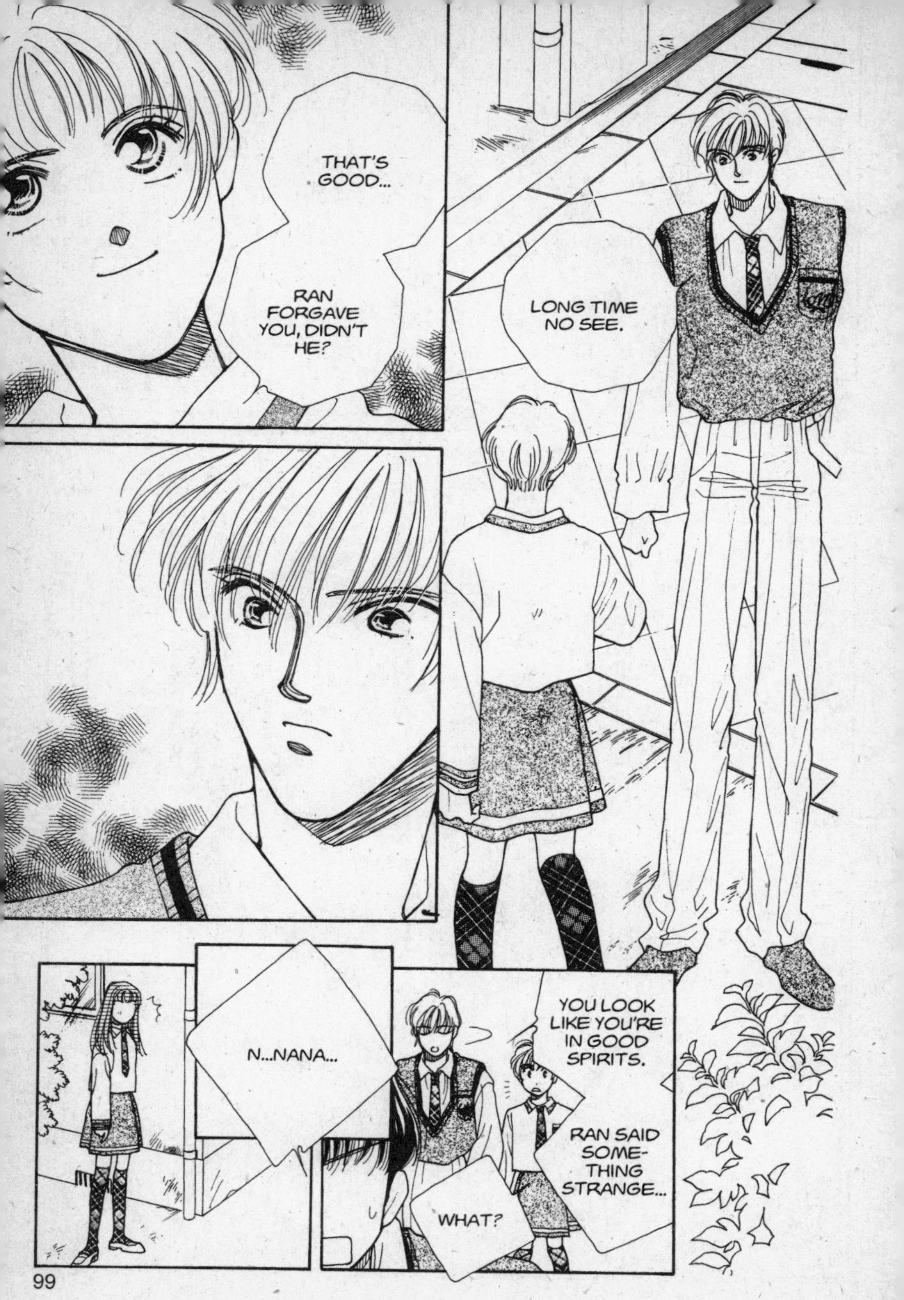
LONG TIME NO SEE.
THAT'S GOOD...
RAN FORGAVE YOU, DIDN'T HE?
YOU LOOK LIKE YOU'RE IN GOOD SPIRITS.
RAN SAID SOME-THING STRANGE...
WHAT?
N...NANA...

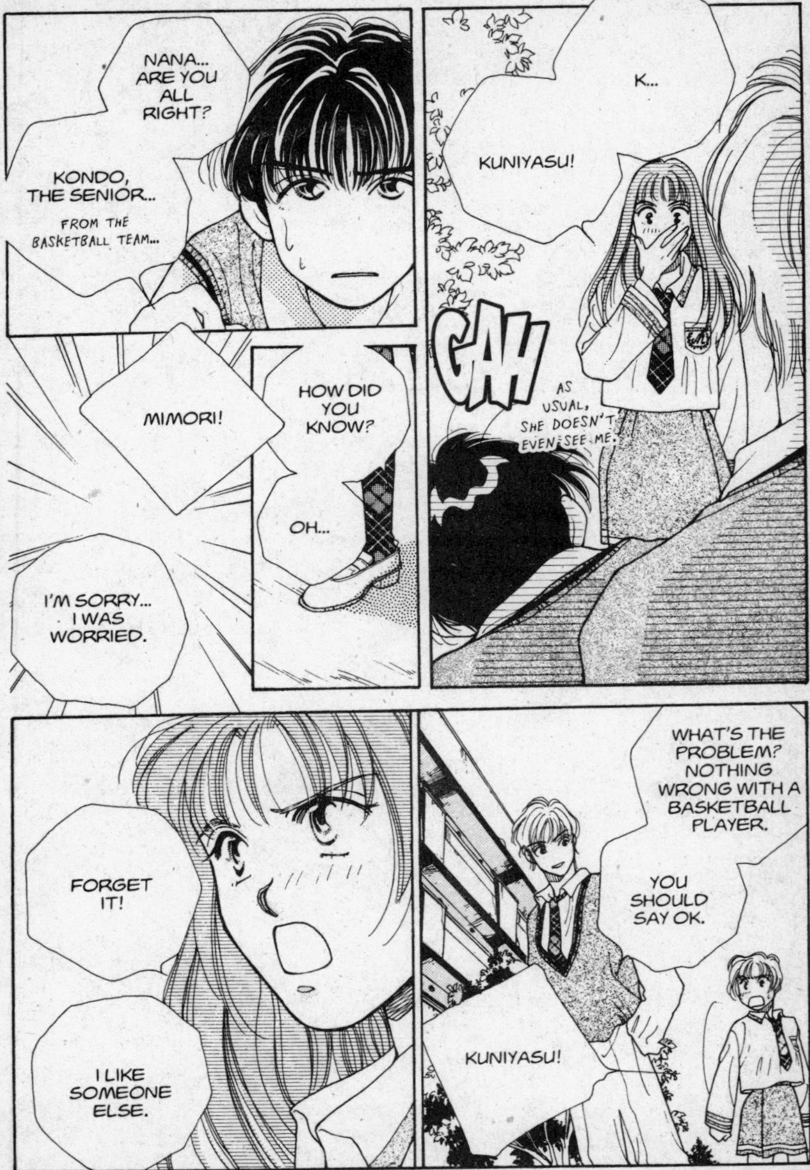
K...
KUNIYASU!
GAH
AS USUAL, SHE DOESN'T EVEN SEE ME.
NANA... ARE YOU ALL RIGHT?
KONDO, THE SENIOR...
FROM THE BASKETBALL TEAM...
HOW DID YOU KNOW?
OH...
MIMORI!
I'M SORRY... I WAS WORRIED.
WHAT'S THE PROBLEM? NOTHING WRONG WITH A BASKETBALL PLAYER.
YOU SHOULD SAY OK.
KUNIYASU!
FORGET IT!
I LIKE SOMEONE ELSE.

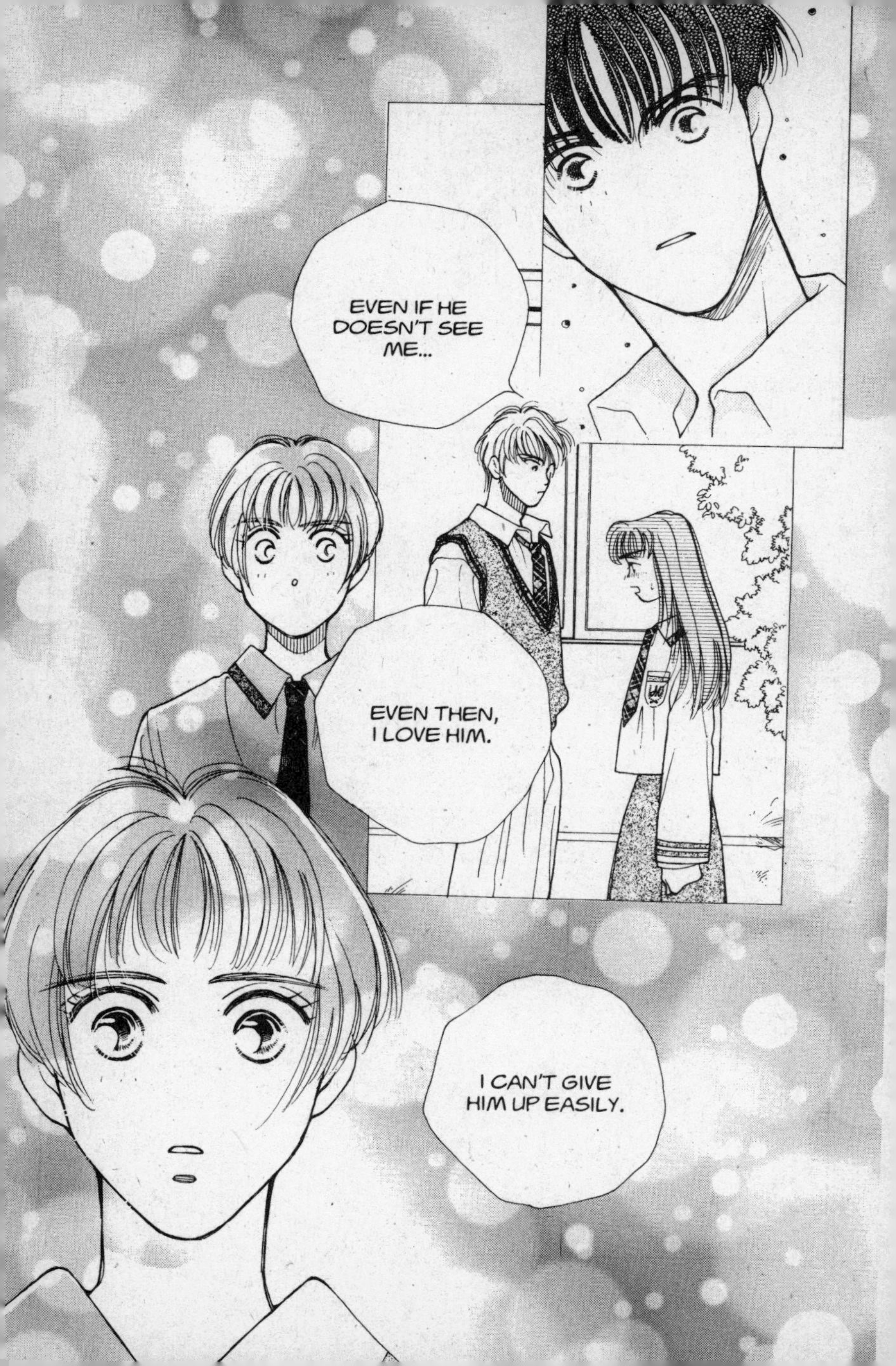
EVEN IF HE DOESN'T SEE ME...
EVEN THEN, I LOVE HIM.
I CAN'T GIVE HIM UP EASILY.

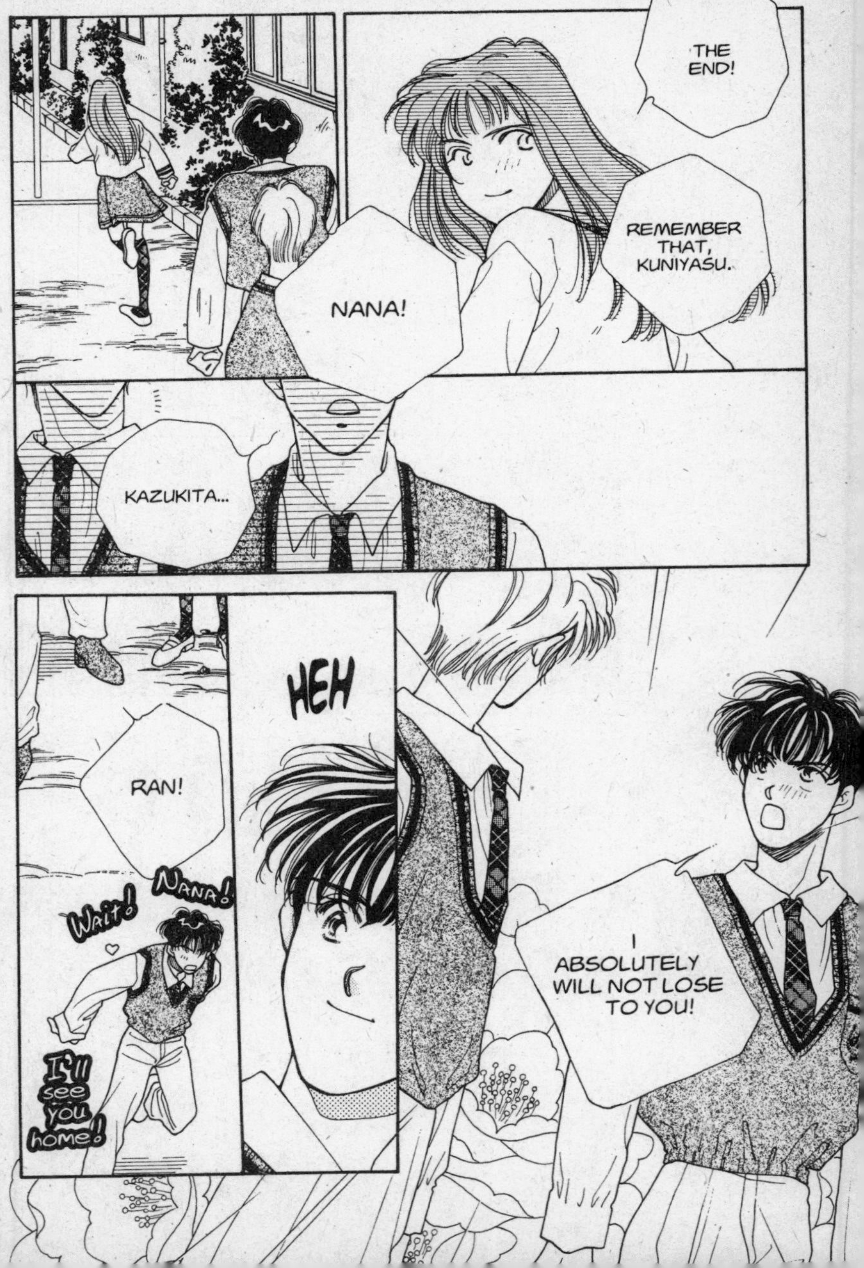
THE END!
REMEMBER THAT, KUNIYASU.
NANA!
KAZUKITA...
I ABSOLUTELY WILL NOT LOSE TO YOU!
HEH
RAN!
Nana!
Wait!
I'll see you home!

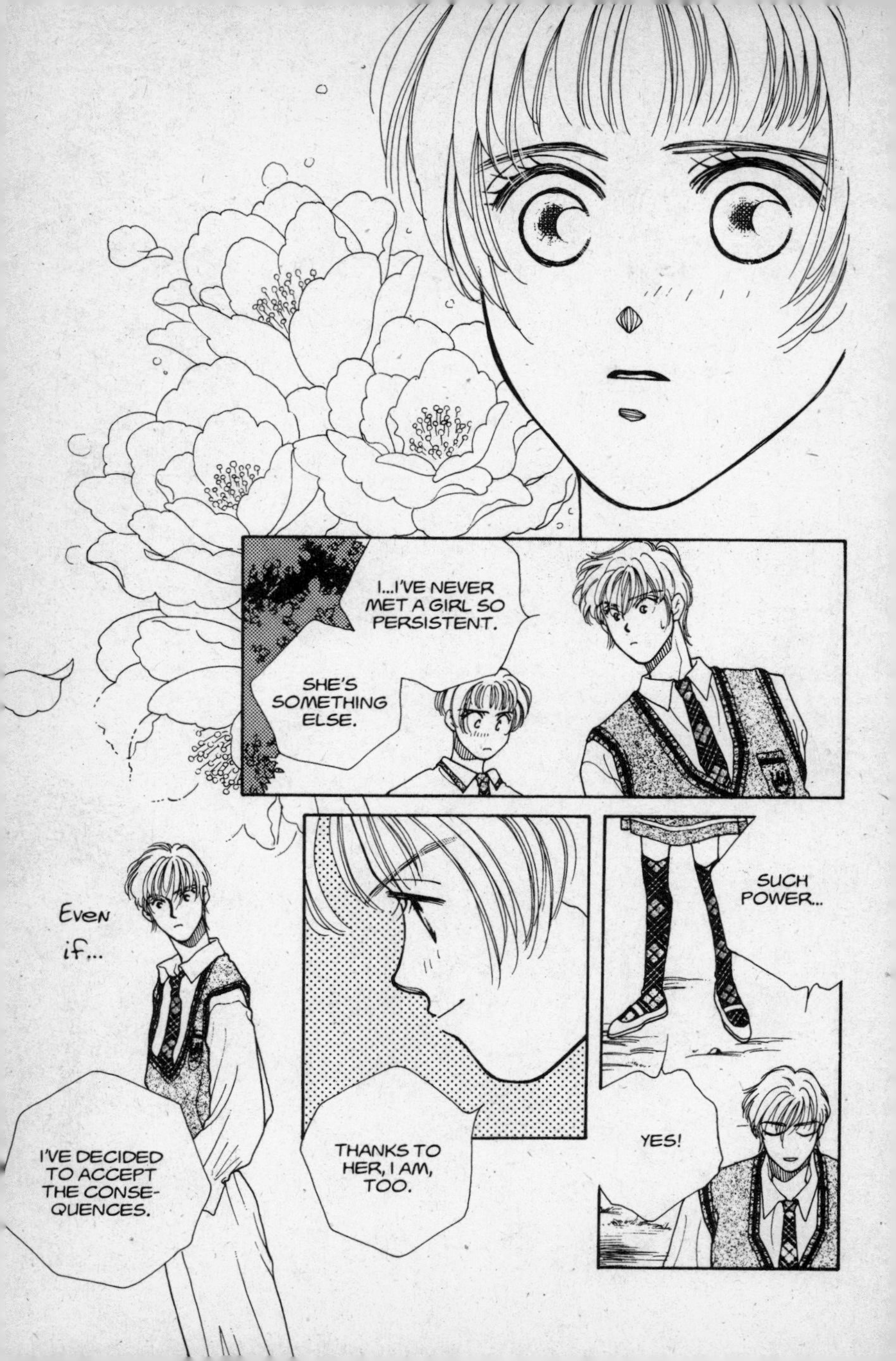
I...I'VE NEVER MET A GIRL SO PERSISTENT.
SHE'S SOMETHING ELSE.
SUCH POWER...
YES!
THANKS TO HER, I AM, TOO.
Even if...
I'VE DECIDED TO ACCEPT THE CONSE-QUENCES.

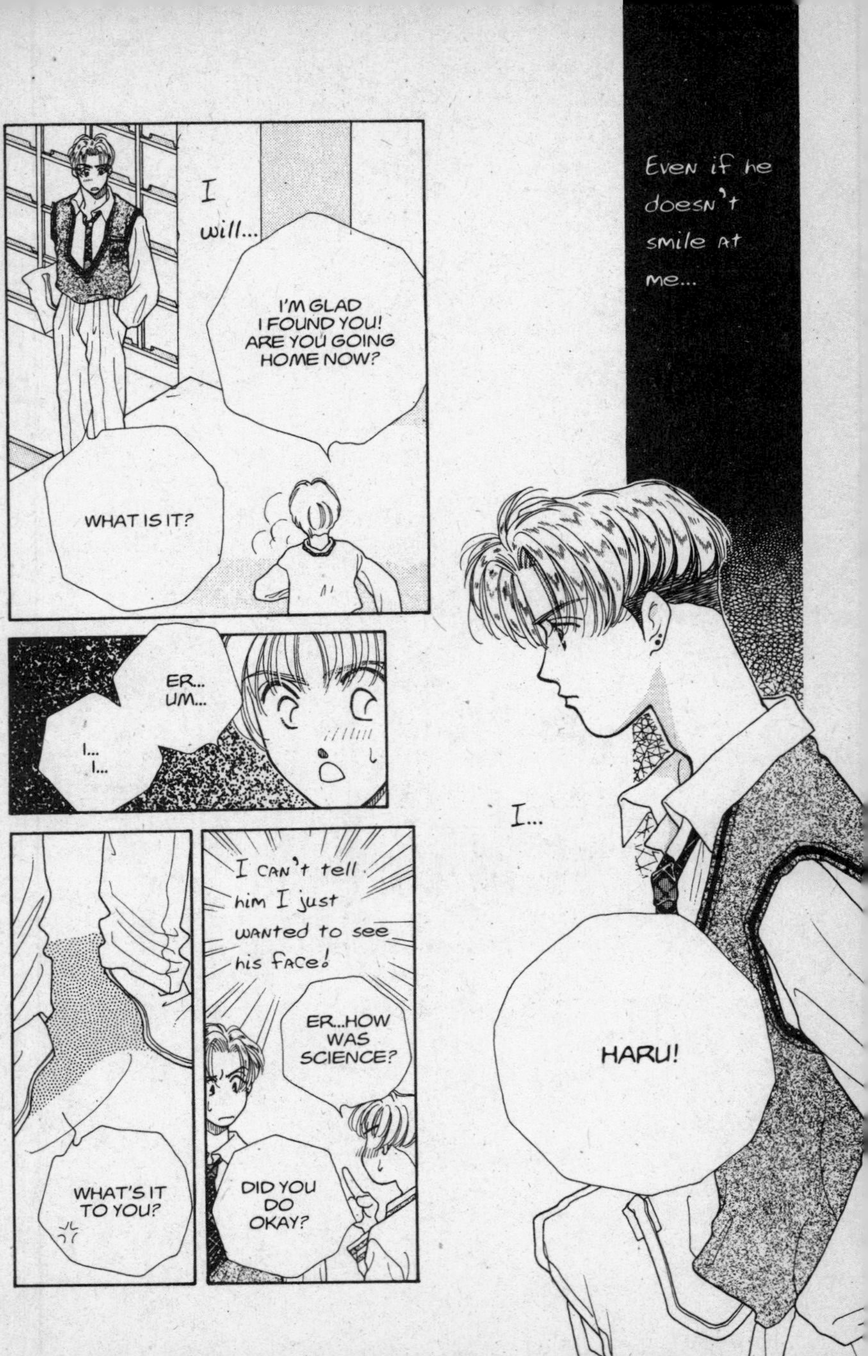
Even if he doesn't smile at me...
I...
HARU!
I will...
I'M GLAD I FOUND YOU! ARE YOU GOING HOME NOW?
WHAT IS IT?
ER... UM...
I... I...
I can't tell him I just wanted to see his face!
ER...HOW WAS SCIENCE?
DID YOU DO OKAY?
WHAT'S IT TO YOU?

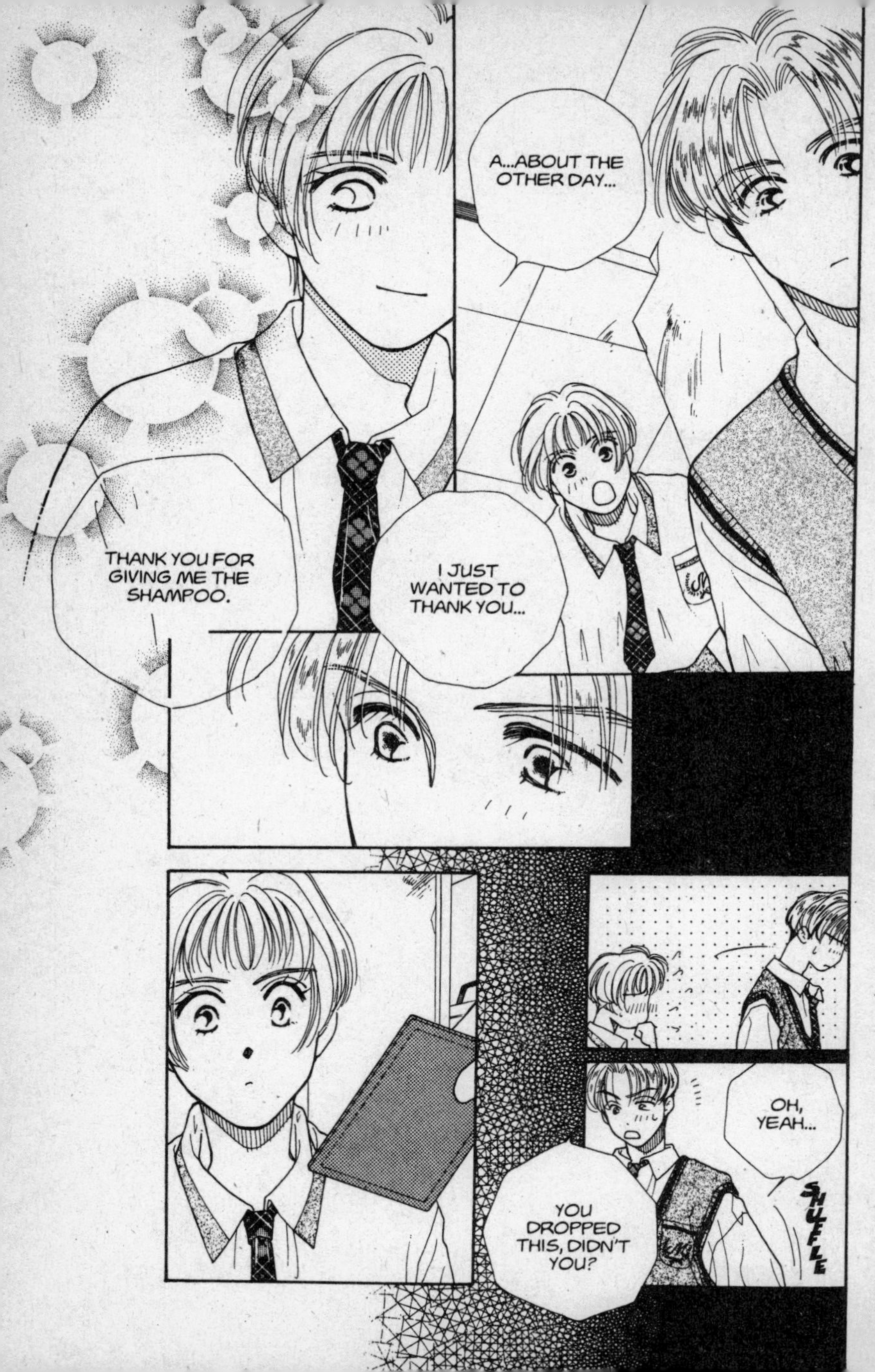
A...ABOUT THE OTHER DAY...
I JUST WANTED TO THANK YOU...
THANK YOU FOR GIVING ME THE SHAMPOO.
OH, YEAH...
SHUFFLE
YOU DROPPED THIS, DIDN'T YOU?

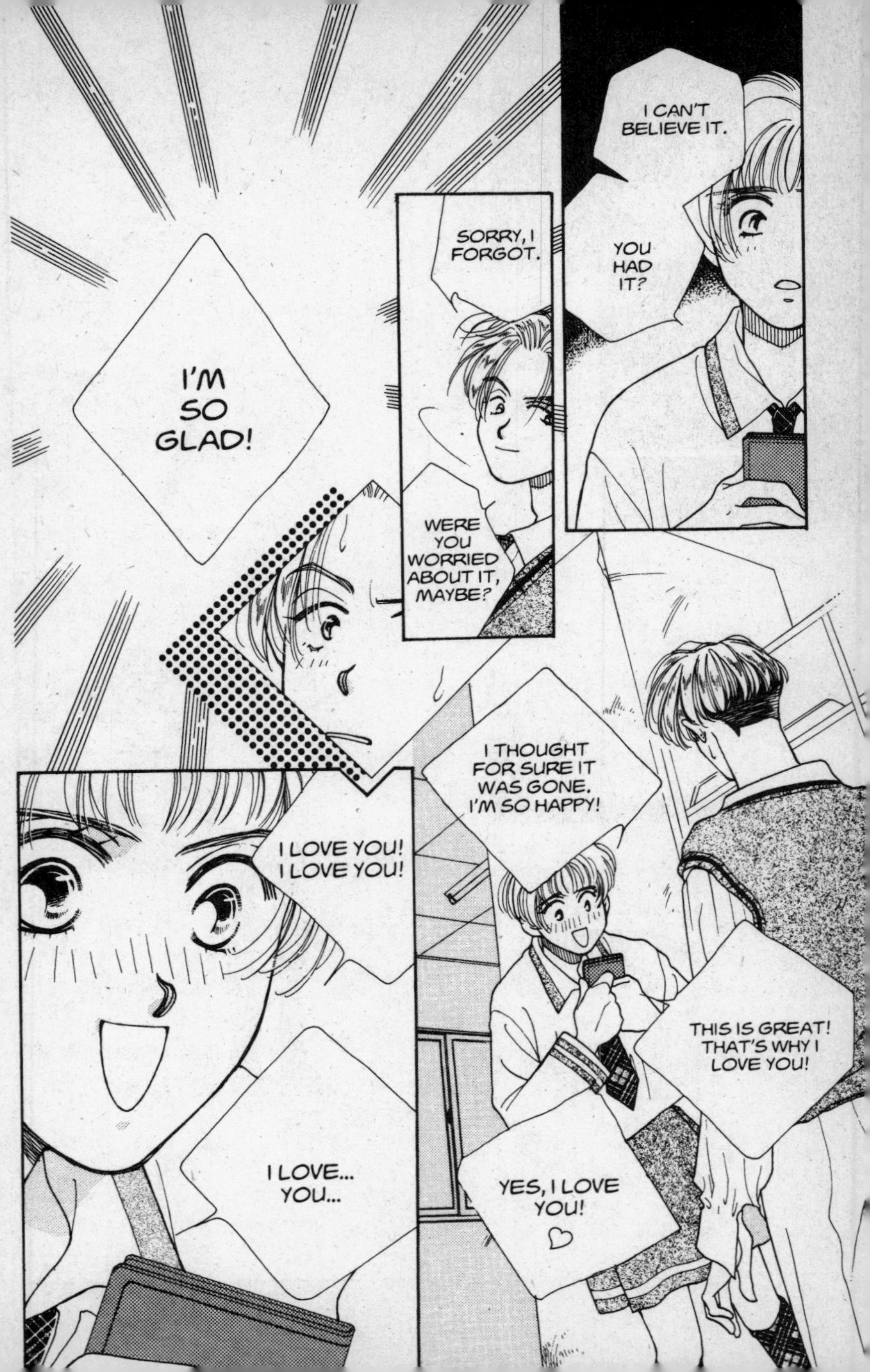
I CAN'T BELIEVE IT.
YOU HAD IT?
SORRY, I FORGOT.
WERE YOU WORRIED ABOUT IT, MAYBE?
I'M SO GLAD!
I THOUGHT FOR SURE IT WAS GONE. I'M SO HAPPY!
THIS IS GREAT! THAT'S WHY I LOVE YOU!
YES, I LOVE YOU! ♡
I LOVE YOU! I LOVE YOU!
I LOVE... YOU...

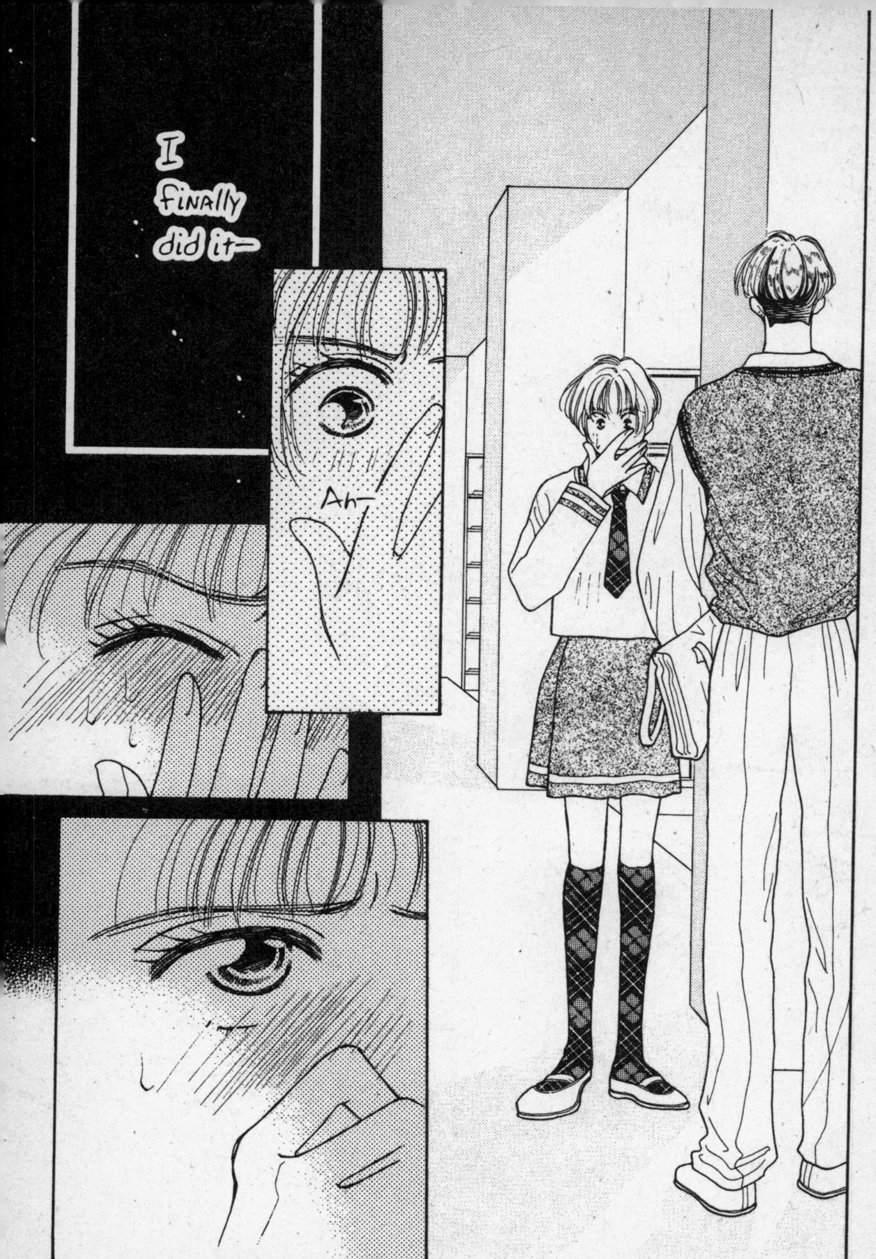
I finally did it—
Ah—

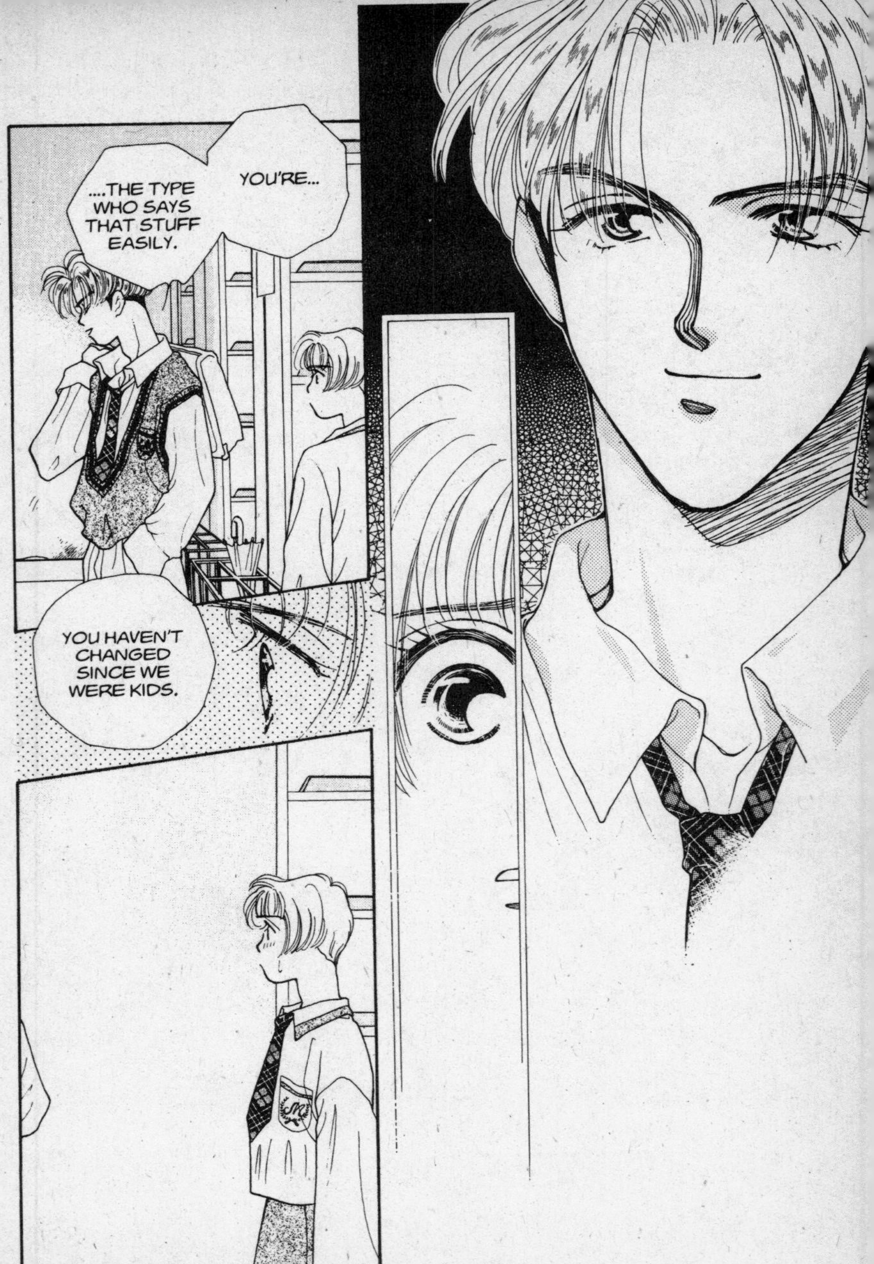
YOU'RE...
....THE TYPE WHO SAYS THAT STUFF EASILY.
YOU HAVEN'T CHANGED SINCE WE WERE KIDS.

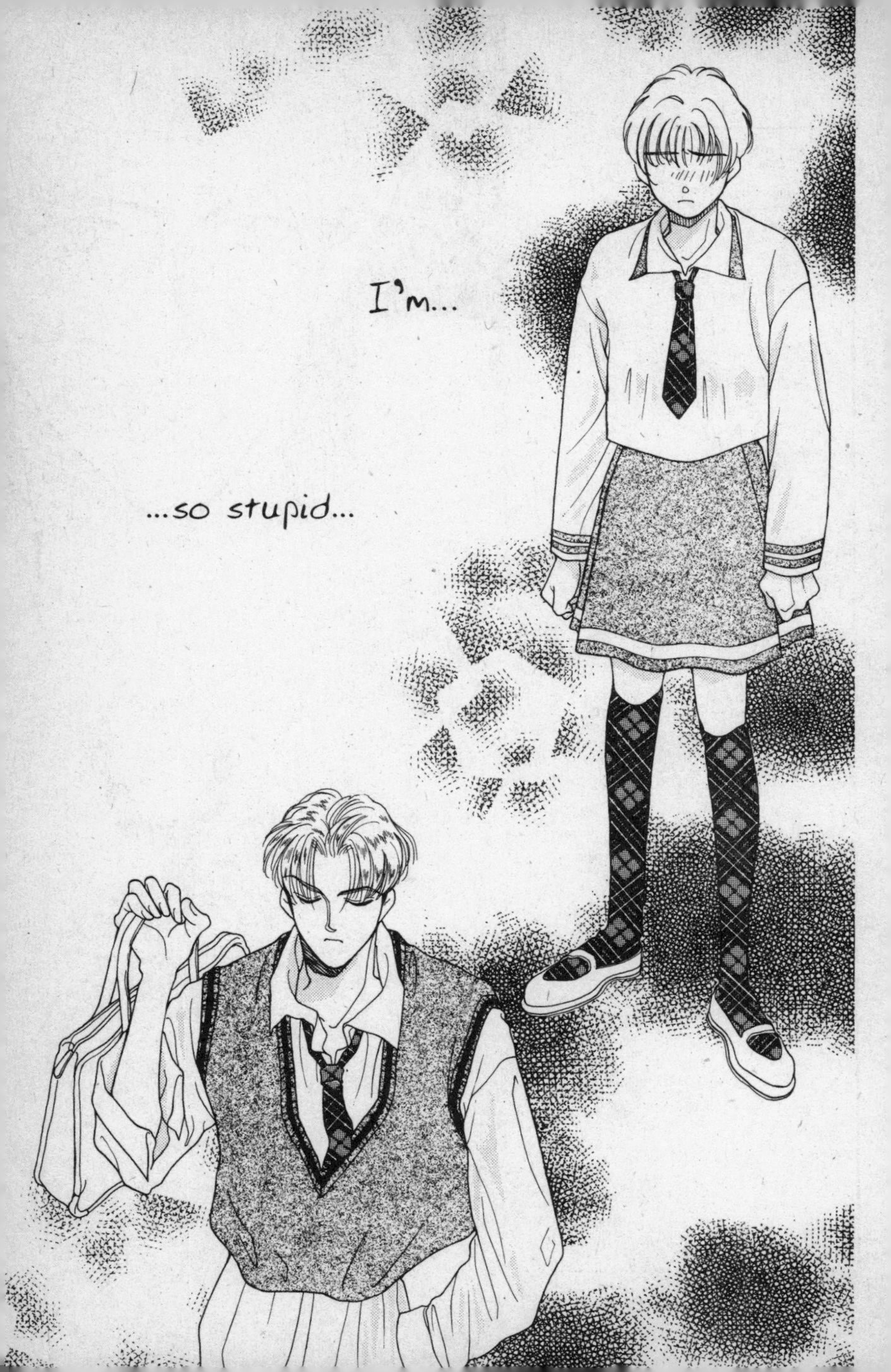
I'm...
...so stupid...

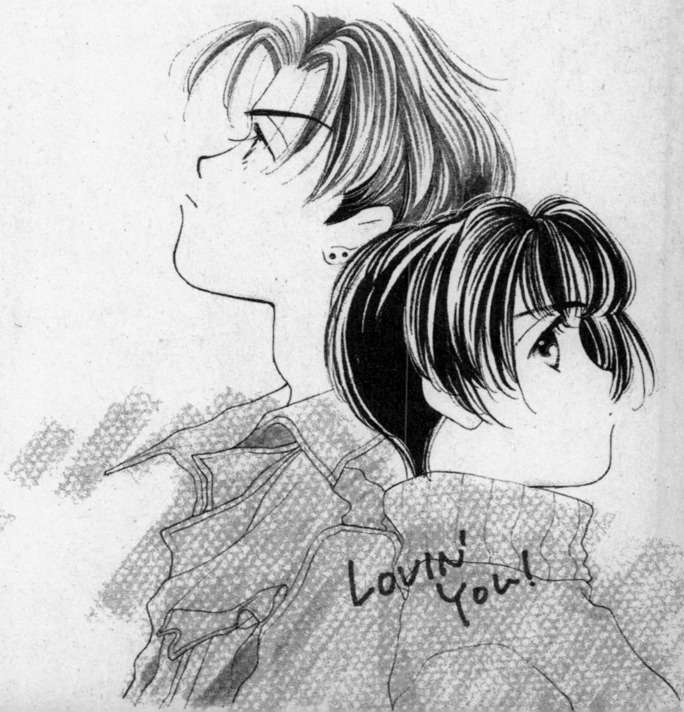
Lovin' You!

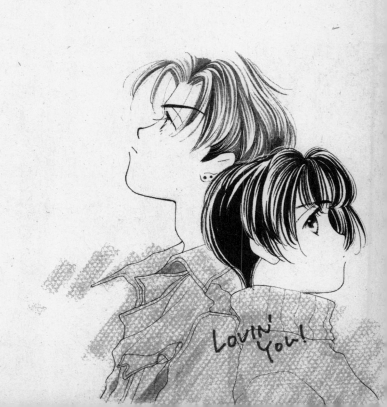

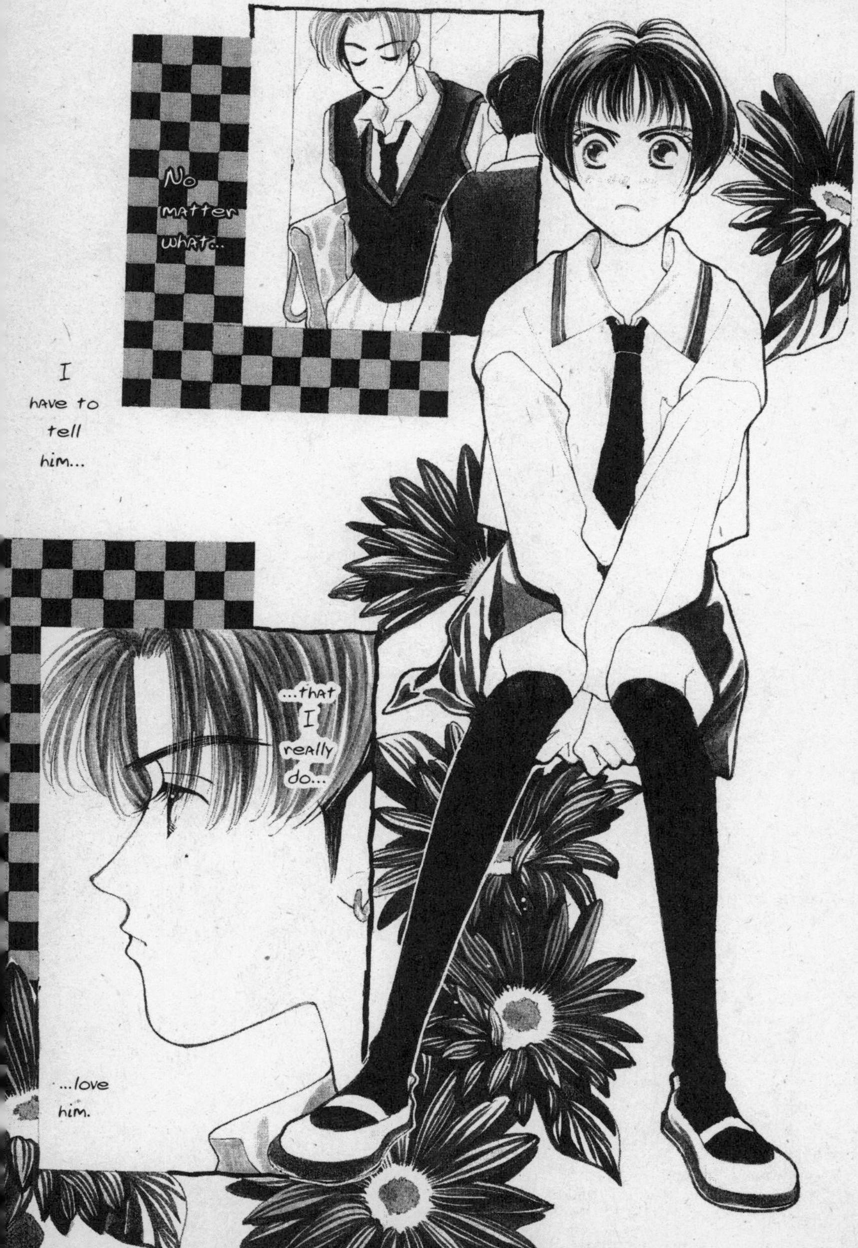
No matter what...
I have to tell him...
...that I really do...
...love him.

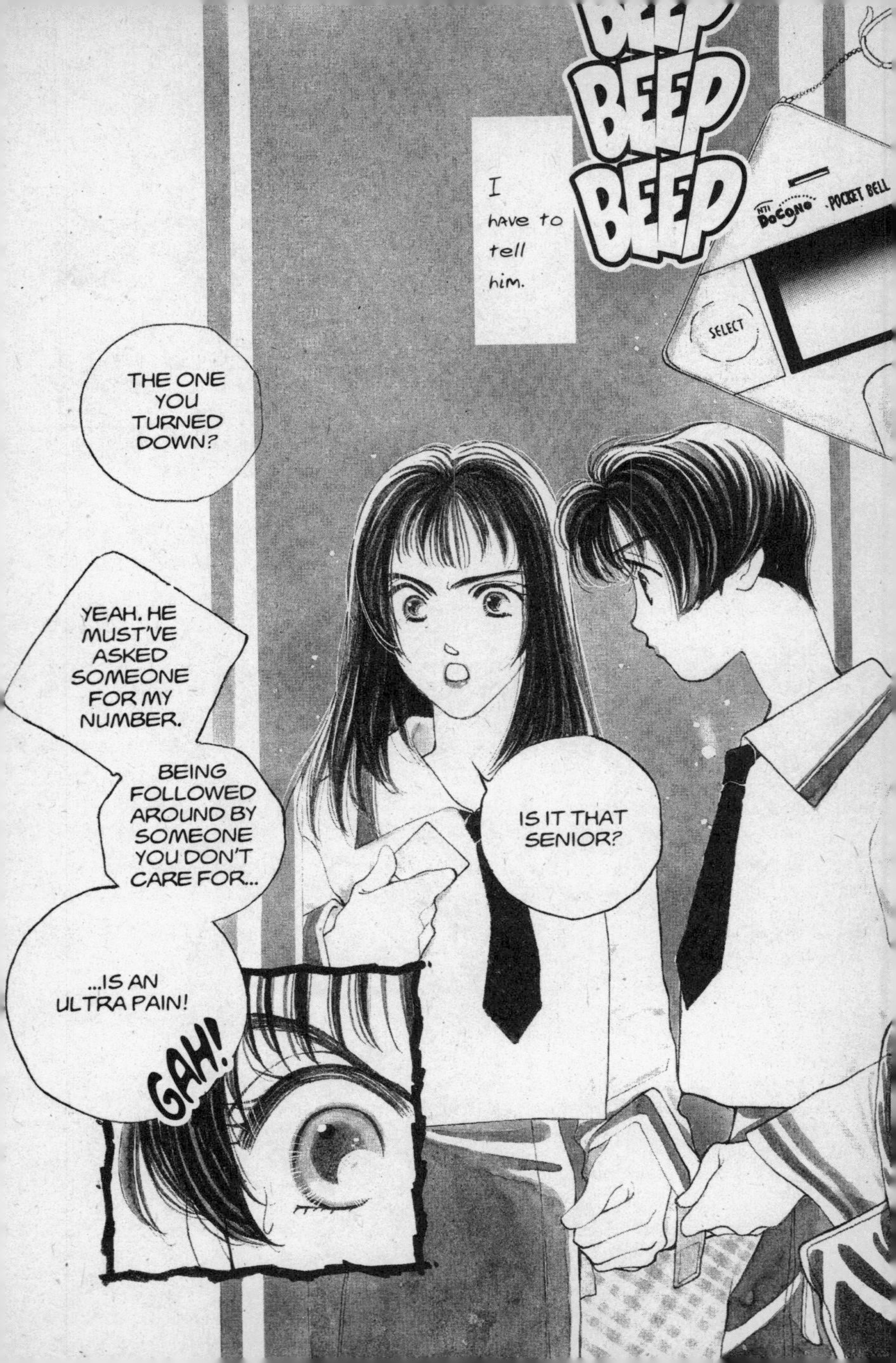
BEEP BEEP BEEP
POCKET BELL
SELECT
I have to tell him.
IS IT THAT SENIOR?
THE ONE YOU TURNED DOWN?
YEAH. HE MUST'VE ASKED SOMEONE FOR MY NUMBER.
BEING FOLLOWED AROUND BY SOMEONE YOU DON'T CARE FOR...
...IS AN ULTRA PAIN!
GAH!

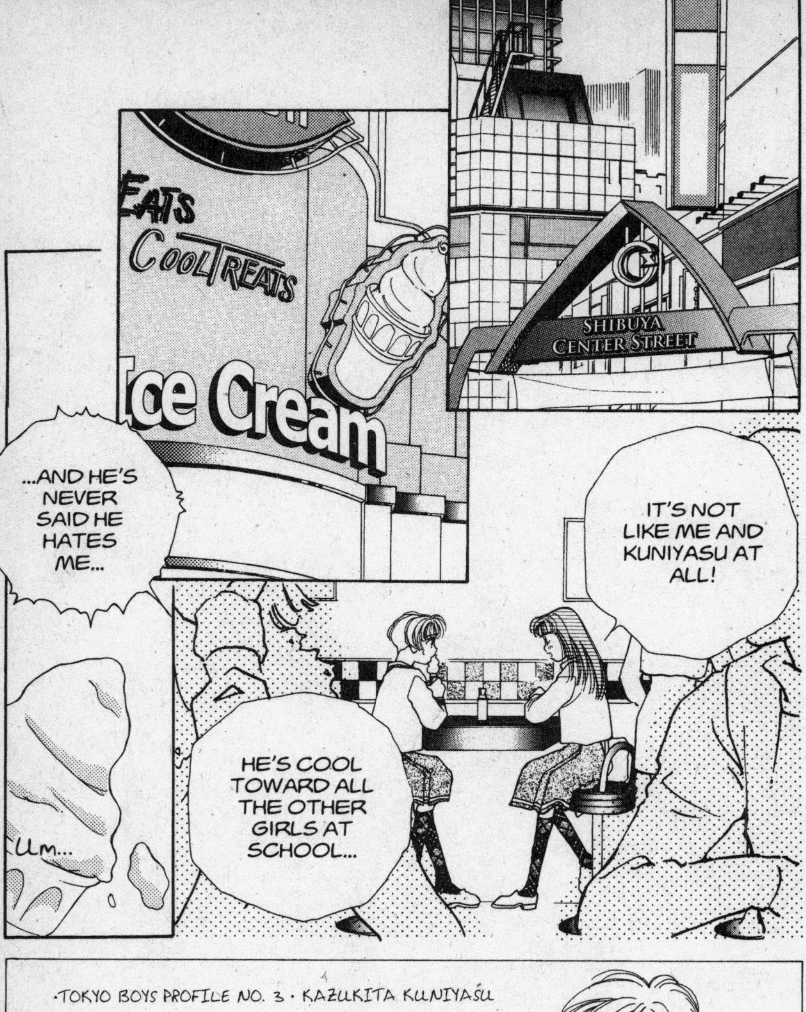
SHIBUYA CENTER STREET
EATS
COOL TREATS
Ice Cream
IT'S NOT LIKE ME AND KUNIYASU AT ALL!
HE'S COOL TOWARD ALL THE OTHER GIRLS AT SCHOOL...
...AND HE'S NEVER SAID HE HATES ME...
Um...

·TOKYO BOYS PROFILE NO. 3 · KAZUKITA KUNIYASU

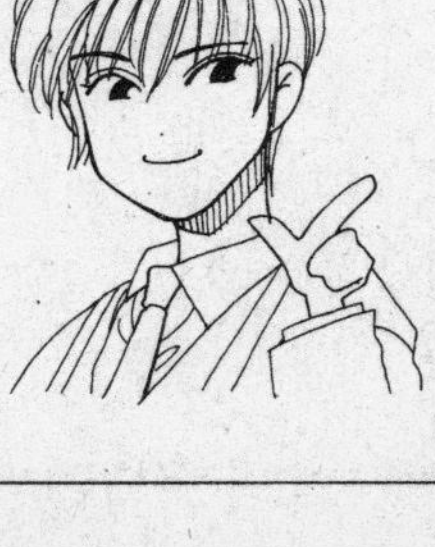

LIVES IN SETAGAYA-KU, TOKYO
HEIGHT: 181 CM   WEIGHT: 61KG (GIVE OR TAKE A FEW)
BLOOD TYPE: AB   FAMILY: FATHER, ELDER BROTHER, GRANDMOTHER, 2 EMPLOYEES
INTERESTS: NONE. LEAVES THINGS TO OTHERS. HE WON'T ADMIT IT, BUT HE HATES BEING ALONE. HE HAS A LOT OF GIRLFRIENDS HE DOESN'T ESPECIALLY LIKE.

HE'S BEEN FRIENDS WITH RAN SINCE JUNIOR HIGH. THEY WEREN'T FRIENDS IN ELEMENTARY SCHOOL, BUT THEY KNEW EACH OTHER.

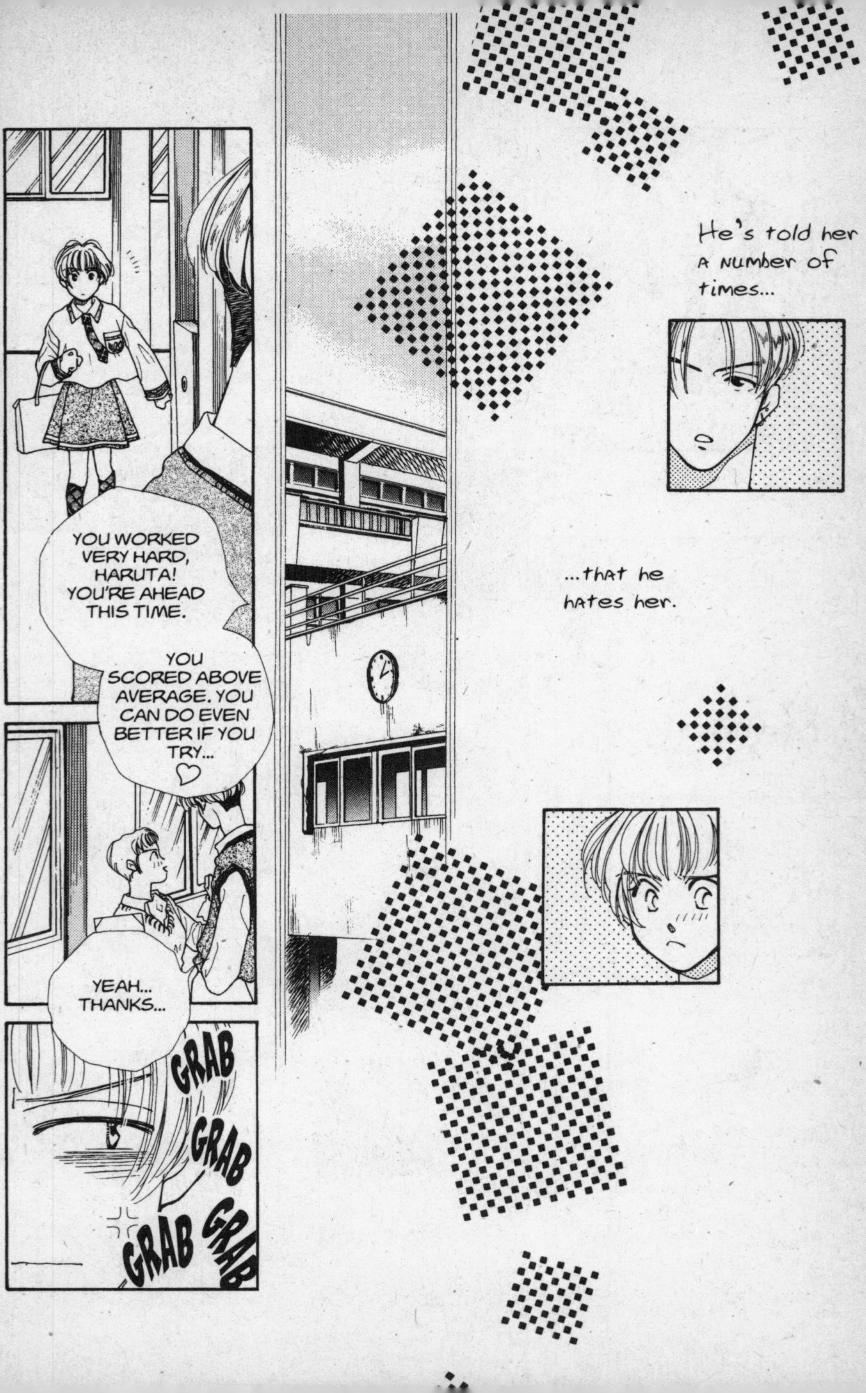
He's told her a number of times...
...that he hates her.
YOU WORKED VERY HARD, HARUTA! YOU'RE AHEAD THIS TIME.
YOU SCORED ABOVE AVERAGE. YOU CAN DO EVEN BETTER IF YOU TRY... ♡
YEAH... THANKS...
GRAB GRAB GRAB GRAB GRAB

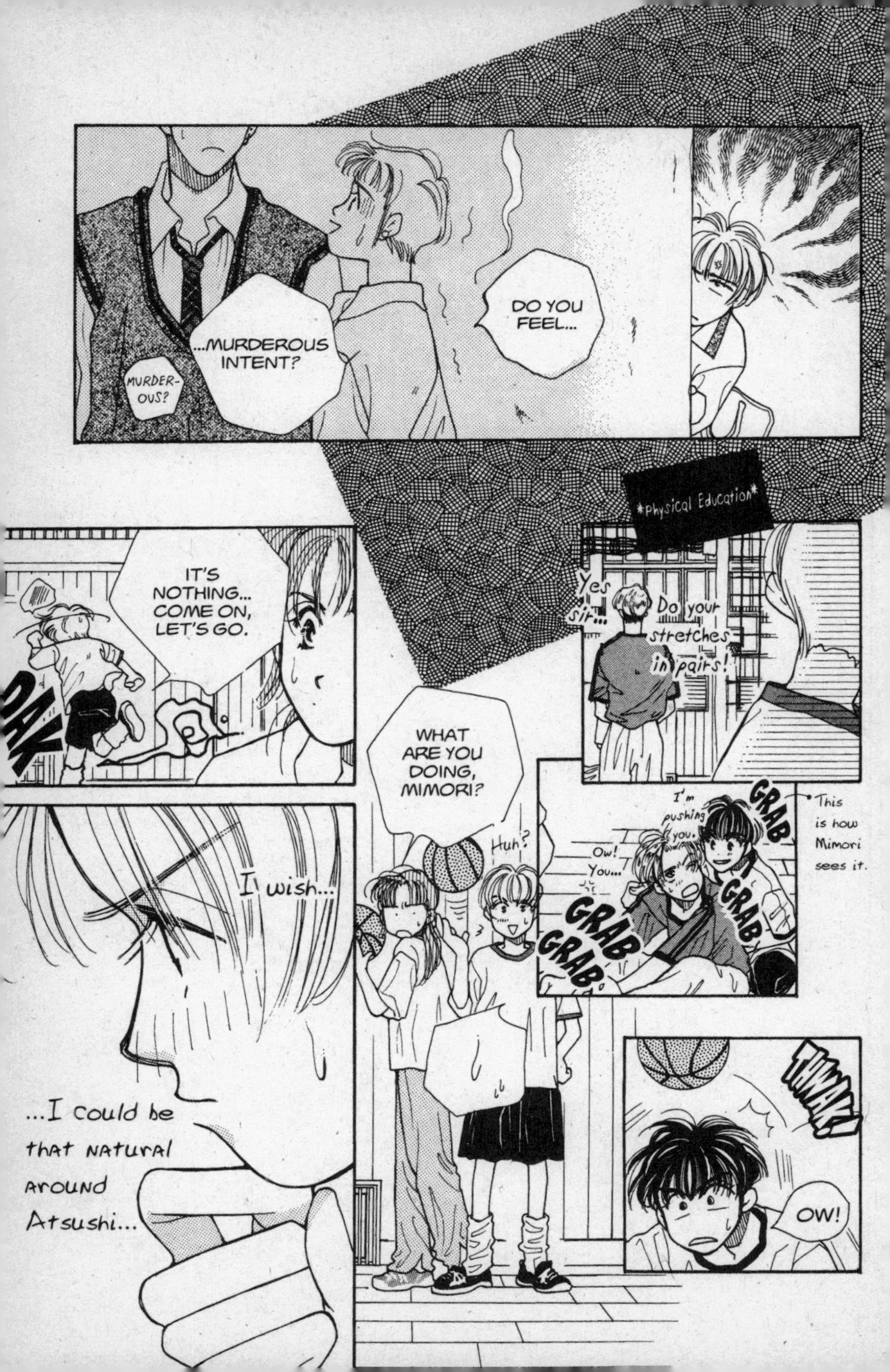
DO YOU FEEL...
...MURDEROUS INTENT?
MURDER-OUS?
Physical Education
Do your stretches in pairs!
Yes sir...
IT'S NOTHING... COME ON, LET'S GO.
GRAB
I'm pushing you.
This is how Mimori sees it.
GRAB
Ow! You...
GRAB
GRAB
GRAB
THWAK!
OW!
WHAT ARE YOU DOING, MIMORI?
Huh?
I wish...
...I could be that natural around Atsushi...

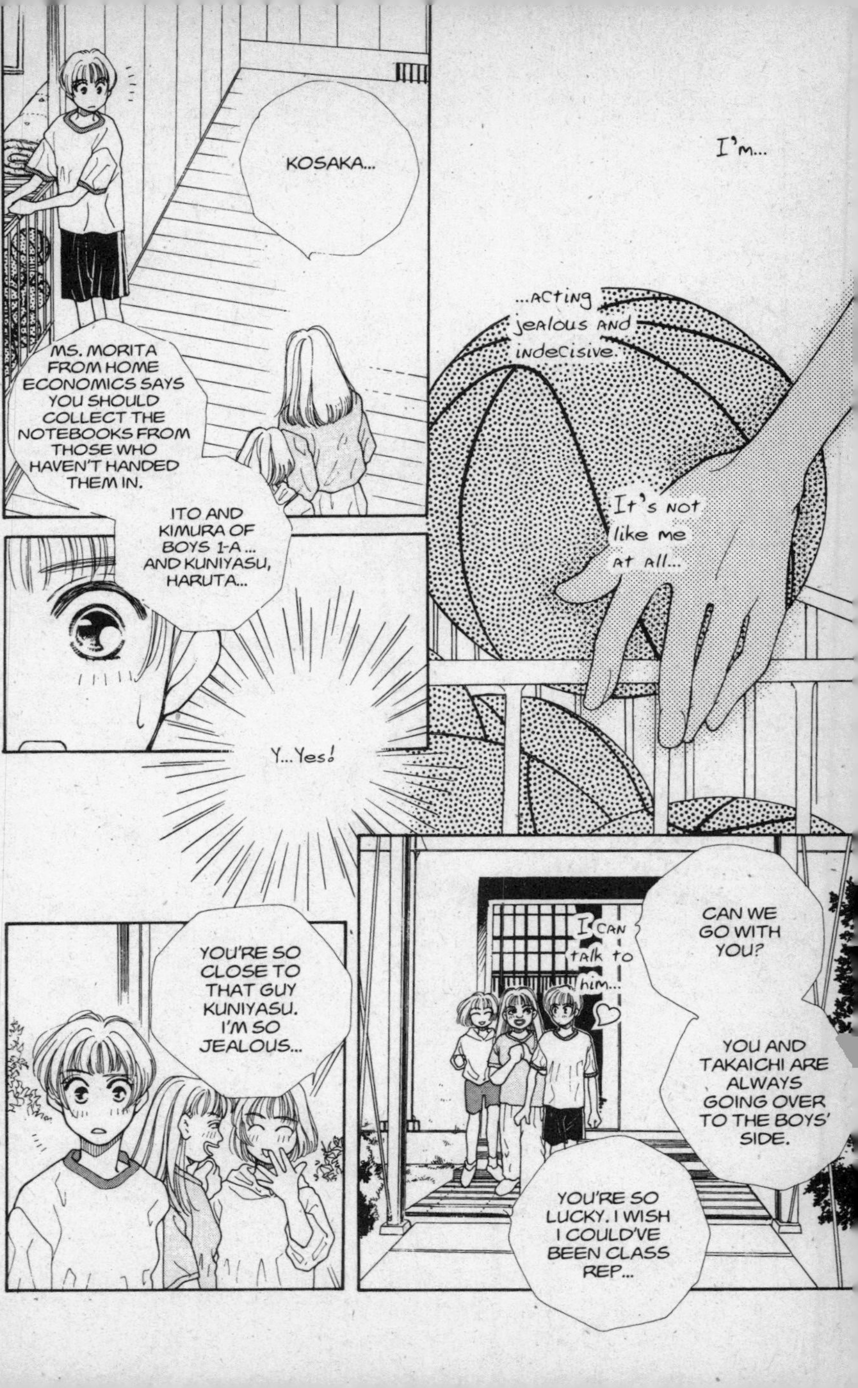
I'm...
...acting jealous and indecisive.
It's not like me at all...
KOSAKA...
MS. MORITA FROM HOME ECONOMICS SAYS YOU SHOULD COLLECT THE NOTEBOOKS FROM THOSE WHO HAVEN'T HANDED THEM IN.
ITO AND KIMURA OF BOYS 1-A ... AND KUNIYASU, HARUTA...
Y...Yes!
CAN WE GO WITH YOU?
YOU AND TAKAICHI ARE ALWAYS GOING OVER TO THE BOYS' SIDE.
I can talk to him...
YOU'RE SO LUCKY. I WISH I COULD'VE BEEN CLASS REP...
YOU'RE SO CLOSE TO THAT GUY KUNIYASU. I'M SO JEALOUS...

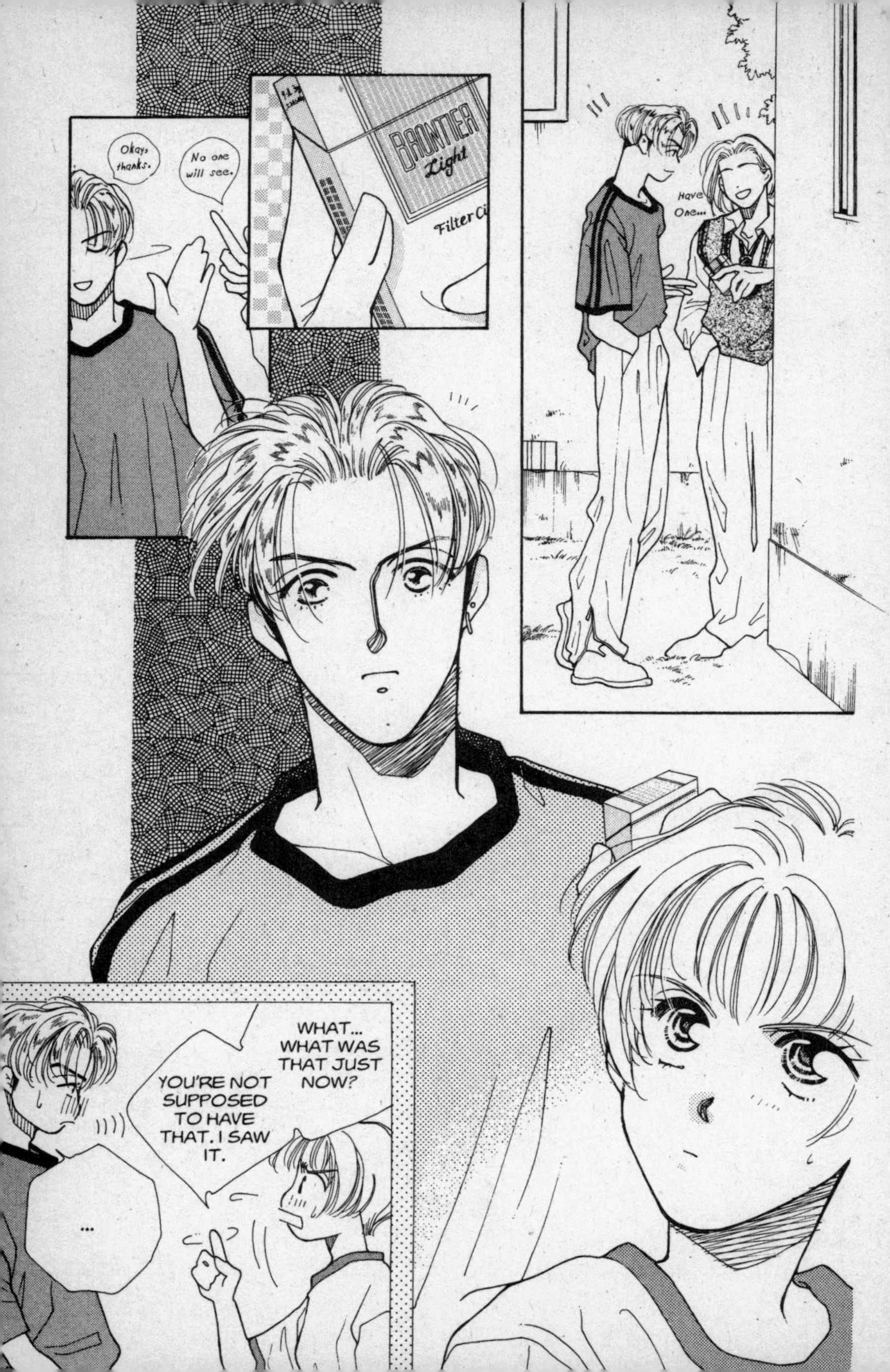
Have One...
BRONTIER
Light
No one will see.
Okay, thanks.
WHAT... WHAT WAS THAT JUST NOW?
YOU'RE NOT SUPPOSED TO HAVE THAT. I SAW IT.
...

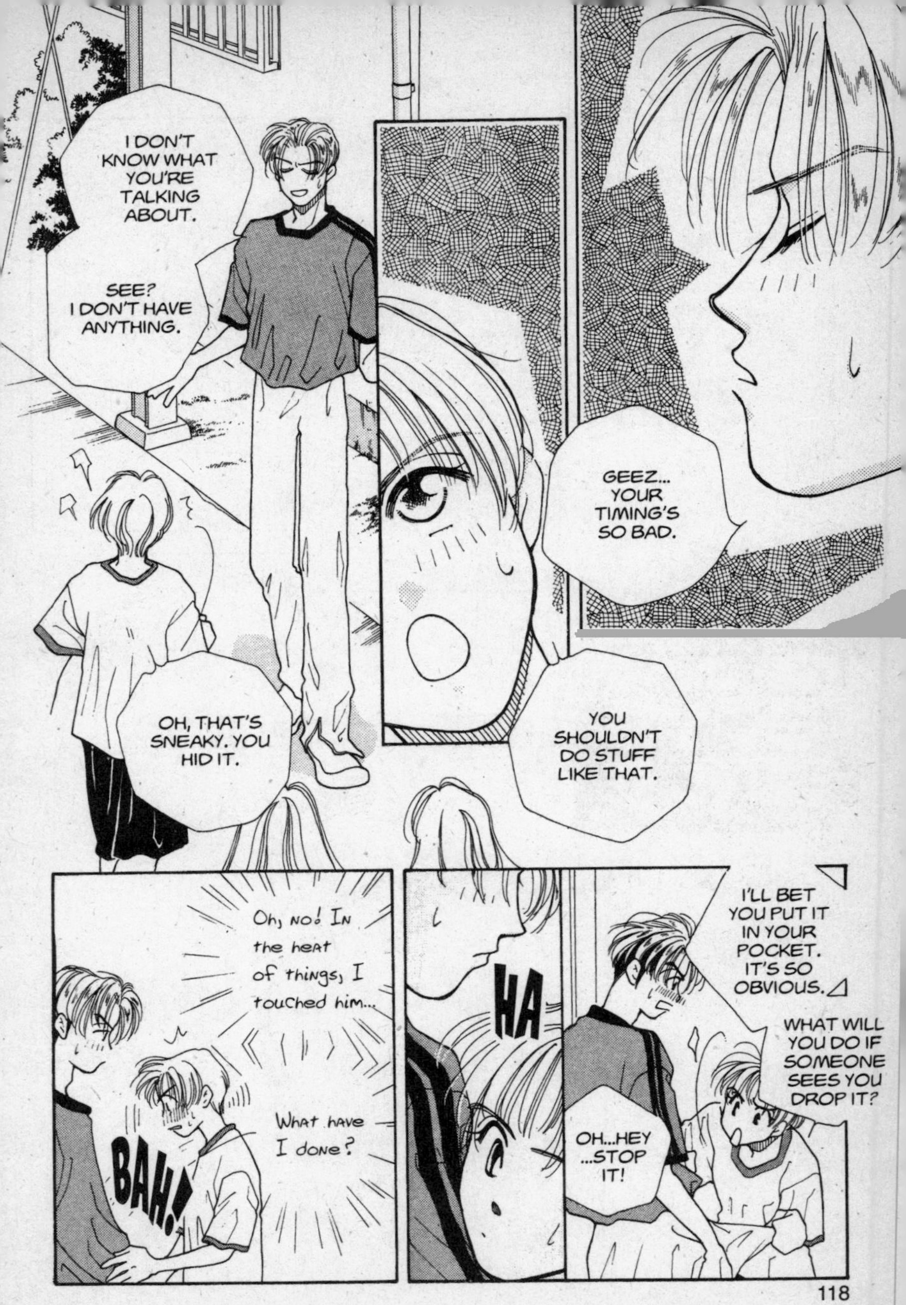
GEEZ... YOUR TIMING'S SO BAD.
YOU SHOULDN'T DO STUFF LIKE THAT.
I DON'T KNOW WHAT YOU'RE TALKING ABOUT.
SEE? I DON'T HAVE ANYTHING.
OH, THAT'S SNEAKY. YOU HID IT.
I'LL BET YOU PUT IT IN YOUR POCKET. IT'S SO OBVIOUS.
WHAT WILL YOU DO IF SOMEONE SEES YOU DROP IT?
HA
OH...HEY ...STOP IT!
Oh, no! In the heat of things, I touched him...
BAH!
What have I done?

TOKYO BOYS GIRLS

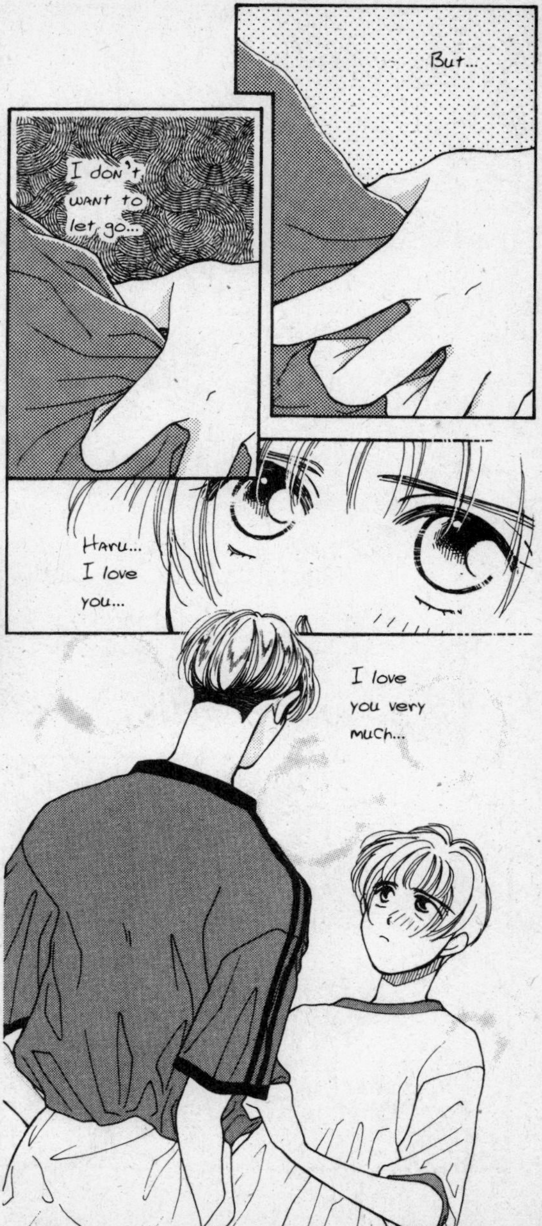

But...
I don't want to let go...
Haru... I love you...
I love you very much...

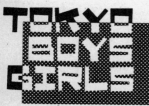

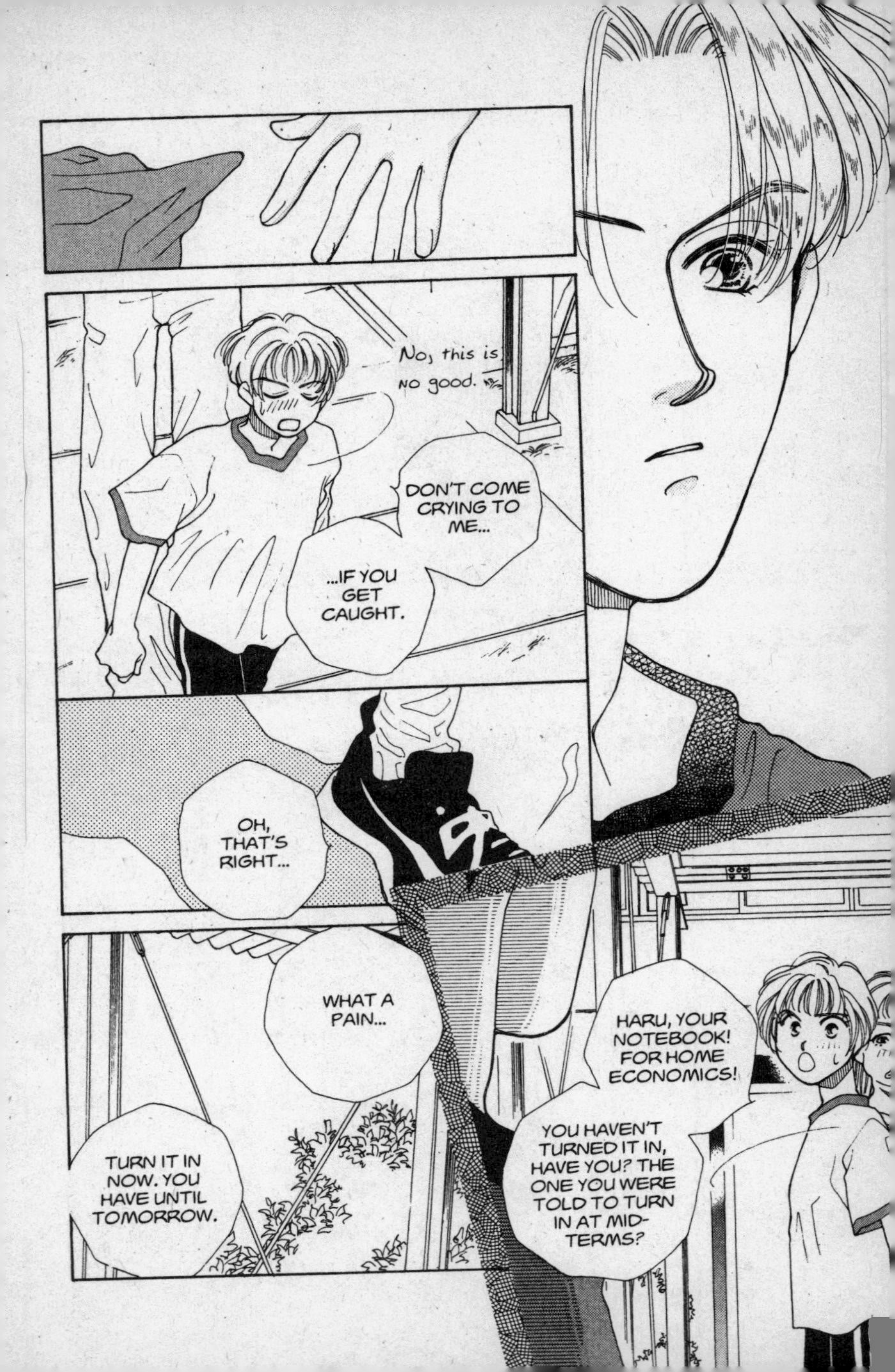
No, this is no good.
DON'T COME CRYING TO ME...
...IF YOU GET CAUGHT.
OH, THAT'S RIGHT...
HARU, YOUR NOTEBOOK! FOR HOME ECONOMICS!
YOU HAVEN'T TURNED IT IN, HAVE YOU? THE ONE YOU WERE TOLD TO TURN IN AT MID-TERMS?
WHAT A PAIN...
TURN IT IN NOW. YOU HAVE UNTIL TOMORROW.

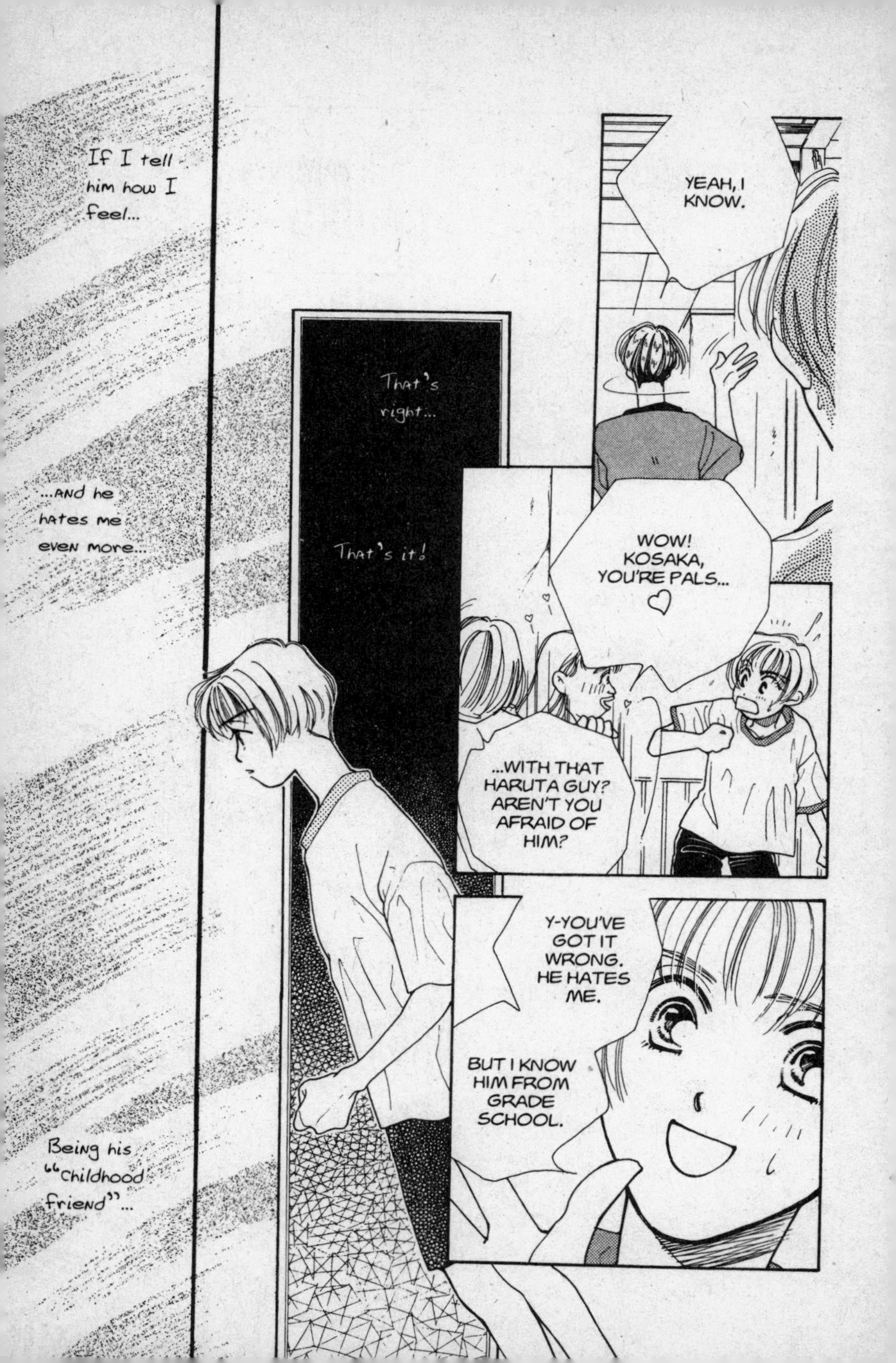
YEAH, I KNOW.
WOW! KOSAKA, YOU'RE PALS... ♡
...WITH THAT HARUTA GUY? AREN'T YOU AFRAID OF HIM?
Y-YOU'VE GOT IT WRONG. HE HATES ME.
BUT I KNOW HIM FROM GRADE SCHOOL.
That's right...
That's it!
If I tell him how I feel...
...and he hates me even more...
Being his "childhood friend"...

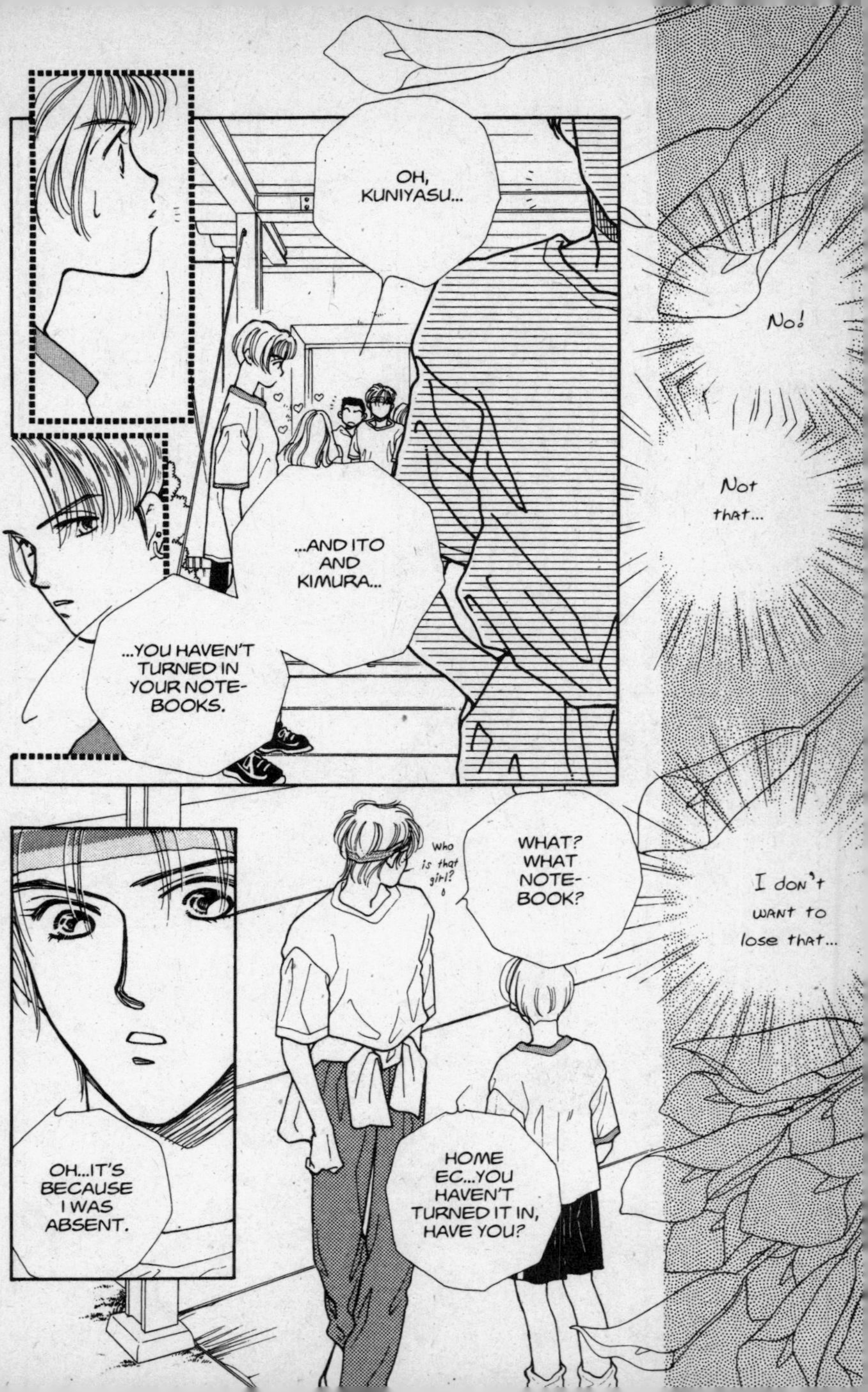
No!
Not that...
I don't want to lose that...
OH, KUNIYASU...
...AND ITO AND KIMURA...
...YOU HAVEN'T TURNED IN YOUR NOTE-BOOKS.
WHAT? WHAT NOTE-BOOK?
Who is that girl?
HOME EC...YOU HAVEN'T TURNED IT IN, HAVE YOU?
OH...IT'S BECAUSE I WAS ABSENT.

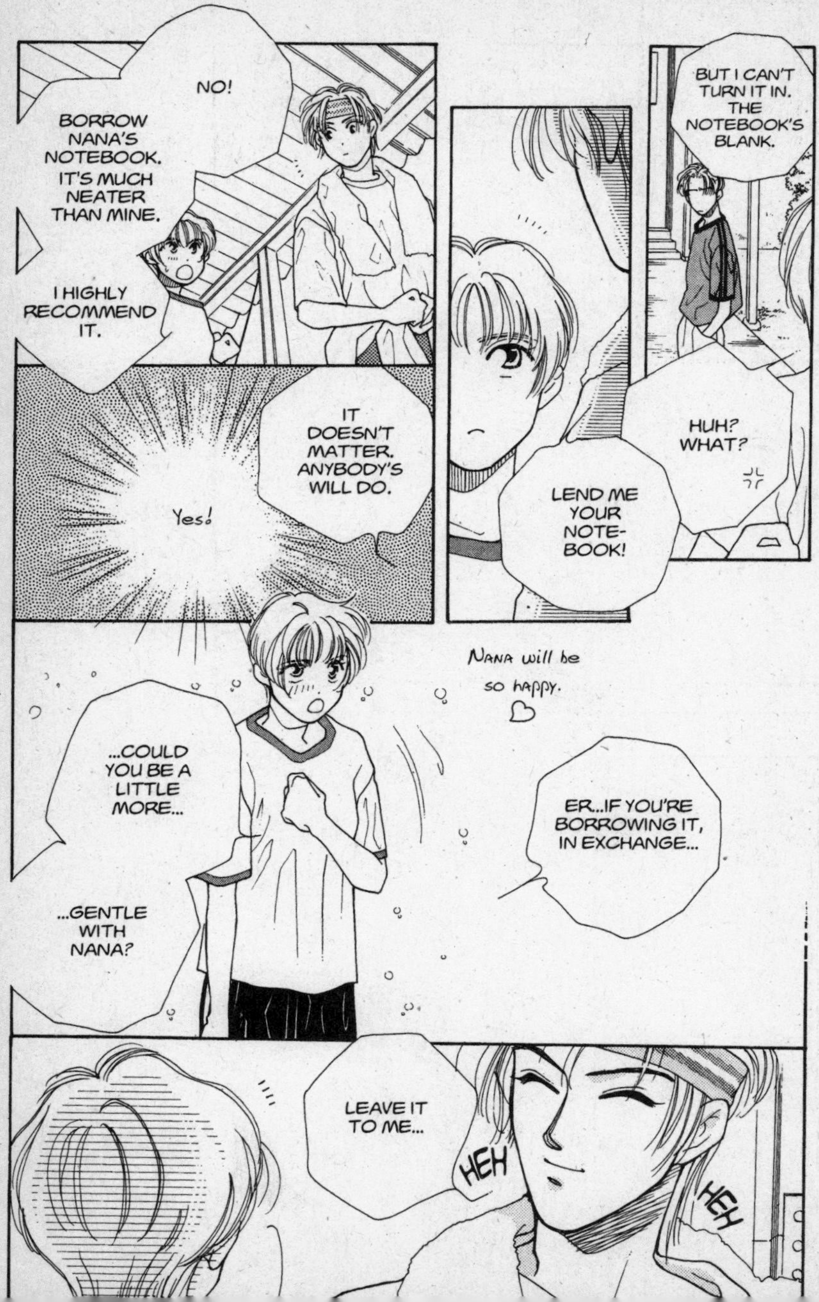

BUT I CAN'T TURN IT IN. THE NOTEBOOK'S BLANK.
HUH? WHAT?
LEND ME YOUR NOTE-BOOK!
NO!
BORROW NANA'S NOTEBOOK. IT'S MUCH NEATER THAN MINE.
I HIGHLY RECOMMEND IT.
IT DOESN'T MATTER. ANYBODY'S WILL DO.
Yes!
Nana will be so happy.
ER...IF YOU'RE BORROWING IT, IN EXCHANGE...
...COULD YOU BE A LITTLE MORE...
...GENTLE WITH NANA?
LEAVE IT TO ME...
HEH
HEH

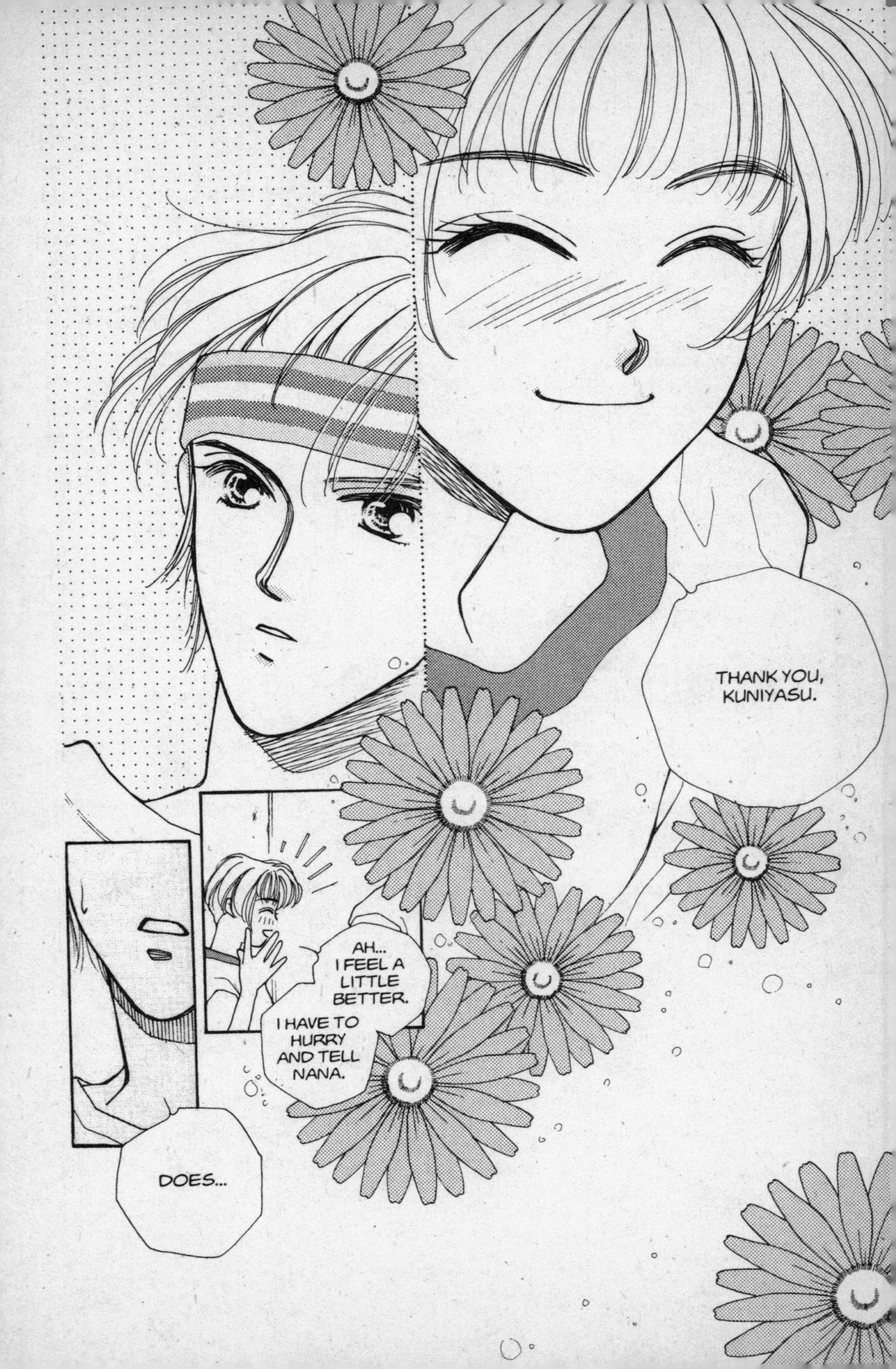
THANK YOU, KUNIYASU.
AH... I FEEL A LITTLE BETTER.
I HAVE TO HURRY AND TELL NANA.
DOES...

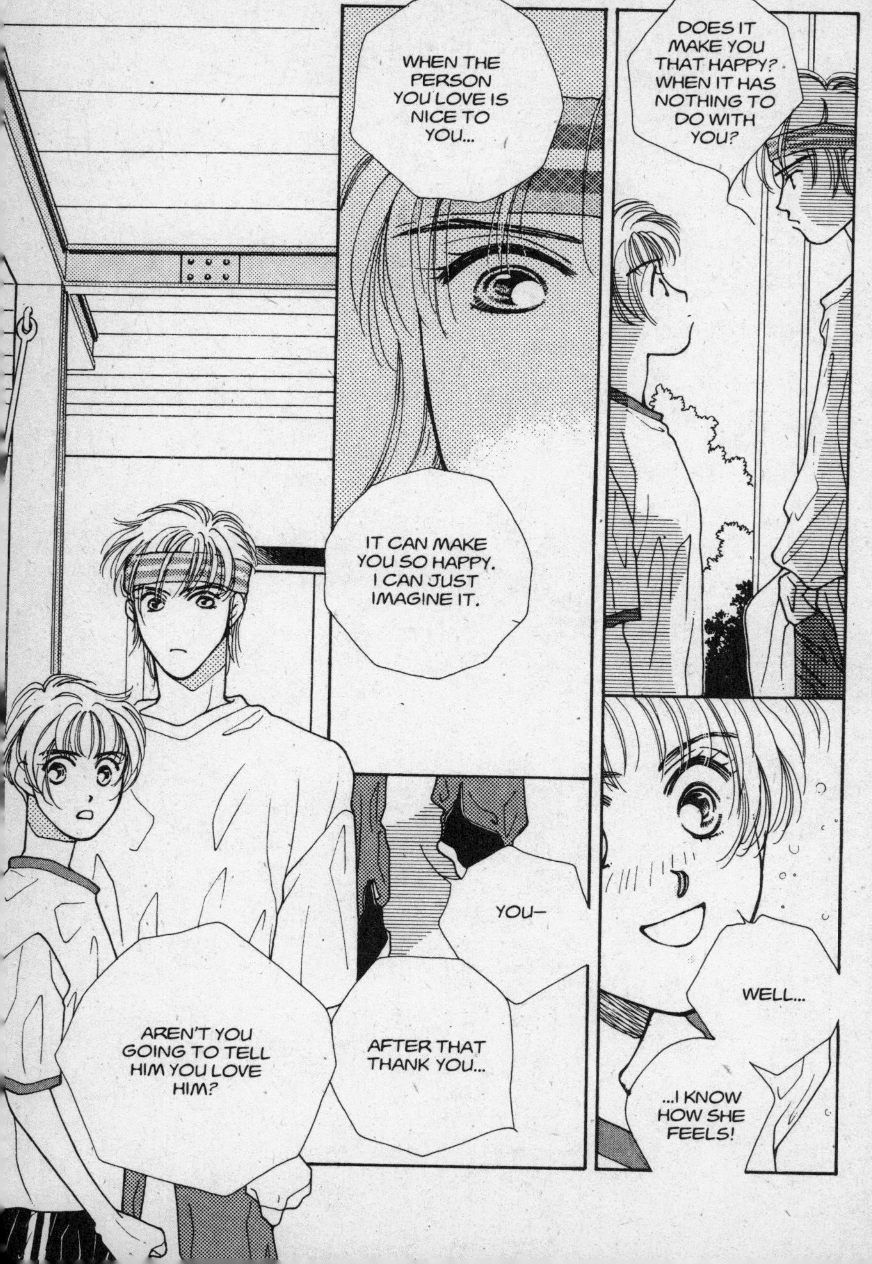
DOES IT MAKE YOU THAT HAPPY? WHEN IT HAS NOTHING TO DO WITH YOU?
WELL...
...I KNOW HOW SHE FEELS!
WHEN THE PERSON YOU LOVE IS NICE TO YOU...
IT CAN MAKE YOU SO HAPPY. I CAN JUST IMAGINE IT.
YOU—
AFTER THAT THANK YOU...
AREN'T YOU GOING TO TELL HIM YOU LOVE HIM?

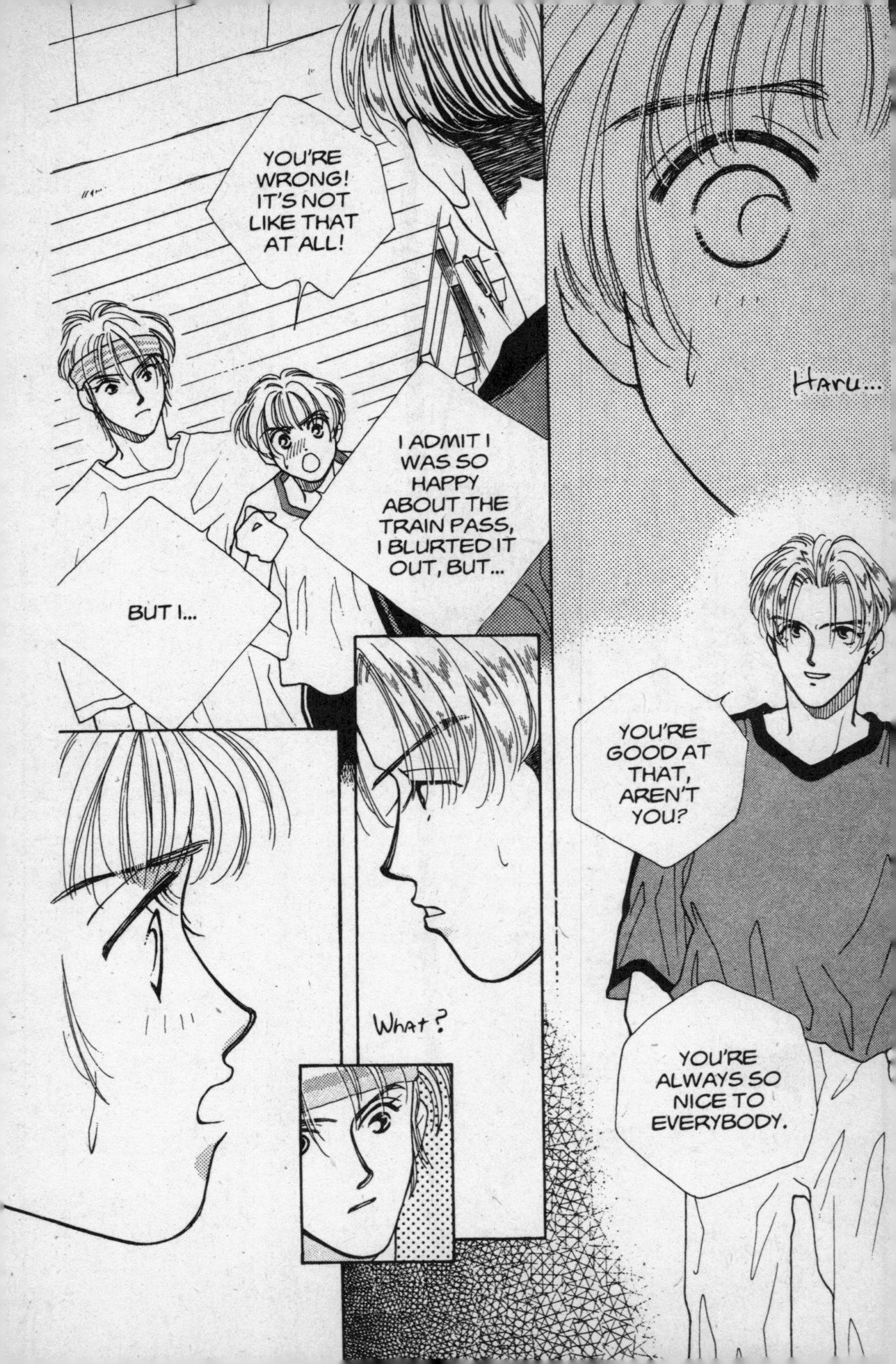
Haru...
YOU'RE GOOD AT THAT, AREN'T YOU?
YOU'RE ALWAYS SO NICE TO EVERYBODY.
YOU'RE WRONG! IT'S NOT LIKE THAT AT ALL!
I ADMIT I WAS SO HAPPY ABOUT THE TRAIN PASS, I BLURTED IT OUT, BUT...
BUT I...
What?

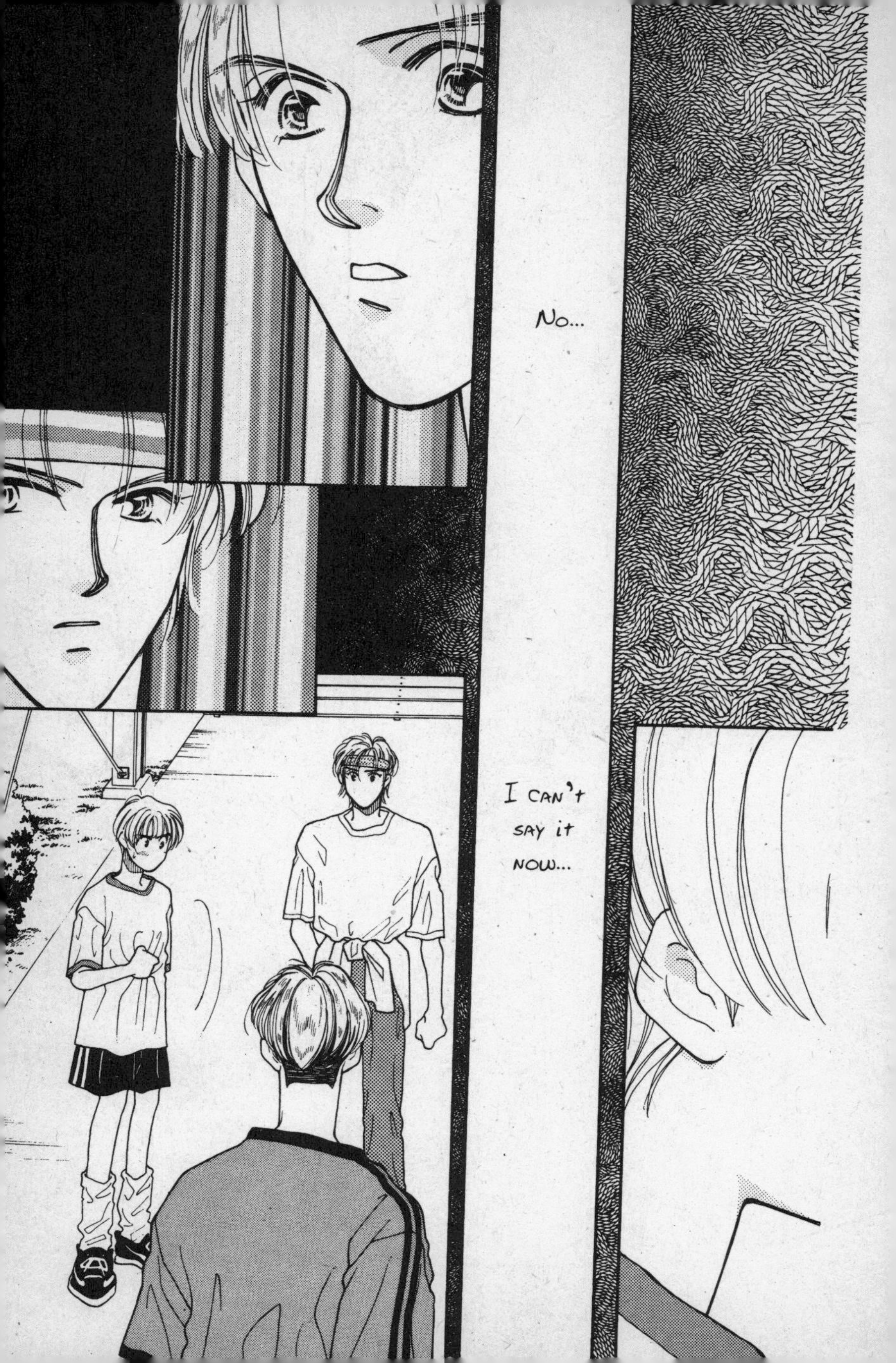
No...
I can't say it now...

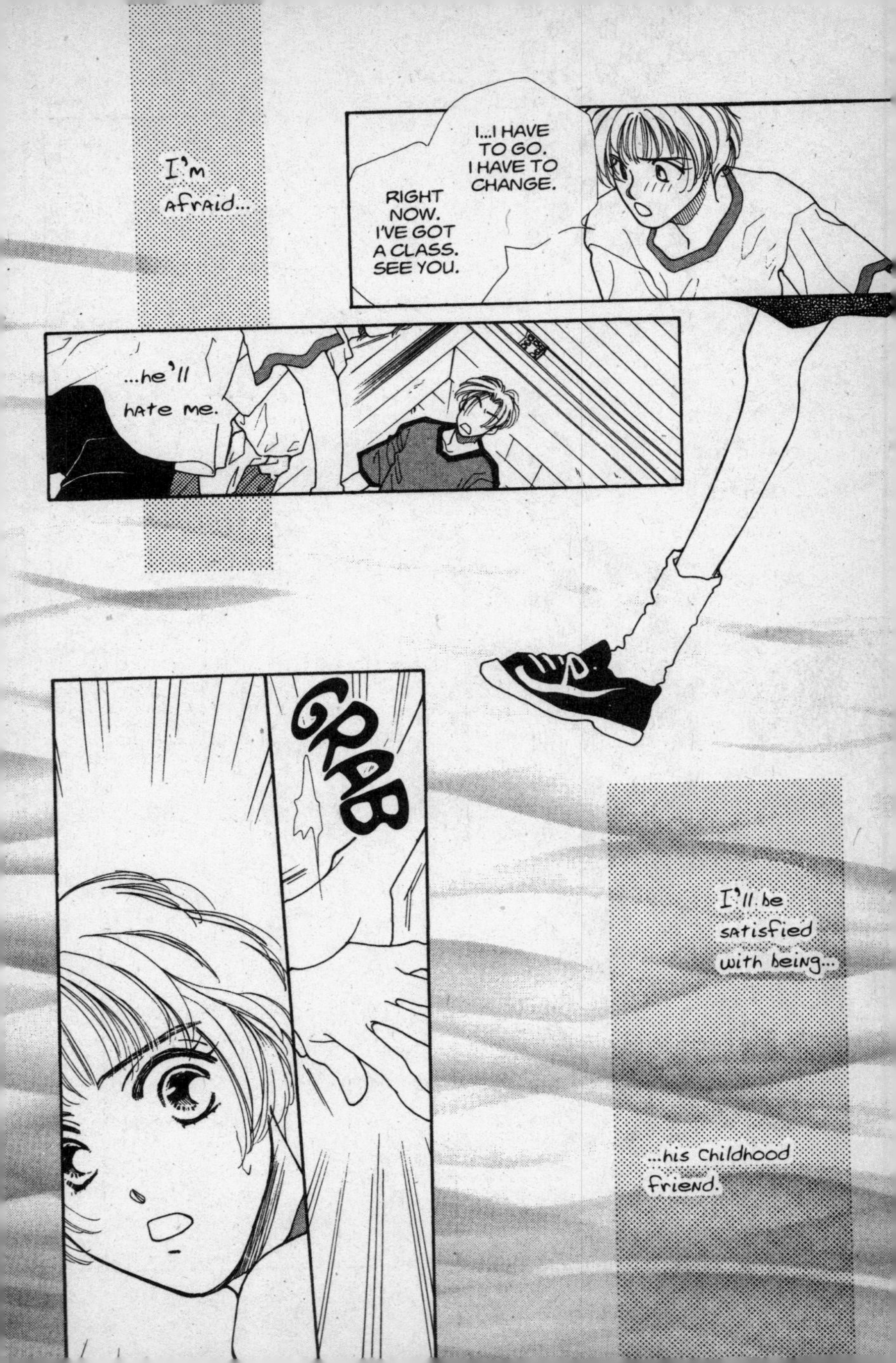
I...I HAVE TO GO. I HAVE TO CHANGE.
RIGHT NOW. I'VE GOT A CLASS. SEE YOU.
I'm afraid...
...he'll hate me.
I'll be satisfied with being...
...his childhood friend.
GRAB

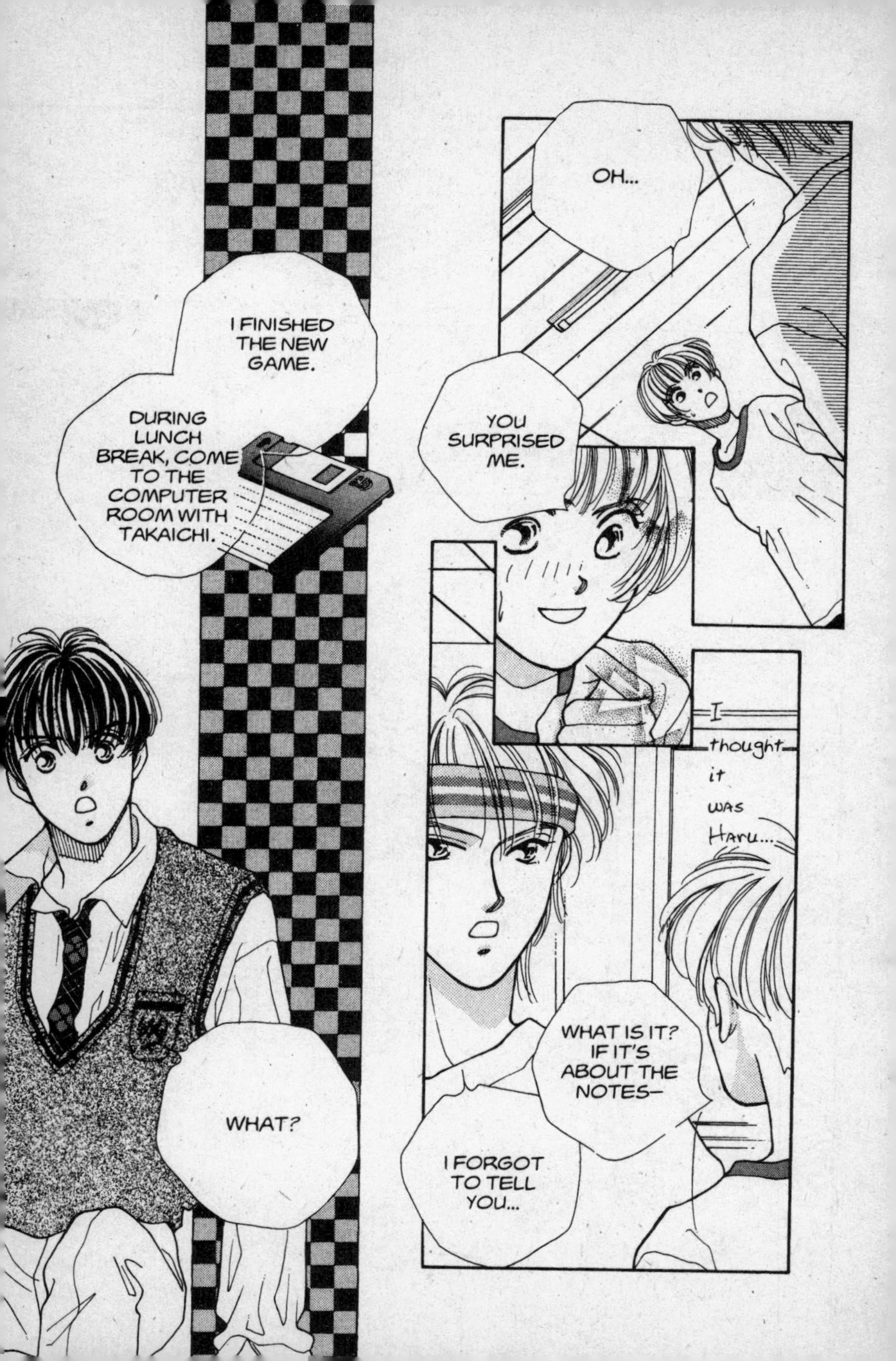
OH...
YOU SURPRISED ME.
I thought it was Haru...
WHAT IS IT? IF IT'S ABOUT THE NOTES—
I FORGOT TO TELL YOU...
I FINISHED THE NEW GAME.
DURING LUNCH BREAK, COME TO THE COMPUTER ROOM WITH TAKAICHI.
WHAT?

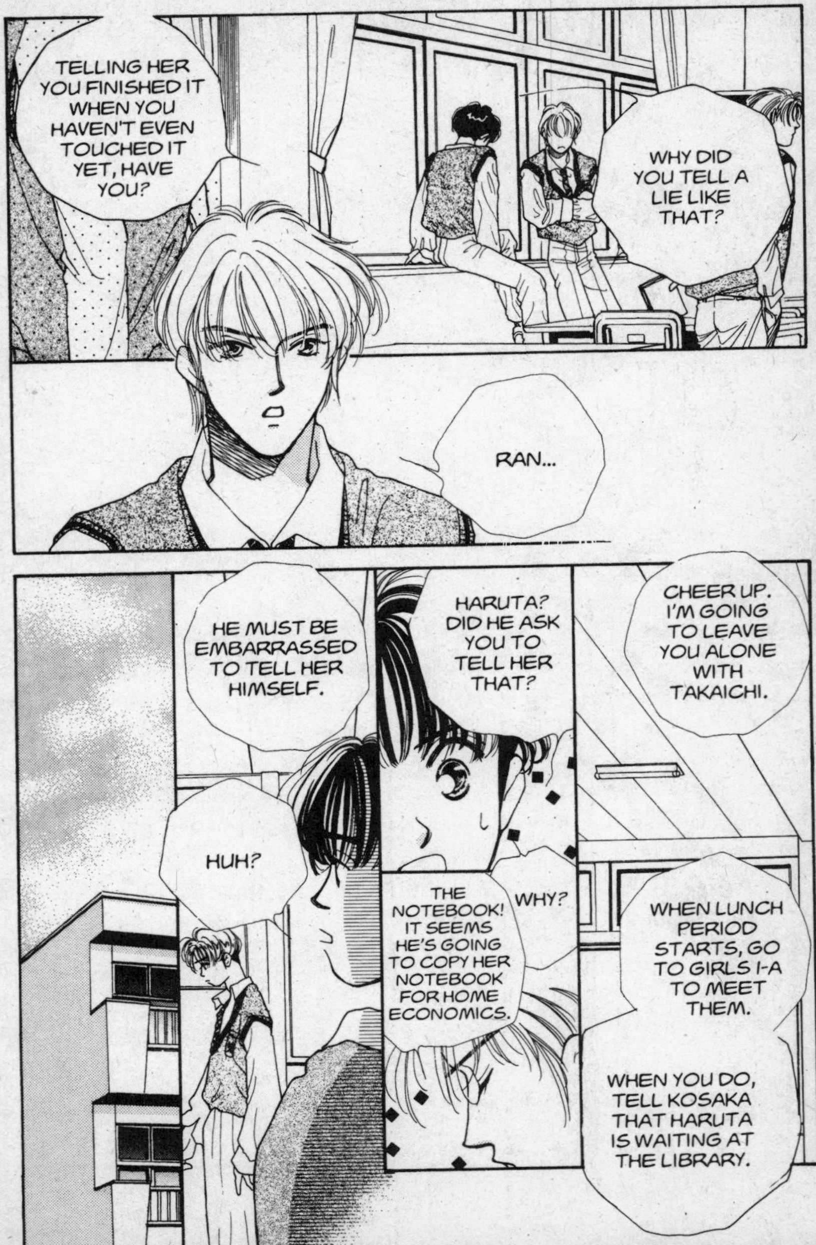
WHY DID YOU TELL A LIE LIKE THAT?
TELLING HER YOU FINISHED IT WHEN YOU HAVEN'T EVEN TOUCHED IT YET, HAVE YOU?
RAN...
CHEER UP. I'M GOING TO LEAVE YOU ALONE WITH TAKAICHI.
WHEN LUNCH PERIOD STARTS, GO TO GIRLS I-A TO MEET THEM.
WHEN YOU DO, TELL KOSAKA THAT HARUTA IS WAITING AT THE LIBRARY.
HARUTA? DID HE ASK YOU TO TELL HER THAT?
WHY?
THE NOTEBOOK! IT SEEMS HE'S GOING TO COPY HER NOTEBOOK FOR HOME ECONOMICS.
HE MUST BE EMBARRASSED TO TELL HER HIMSELF.
HUH?

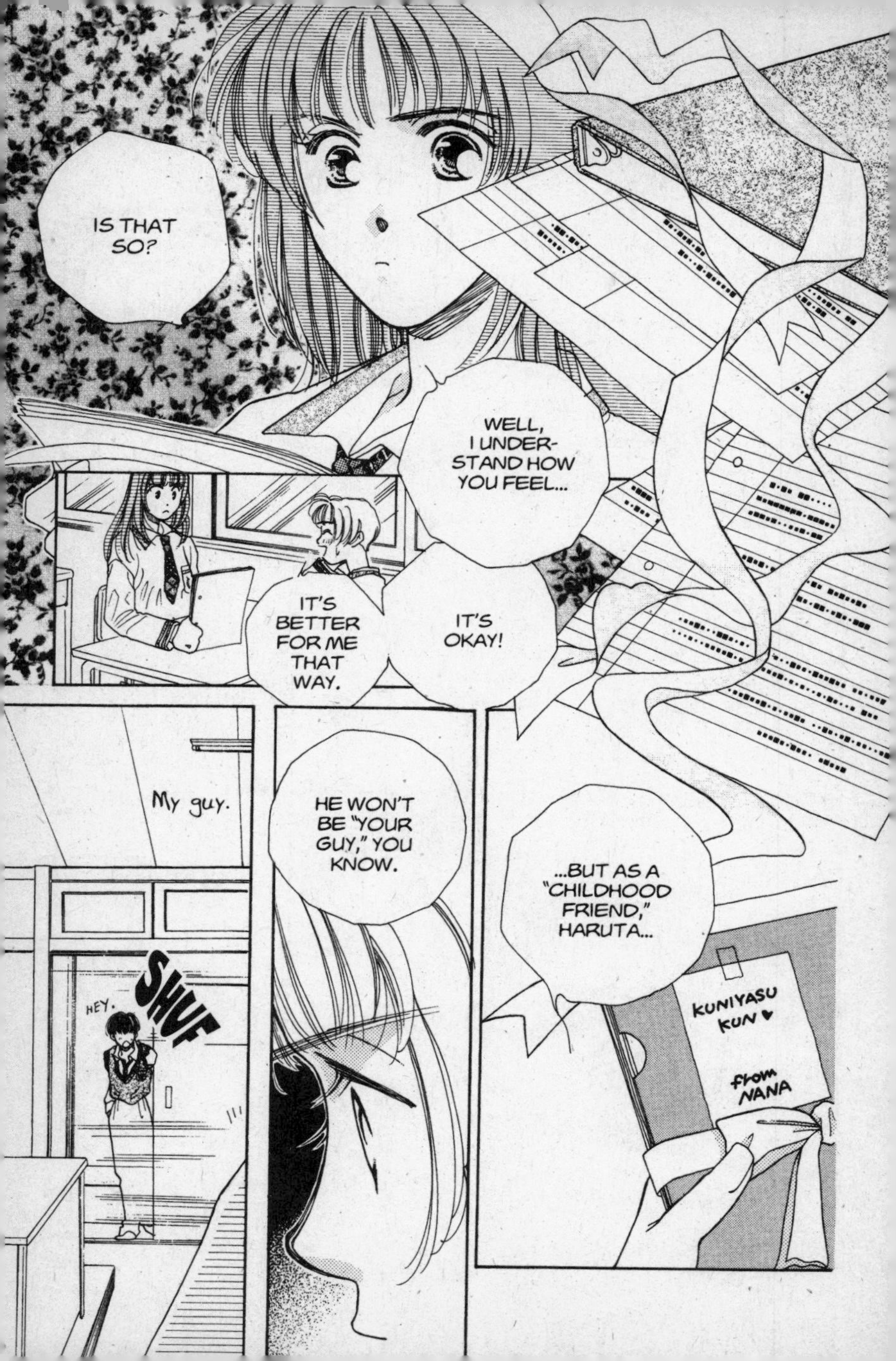

IS THAT SO?
WELL, I UNDER-STAND HOW YOU FEEL...
IT'S OKAY!
IT'S BETTER FOR ME THAT WAY.
...BUT AS A "CHILDHOOD FRIEND," HARUTA...
KUNIYASU KUN ♥
from NANA
HE WON'T BE "YOUR GUY," YOU KNOW.
My guy.
SHUF
HEY.

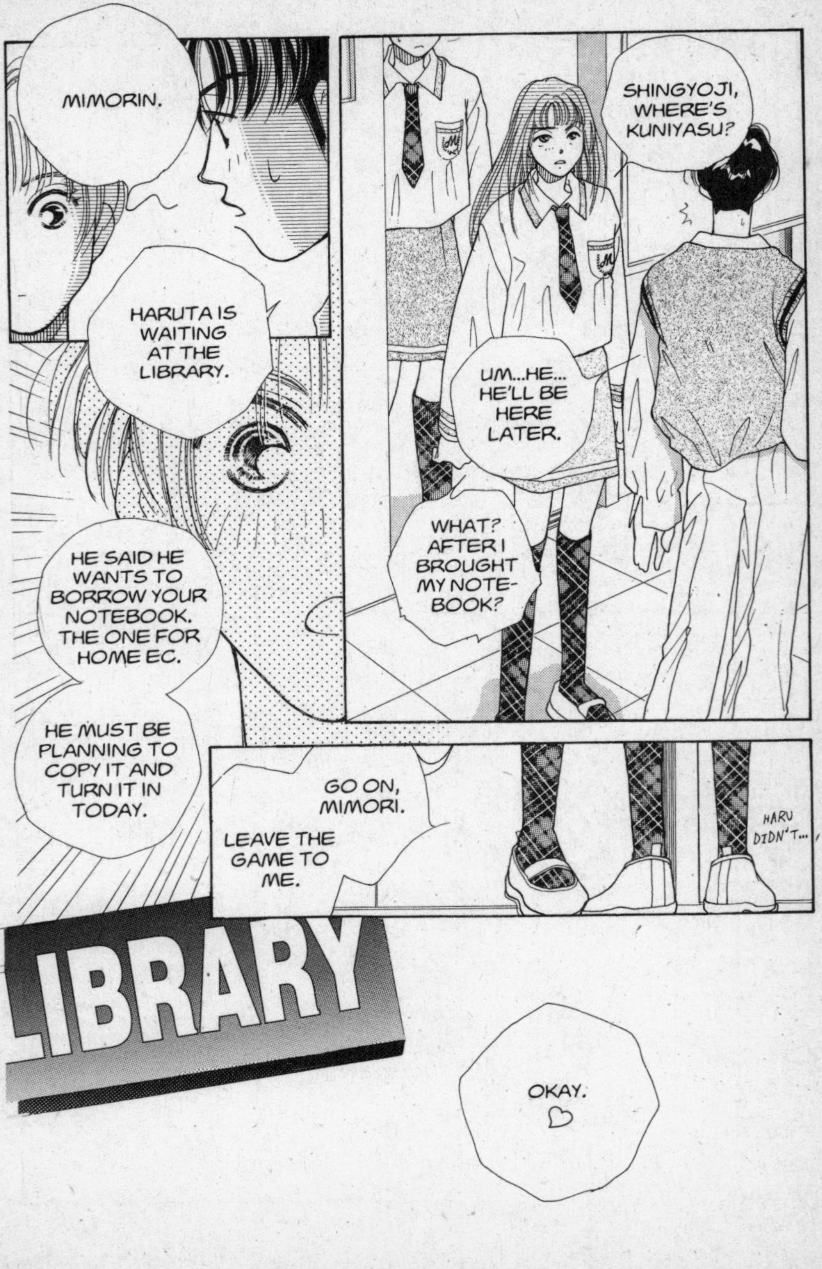
SHINGYOJI, WHERE'S KUNIYASU?
UM...HE... HE'LL BE HERE LATER.
WHAT? AFTER I BROUGHT MY NOTEBOOK?
MIMORIN.
HARUTA IS WAITING AT THE LIBRARY.
HE SAID HE WANTS TO BORROW YOUR NOTEBOOK. THE ONE FOR HOME EC.
HE MUST BE PLANNING TO COPY IT AND TURN IT IN TODAY.
HARU DIDN'T...
GO ON, MIMORI.
LEAVE THE GAME TO ME.
LIBRARY
OKAY. ♡

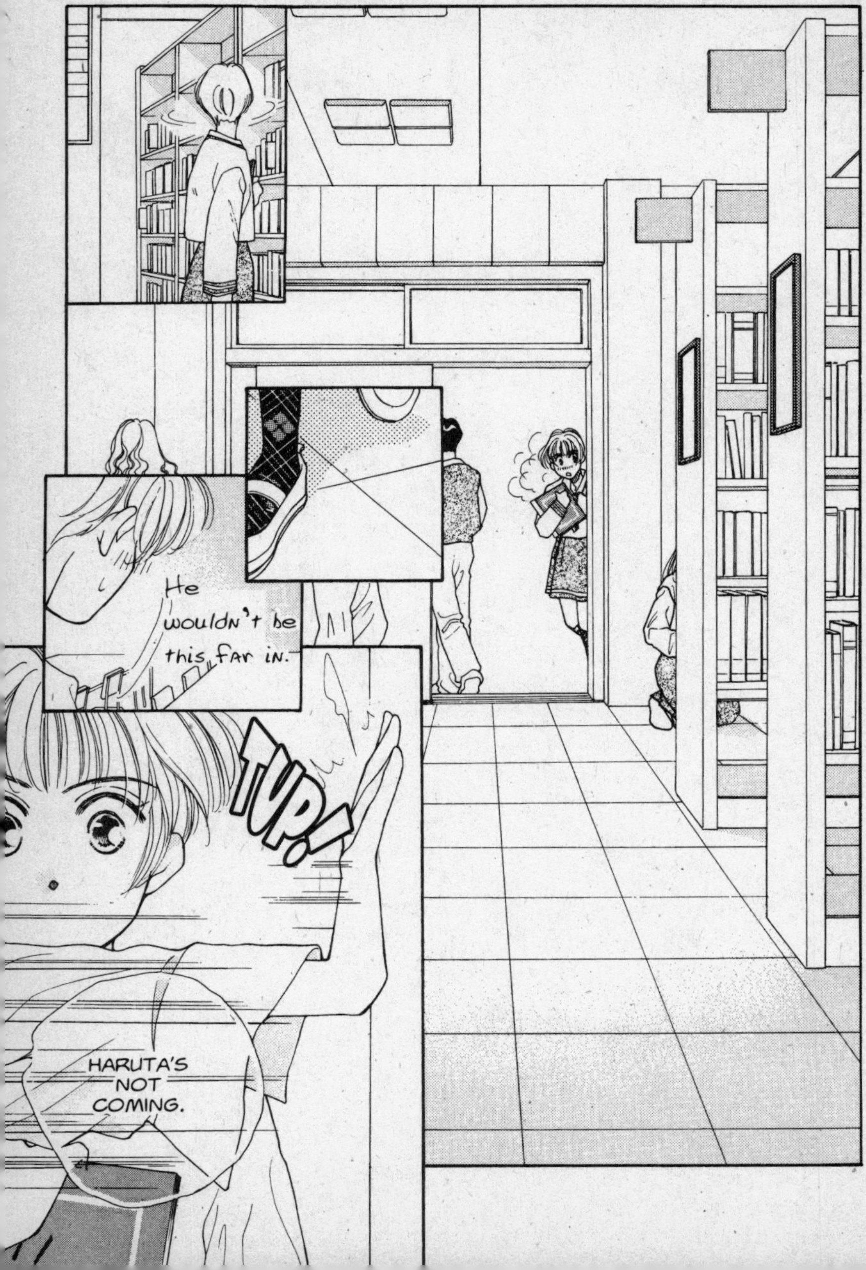
He wouldn't be this far in.
TUP!
HARUTA'S NOT COMING.

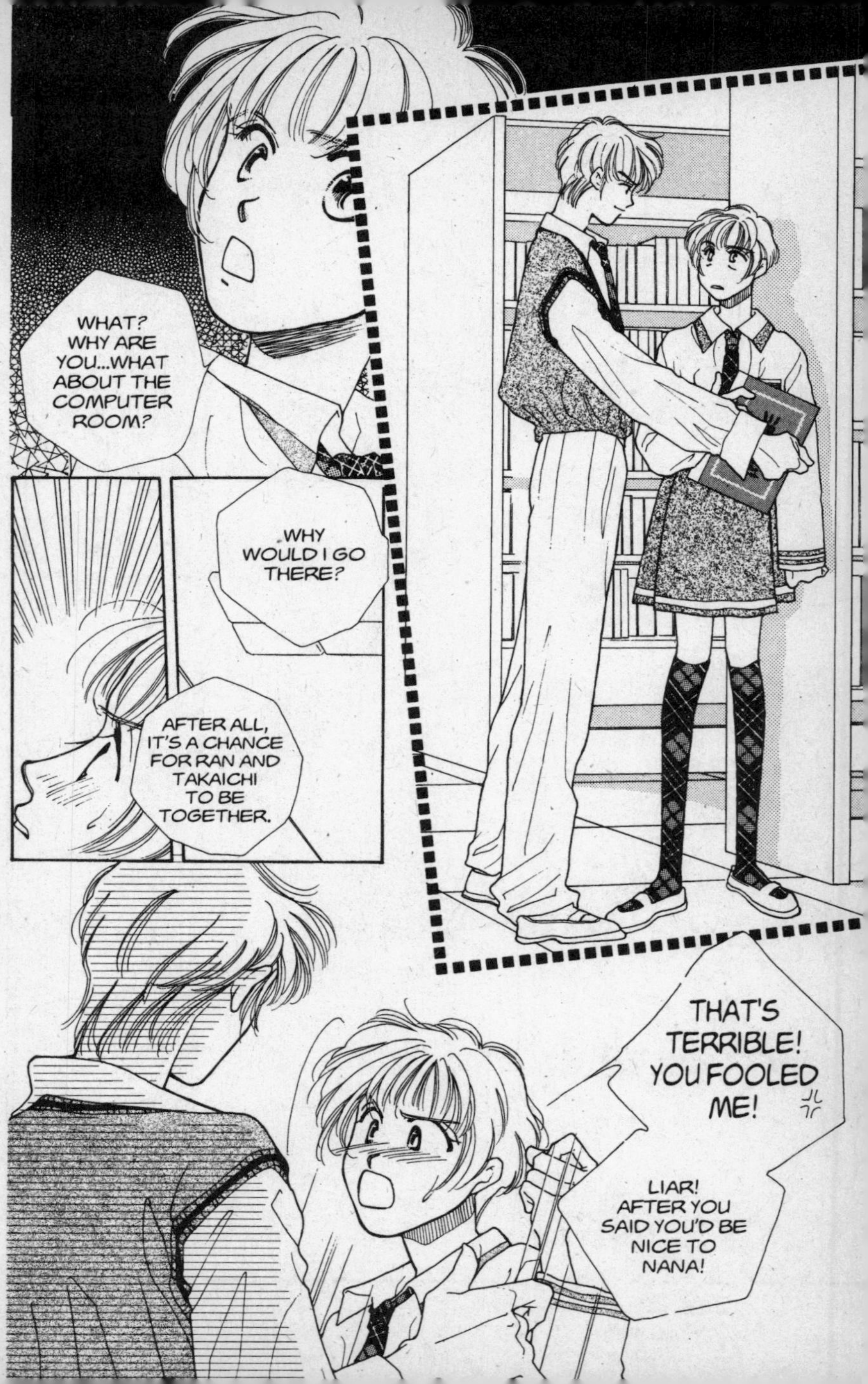
WHAT? WHY ARE YOU...WHAT ABOUT THE COMPUTER ROOM?
.WHY WOULD I GO THERE?
AFTER ALL, IT'S A CHANCE FOR RAN AND TAKAICHI TO BE TOGETHER.
THAT'S TERRIBLE! YOU FOOLED ME!
LIAR! AFTER YOU SAID YOU'D BE NICE TO NANA!

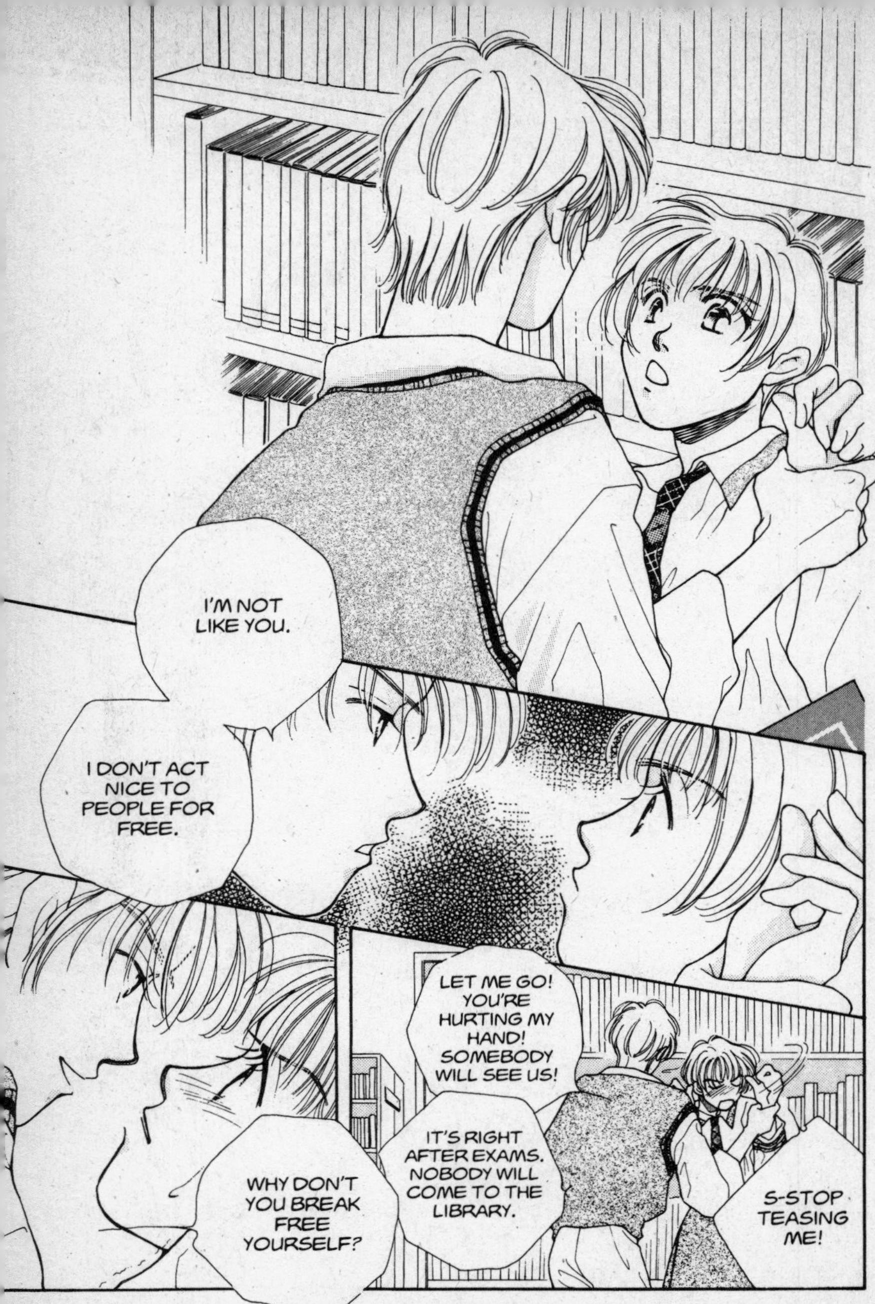

I'M NOT LIKE YOU.
I DON'T ACT NICE TO PEOPLE FOR FREE.
LET ME GO! YOU'RE HURTING MY HAND! SOMEBODY WILL SEE US!
IT'S RIGHT AFTER EXAMS. NOBODY WILL COME TO THE LIBRARY.
S-STOP TEASING ME!
WHY DON'T YOU BREAK FREE YOURSELF?

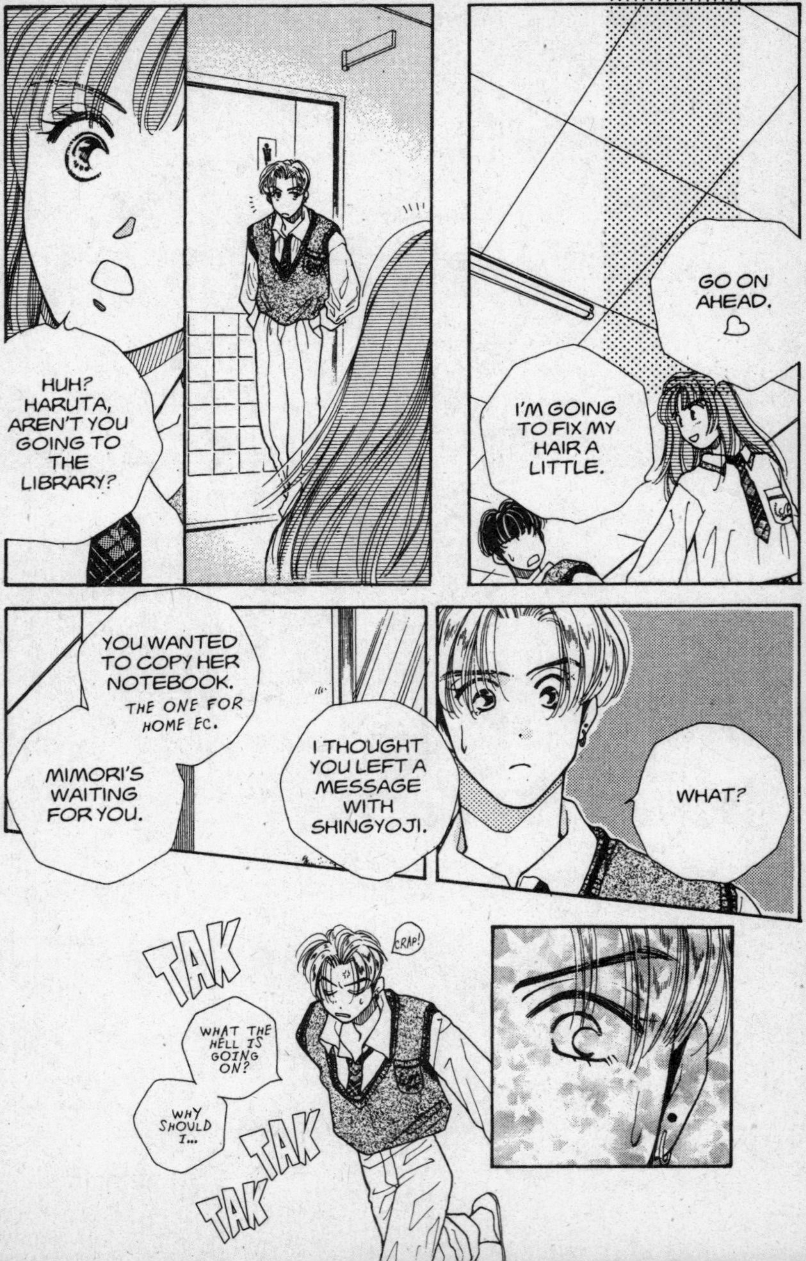
GO ON AHEAD. ♡
I'M GOING TO FIX MY HAIR A LITTLE.
HUH? HARUTA, AREN'T YOU GOING TO THE LIBRARY?
WHAT?
I THOUGHT YOU LEFT A MESSAGE WITH SHINGYOJI.
YOU WANTED TO COPY HER NOTEBOOK. THE ONE FOR HOME EC.
MIMORI'S WAITING FOR YOU.
CRAP!
TAK
WHAT THE HELL IS GOING ON?
WHY SHOULD I...
TAK
TAK

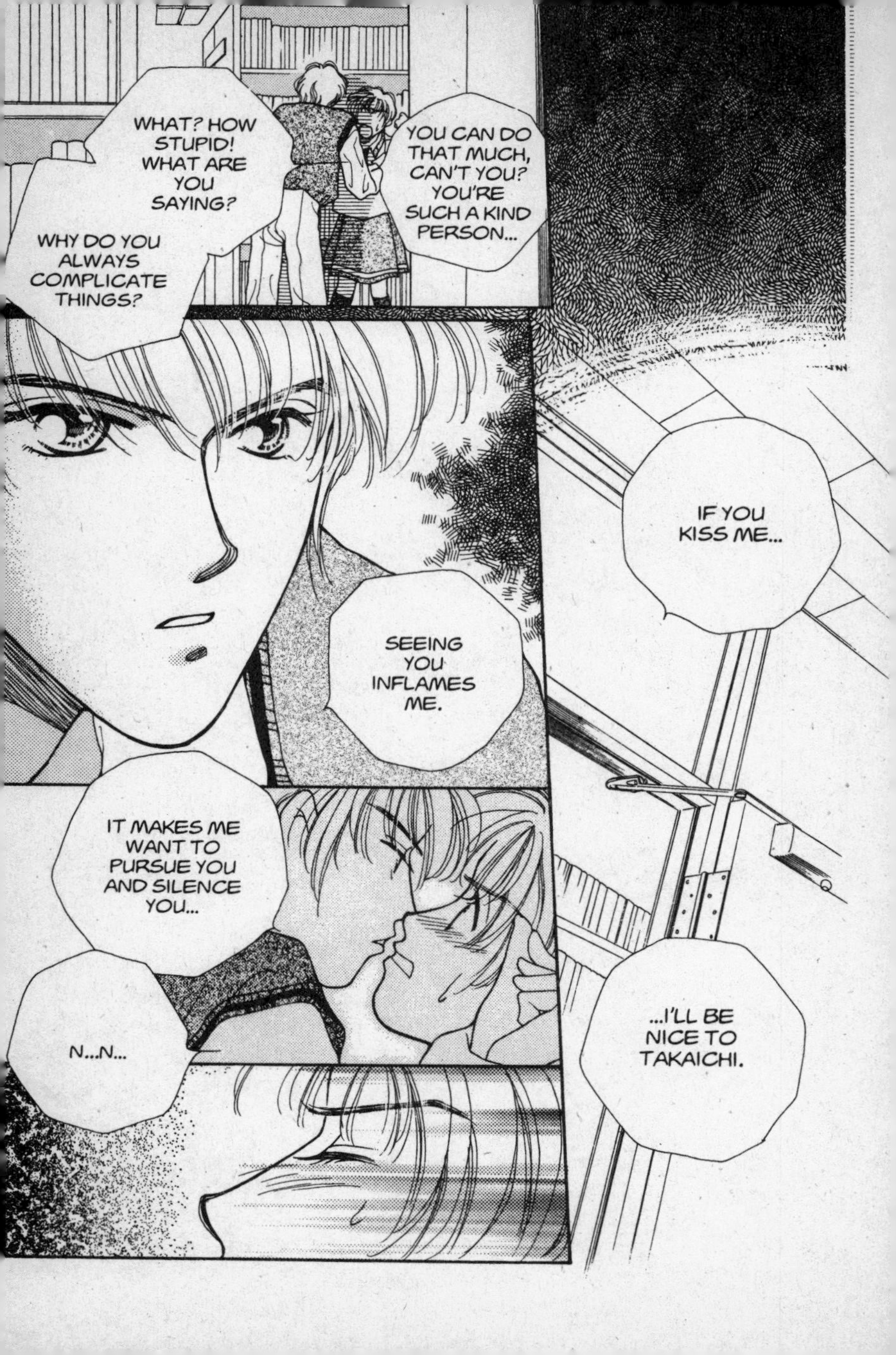
IF YOU KISS ME...
...I'LL BE NICE TO TAKAICHI.
YOU CAN DO THAT MUCH, CAN'T YOU? YOU'RE SUCH A KIND PERSON...
WHAT? HOW STUPID! WHAT ARE YOU SAYING?
WHY DO YOU ALWAYS COMPLICATE THINGS?
SEEING YOU INFLAMES ME.
IT MAKES ME WANT TO PURSUE YOU AND SILENCE YOU...
N...N...

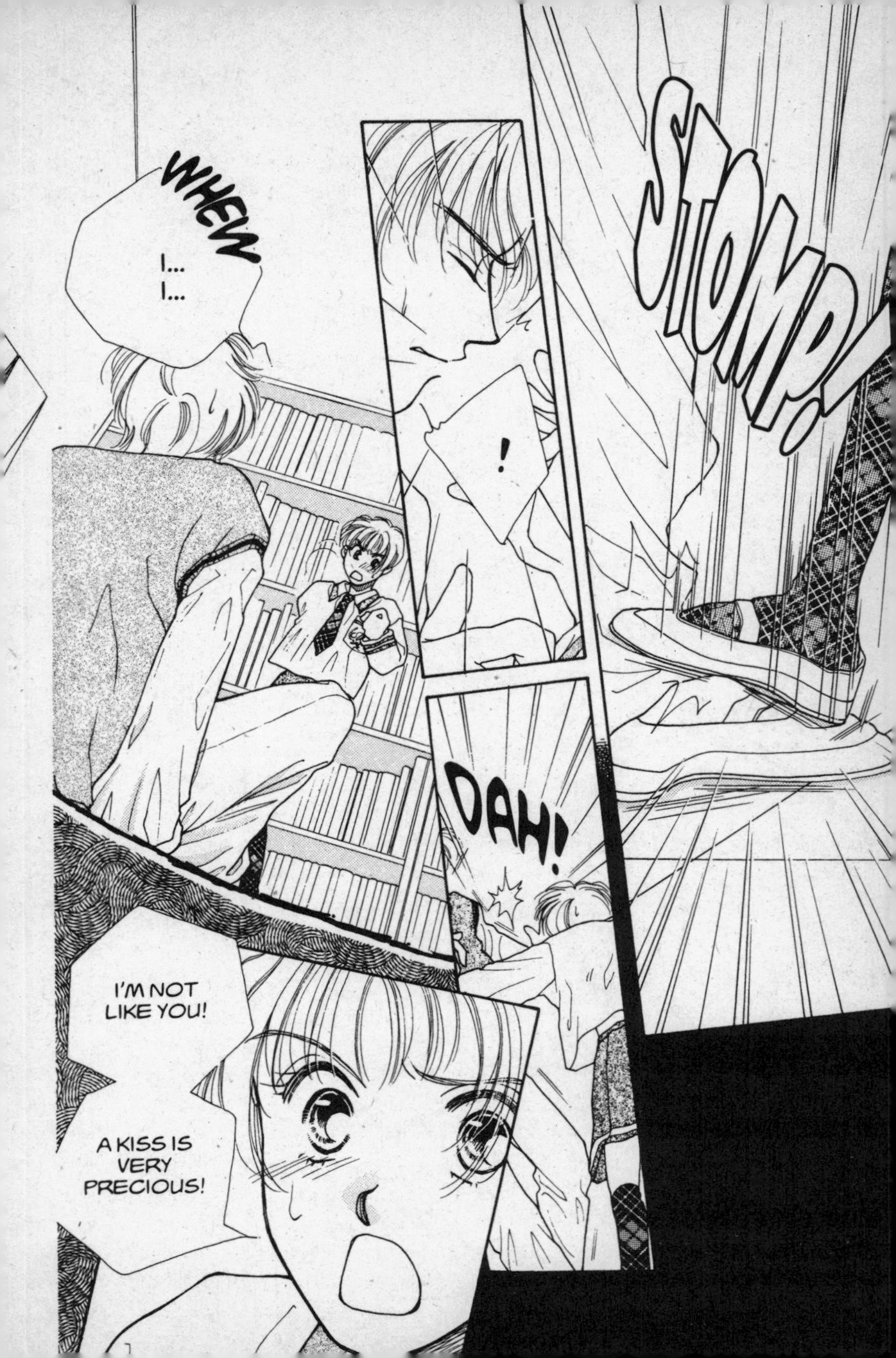
STOMP!
!
DAH!
WHEW
I...
I...
I'M NOT LIKE YOU!
A KISS IS VERY PRECIOUS!

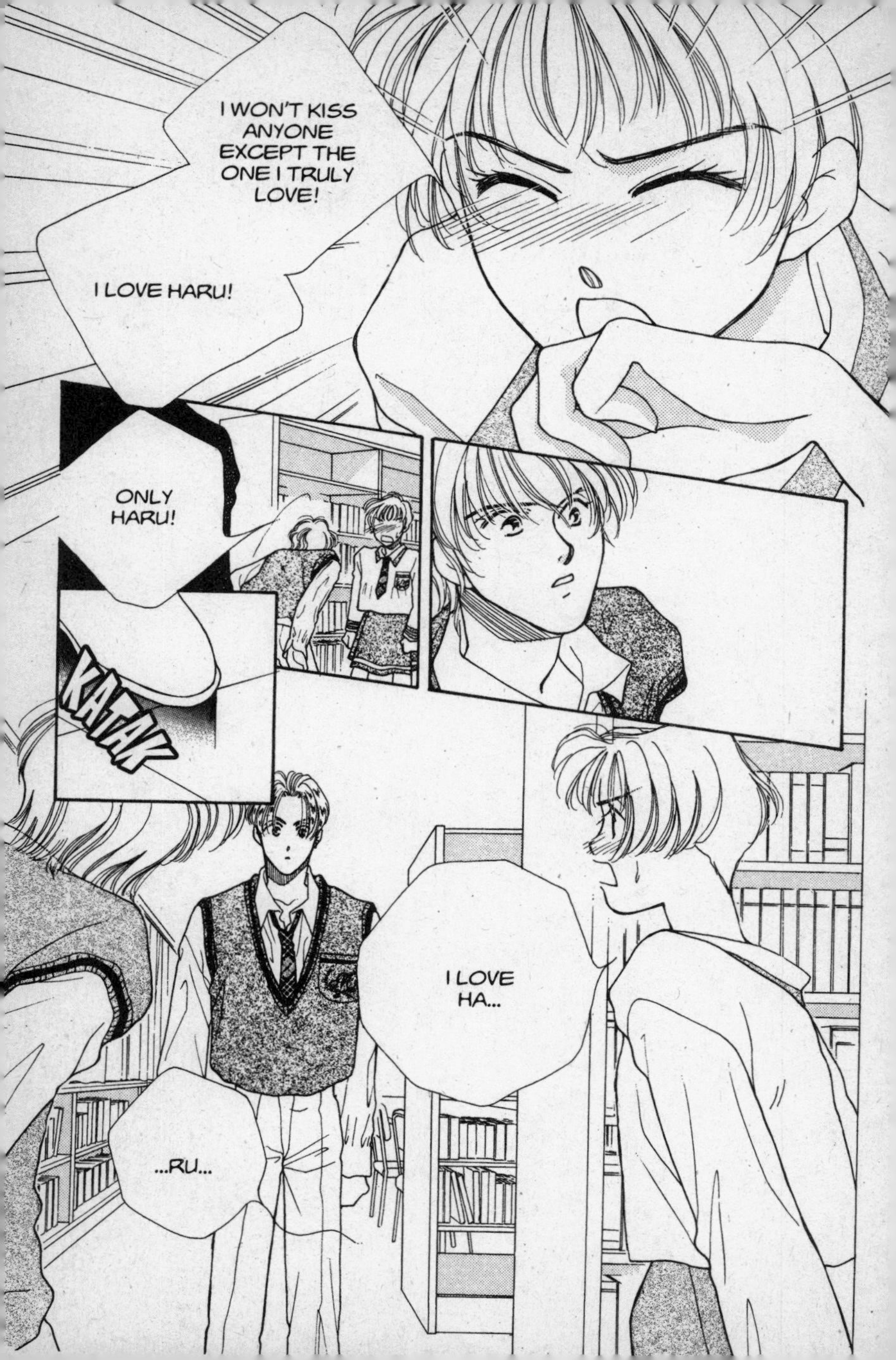
I WON'T KISS ANYONE EXCEPT THE ONE I TRULY LOVE!
I LOVE HARU!
ONLY HARU!
KATAK
I LOVE HA...
...RU...

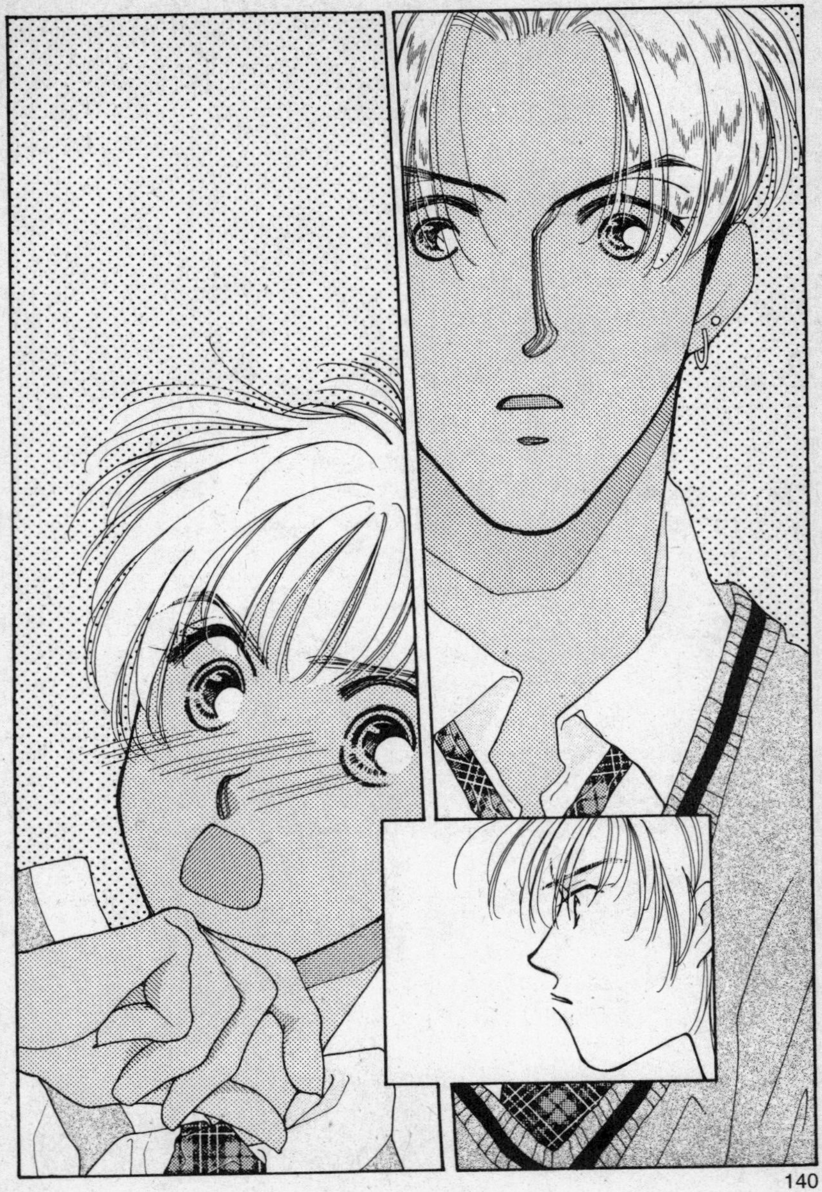

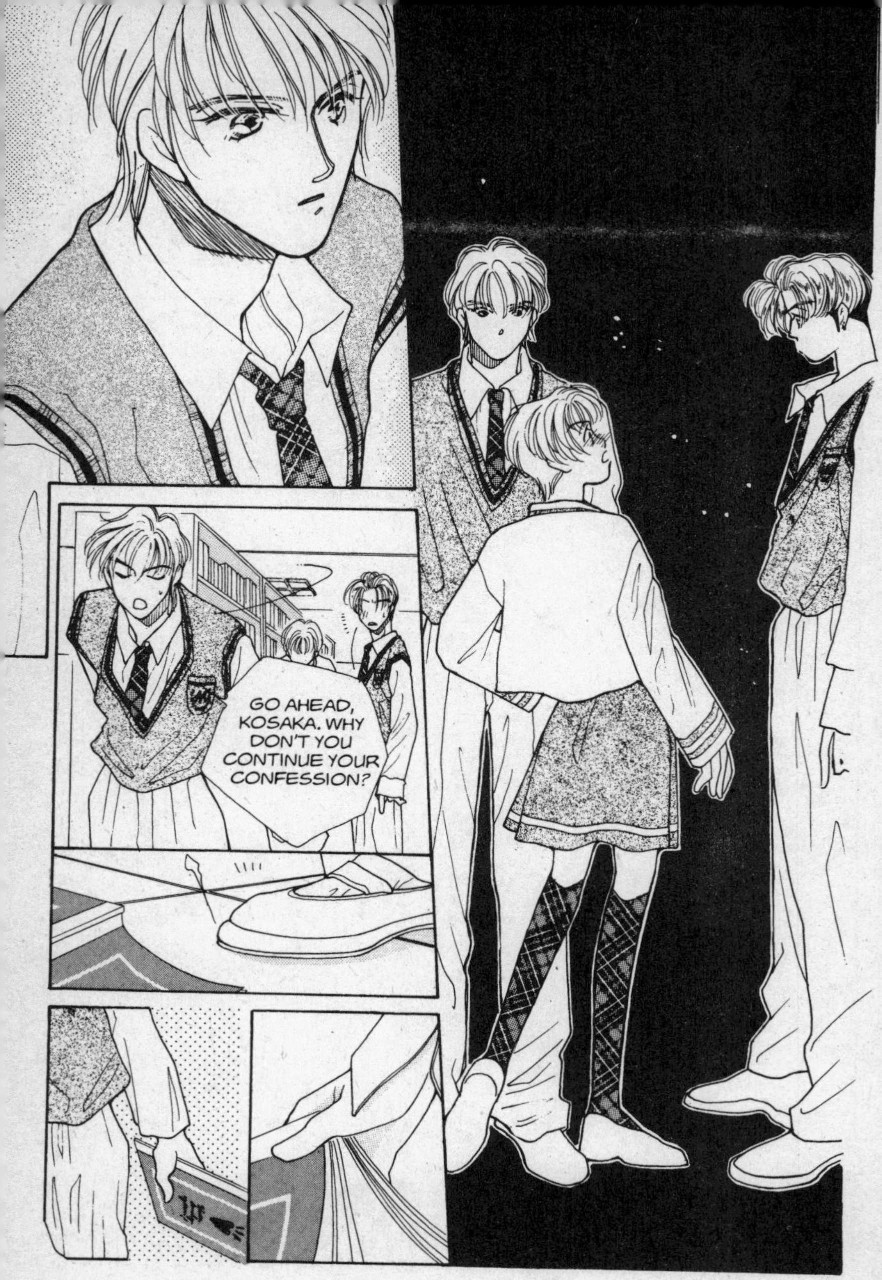
GO AHEAD, KOSAKA. WHY DON'T YOU CONTINUE YOUR CONFESSION?

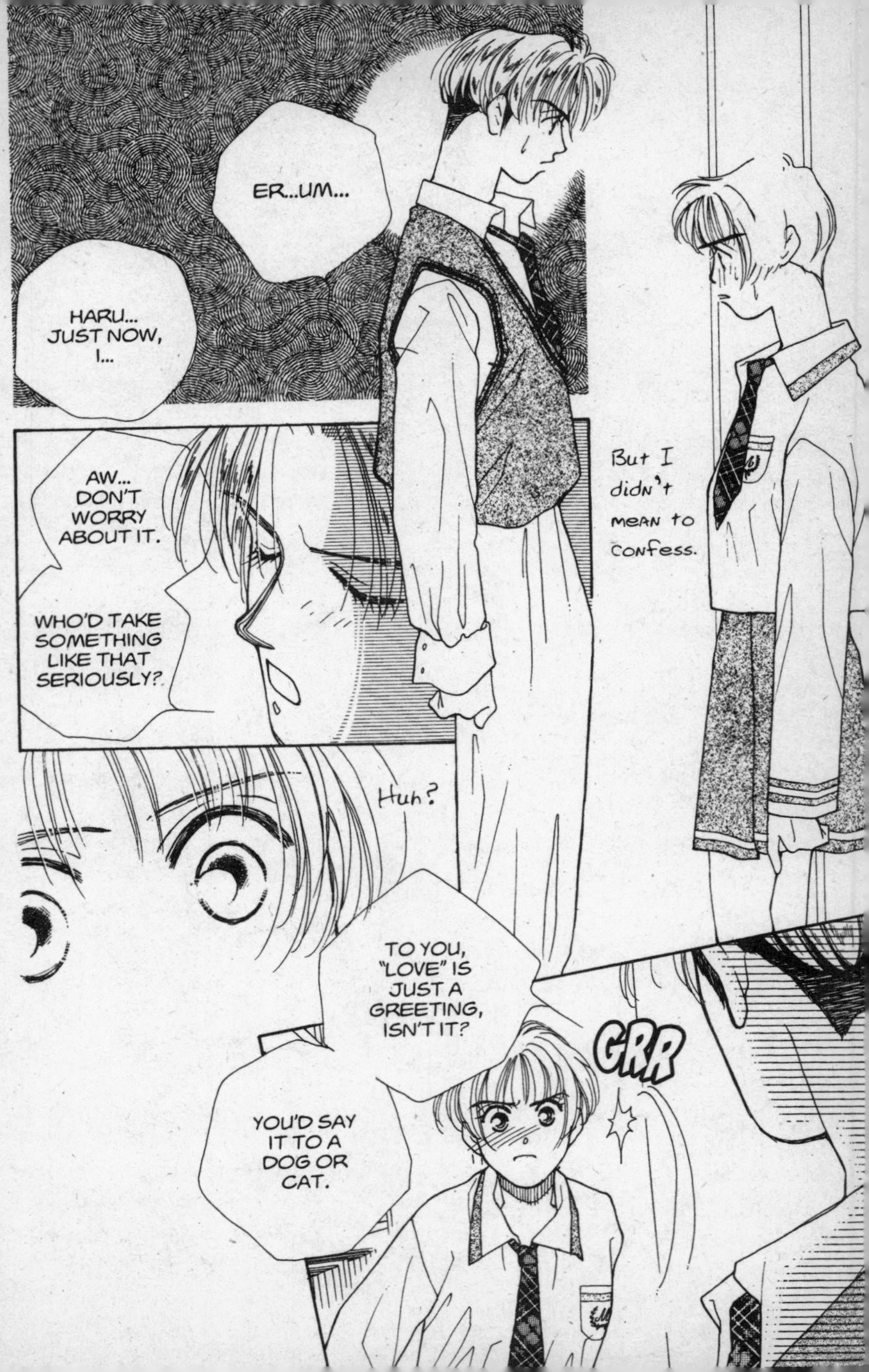
But I didn't mean to confess.
ER...UM...
HARU... JUST NOW, I...
AW... DON'T WORRY ABOUT IT.
WHO'D TAKE SOMETHING LIKE THAT SERIOUSLY?
Huh?
TO YOU, "LOVE" IS JUST A GREETING, ISN'T IT?
YOU'D SAY IT TO A DOG OR CAT.
GRR

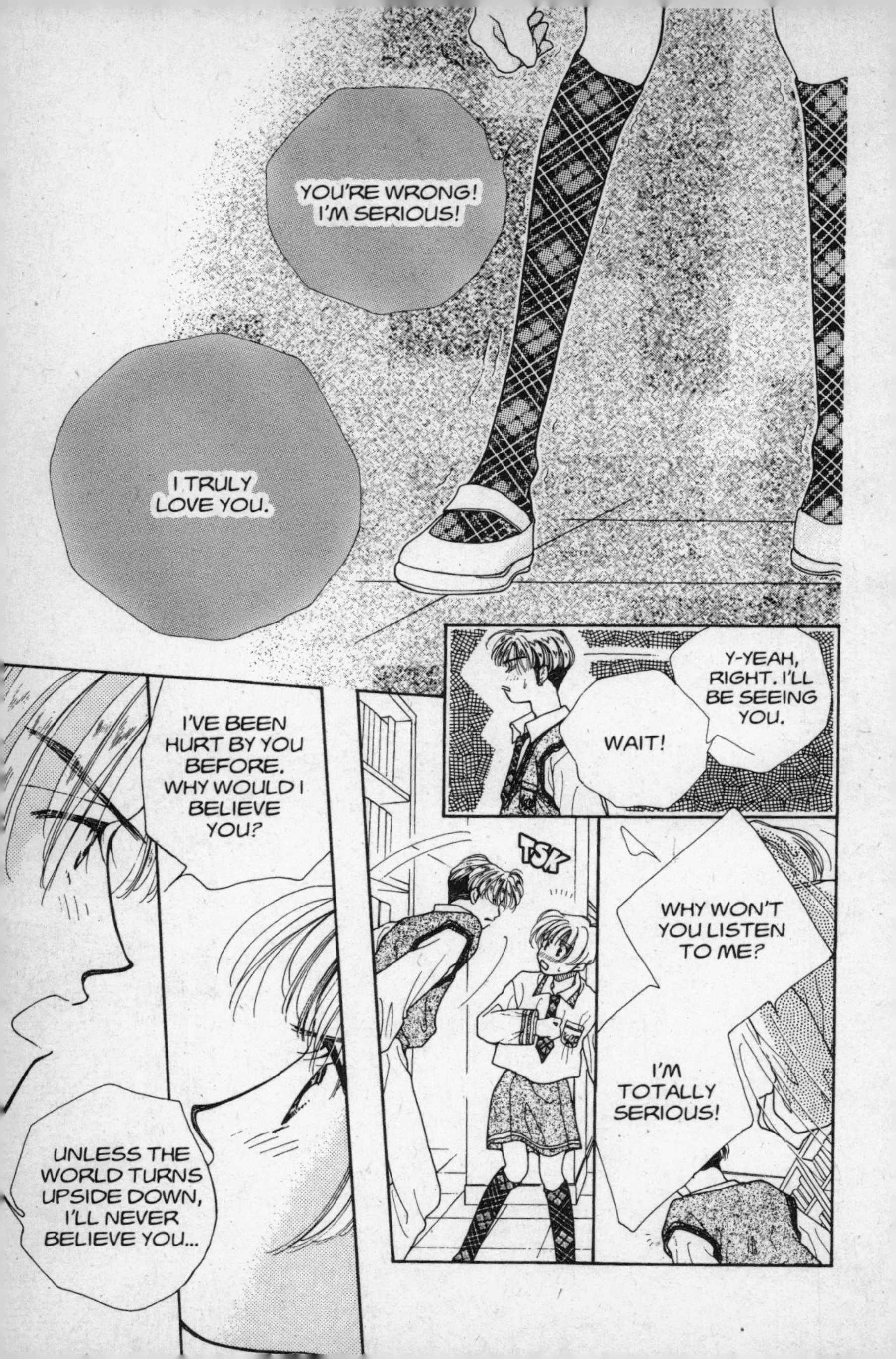
YOU'RE WRONG! I'M SERIOUS!
I TRULY LOVE YOU.
Y-YEAH, RIGHT. I'LL BE SEEING YOU.
WAIT!
WHY WON'T YOU LISTEN TO ME?
I'M TOTALLY SERIOUS!
TSK
I'VE BEEN HURT BY YOU BEFORE. WHY WOULD I BELIEVE YOU?
UNLESS THE WORLD TURNS UPSIDE DOWN, I'LL NEVER BELIEVE YOU...

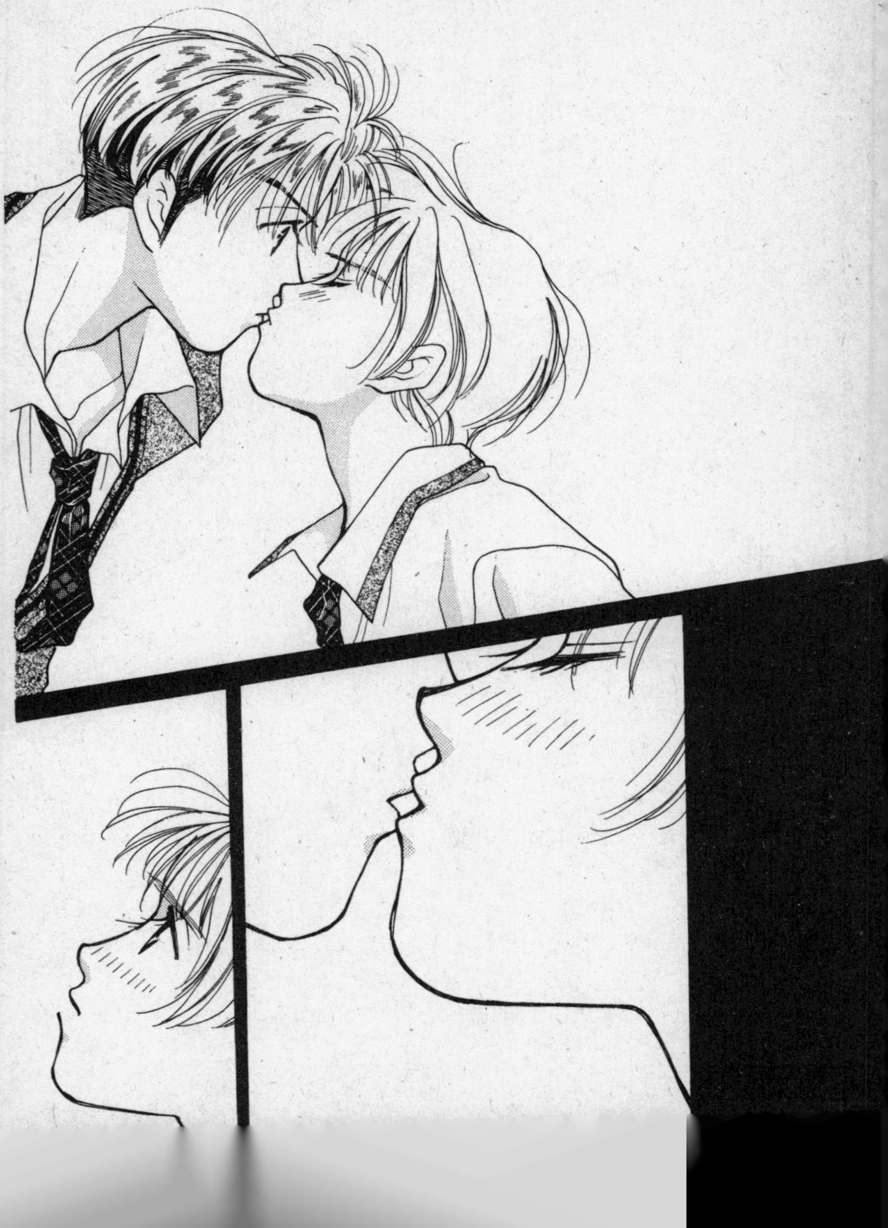

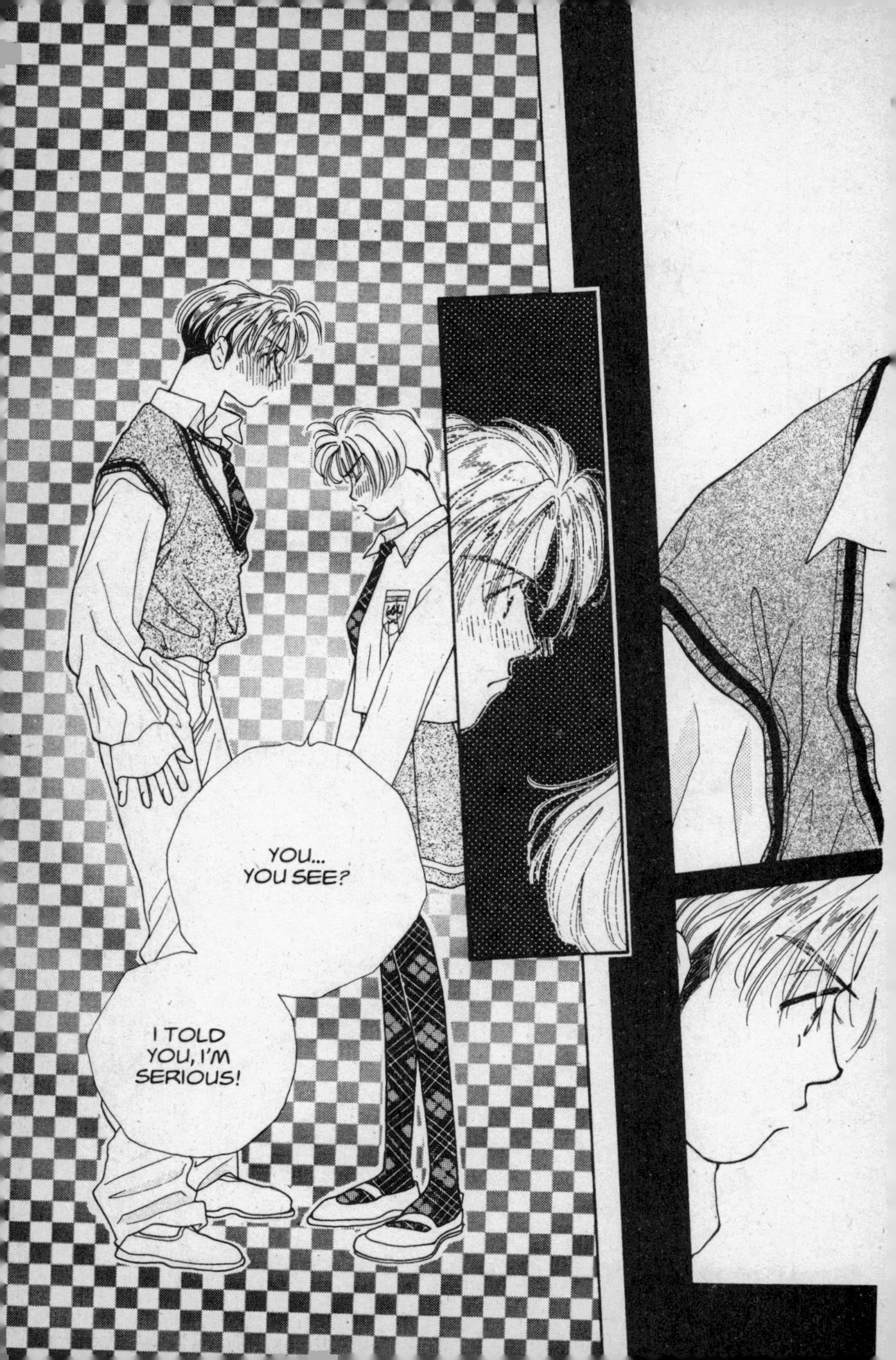
YOU... YOU SEE?
I TOLD YOU, I'M SERIOUS!

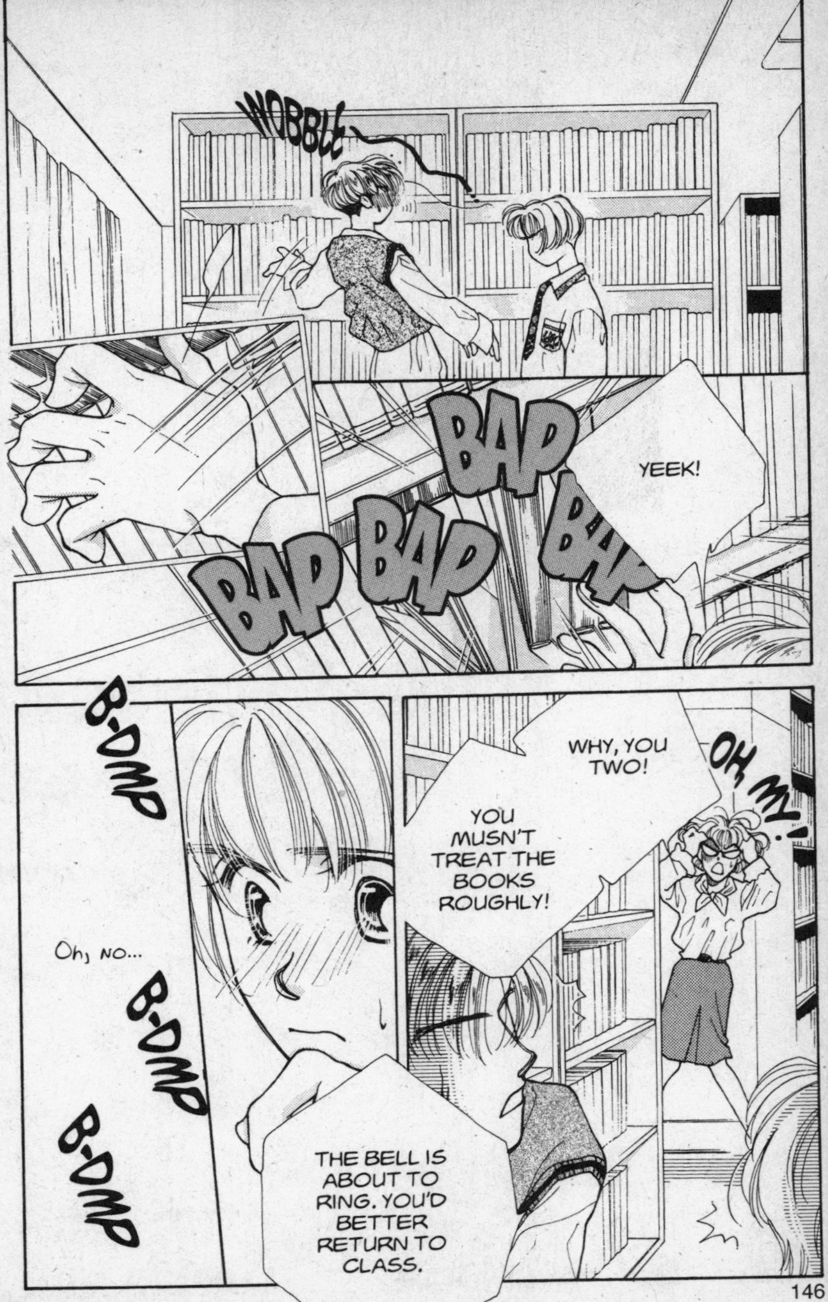
WOBBLE
YEEK!
BAP
BAP
BAP
BAP
WHY, YOU TWO!
OH, MY!
YOU MUSN'T TREAT THE BOOKS ROUGHLY!
THE BELL IS ABOUT TO RING. YOU'D BETTER RETURN TO CLASS.
B-DMP
Oh, no...
B-DMP
B-DMP

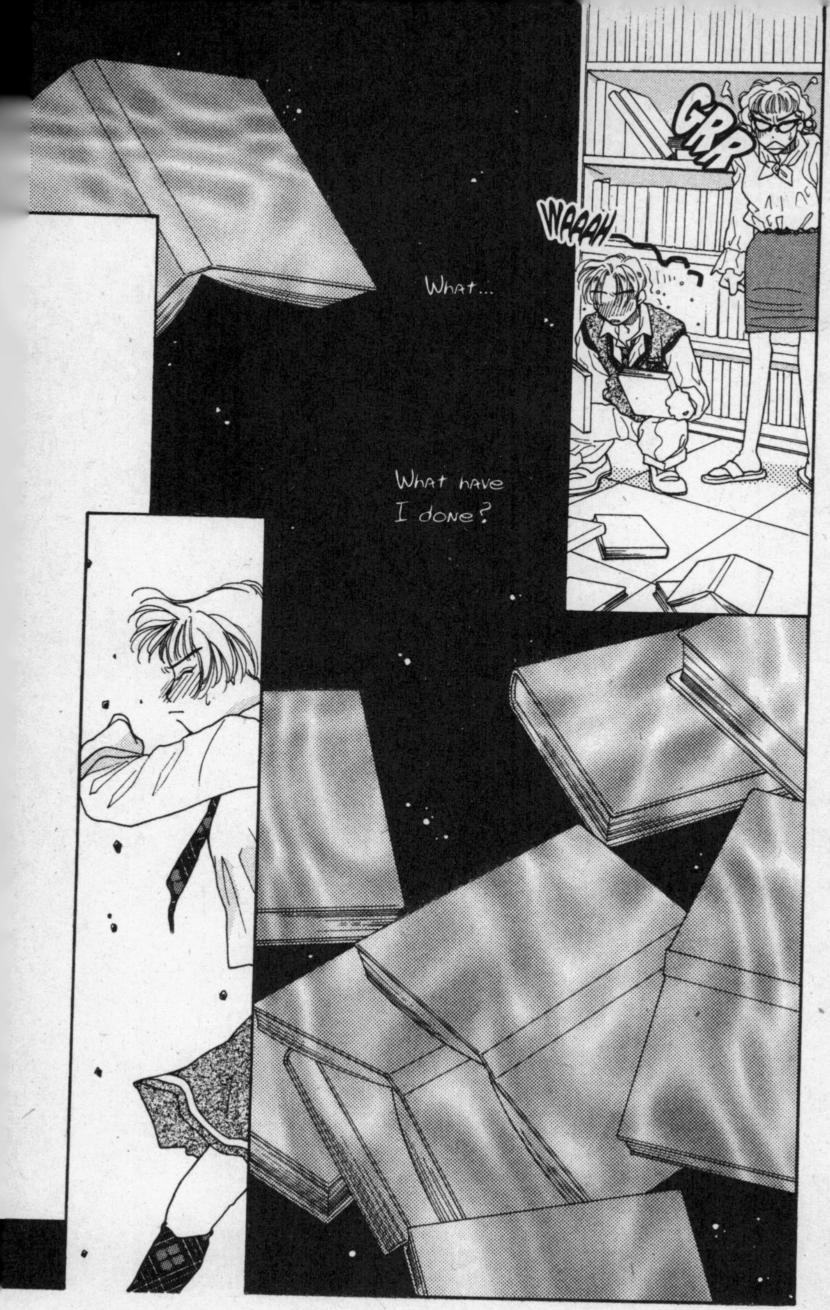
GRR
WAAAH
What...
What have I done?

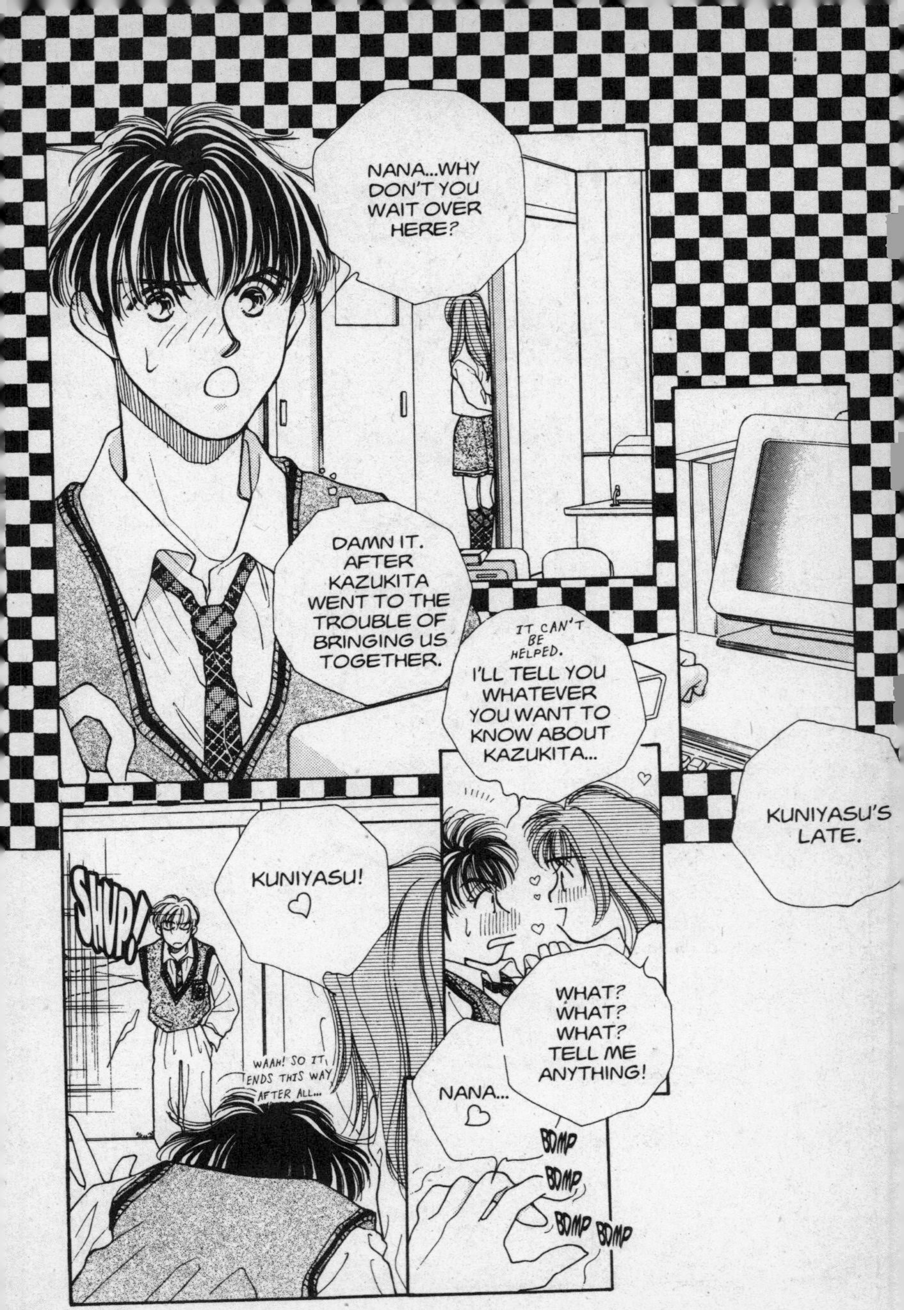
KUNIYASU'S LATE.
NANA...WHY DON'T YOU WAIT OVER HERE?
DAMN IT. AFTER KAZUKITA WENT TO THE TROUBLE OF BRINGING US TOGETHER.
IT CAN'T BE HELPED.
I'LL TELL YOU WHATEVER YOU WANT TO KNOW ABOUT KAZUKITA...
WHAT? WHAT? WHAT? TELL ME ANYTHING!
NANA... ♡
BDMP BDMP BDMP BDMP
SHUP!
KUNIYASU! ♡
WAAH! SO IT ENDS THIS WAY AFTER ALL...

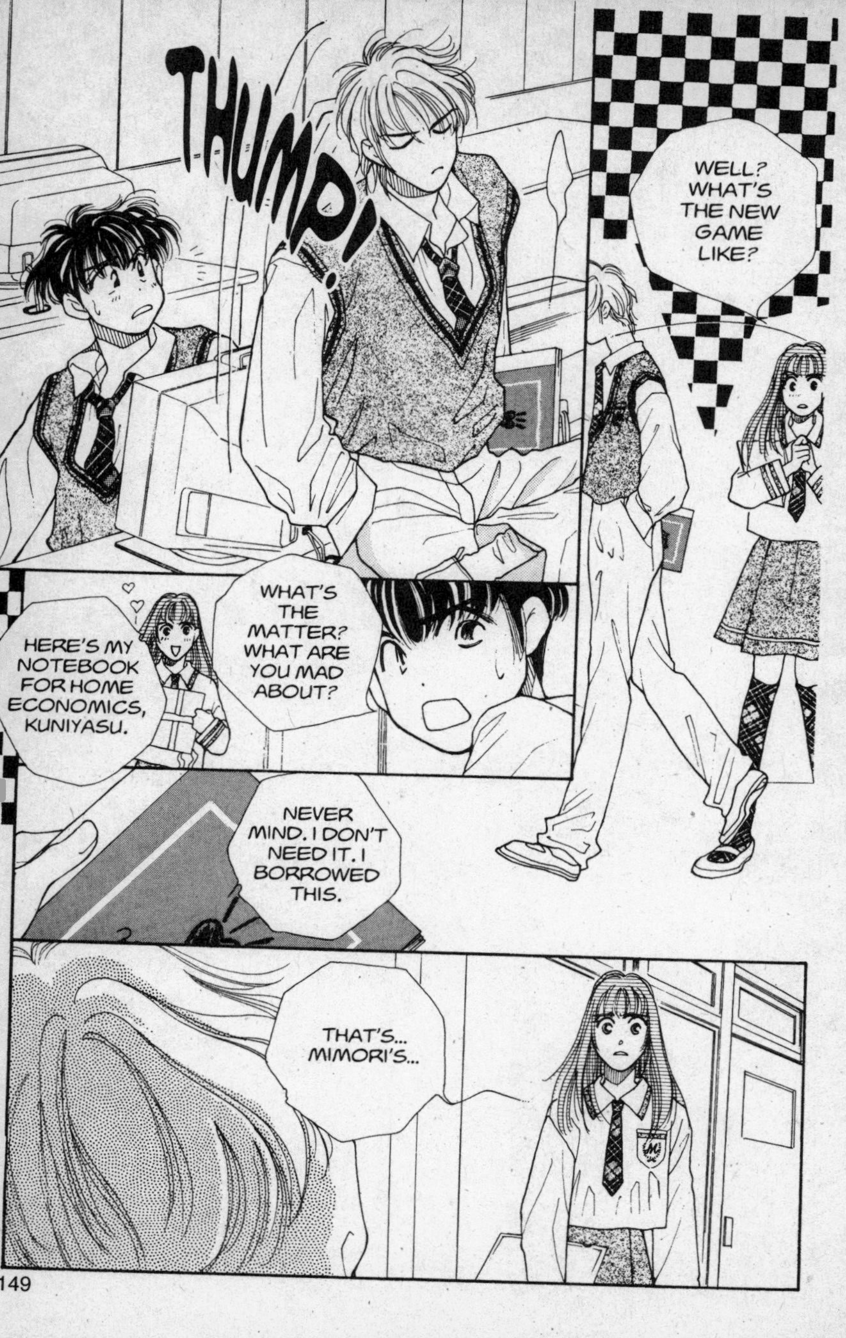
WELL? WHAT'S THE NEW GAME LIKE?
THUMP!
WHAT'S THE MATTER? WHAT ARE YOU MAD ABOUT?
HERE'S MY NOTEBOOK FOR HOME ECONOMICS, KUNIYASU.
NEVER MIND. I DON'T NEED IT. I BORROWED THIS.
THAT'S... MIMORI'S...

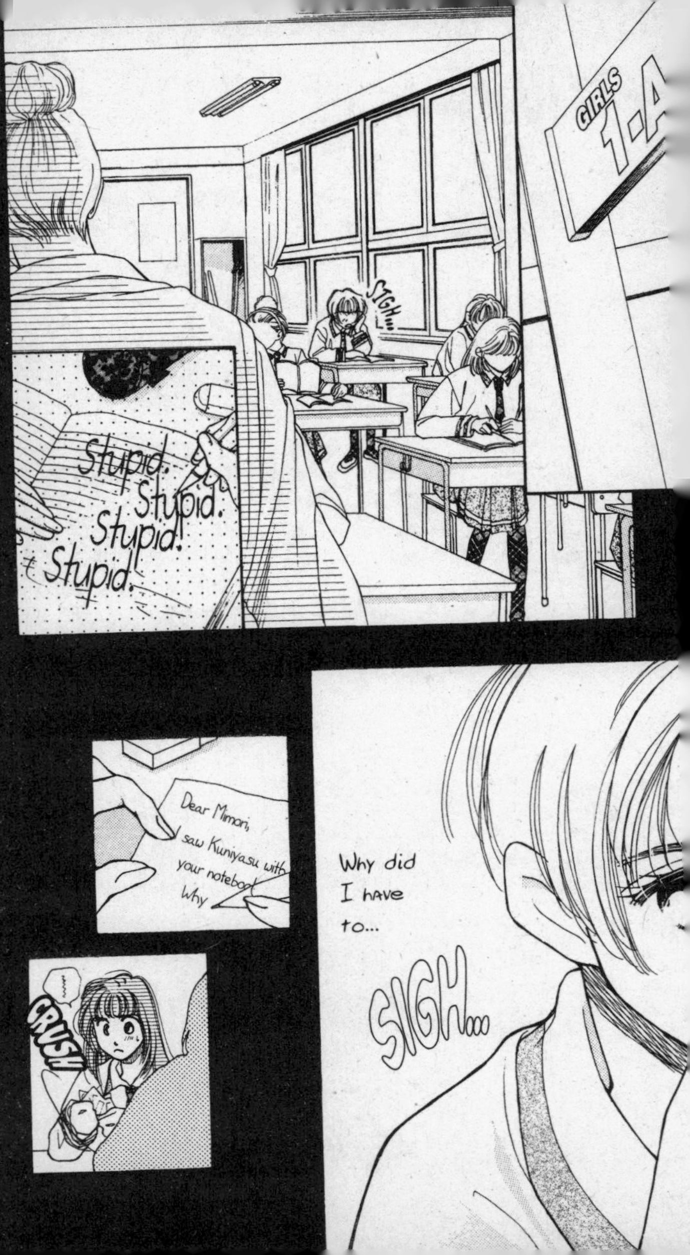
GIRLS 1-A
SIGH...
Stupid. Stupid. Stupid! Stupid.
Why did I have to...
SIGH...
Dear Mimori,
I saw Kuniyasu with
your
Why
CRUSH

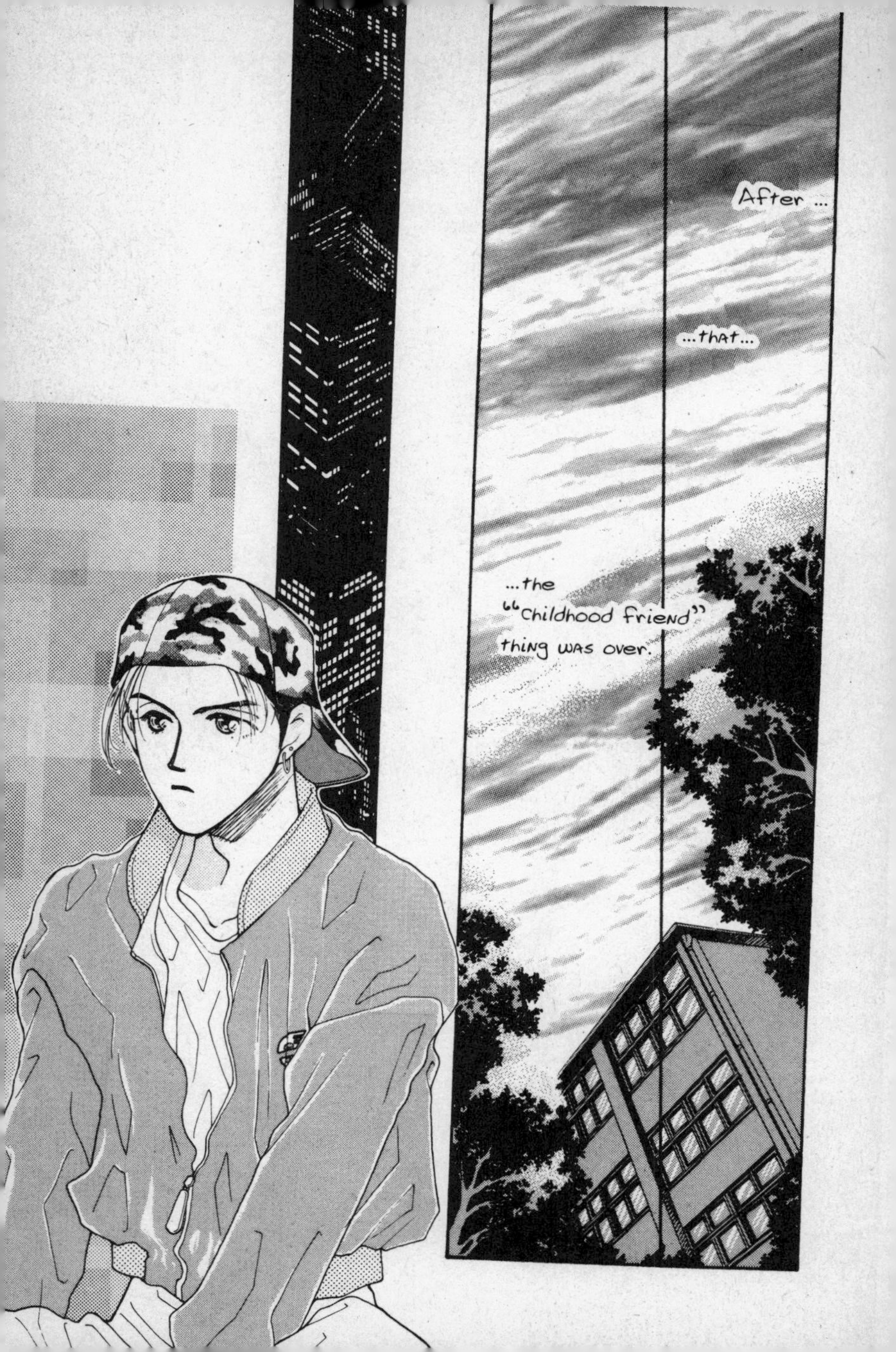
After ...
...that...
...the "childhood friend" thing was over.

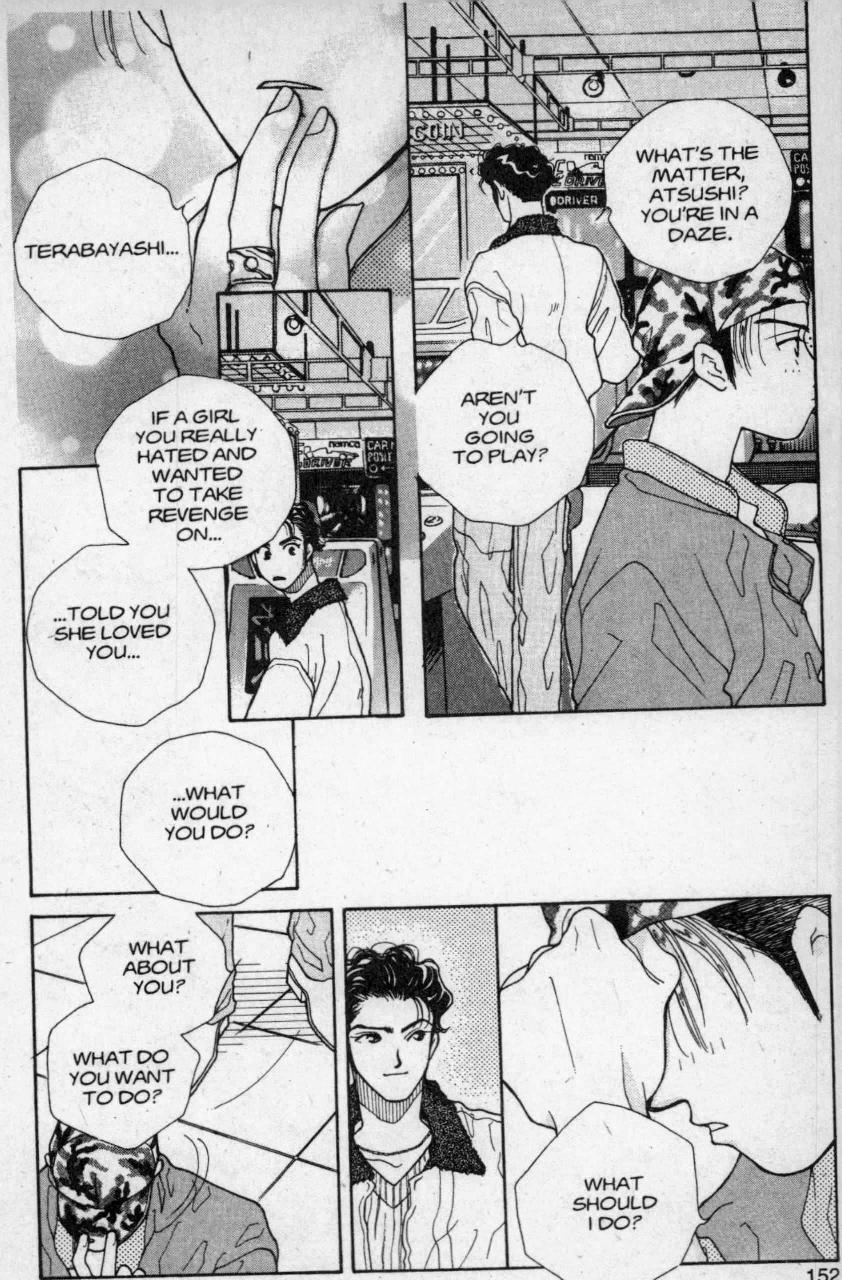
WHAT'S THE MATTER, ATSUSHI? YOU'RE IN A DAZE.
AREN'T YOU GOING TO PLAY?
TERABAYASHI...
IF A GIRL YOU REALLY HATED AND WANTED TO TAKE REVENGE ON...
...TOLD YOU SHE LOVED YOU...
...WHAT WOULD YOU DO?
WHAT SHOULD I DO?
WHAT ABOUT YOU?
WHAT DO YOU WANT TO DO?

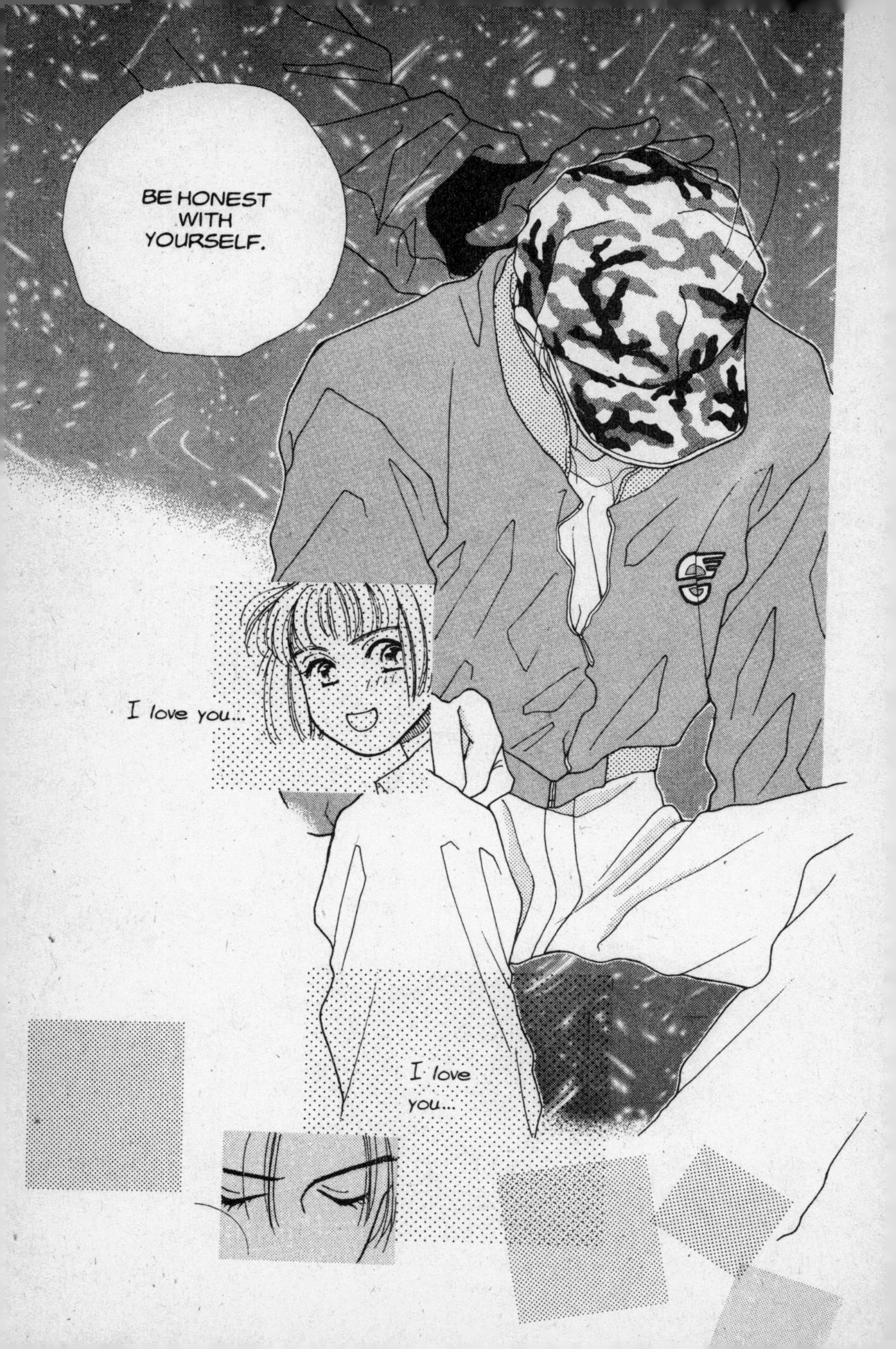
BE HONEST WITH YOURSELF.
I love you...
I love you...

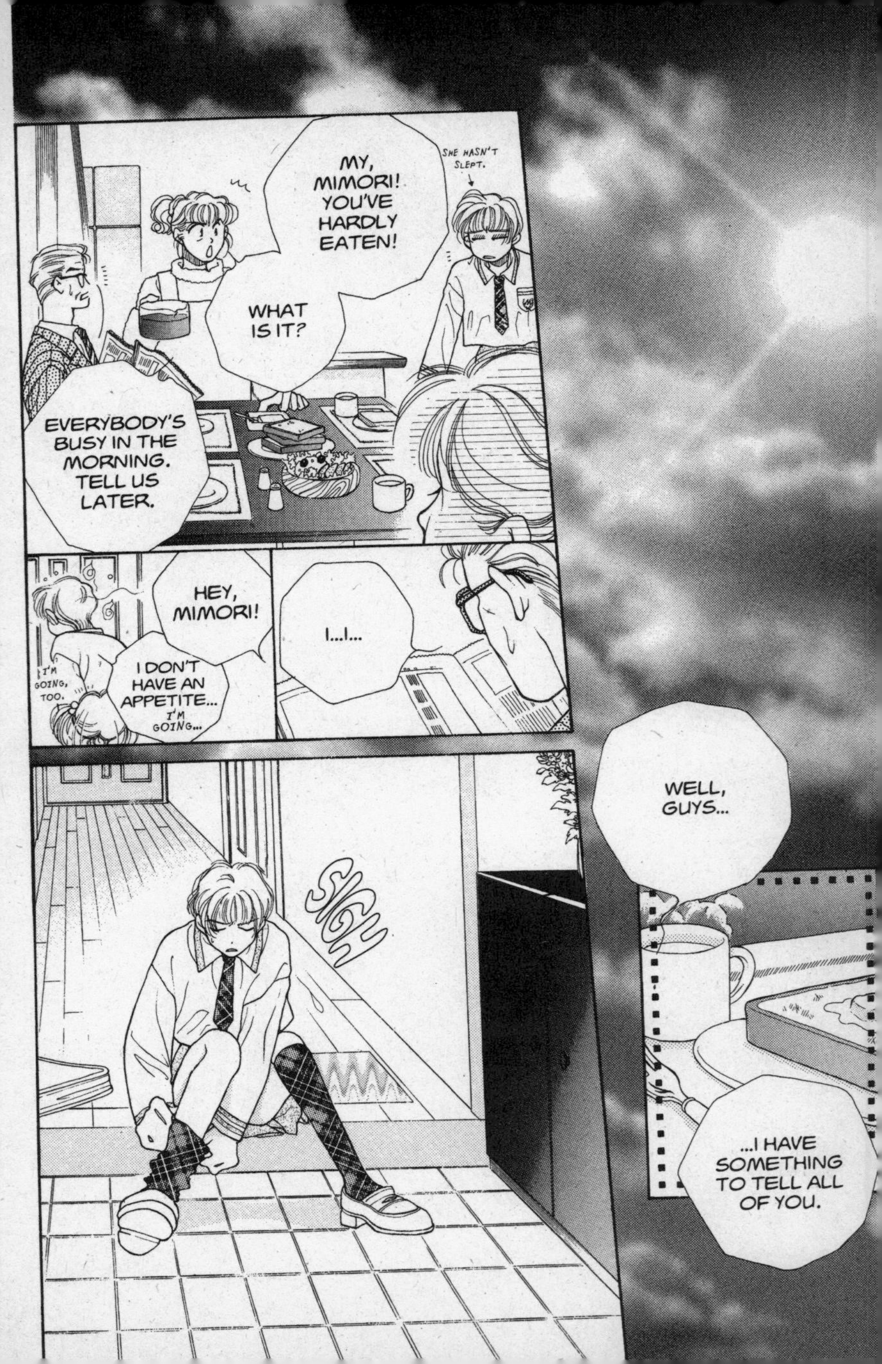
WELL, GUYS...
...I HAVE SOMETHING TO TELL ALL OF YOU.
SHE HASN'T SLEPT.
MY, MIMORI! YOU'VE HARDLY EATEN!
WHAT IS IT?
EVERYBODY'S BUSY IN THE MORNING. TELL US LATER.
I...I...
HEY, MIMORI!
I DON'T HAVE AN APPETITE...
I'M GOING...
I'M GOING, TOO.
SIGH

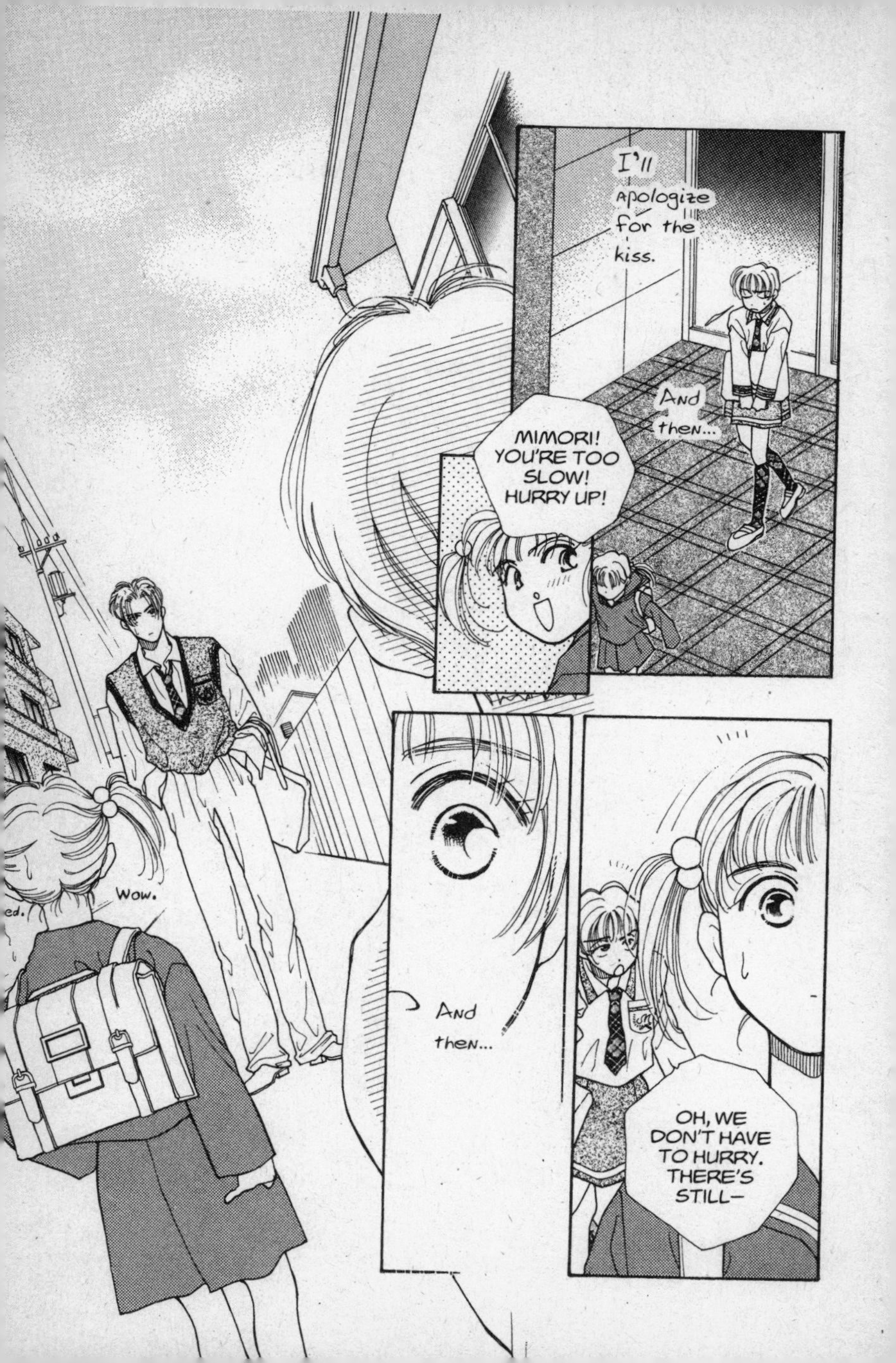
I'll apologize for the kiss.
And then...
MIMORI! YOU'RE TOO SLOW! HURRY UP!
OH, WE DON'T HAVE TO HURRY. THERE'S STILL—
And then...
Wow.

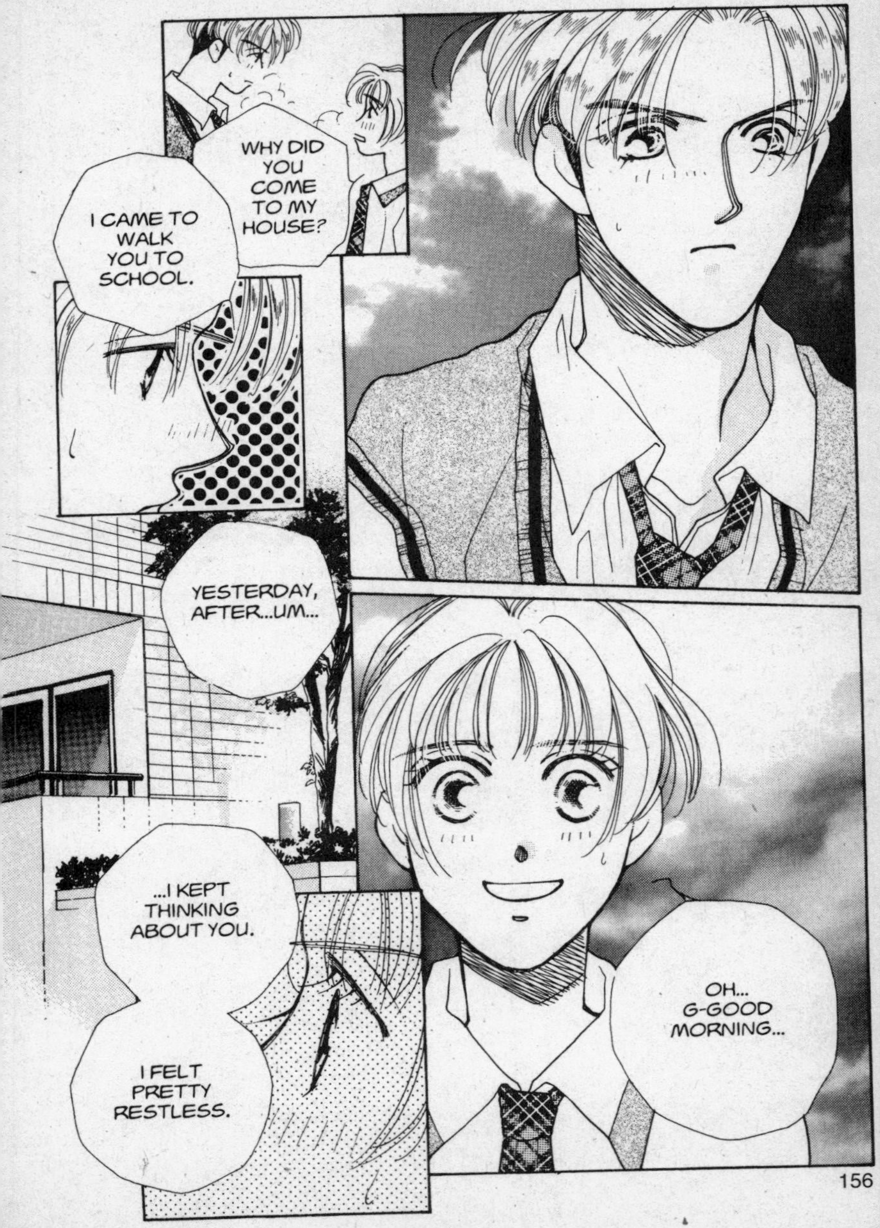
WHY DID YOU COME TO MY HOUSE?
I CAME TO WALK YOU TO SCHOOL.
OH... G-GOOD MORNING...
YESTERDAY, AFTER...UM...
...I KEPT THINKING ABOUT YOU.
I FELT PRETTY RESTLESS.

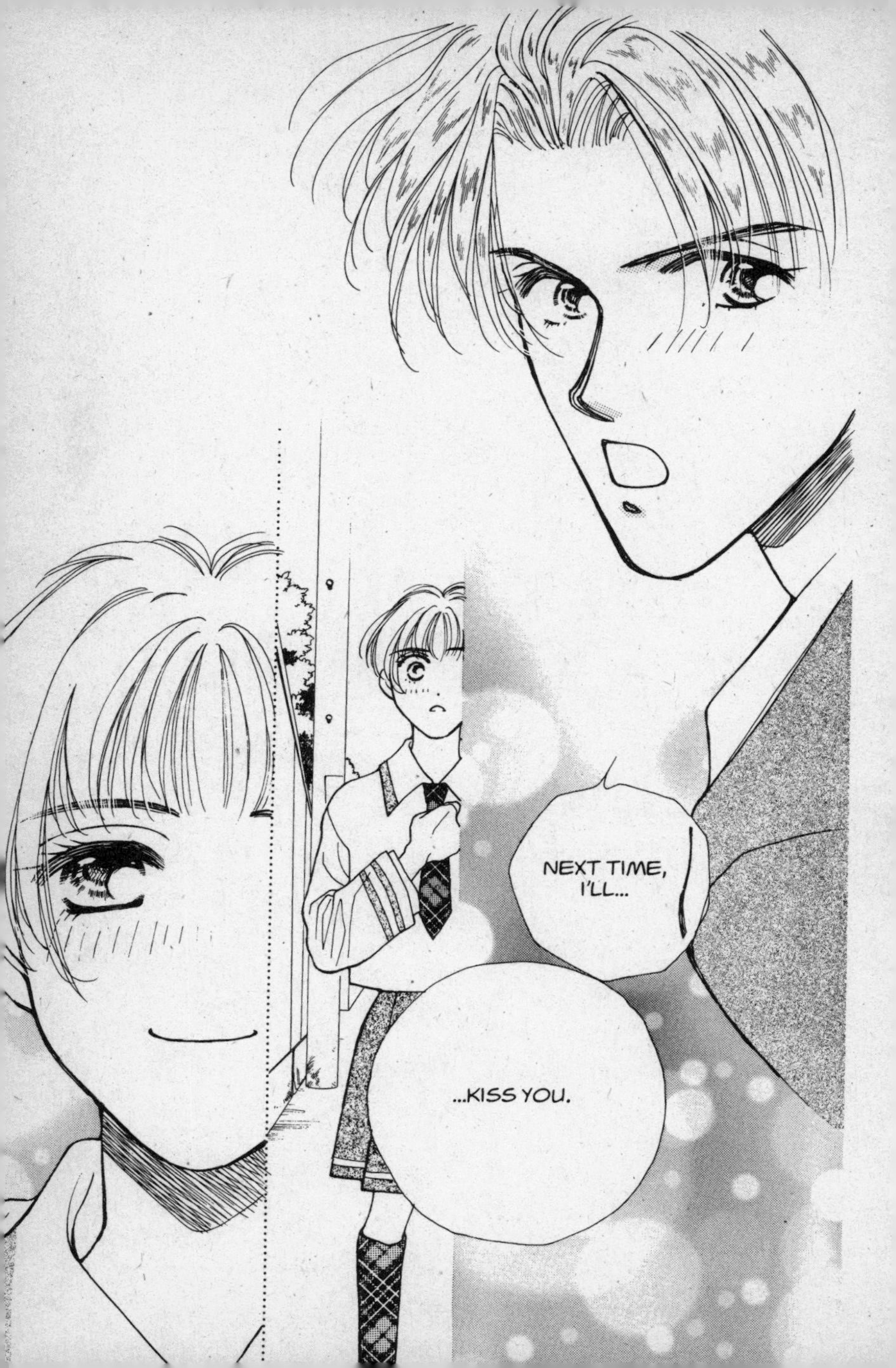
NEXT TIME, I'LL...
...KISS YOU.

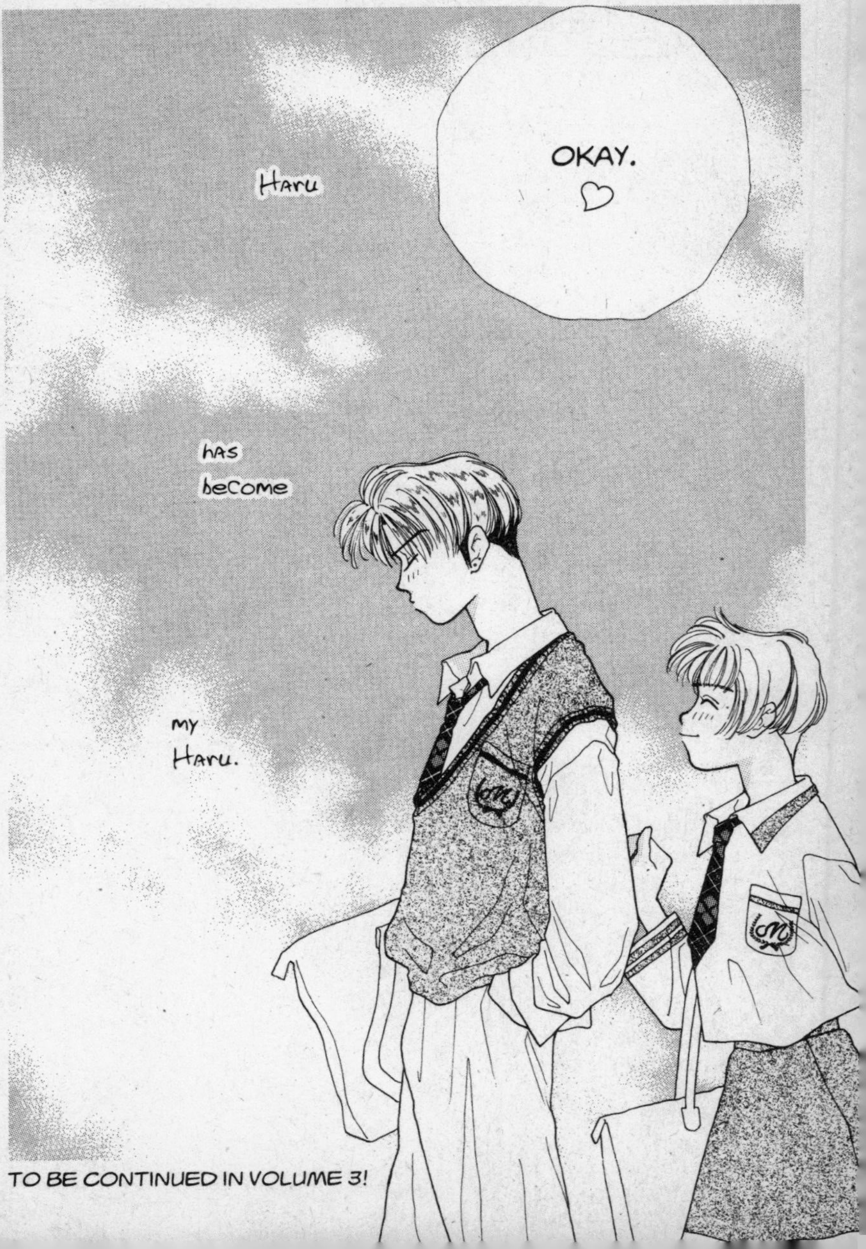
OKAY. ♡
Haru
has become
my Haru.

TO BE CONTINUED IN VOLUME 3!

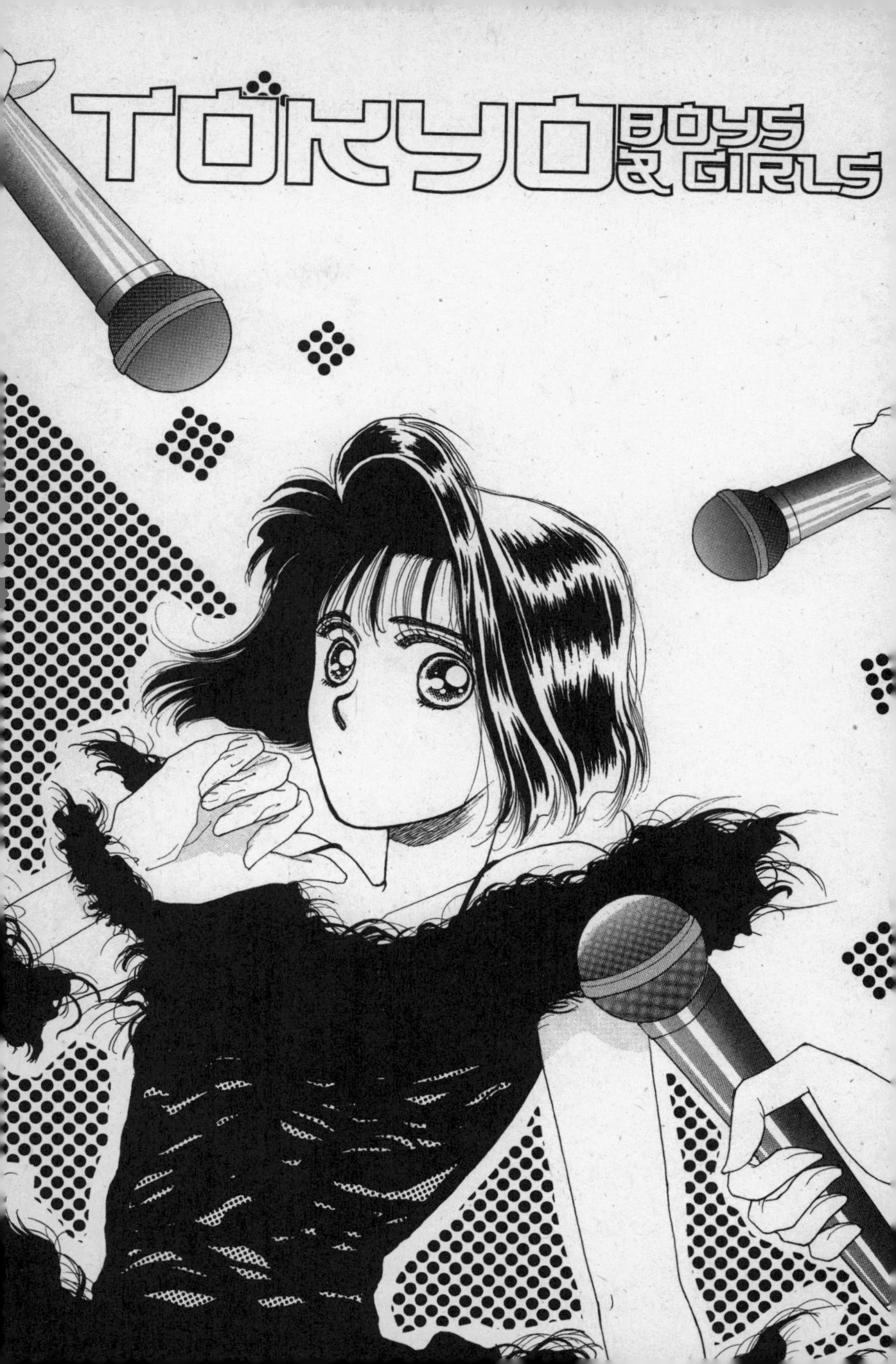
TOKYO BOYS & GIRLS

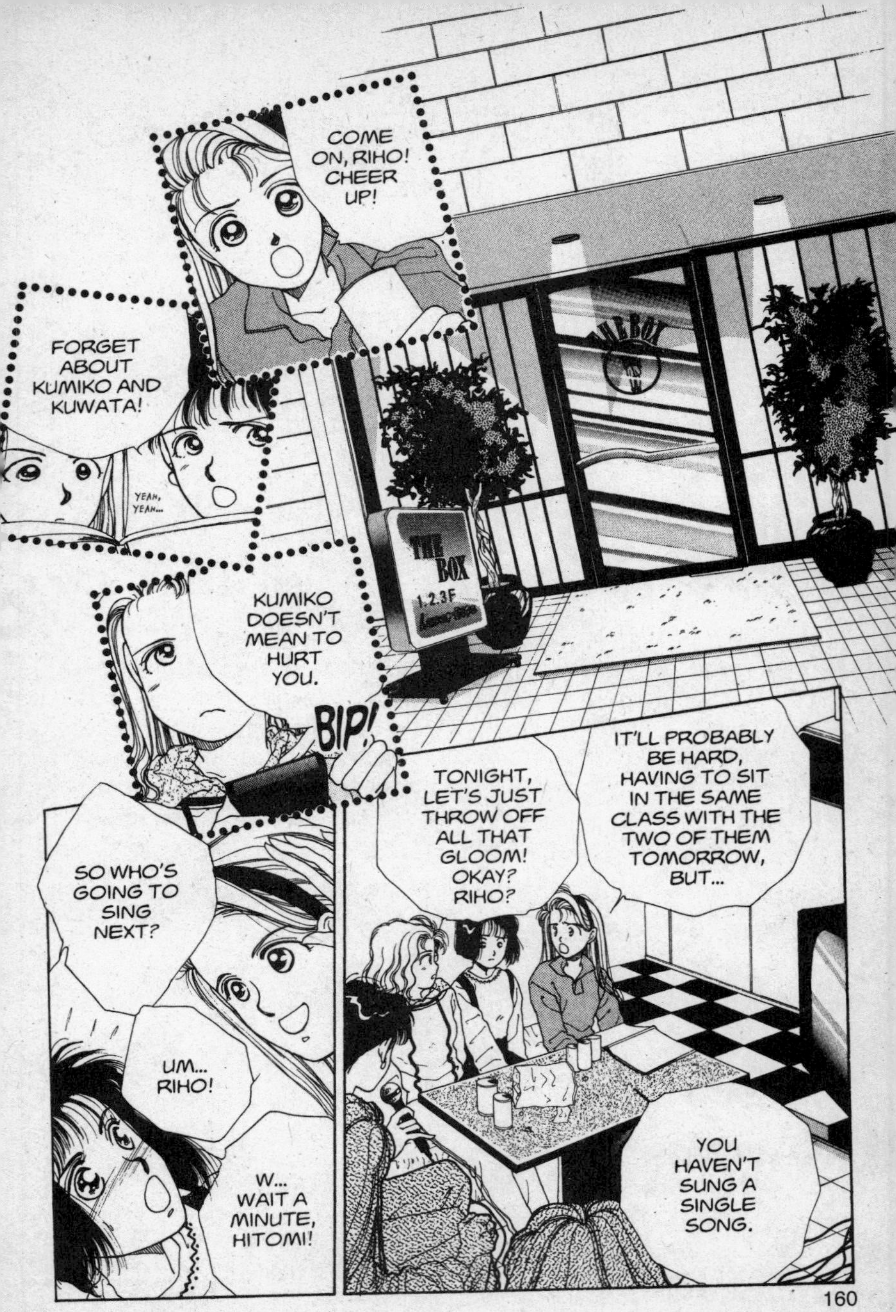
COME ON, RIHO! CHEER UP!
FORGET ABOUT KUMIKO AND KUWATA!
YEAH, YEAH...
KUMIKO DOESN'T MEAN TO HURT YOU.
THE BOX
1.2.3F
BIP!
IT'LL PROBABLY BE HARD, HAVING TO SIT IN THE SAME CLASS WITH THE TWO OF THEM TOMORROW, BUT...
TONIGHT, LET'S JUST THROW OFF ALL THAT GLOOM! OKAY? RIHO?
YOU HAVEN'T SUNG A SINGLE SONG.
SO WHO'S GOING TO SING NEXT?
UM... RIHO!
W... WAIT A MINUTE, HITOMI!

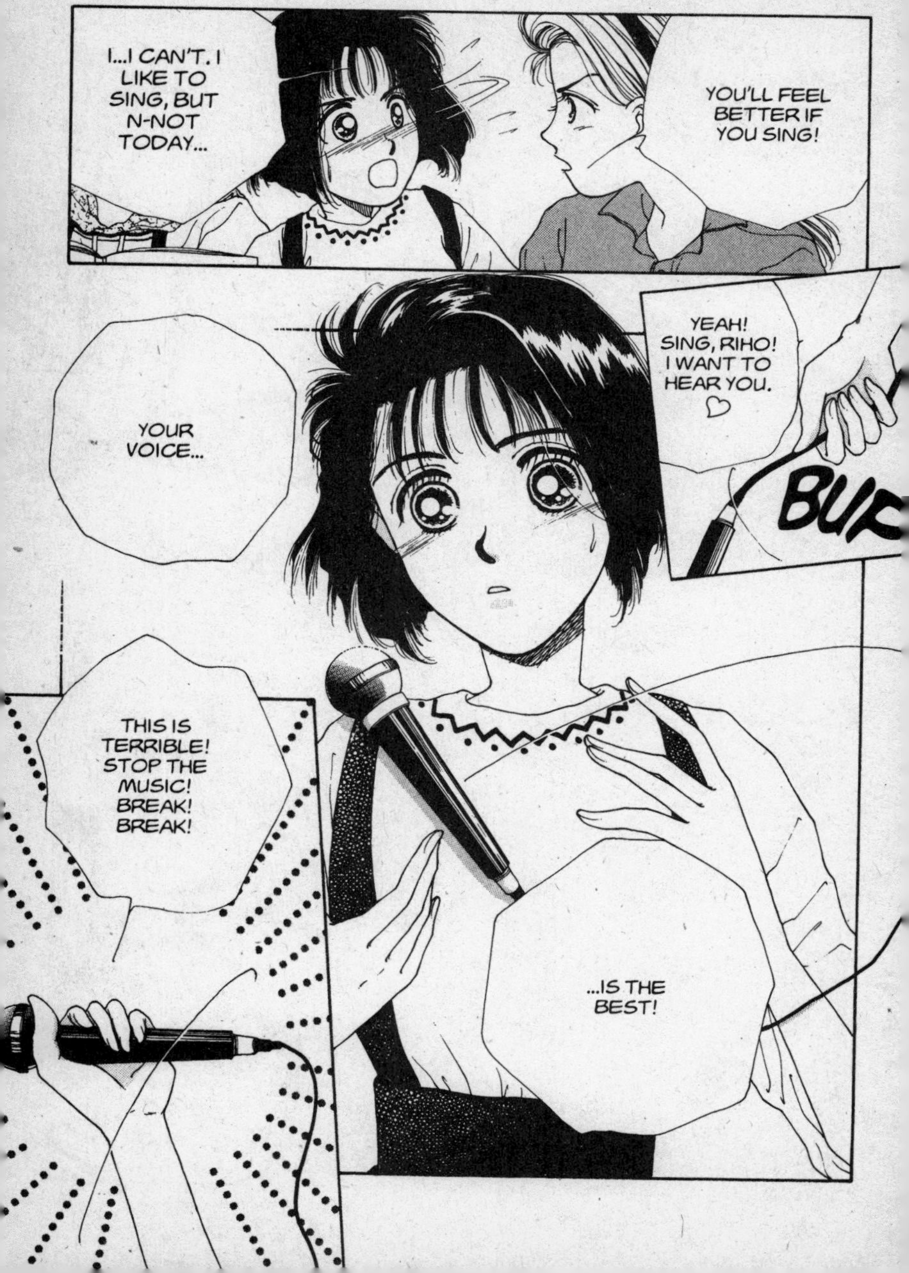
YOU'LL FEEL BETTER IF YOU SING!
I...I CAN'T. I LIKE TO SING, BUT N-NOT TODAY...
YEAH! SING, RIHO! I WANT TO HEAR YOU. ♡
BUR
YOUR VOICE...
...IS THE BEST!
THIS IS TERRIBLE! STOP THE MUSIC! BREAK! BREAK!

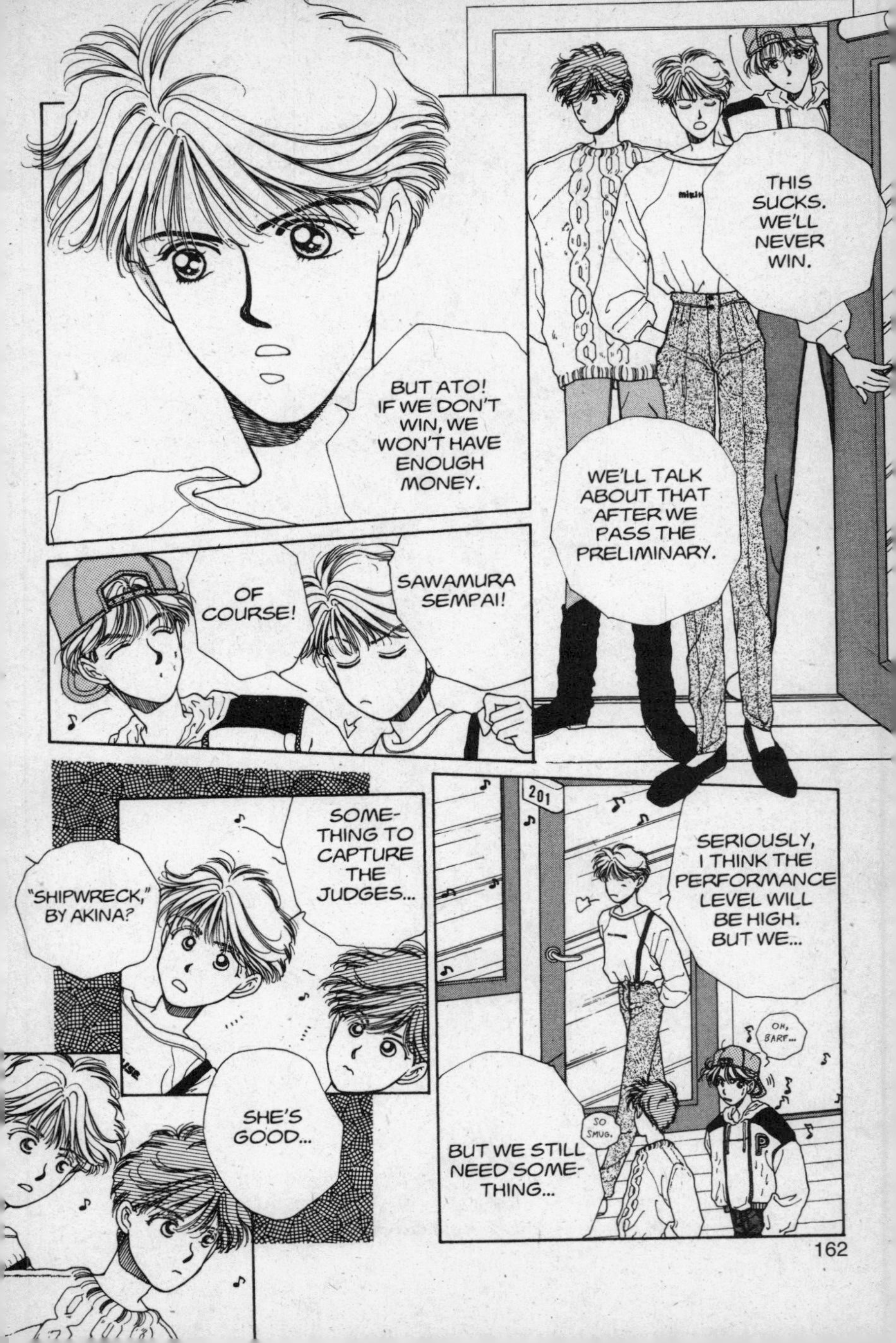

THIS SUCKS. WE'LL NEVER WIN.
WE'LL TALK ABOUT THAT AFTER WE PASS THE PRELIMINARY.
BUT ATO! IF WE DON'T WIN, WE WON'T HAVE ENOUGH MONEY.
SAWAMURA SEMPAI!
OF COURSE!
SERIOUSLY, I THINK THE PERFORMANCE LEVEL WILL BE HIGH. BUT WE...
OH, BARF...
SO SMUG.
BUT WE STILL NEED SOME-THING...
SOME-THING TO CAPTURE THE JUDGES...
"SHIPWRECK," BY AKINA?
SHE'S GOOD...

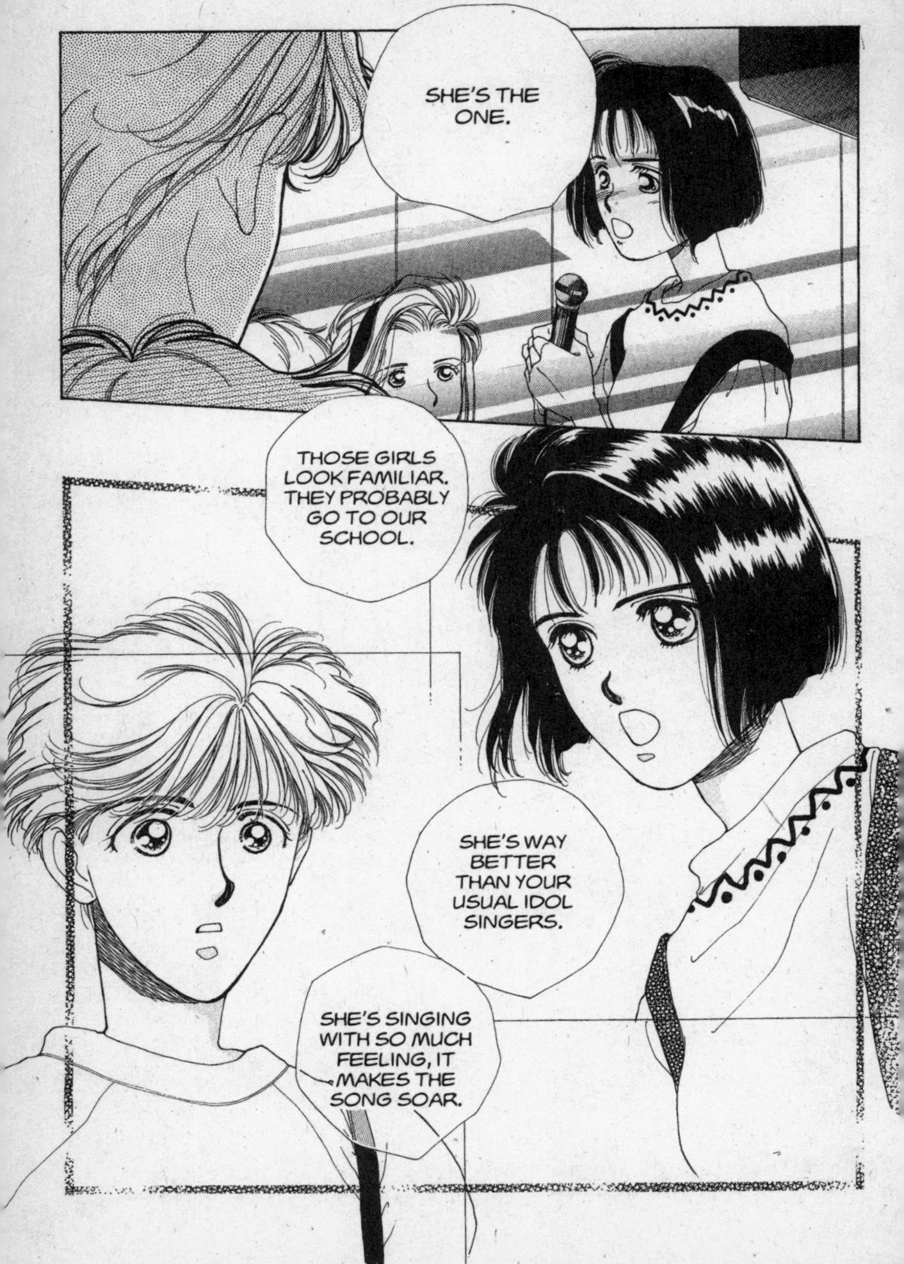
SHE'S THE ONE.
THOSE GIRLS LOOK FAMILIAR. THEY PROBABLY GO TO OUR SCHOOL.
SHE'S WAY BETTER THAN YOUR USUAL IDOL SINGERS.
SHE'S SINGING WITH SO MUCH FEELING, IT MAKES THE SONG SOAR.

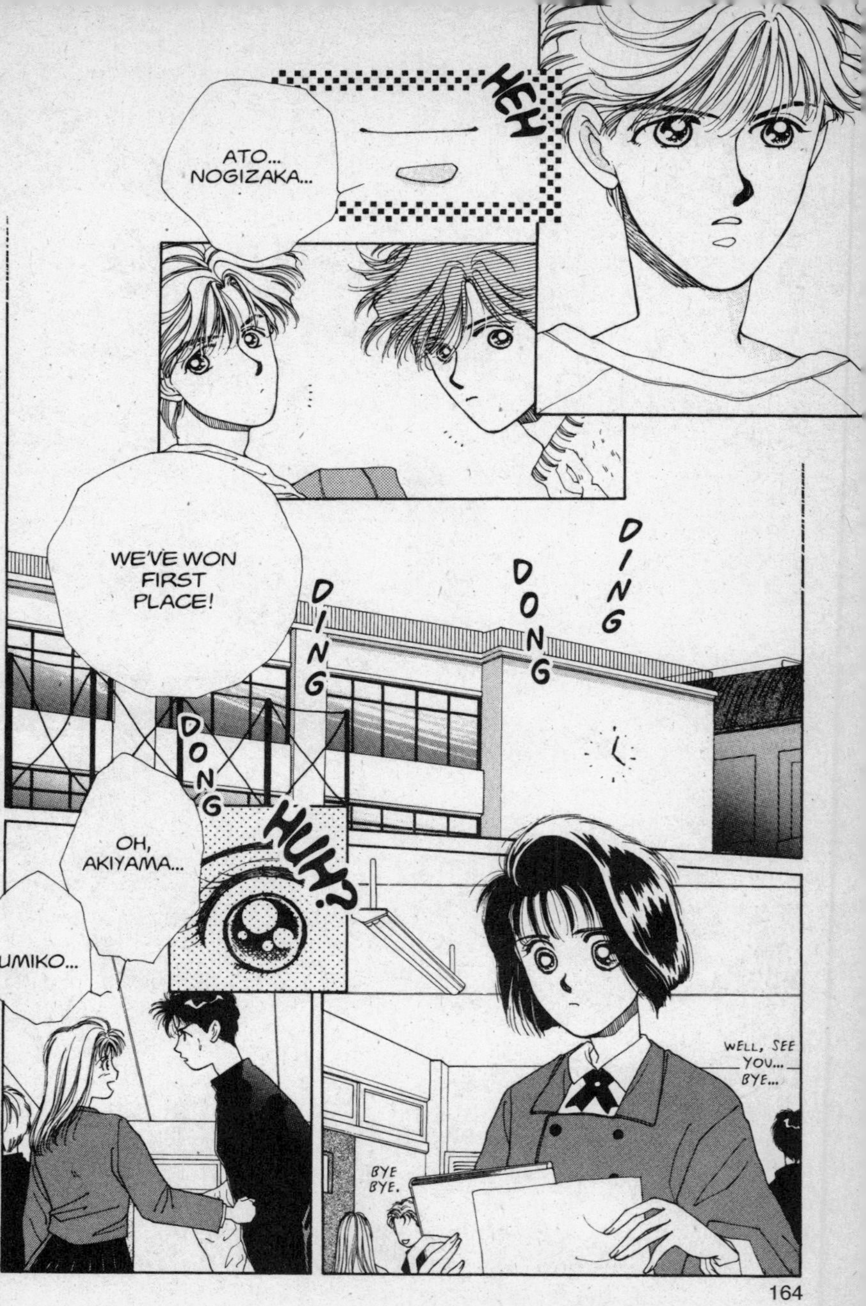
HEH
ATO... NOGIZAKA...
WE'VE WON FIRST PLACE!
DING
DONG
DING
DONG
WELL, SEE YOU... BYE...
BYE BYE.
HUH?
OH, AKIYAMA...
KUMIKO...

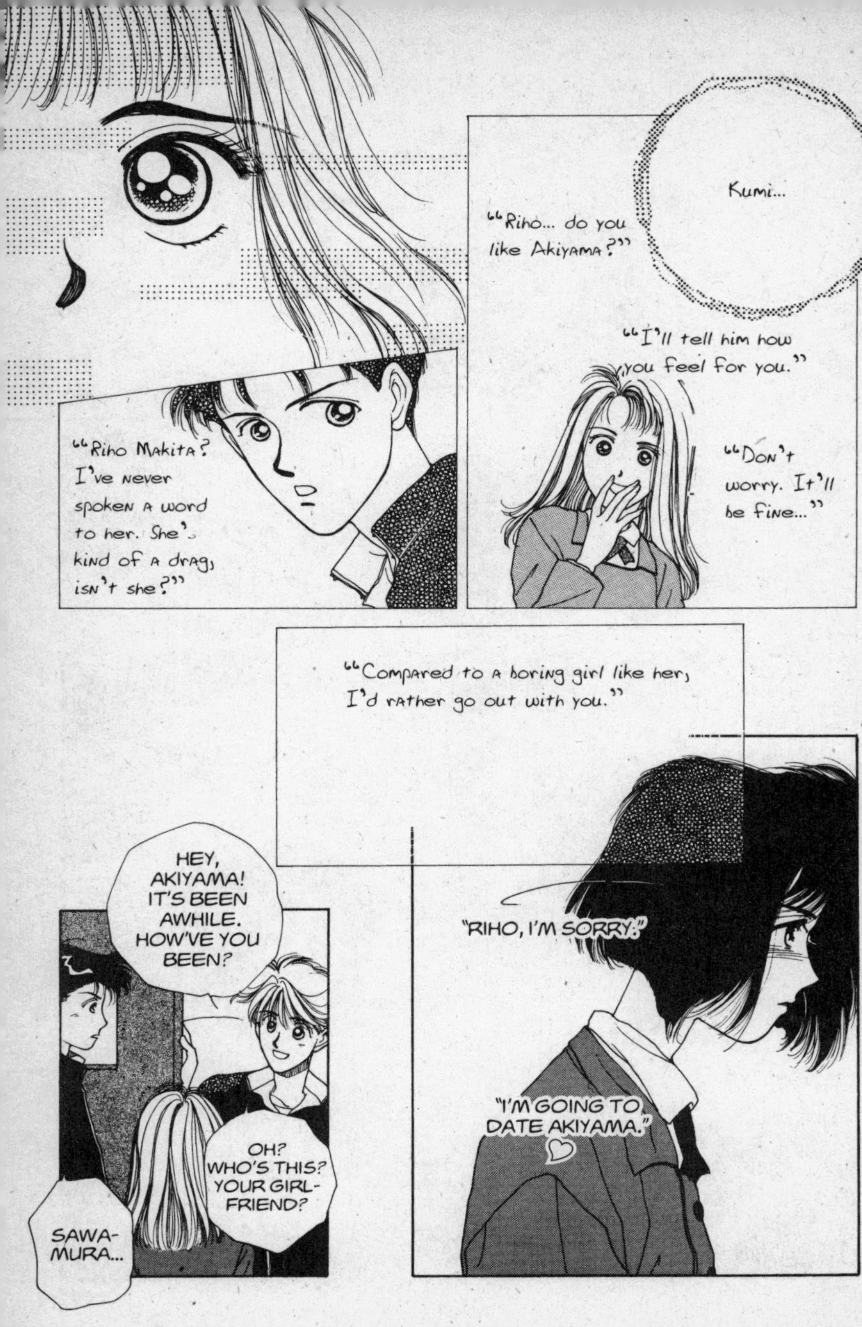
Kumi...
"Riho... do you like Akiyama?"
"I'll tell him how you feel for you."
"Don't worry. It'll be fine..."
"Riho Makita? I've never spoken a word to her. She's kind of a drag, isn't she?"
"Compared to a boring girl like her, I'd rather go out with you."
"RIHO, I'M SORRY."
"I'M GOING TO DATE AKIYAMA."
HEY, AKIYAMA! IT'S BEEN AWHILE. HOW'VE YOU BEEN?
OH? WHO'S THIS? YOUR GIRL-FRIEND?
SAWAMURA...

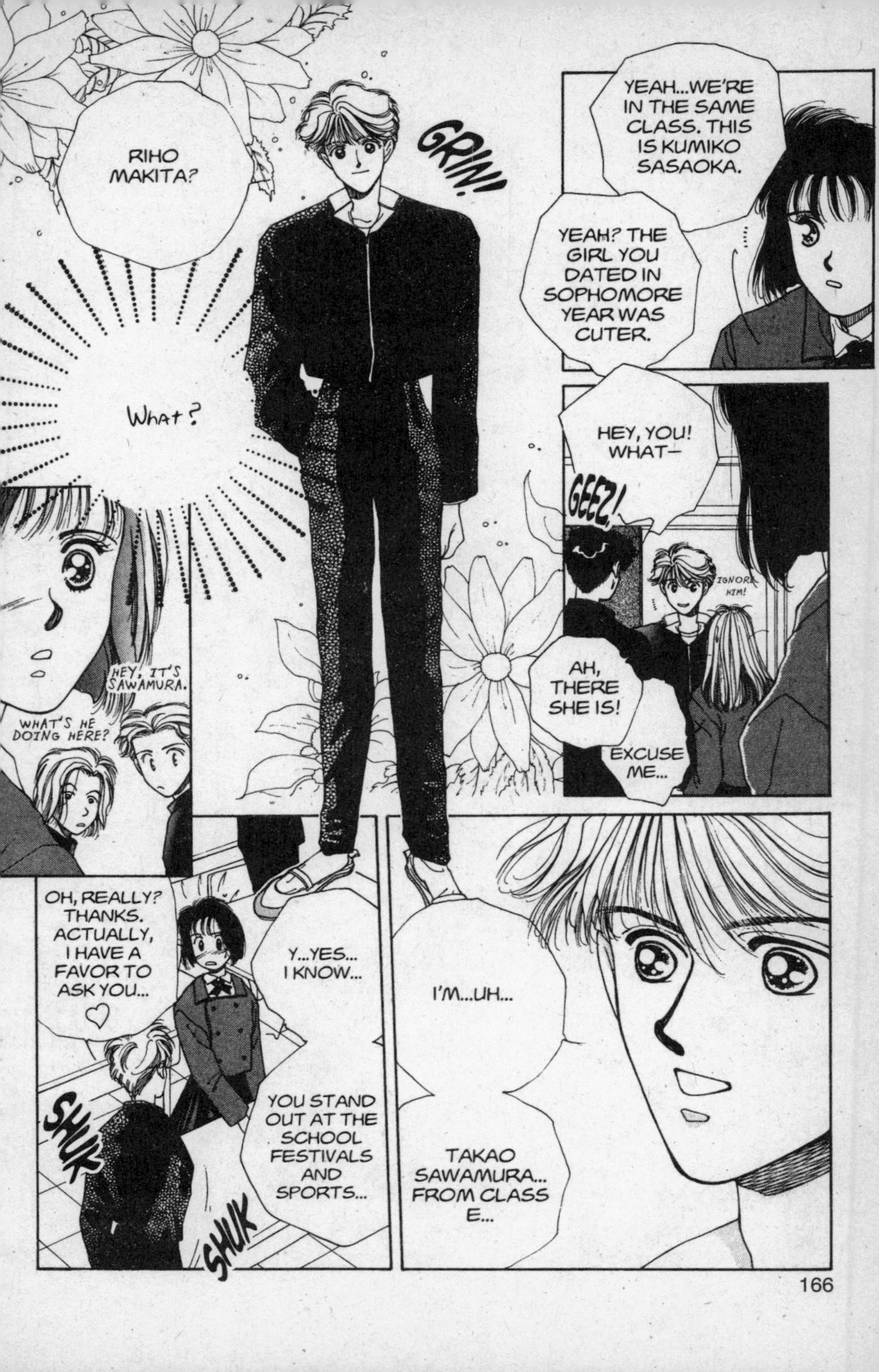
YEAH...WE'RE IN THE SAME CLASS. THIS IS KUMIKO SASAOKA.
YEAH? THE GIRL YOU DATED IN SOPHOMORE YEAR WAS CUTER.
HEY, YOU! WHAT—
GEEZ!
IGNORE HIM!
AH, THERE SHE IS!
EXCUSE ME...
RIHO MAKITA?
GRIN!
What?
HEY, IT'S SAWAMURA.
WHAT'S HE DOING HERE?
I'M...UH...
TAKAO SAWAMURA... FROM CLASS E...
Y...YES... I KNOW...
YOU STAND OUT AT THE SCHOOL FESTIVALS AND SPORTS...
OH, REALLY? THANKS. ACTUALLY, I HAVE A FAVOR TO ASK YOU... ♡
SHUK
SHUK

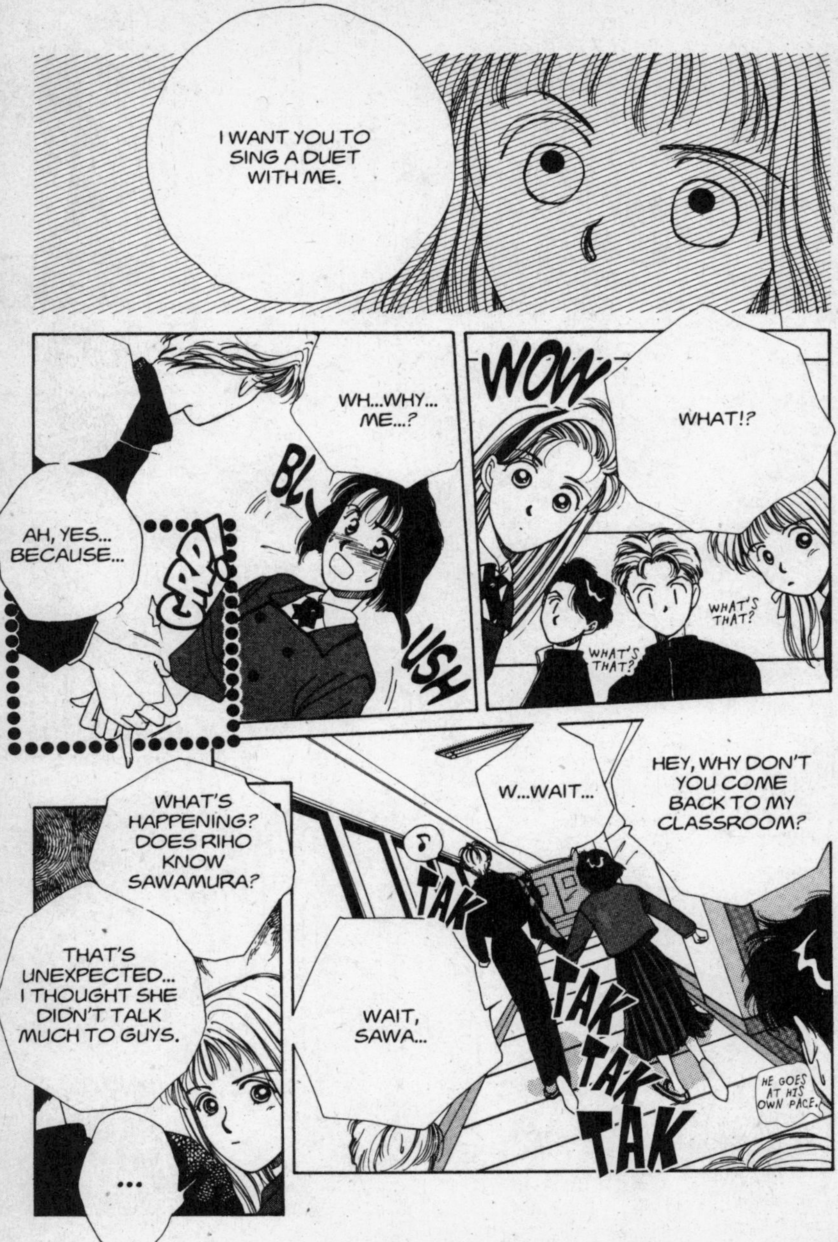
I WANT YOU TO SING A DUET WITH ME.
WOW
WHAT!?
WHAT'S THAT?
WHAT'S THAT?
WH...WHY... ME...?
BLUSH
GRP!
AH, YES... BECAUSE...
HEY, WHY DON'T YOU COME BACK TO MY CLASSROOM?
W...WAIT...
TAK
TAK
TAK
TAK
HE GOES AT HIS OWN PACE.
WAIT, SAWA...
WHAT'S HAPPENING? DOES RIHO KNOW SAWAMURA?
THAT'S UNEXPECTED... I THOUGHT SHE DIDN'T TALK MUCH TO GUYS.
...

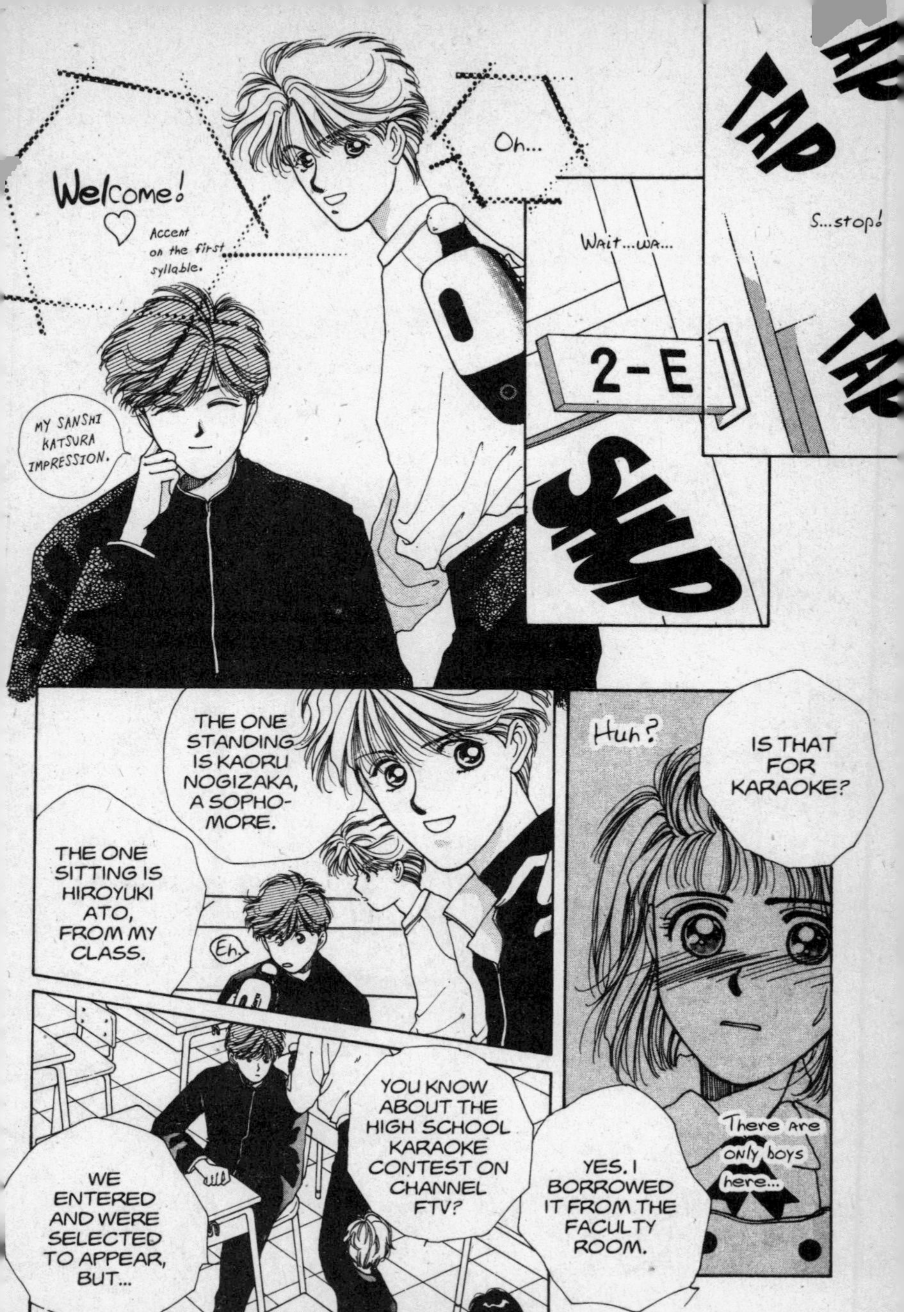
TAP
TAP
S...stop!
TAP
Wait...wa...
2-E
SHUP
Oh...
Welcome!
Accent on the first syllable.
MY SANSHI KATSURA IMPRESSION.
IS THAT FOR KARAOKE?
Huh?
There are only boys here...
THE ONE STANDING IS KAORU NOGIZAKA, A SOPHOMORE.
THE ONE SITTING IS HIROYUKI ATO, FROM MY CLASS.
Eh.
YES. I BORROWED IT FROM THE FACULTY ROOM.
YOU KNOW ABOUT THE HIGH SCHOOL KARAOKE CONTEST ON CHANNEL FTV?
WE ENTERED AND WERE SELECTED TO APPEAR, BUT...

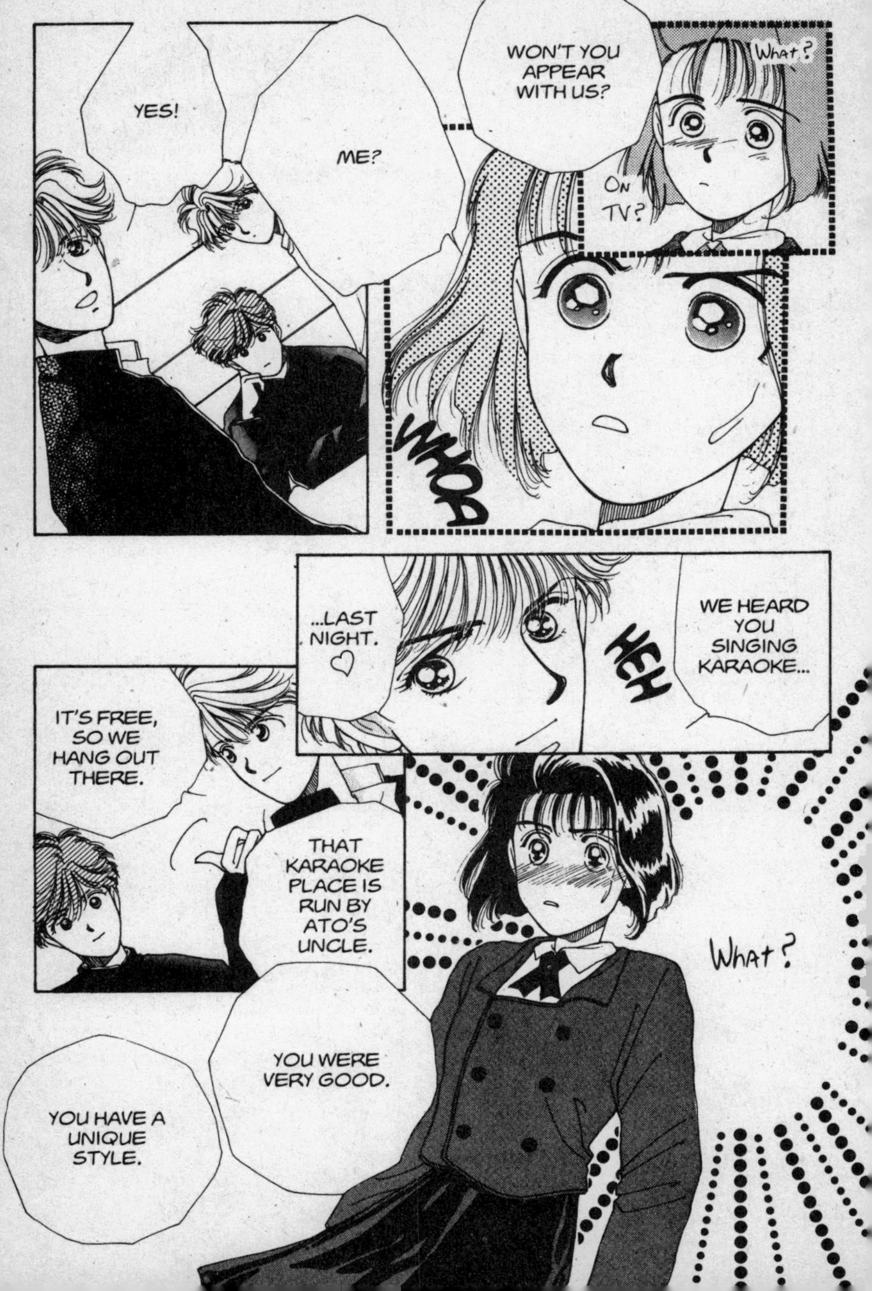
WON'T YOU APPEAR WITH US?
What?
ON TV?
WHOA
ME?
YES!
WE HEARD YOU SINGING KARAOKE...
HEH
...LAST NIGHT. ♡
THAT KARAOKE PLACE IS RUN BY ATO'S UNCLE.
IT'S FREE, SO WE HANG OUT THERE.
What?
YOU WERE VERY GOOD.
YOU HAVE A UNIQUE STYLE.

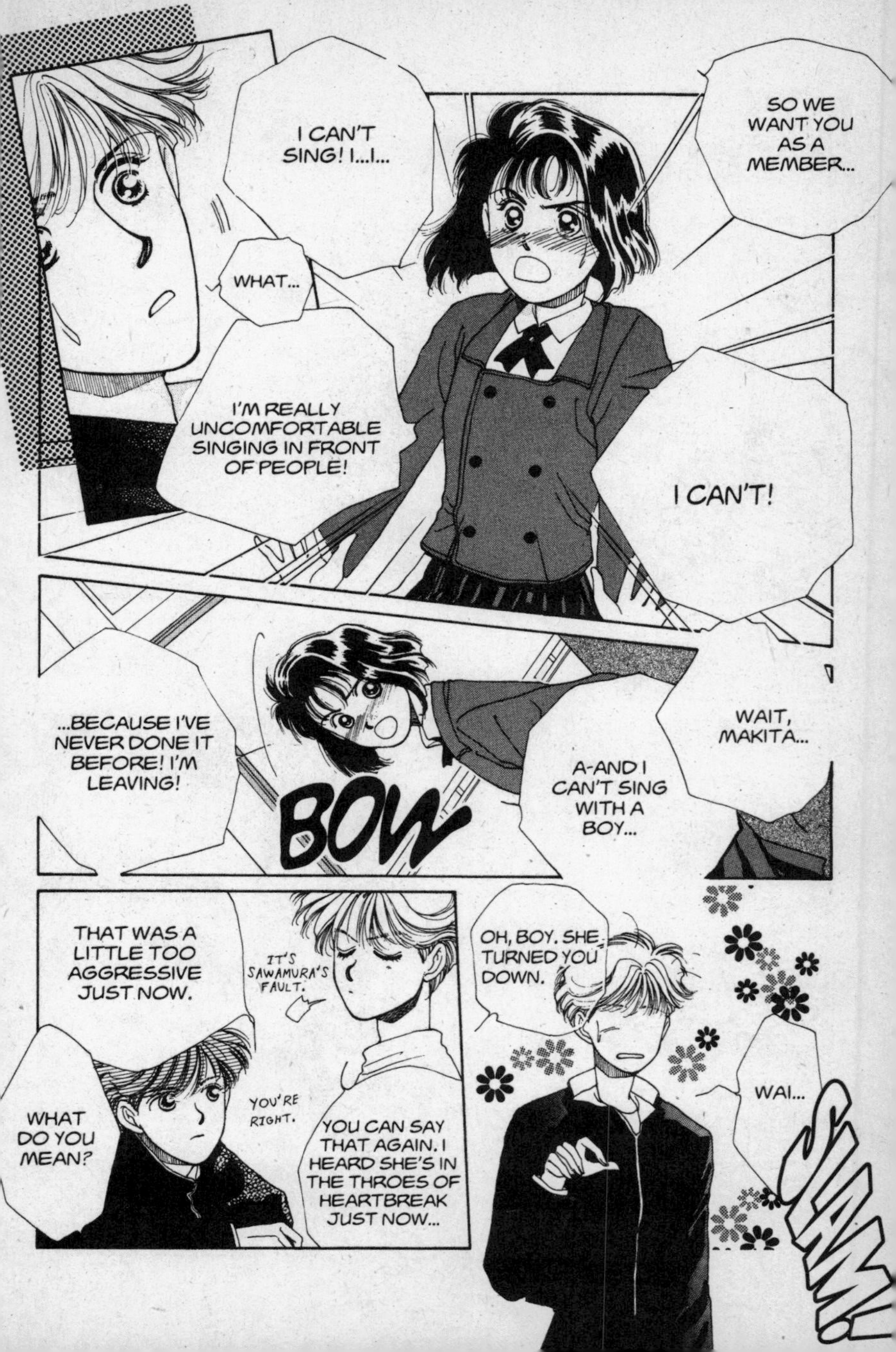
SO WE WANT YOU AS A MEMBER...
I CAN'T!
I CAN'T SING! I...I...
WHAT...
I'M REALLY UNCOMFORTABLE SINGING IN FRONT OF PEOPLE!
WAIT, MAKITA...
A-AND I CAN'T SING WITH A BOY...
...BECAUSE I'VE NEVER DONE IT BEFORE! I'M LEAVING!
BOW
WAI...
SLAM!
OH, BOY. SHE TURNED YOU DOWN.
IT'S SAWAMURA'S FAULT.
THAT WAS A LITTLE TOO AGGRESSIVE JUST NOW.
YOU CAN SAY THAT AGAIN. I HEARD SHE'S IN THE THROES OF HEARTBREAK JUST NOW...
YOU'RE RIGHT.
WHAT DO YOU MEAN?

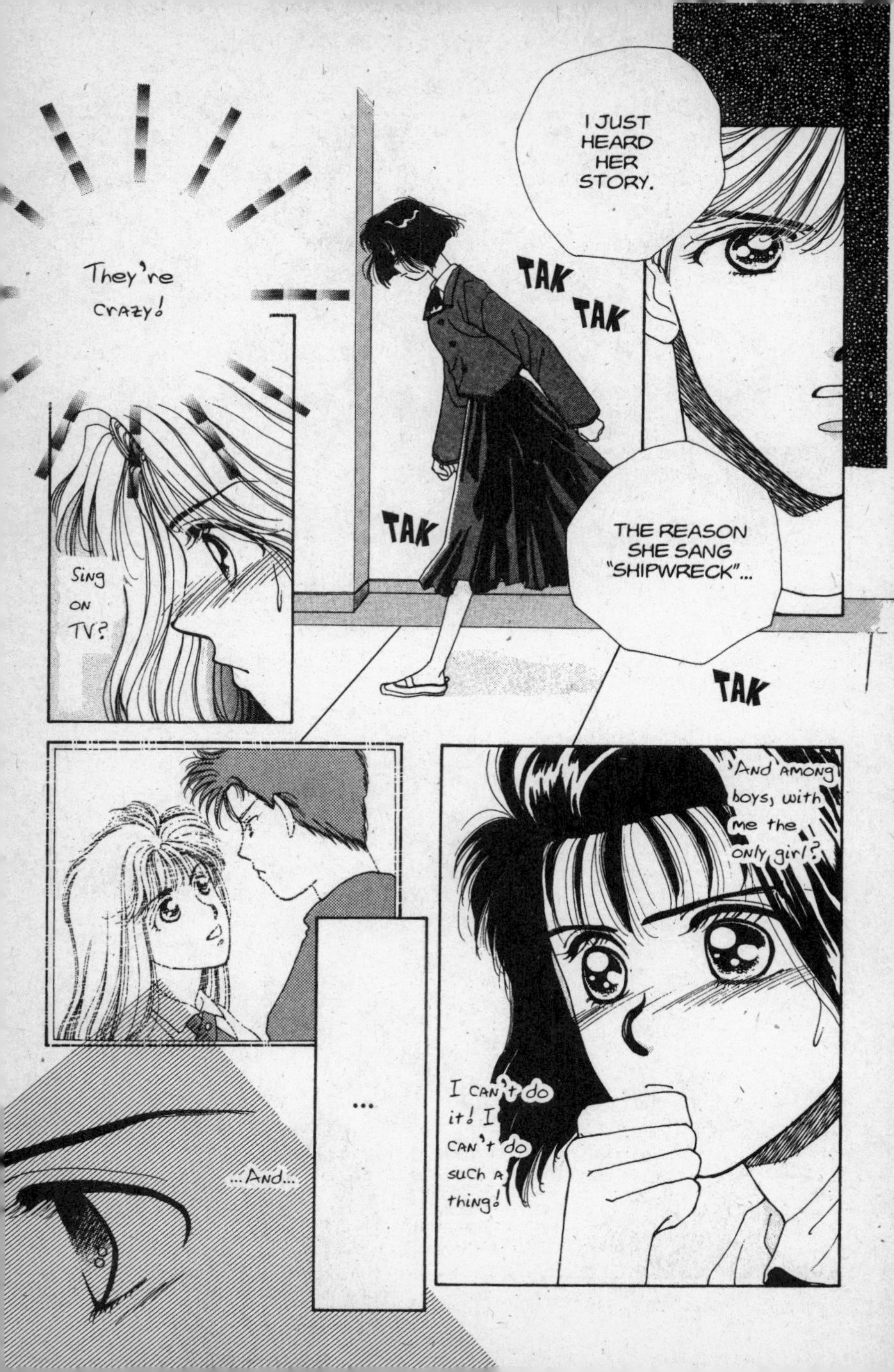
I JUST HEARD HER STORY.
TAK
TAK
THE REASON SHE SANG "SHIPWRECK"...
TAK
TAK
They're crazy!
Sing on TV?
And among boys, with me the only girl?
I can't do it! I can't do such a thing!
...
...And...

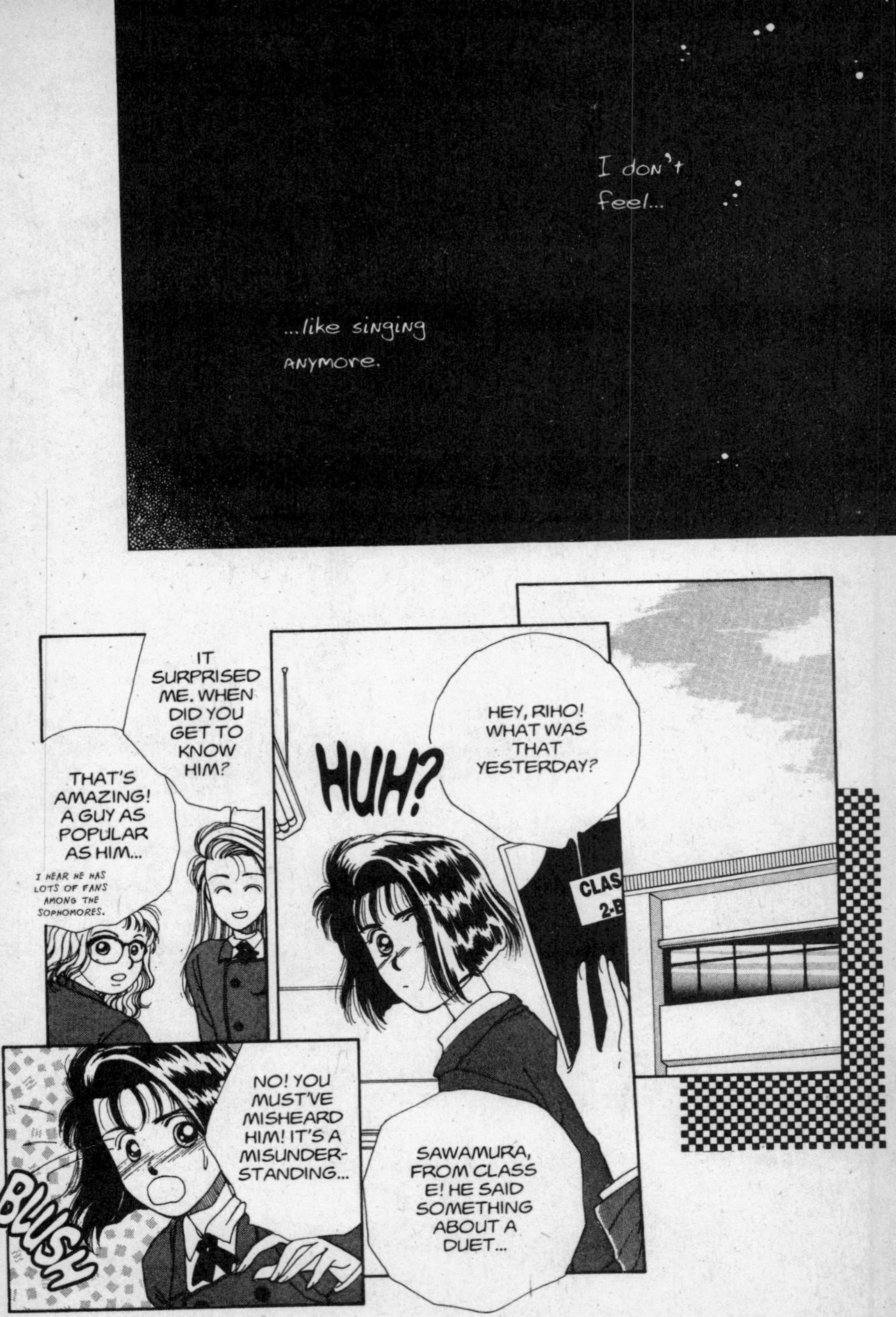
I don't feel...
...like singing anymore.
HEY, RIHO! WHAT WAS THAT YESTERDAY?
HUH?
IT SURPRISED ME. WHEN DID YOU GET TO KNOW HIM?
THAT'S AMAZING! A GUY AS POPULAR AS HIM...
I HEAR HE HAS LOTS OF FANS AMONG THE SOPHOMORES.
SAWAMURA, FROM CLASS E! HE SAID SOMETHING ABOUT A DUET...
NO! YOU MUST'VE MISHEARD HIM! IT'S A MISUNDER-STANDING...
BLUSH

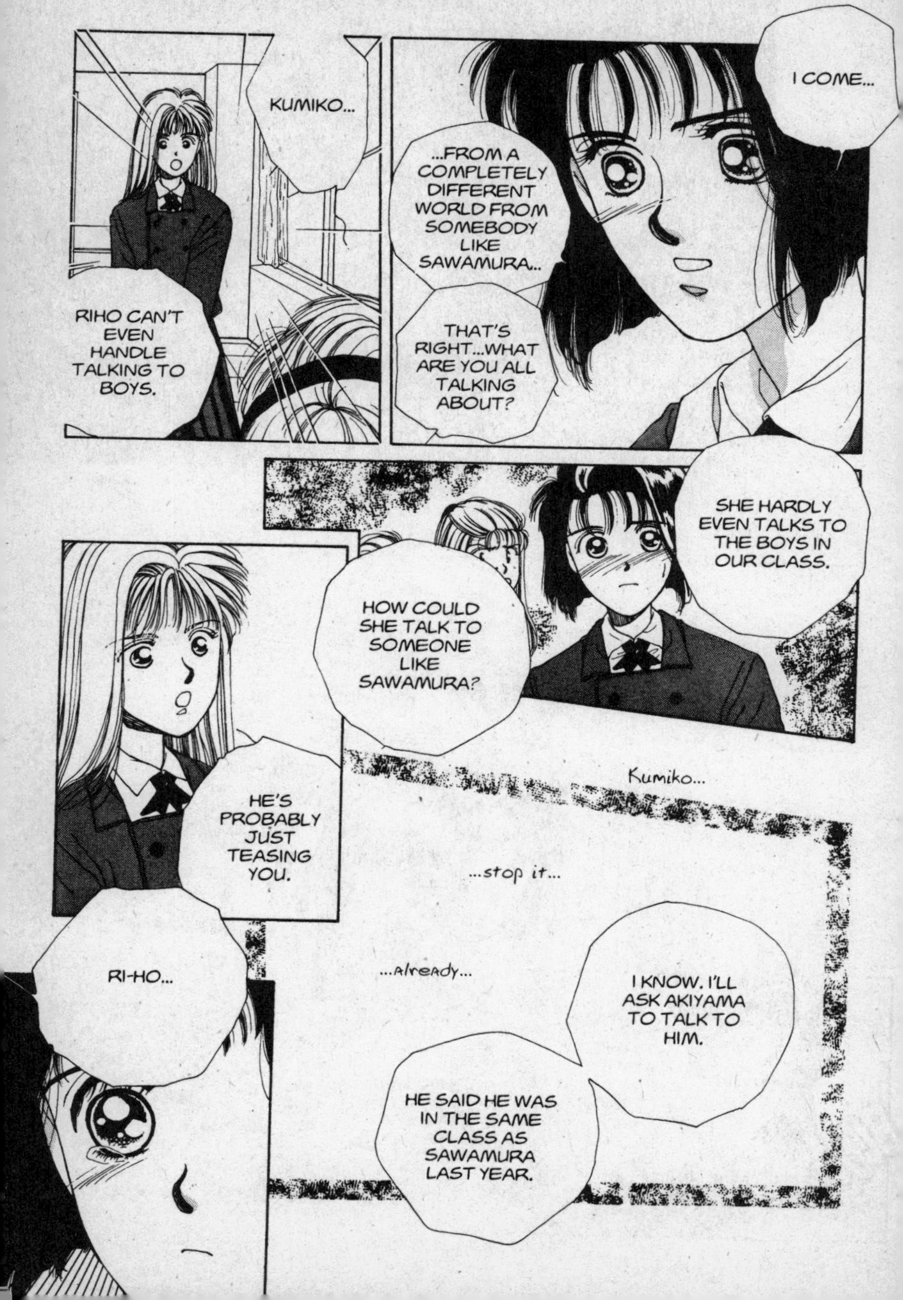
I COME...
...FROM A COMPLETELY DIFFERENT WORLD FROM SOMEBODY LIKE SAWAMURA...
THAT'S RIGHT...WHAT ARE YOU ALL TALKING ABOUT?
KUMIKO...
RIHO CAN'T EVEN HANDLE TALKING TO BOYS.
SHE HARDLY EVEN TALKS TO THE BOYS IN OUR CLASS.
HOW COULD SHE TALK TO SOMEONE LIKE SAWAMURA?
HE'S PROBABLY JUST TEASING YOU.
Kumiko...
...stop it...
...already...
I KNOW. I'LL ASK AKIYAMA TO TALK TO HIM.
HE SAID HE WAS IN THE SAME CLASS AS SAWAMURA LAST YEAR.
RI-HO...

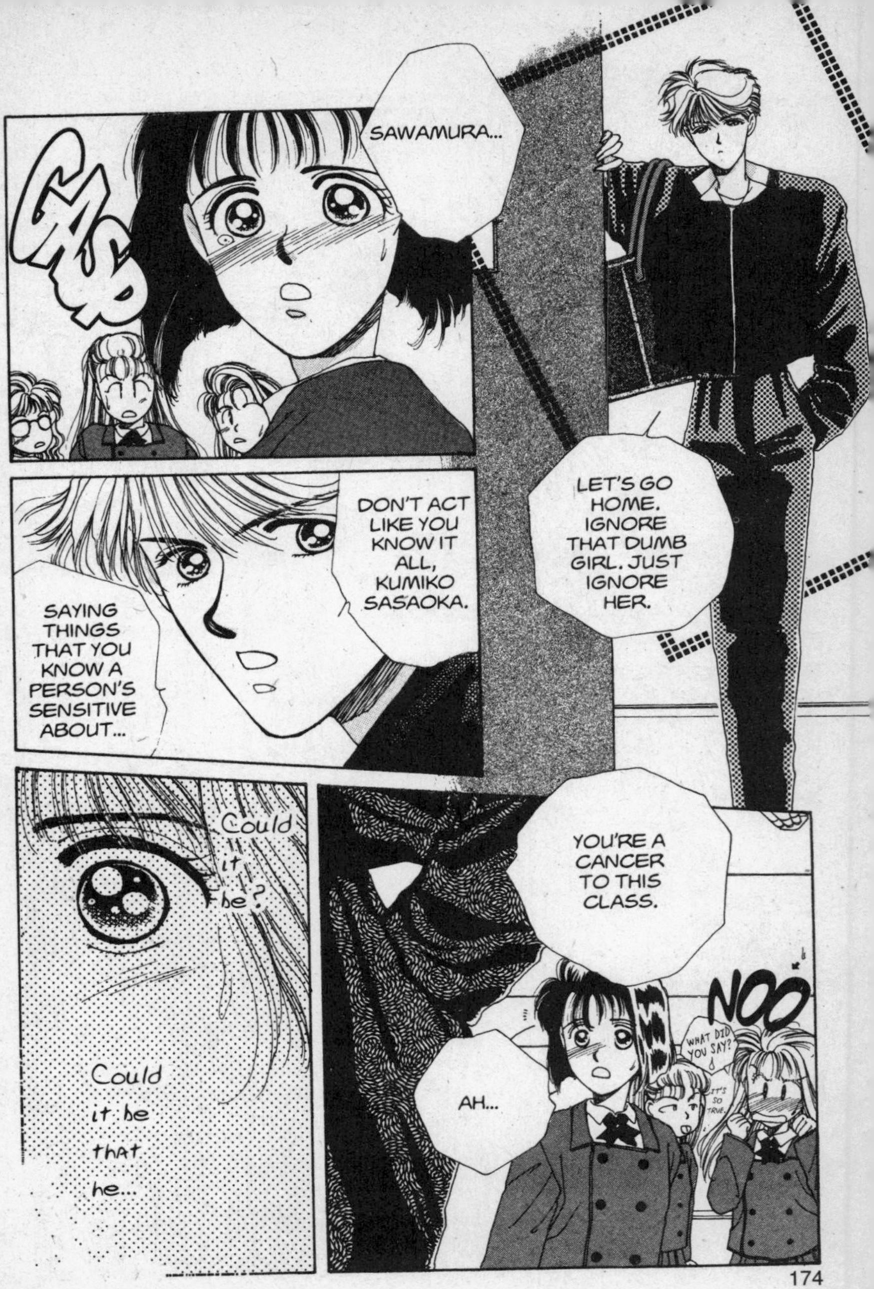
SAWAMURA...
GASP
DON'T ACT LIKE YOU KNOW IT ALL, KUMIKO SASAOKA.
SAYING THINGS THAT YOU KNOW A PERSON'S SENSITIVE ABOUT...
LET'S GO HOME. IGNORE THAT DUMB GIRL. JUST IGNORE HER.
YOU'RE A CANCER TO THIS CLASS.
NOO
WHAT DID YOU SAY?
IT'S SO TRUE.
AH...
Could it be?
Could it be that he...

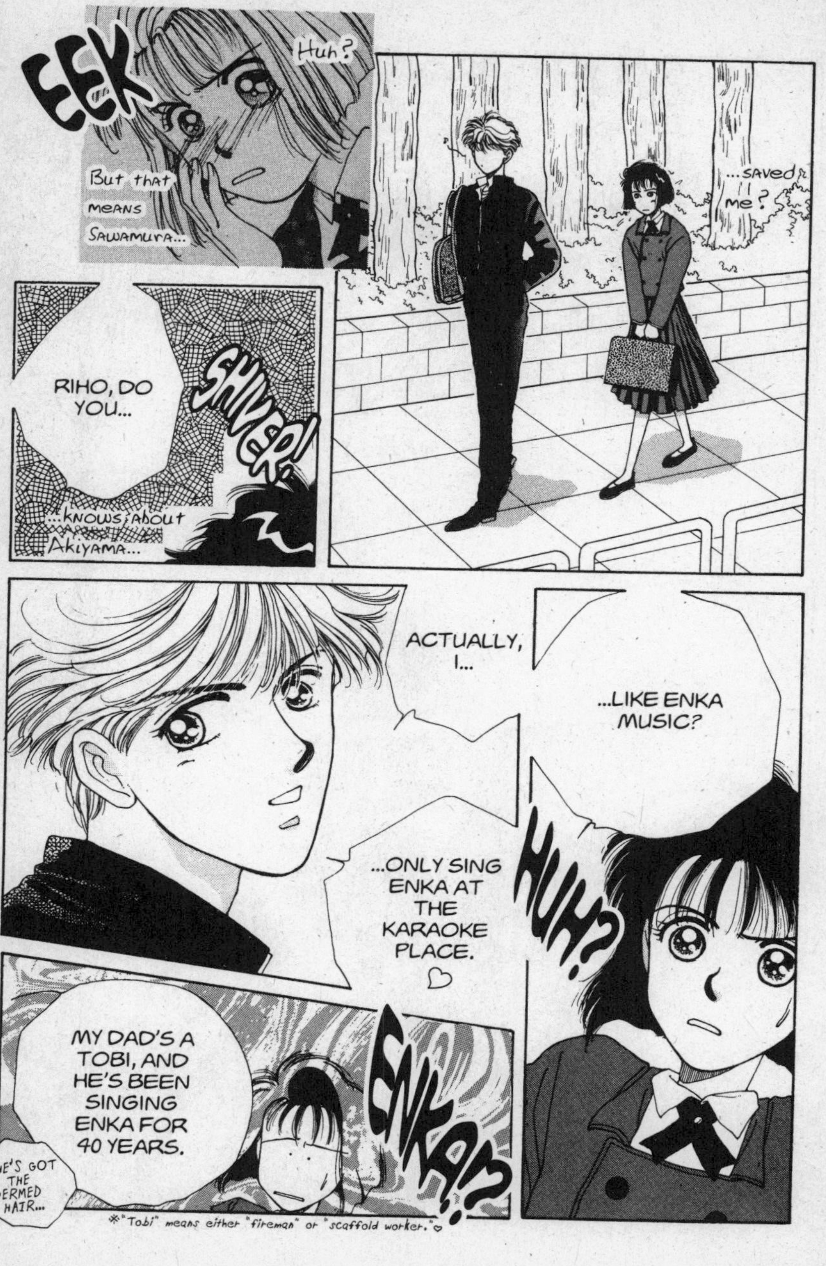
...saved me?
Huh?
But that means Sawamura...
EEK
RIHO, DO YOU...
SHIVER!
...knows about Akiyama...
...LIKE ENKA MUSIC?
HUH?
ACTUALLY, I...
...ONLY SING ENKA AT THE KARAOKE PLACE. ♡
MY DAD'S A TOBI, AND HE'S BEEN SINGING ENKA FOR 40 YEARS.
ENKA!?
HE'S GOT THE PERMED HAIR...
※"Tobi" means either "fireman" or "scaffold worker." ♡

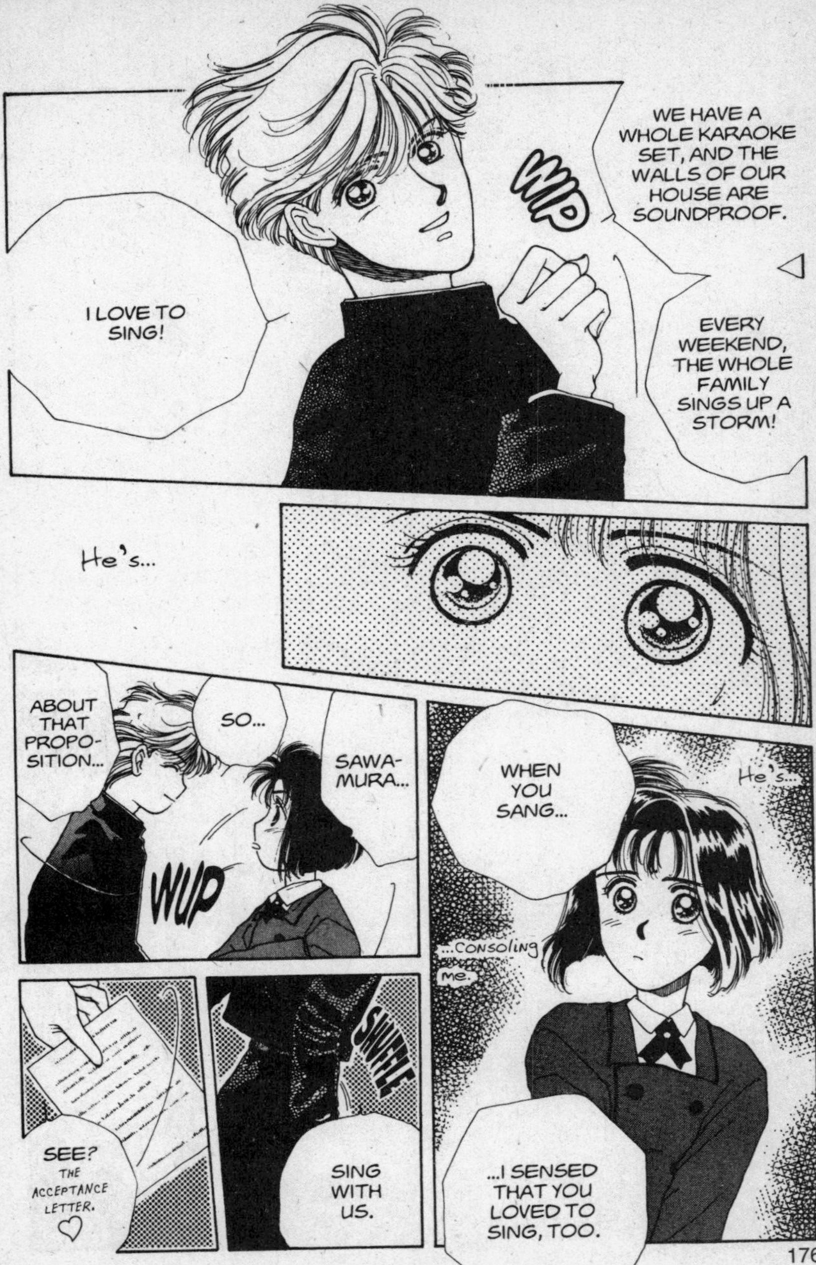
WE HAVE A WHOLE KARAOKE SET, AND THE WALLS OF OUR HOUSE ARE SOUNDPROOF.
WIP
EVERY WEEKEND, THE WHOLE FAMILY SINGS UP A STORM!
I LOVE TO SING!
He's...
WHEN YOU SANG...
He's...
...CONSOLING me.
...I SENSED THAT YOU LOVED TO SING, TOO.
SAWAMURA...
SO...
ABOUT THAT PROPOSITION...
WUP
SHUFFLE
SING WITH US.
SEE? THE ACCEPTANCE LETTER. ♡

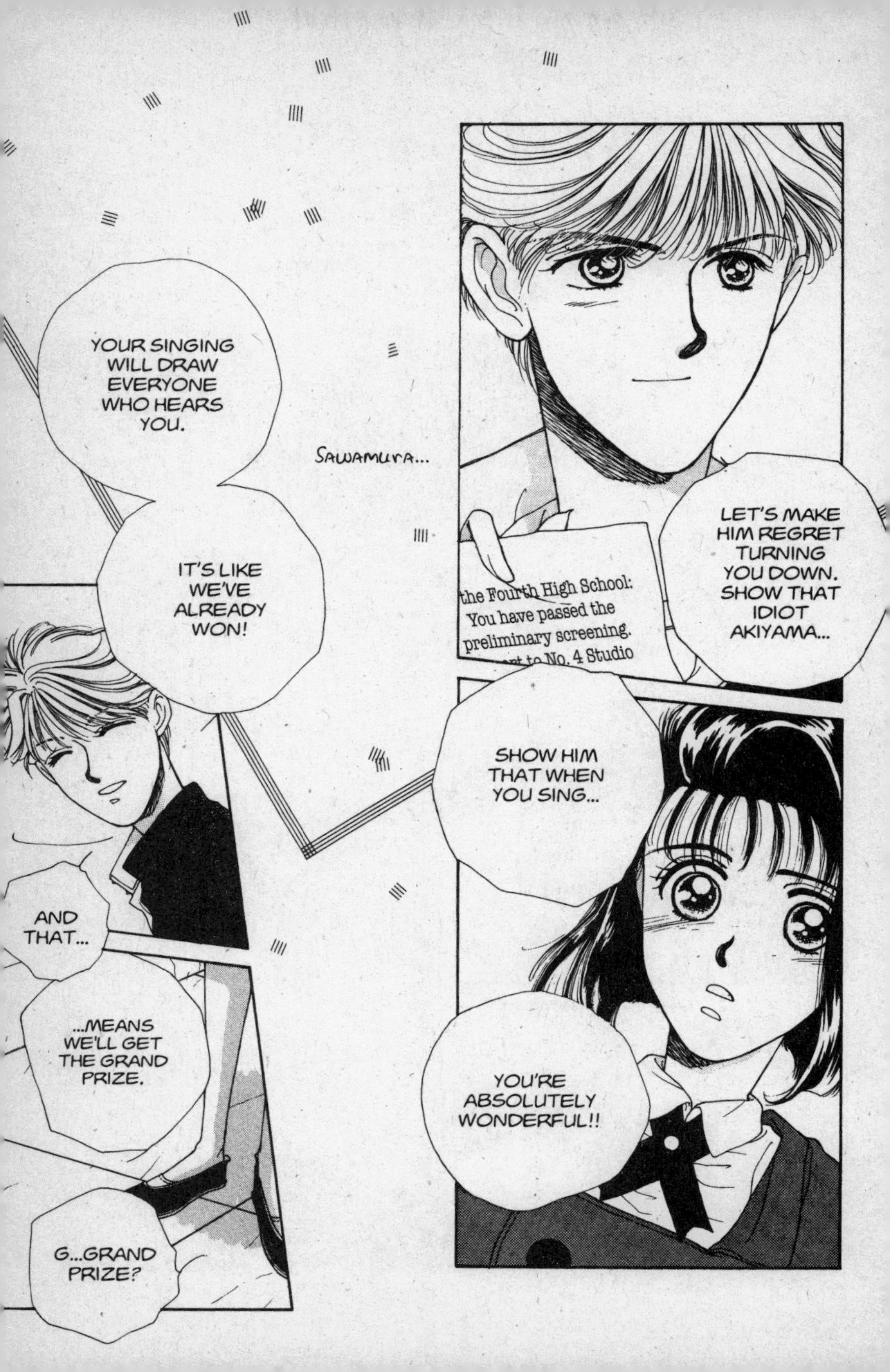
the Fourth High School:
You have passed the
preliminary screening.
LET'S MAKE HIM REGRET TURNING YOU DOWN. SHOW THAT IDIOT AKIYAMA...
SHOW HIM THAT WHEN YOU SING...
YOU'RE ABSOLUTELY WONDERFUL!!
SAWAMURA...
YOUR SINGING WILL DRAW EVERYONE WHO HEARS YOU.
IT'S LIKE WE'VE ALREADY WON!
AND THAT...
...MEANS WE'LL GET THE GRAND PRIZE.
G...GRAND PRIZE?

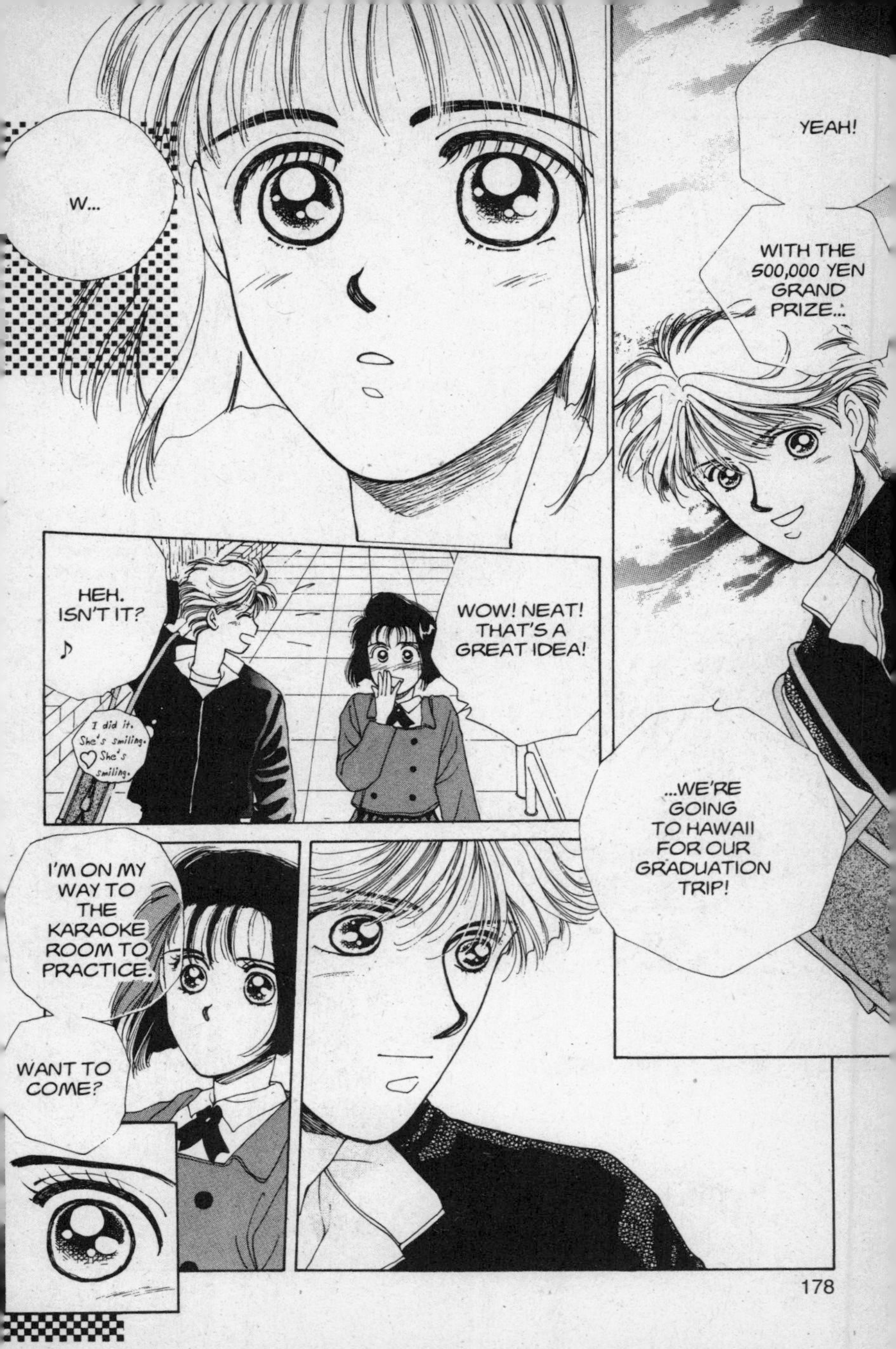
YEAH!
WITH THE 500,000 YEN GRAND PRIZE...
...WE'RE GOING TO HAWAII FOR OUR GRADUATION TRIP!
W...
WOW! NEAT! THAT'S A GREAT IDEA!
HEH. ISN'T IT? ♪
I did it. She's smiling. ♡ She's smiling.
I'M ON MY WAY TO THE KARAOKE ROOM TO PRACTICE.
WANT TO COME?

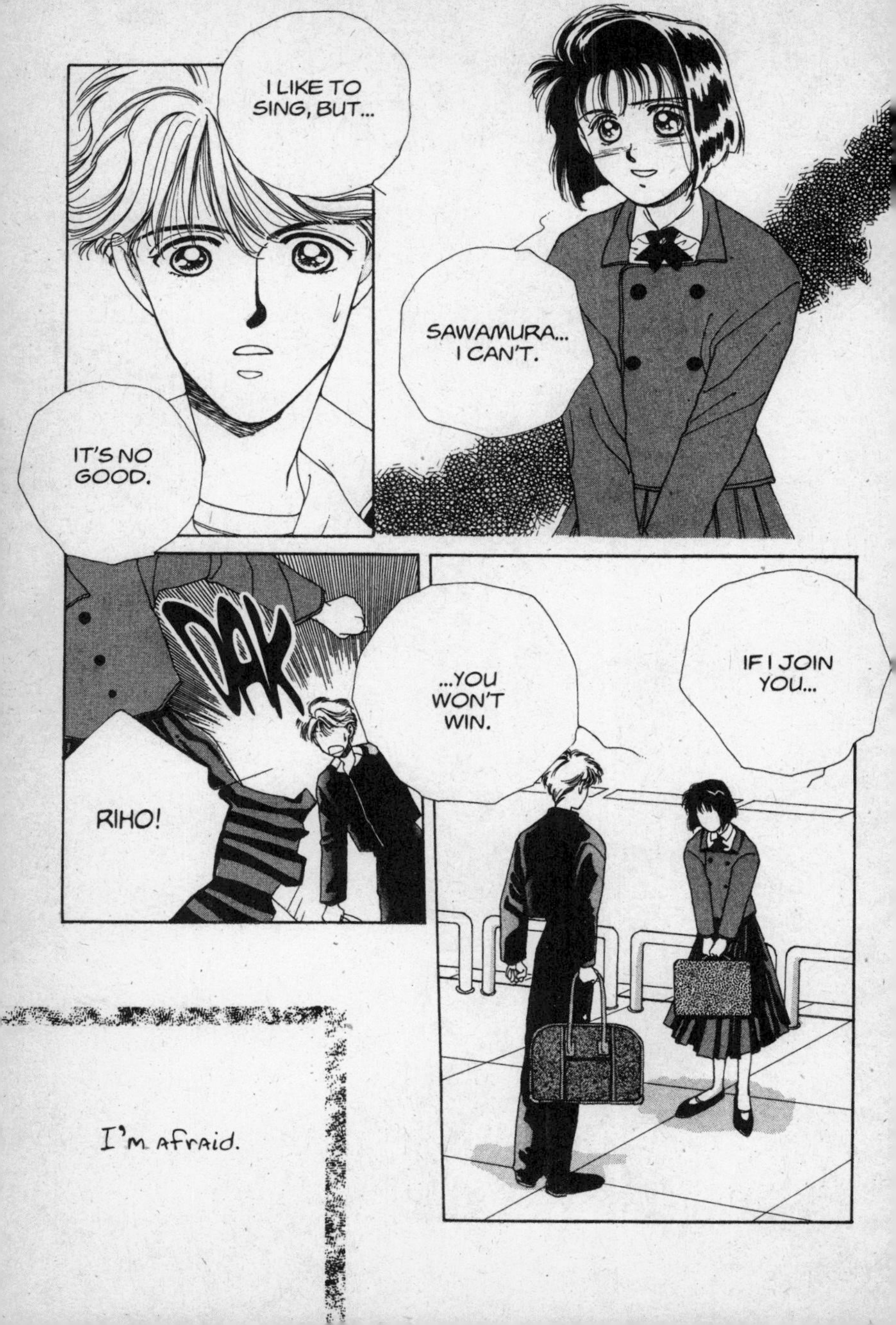
SAWAMURA... I CAN'T.
I LIKE TO SING, BUT...
IT'S NO GOOD.
IF I JOIN YOU...
...YOU WON'T WIN.
DAK
RIHO!
I'm afraid.

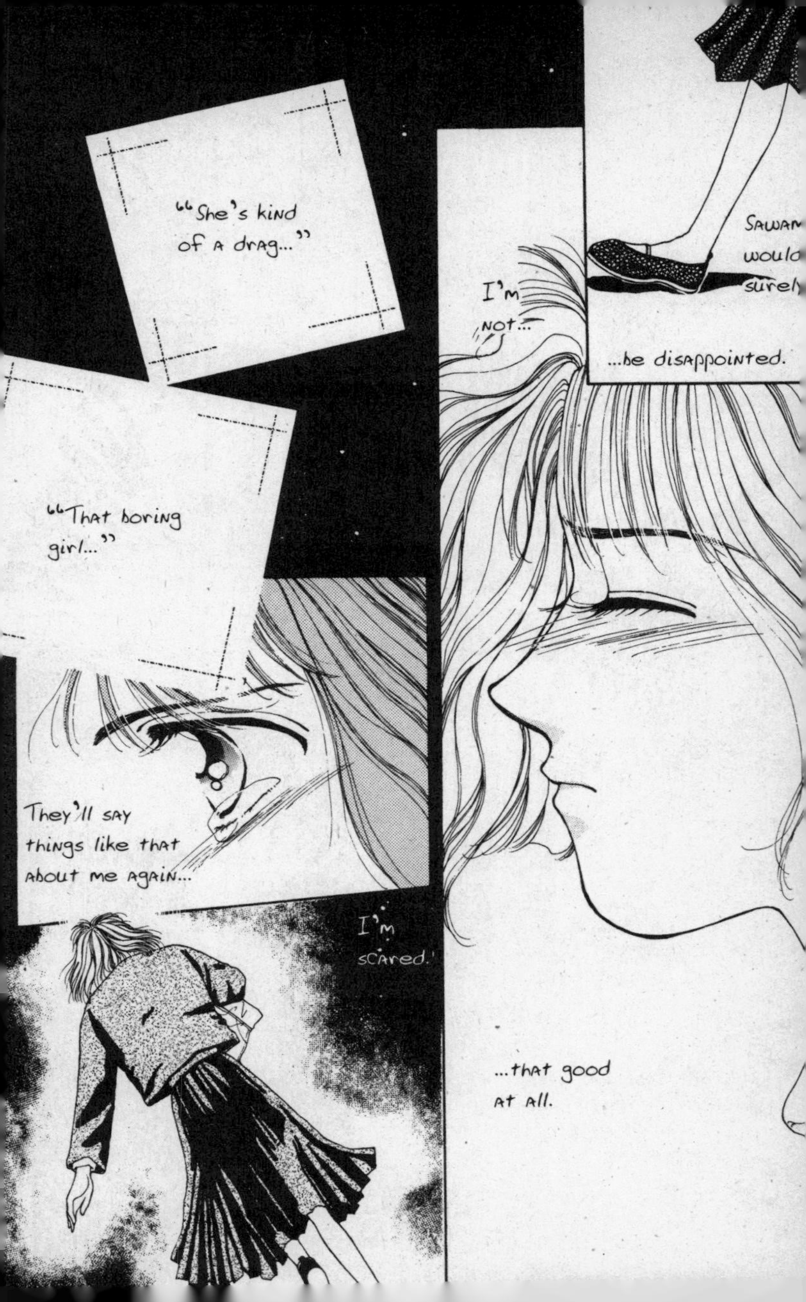

...be disappointed.
I'm not...
...that good at all.
"She's kind of a drag..."
"That boring girl..."
They'll say things like that about me again...
I'm scared.

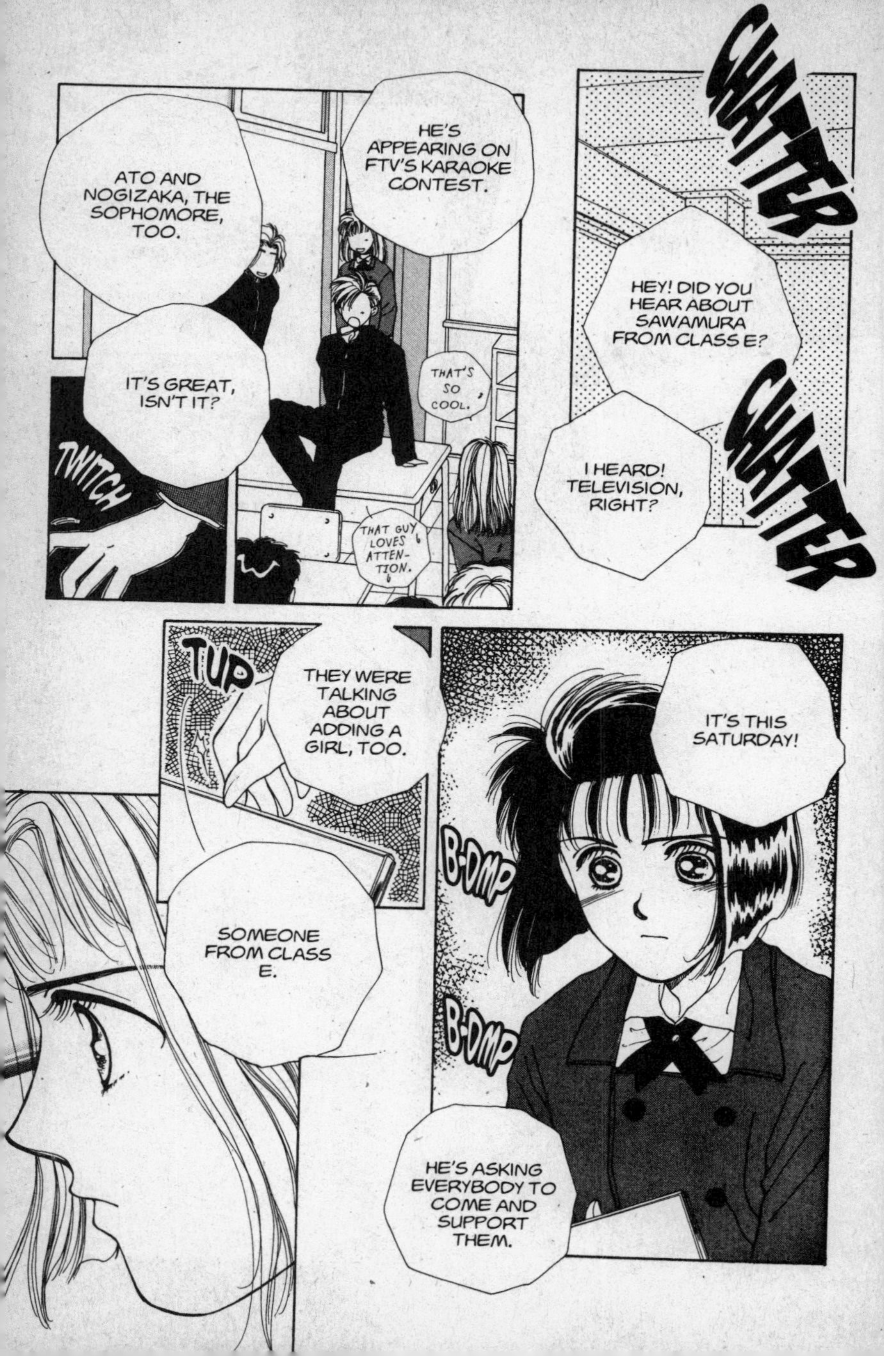
CHATTER
CHATTER
HEY! DID YOU HEAR ABOUT SAWAMURA FROM CLASS E?
I HEARD! TELEVISION, RIGHT?
HE'S APPEARING ON FTV'S KARAOKE CONTEST.
ATO AND NOGIZAKA, THE SOPHOMORE, TOO.
THAT'S SO COOL.
THAT GUY LOVES ATTENTION.
IT'S GREAT, ISN'T IT?
TWITCH
IT'S THIS SATURDAY!
B-DMP
B-DMP
HE'S ASKING EVERYBODY TO COME AND SUPPORT THEM.
TUP
THEY WERE TALKING ABOUT ADDING A GIRL, TOO.
SOMEONE FROM CLASS E.

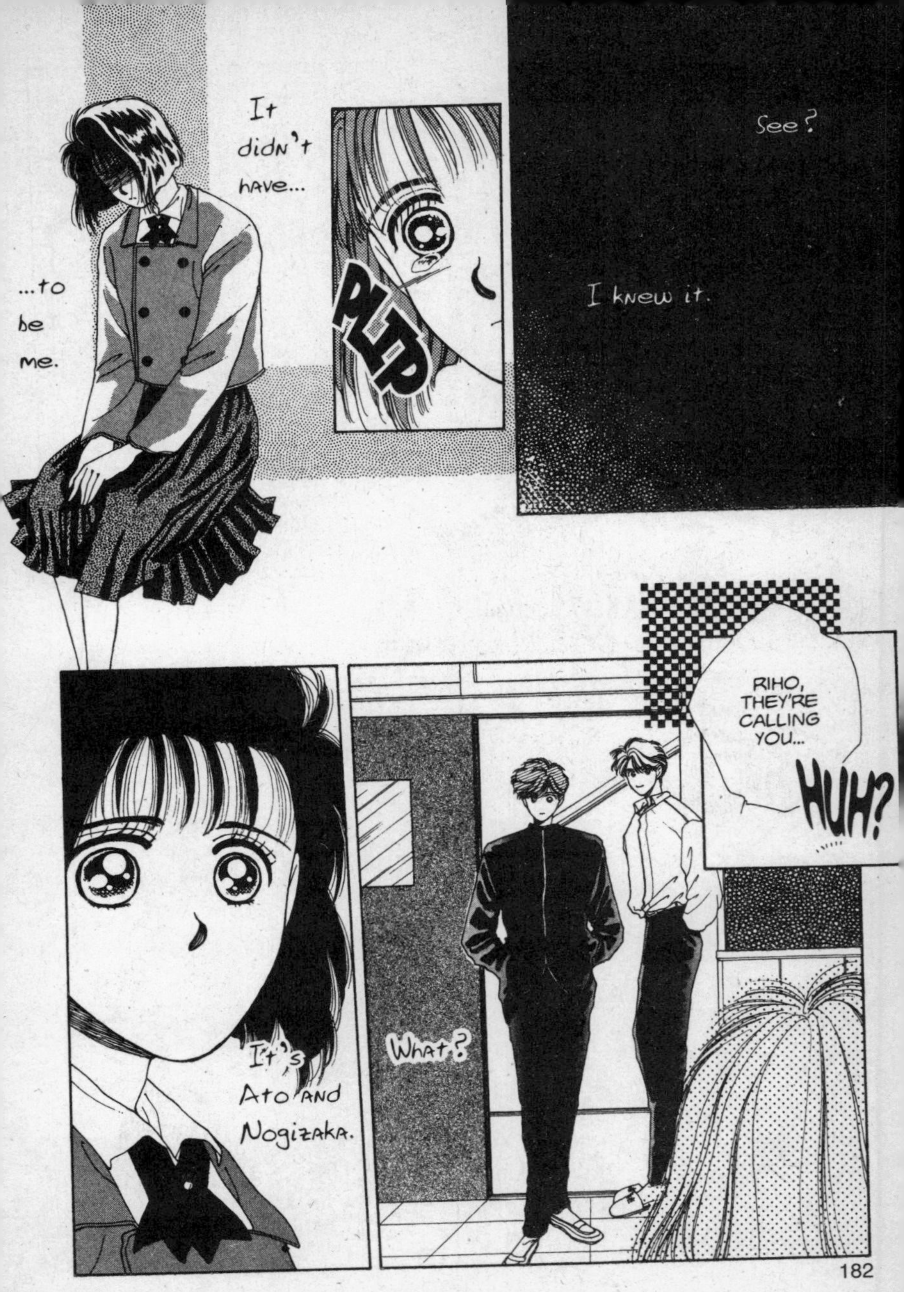

See?
I knew it.
PLIP
It didn't have...
...to be me.
RIHO, THEY'RE CALLING YOU...
HUH?
What?
It's Ato and Nogizaka.

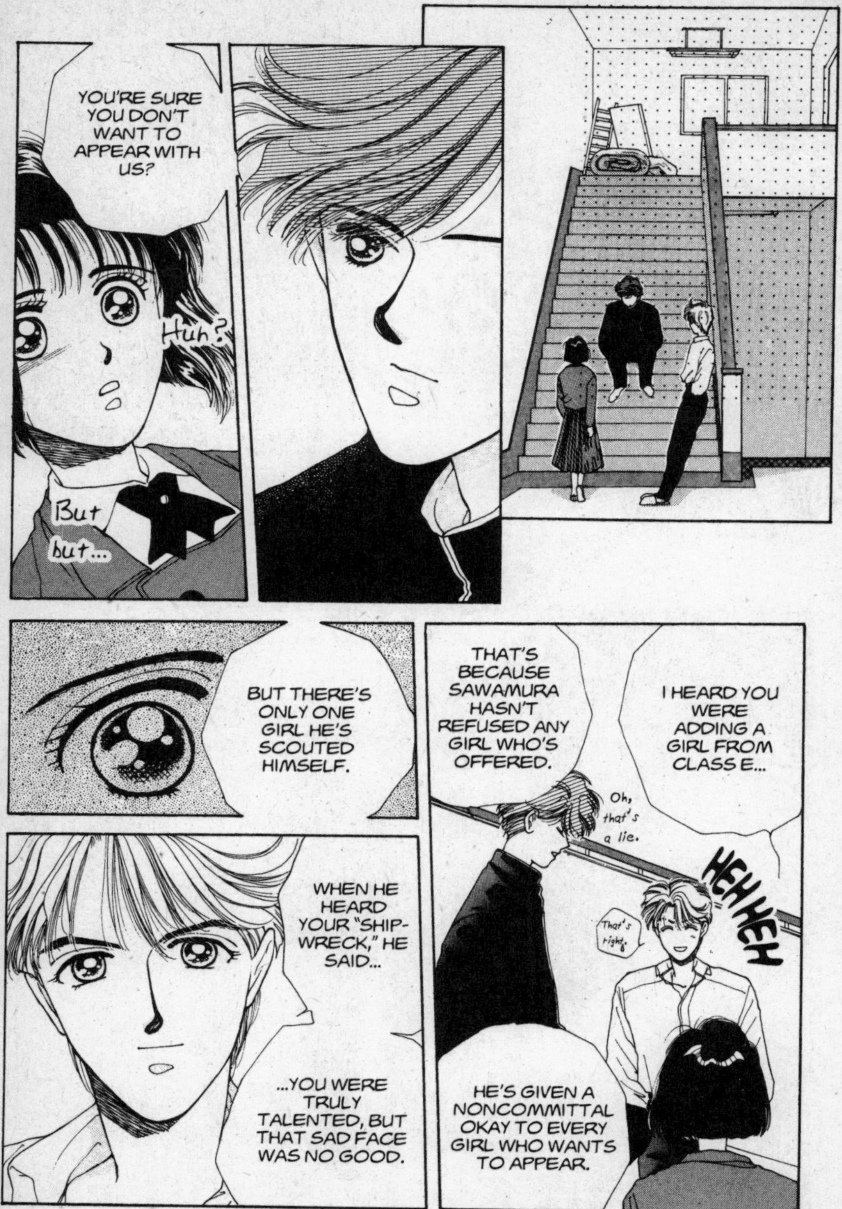
YOU'RE SURE YOU DON'T WANT TO APPEAR WITH US?
Huh?
But but...
I HEARD YOU WERE ADDING A GIRL FROM CLASS E...
THAT'S BECAUSE SAWAMURA HASN'T REFUSED ANY GIRL WHO'S OFFERED.
Oh, that's a lie.
HEH HEH
That's right.
HE'S GIVEN A NONCOMMITTAL OKAY TO EVERY GIRL WHO WANTS TO APPEAR.
BUT THERE'S ONLY ONE GIRL HE'S SCOUTED HIMSELF.
WHEN HE HEARD YOUR "SHIP-WRECK," HE SAID...
...YOU WERE TRULY TALENTED, BUT THAT SAD FACE WAS NO GOOD.

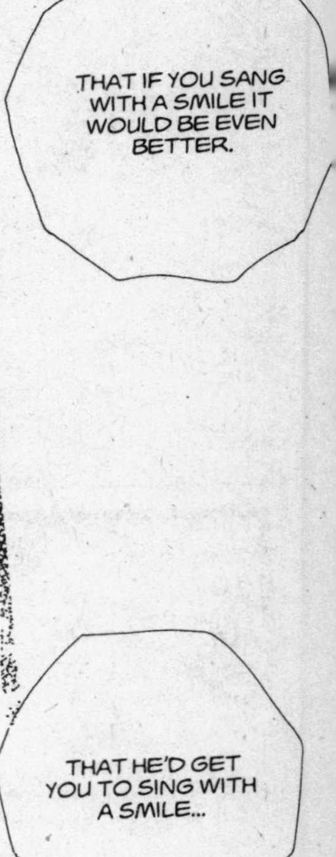
THAT IF YOU SANG WITH A SMILE IT WOULD BE EVEN BETTER.
THAT HE'D GET YOU TO SING WITH A SMILE...

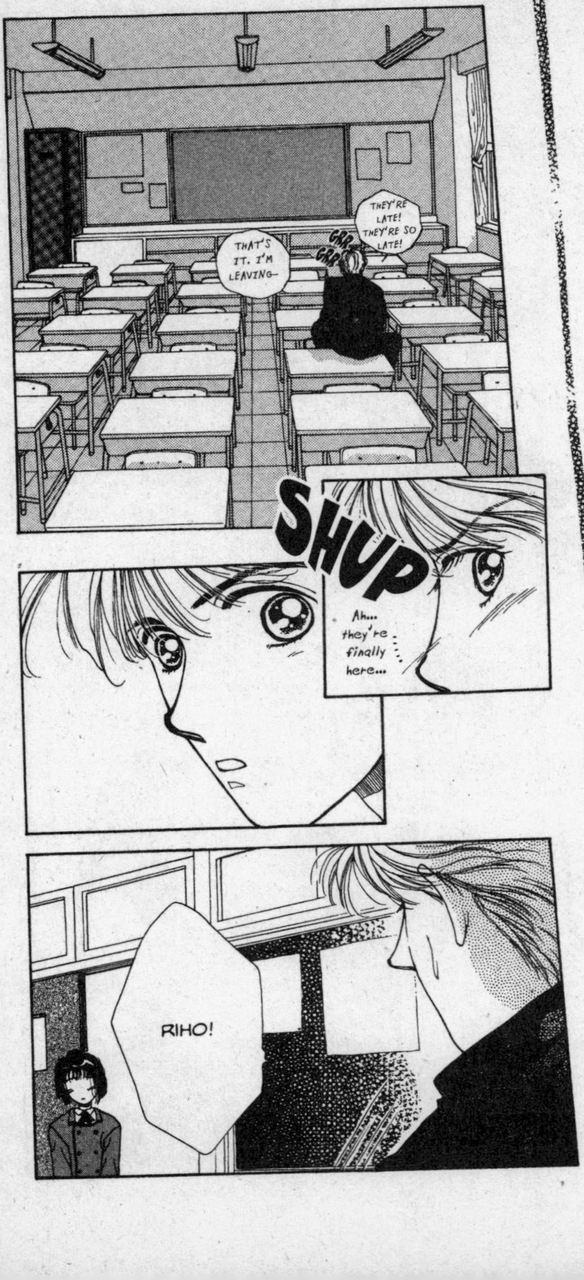
THEY'RE LATE! THEY'RE SO LATE!
GRR GRR
THAT'S IT. I'M LEAVING—
SHUP
Ah... they're finally here...
RIHO!

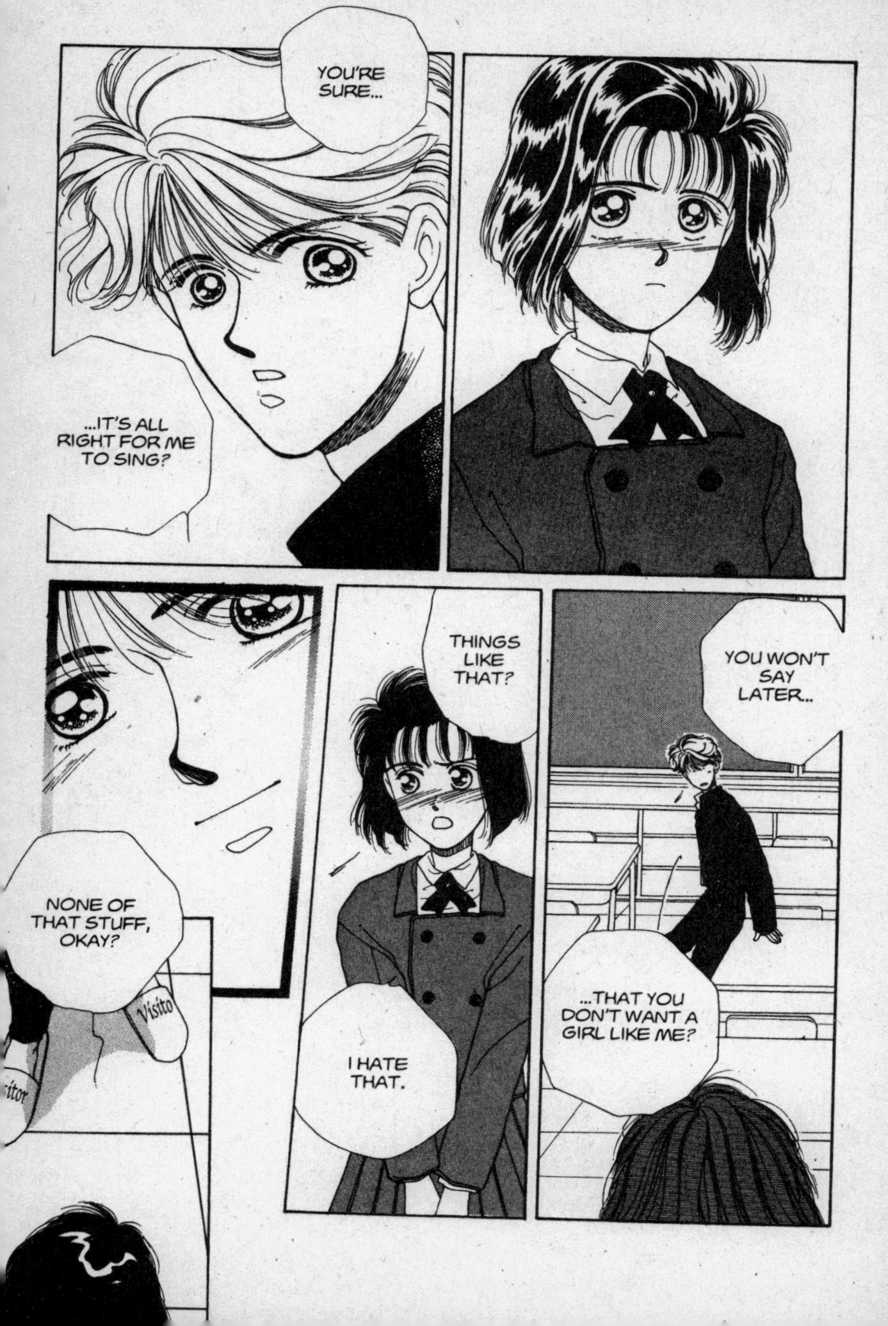
YOU'RE SURE...
...IT'S ALL RIGHT FOR ME TO SING?
YOU WON'T SAY LATER...
...THAT YOU DON'T WANT A GIRL LIKE ME?
THINGS LIKE THAT?
I HATE THAT.
NONE OF THAT STUFF, OKAY?

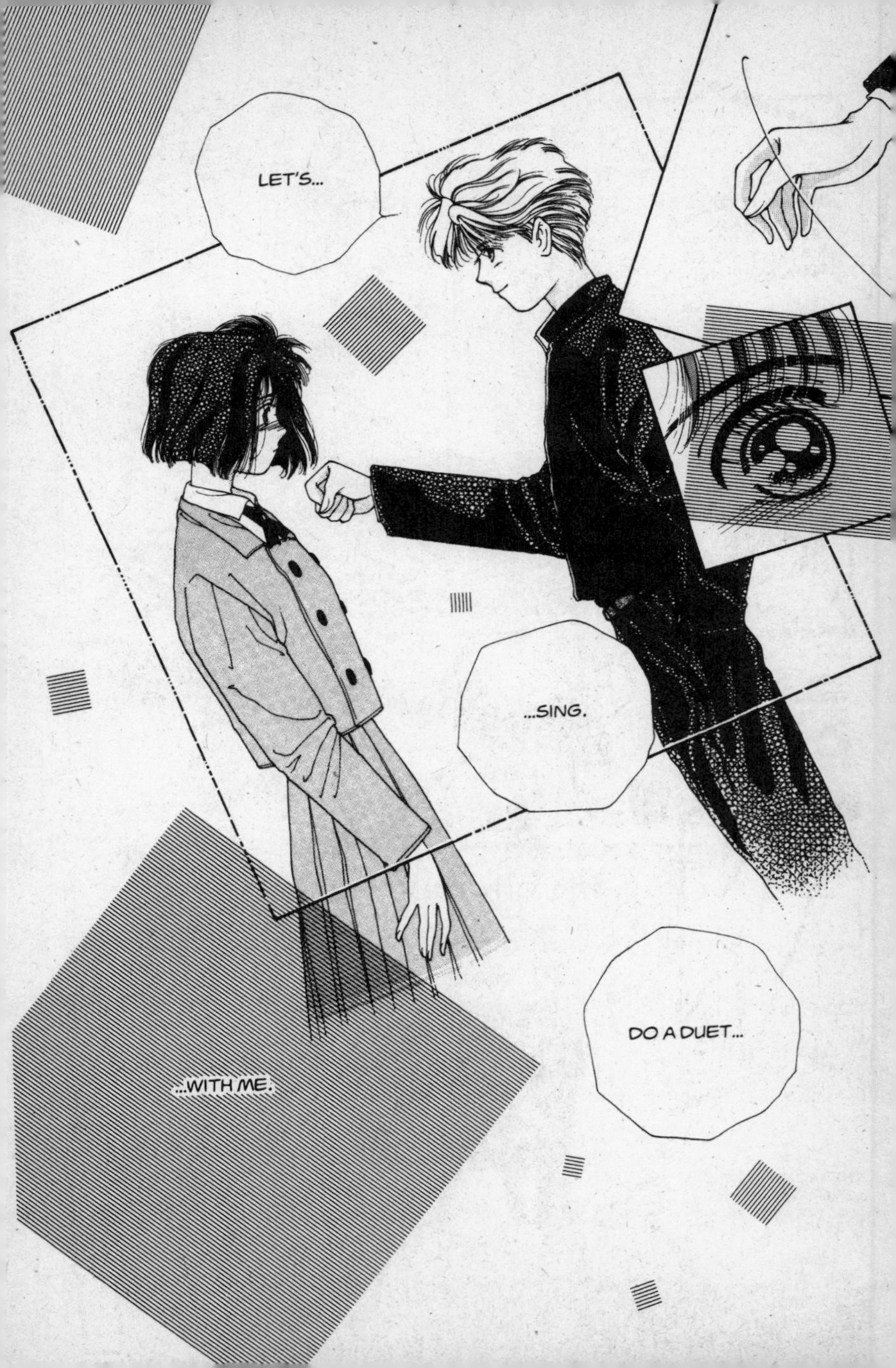
LET'S...
...SING.
DO A DUET...
...WITH ME.

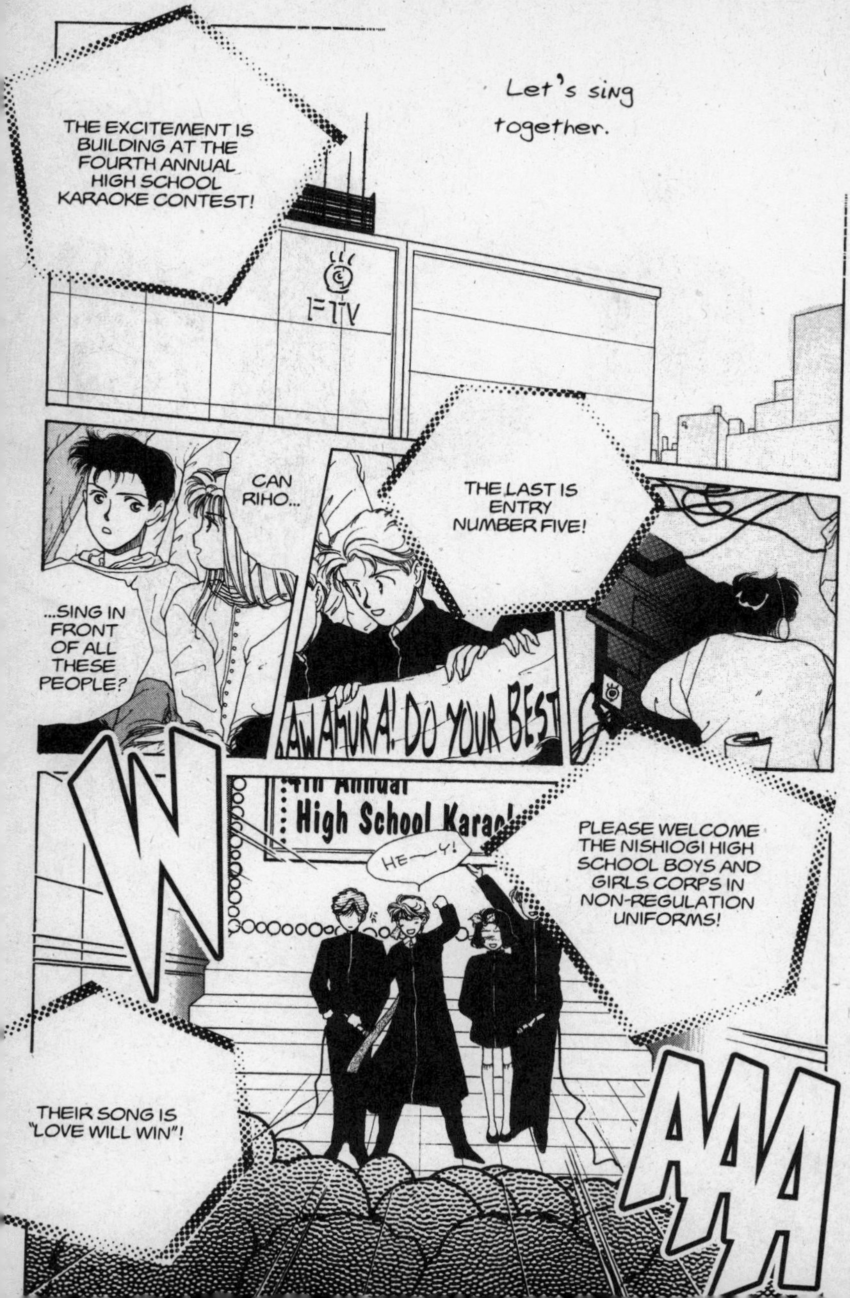
Let's sing together.
THE EXCITEMENT IS BUILDING AT THE FOURTH ANNUAL HIGH SCHOOL KARAOKE CONTEST!
FTV
THE LAST IS ENTRY NUMBER FIVE!
CAN RIHO...
...SING IN FRONT OF ALL THESE PEOPLE?
AWAMURA! DO YOUR BEST
High School Karao
HE—Y!
PLEASE WELCOME THE NISHIOGI HIGH SCHOOL BOYS AND GIRLS CORPS IN NON-REGULATION UNIFORMS!
W
THEIR SONG IS "LOVE WILL WIN"!
AAA

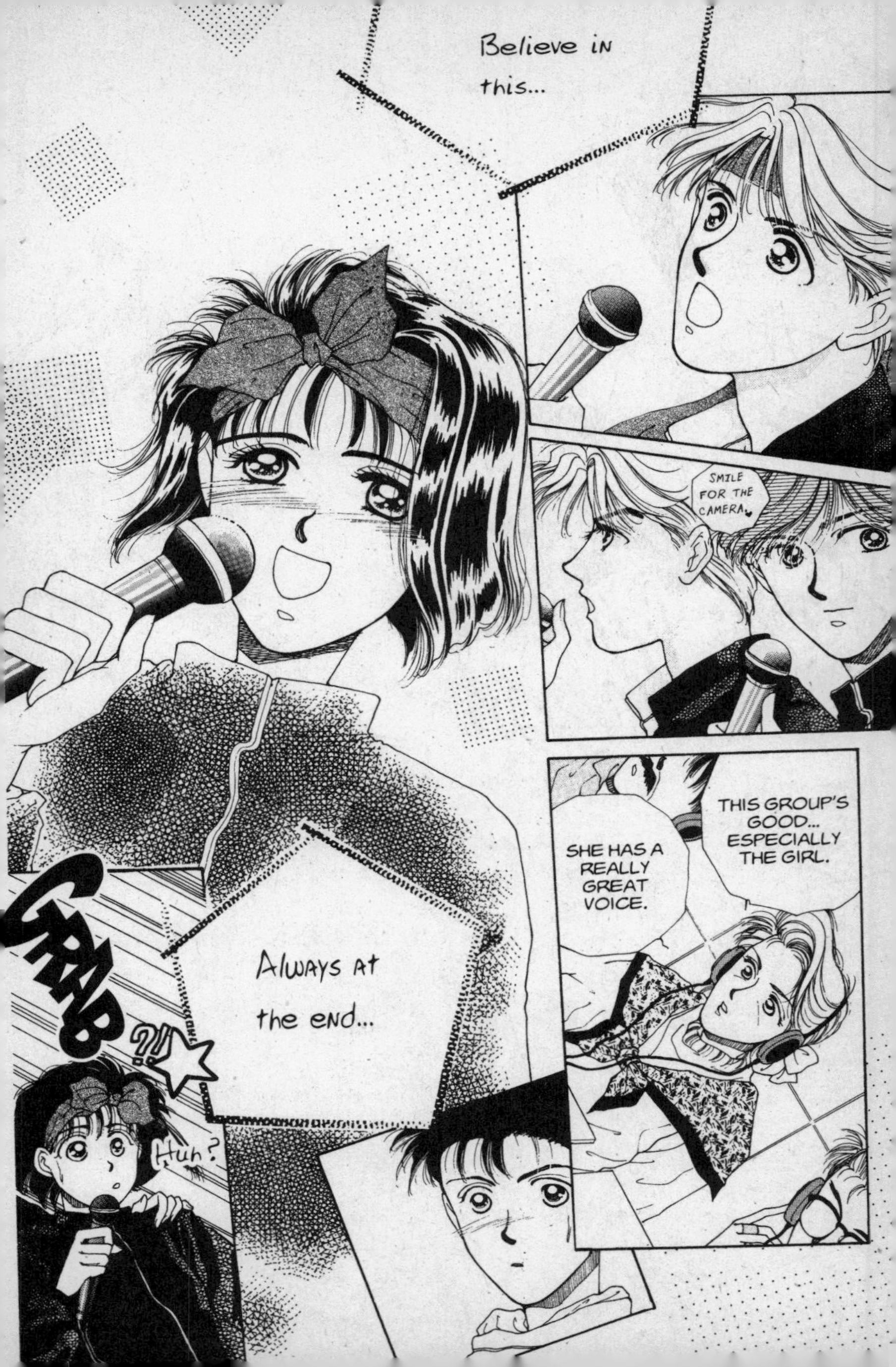
Believe in this...
SMILE FOR THE CAMERA♥
THIS GROUP'S GOOD... ESPECIALLY THE GIRL.
SHE HAS A REALLY GREAT VOICE.
Always at the end...
GRAB
?!
Huh?

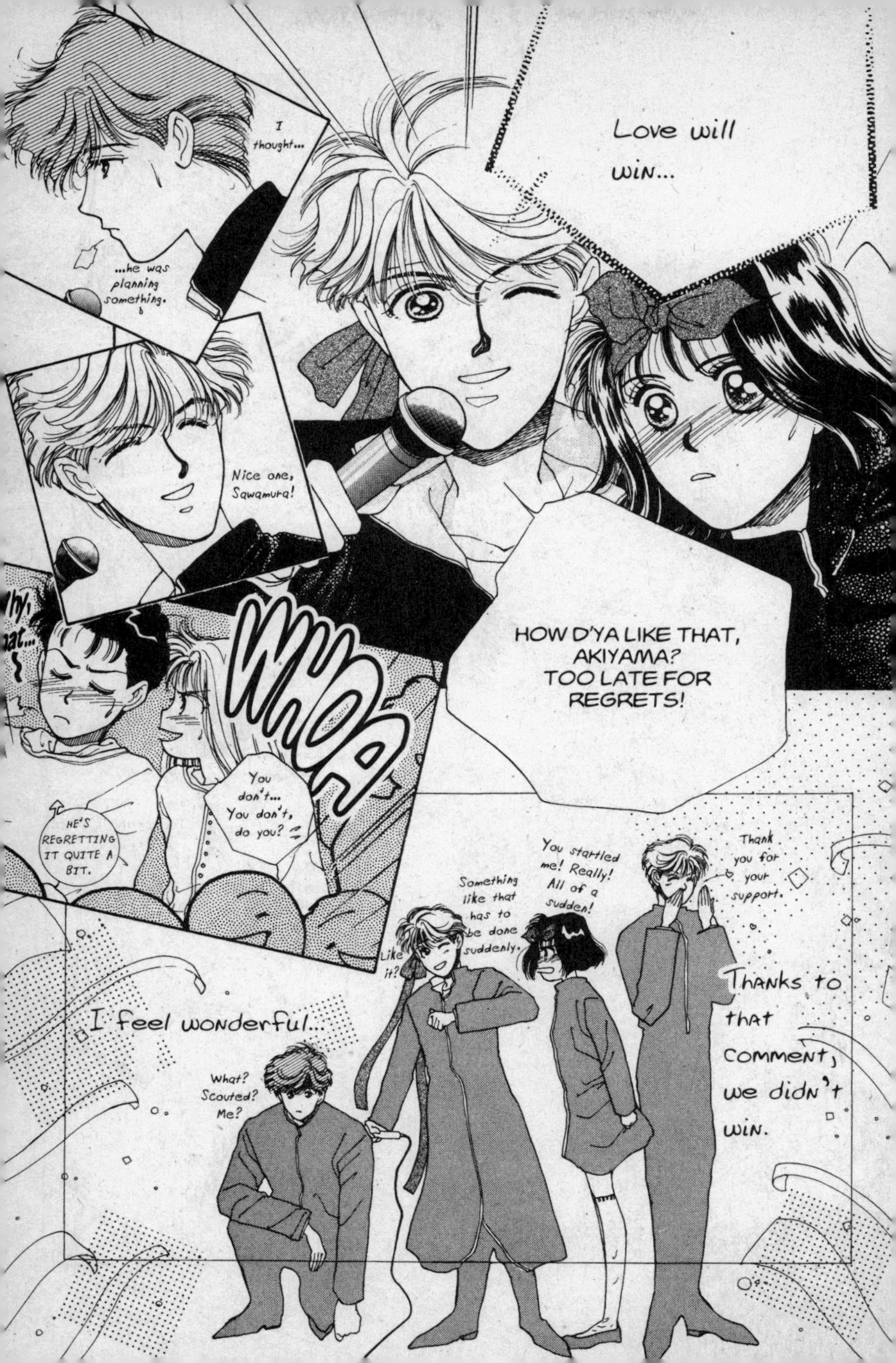
Love will win...
HOW D'YA LIKE THAT, AKIYAMA? TOO LATE FOR REGRETS!
I thought...
...he was planning something.
Nice one, Sawamura!
WHOA
You don't... You don't, do you?
HE'S REGRETTING IT QUITE A BIT.
Thanks to that comment, we didn't win.
Thank you for your support.
You startled me! Really! All of a sudden!
Something like that has to be done suddenly.
Like it?
What? Scouted? Me?
I feel wonderful...

Miki Aihara was born in the Shizuoka prefecture of Japan and currently lives in Tokyo. She made her debut in 1991 with *Lip Conscious!*, published in *Bessatsu Shojo* Comic. Her immensely popular manga *Hot Gimmick* is published in English by VIZ Media. Aihara moves houses frequently, and loves to go to movies and shop for clothes. One of her hobbies is keeping tropical fish.

Shojo Beat

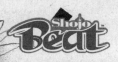

TOKYO BOYS & GIRLS VOLUME 2
The Shojo Beat Manga Edition

STORY AND ART BY
MIKI AIHARA

English Adaptation/Shaenon Garrity
Translation/JN Productions
Touch-up Art & Lettering/Bill Schuch
Design/Courtney Utt
Editor/Urian Brown

Managing Editor/Megan Bates
Director of Production/Noboru Watanabe
Vice President of Publishing/Alvin Lu
Vice President & Editor in Chief/Yumi Hoashi
Sr. Director of Acquisitions/Rika Inouye
Vice President of Sales & Marketing/Liza Coppola
Publisher/Hyoe Narita

Printed in the U.S.A.

Published by VIZ Media, LLC
P.O. Box 77010
San Francisco, CA 94107

Shojo Beat Manga Edition
10 9 8 7 6 5 4 3 2 1
First printing, September 2005

VIZ MEDIA

RATED T+ FOR OLDER TEEN

PARENTAL ADVISORY
TOKYO BOYS & GIRLS is rated T+ for Older Teen and is recommeded for ages 16 & up. This volume contains strong language and sexual themes.

store.viz.com

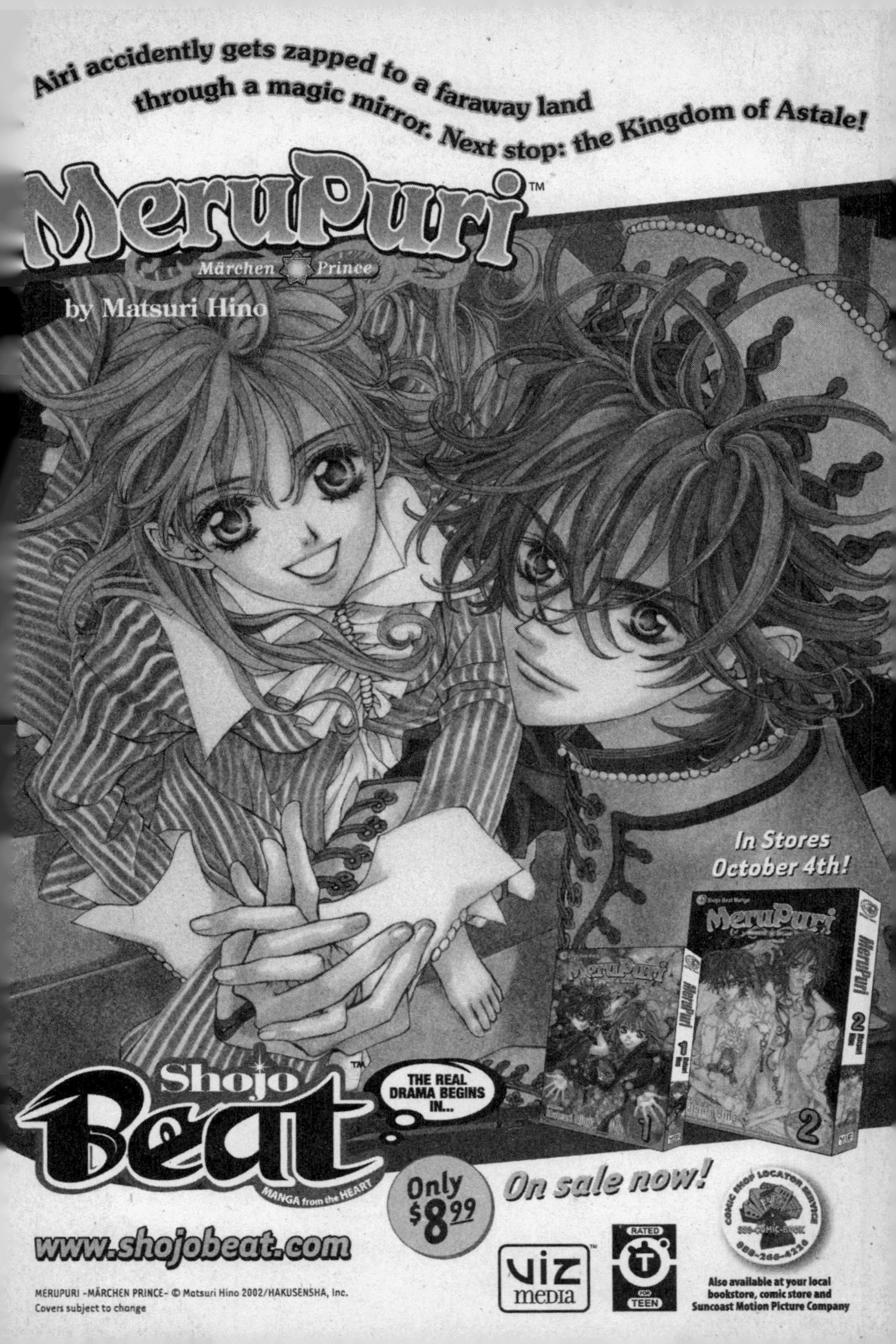
Airi accidently gets zapped to a faraway land
through a magic mirror. Next stop: the Kingdom of Astale!
MeruPuri™
Märchen Prince
by Matsuri Hino
In Stores
October 4th!
Shojo Beat Manga
MeruPuri
Shojo Beat™
MANGA from the HEART
THE REAL DRAMA BEGINS IN...
Only $8.99
On sale now!
www.shojobeat.com
VIZ media™
RATED T FOR TEEN
COMIC SHOP LOCATOR SERVICE
888-COMIC-BOOK
888-266-4226
Also available at your local bookstore, comic store and Suncoast Motion Picture Company
MERUPURI -MÄRCHEN PRINCE- © Matsuri Hino 2002/HAKUSENSHA, Inc.
Covers subject to change

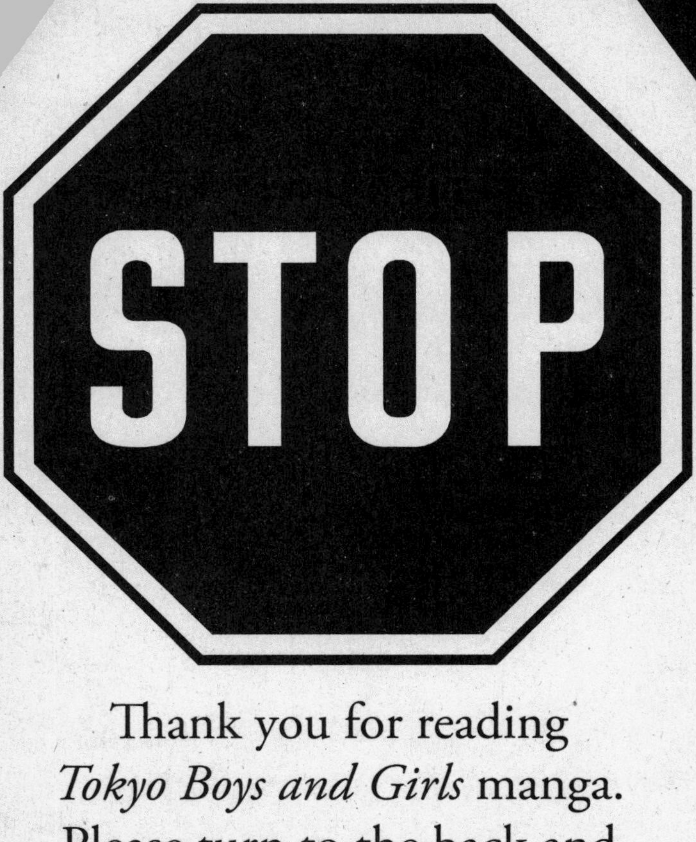
STOP

Thank you for reading
Tokyo Boys and Girls manga.
Please turn to the back and
enjoy a special sample of the
Socrates in Love novel,
written by Kyoichi Katayama.

"Thanks a lot, huh?"

"Hey, Ryunosuke isn't so bad. Coulda been worse."

"Like what?"

"What if they'd named you Kinnosuke?"

"Kinnosuke? Why?"

"That's Soseki's real first name."

"Huh. I didn't know that."

"Think about it. If your parents' favorite book'd been *Kokoro*, you'd be Kinnosuke Oki now."

"No way," he said, laughing. "Come on, nobody would name their kid Kinnosuke."

"Hey, just suppose. Suppose your name *was* Kinnosuke Oki. You'd be the laughingstock of the entire school."

Oki's expression darkened.

I went on, "You'd blame your parents, run away from home, and become a pro wrestler."

"A pro wrestler? How come?"

"What else could you do with a name like Kinnosuke Oki?"

"Yeah, you're right!"

Aki put the flowers we'd brought into a vase. Oki and I opened the box of cookies and dug in while we kept on about our oh-so-literary parents.

"Hey, come back soon," Oki called out as we were going. "It gets boring, lying around here all day."

"Don't worry. All the kids from class are gonna start taking turns coming by to fill you in on what you're missing."

"That I could do without."

TO BE CONTINUED...

to visit a classmate named Oki, who'd broken his leg the first day of school. On the way there, we bought cookies and flowers with the money we'd collected from our teacher and classmates.

Oki was lying on his back in bed, with his leg in a huge plaster cast. I hardly knew anything about him, so I kept quiet while Aki, who'd been in the same class with him the year before, did the talking. I stared out the fourth-floor window at the town. A flower shop, fruit market, candy store, and other businesses formed a small shopping area along the bus route. Beyond that, I could see Castle Hill. Its white tower peeped out from behind the trees, which were bright with new leaves.

"Hey, Matsumoto." Oki suddenly turned toward me. "Your first name's Sakutaro, right?"

"Yeah." I turned from the window.

"Must drive you nuts, huh?" he said.

"What drives me nuts?"

"I mean, it's because of Sakutaro Hagiwara, right?"

I didn't answer.

"Know what *my* first name is?"

"Yeah. Ryunosuke."

"Because of Ryunosuke Akutagawa."

I understood what Oki was getting at.

"They should make it illegal to name your kids after famous writers," he said, nodding. He seemed pleased with himself.

"Actually, it was my grandfather," I said.

"Your grandpa picked your name?"

"Yeah."

looked at, Aki was looking at with me, *through* me. But now, no matter what I looked at, I felt nothing. What was I supposed to look at here?

That's what it meant for Aki to be gone, what it meant to lose her. I had nothing to look at anymore, whether in Australia or Alaska, the Mediterranean or the Antarctic. No matter where in the world I went, it would be the same: no landscape could move me, nothing beautiful could please me. The person who'd given me the ability to see, know, and feel—the will to live—was gone. She wasn't with me anymore.

Four months. Everything had happened in the time for one season to change to the next. In that time, one girl had disappeared from this world. If you thought of it as one person out of six billion, it didn't mean a thing. But I wasn't there with the six billion. I was in a place where one death had wiped out every emotion. That was where I was. I didn't see anything, hear anything, or feel anything. But was that where I really was? If not, then where was I?

Two

THE FIRST TIME AKI AND I were in the same class together was our second year of junior high. Until then I'd never even heard of her, but by chance we ended up in the same class, out of nine, and by chance our teacher appointed us male and female class representative.

As class representatives, our first job was to go to the hospital to sad reality, there's a chasm you have to step across, and you can't cross it without shedding tears. It doesn't matter how many times you do it.

The place we'd left was covered in snow, but the place we landed was a city scorching under the summer sun: Cairns, a beautiful town on the Pacific Ocean. A promenade of palm trees and choking tropical vegetation spread their greenery around luxury hotels facing the bay. Large and small cruise ships waited at the wharf. The taxi taking us to our hotel followed the shore, where strolling tourists were out enjoying the sunset.

"It's like Hawaii," Aki's mother said.

To me, the place was cursed. Nothing about it had changed from four months ago, except for the seasons. Australia had gone from early spring to midsummer. That was all. That was all that had happened.

We were going to spend the night at a hotel and take a morning flight the next day. There was hardly any time difference, so the time when we'd left Japan had just continued its flow. After dinner, I sprawled out on my hotel bed and stared up at the ceiling. And I told myself that Aki wasn't here.

When I'd come to Cairns four months ago, Aki hadn't been here, then, either. Our class had come for our high school graduation trip and left her in Japan. We'd flown from a Japanese city close to Australia, to an Australian city close to Japan. That was the only nonstop route, and for this odd reason, this city had entered my life. I'd thought it was a beautiful place. Everything was strange and new and interesting, because everything I'd the treetops fell to the ground with a dry sound. When I looked back, beyond the guardrail, I could see the winter ocean. It was calm and gentle, utterly blue. No matter what I looked at, my memories would suck me in. I closed the lid on my heart and turned my back to the ocean.

The snow in the woods was deep. There were broken branches and hard, stump-like growths that made it hard to walk. Suddenly, somewhere in the grove, a wild bird let out a sharp cry and flew off. I stopped and listened for other noises, but it was as quiet as if the world had nobody left in it. When I closed my eyes, though, I could hear the chains of cars on the nearby road, like the sound of bells. I started not to know where I was or who I was. Then I heard my father calling me.

After we got over the hill, the rest of the drive went smoothly. We arrived at the airport on time, checked in, and headed to the gate.

"Thank you for everything," my father said to Aki's parents.

"We should be thanking you," Aki's father answered, smiling. "I'm sure Aki's very happy to have Sakutaro coming with us."

I glanced at the small urn in Aki's mother's hands. That urn, nestled in its beautiful brocade bag . . . was Aki truly in there?

After the plane took off, I fell asleep and had a dream. It was about Aki when she was still healthy, and in the dream she was smiling, with that slightly embarrassed smile of hers. She called out to me—"Saku-chan." Her voice lingered in my ears. I wished the dream were real, and this reality a dream. But that wasn't the case. And that was why, whenever I woke up, I'd be crying. It wasn't because I was sad. When you return from a happy dream

PART
1

THAT MORNING I woke up crying, as usual. I didn't know anymore whether I was sad or not—my feelings had flowed away with the tears. I lay there listlessly in bed until my mother came in and told me to get up.

It wasn't snowing, but the road was frozen white. Half of the cars we saw had their chains on. My dad drove, while Aki's father sat beside him. Aki's mother and I sat in back. The men up front kept talking about the snow. Would we make it to the airport in time? Would the plane take off on schedule? Aki's mom and I hardly said anything at all. I stared out the window at the passing landscape. The fields on either side of the road were covered in snow as far as the eye could see. Rays of sunlight cut through the clouds, coming down on a distant mountain ridge. Aki's mother held the small urn containing ashes in her lap.

The snow got deeper as we neared the crest of the hill. My father stopped the car, and he and Aki's father went out to put chains on the tires. To pass the time, I went for a short walk. On the other side of the parking area was a grove of trees. Untrampled snow covered the undergrowth, while snow that had piled up on

Socrates
in Love

Kyoichi Katayama

TRANSLATED BY
Akemi Wegmüller

SEKAI NO CHUSHIN DE AI WO SAKEBU *by Kyoichi KATAYAMA*

© Kyoichi KATAYAMA 2001

All Rights Reserverd

Orginal Japanese edition published by Shogakukan Inc.

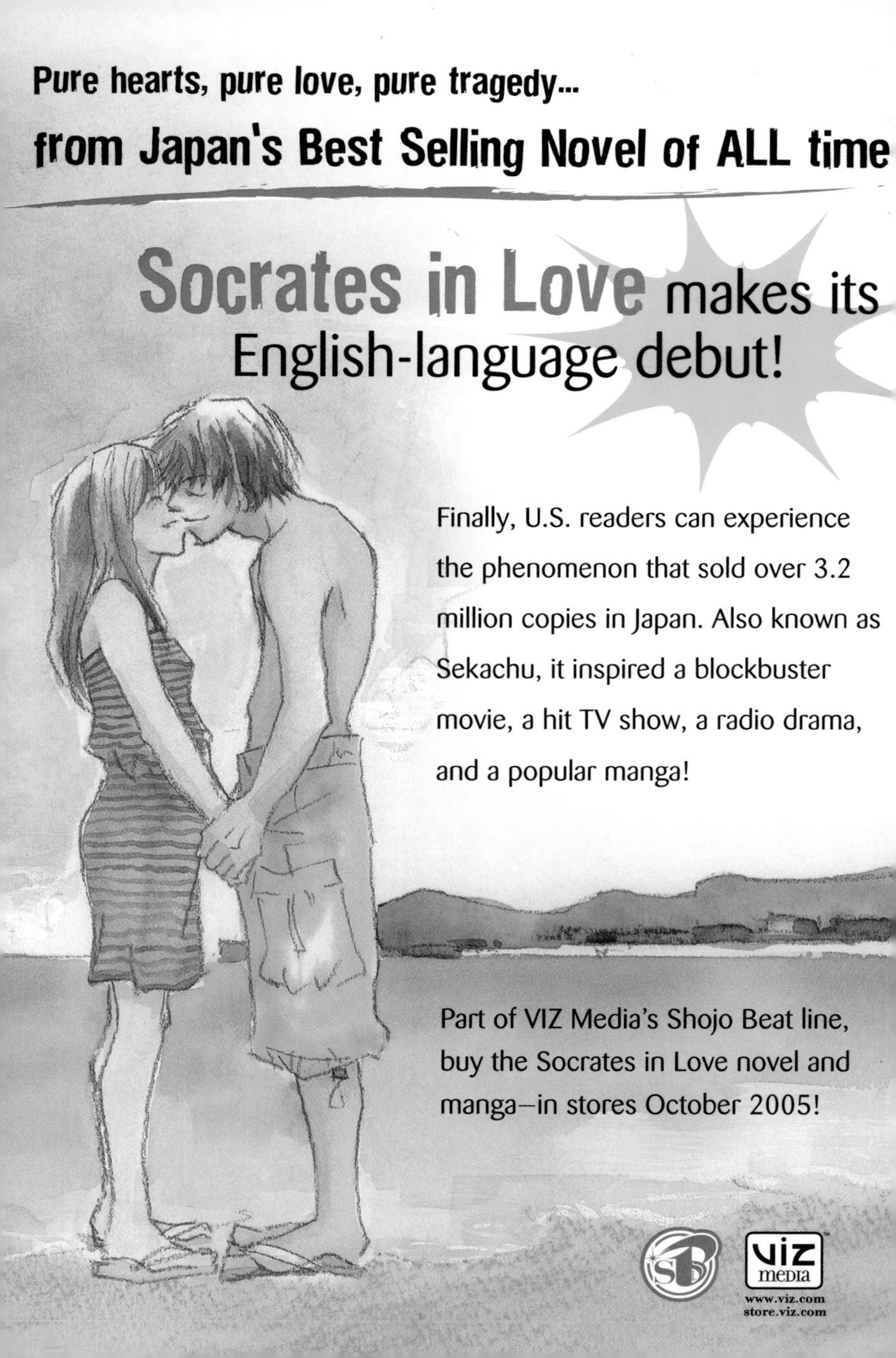
Pure hearts, pure love, pure tragedy...
from Japan's Best Selling Novel of ALL time
Socrates in Love makes its English-language debut!
Finally, U.S. readers can experience the phenomenon that sold over 3.2 million copies in Japan. Also known as Sekachu, it inspired a blockbuster movie, a hit TV show, a radio drama, and a popular manga!
Part of VIZ Media's Shojo Beat line, buy the Socrates in Love novel and manga—in stores October 2005!
VIZ media
www.viz.com
store.viz.com

When an average boy meets a beautiful girl, it's a classic case of young love—instant, all consuming, and enduring. But when a tragedy threatens their romance, they discover just how deep and strong love can be.

Manga

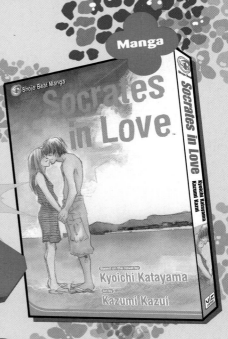

only
$8.99!

Socrates in Love
Story by Kyoichi Katayama
Art by Kazumi Kazui

Novel

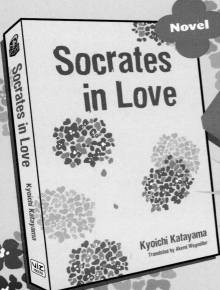

Socrates in Love
Written by Kyoichi Katayama

$17.99
hardcover

www.viz.com
store.viz.com